CANADIAN LAW

Second Edition

CANADIAN LAW

Second Edition

W. H. JENNINGS, B.A., M.Ed.

THOMAS G. ZUBER, B.A.
Judge of the County Court
for the Province of Ontario

McGRAW-HILL RYERSON LIMITED

Toronto
Montreal New York London Sydney Johannesburg Mexico Panama Düsseldorf
Singapore Rio de Janeiro Kuala Lumpur New Delhi

CANADIAN LAW Second Edition

ISBN 0-07-092937-8

3 4 5 6 7 8 9 10 D-72 10 9 8 7 6 5 4 3 2

Drawings by Bob Berger

Printed and bound in Canada

PREFACE

The original edition of *Canadian Law* was prepared for use as a text for the course in law as offered on the secondary school level in Canadian schools. This edition is intended to continue to serve the same purpose; thus, in general, the content of the old text has been retained. Where it has been felt necessary, some areas have been expanded or clarified. Statutory references have been brought up to date (as of the time of going to press).

At the same time, in response to a changing curriculum and the increased emphasis on "personal" law, this edition incorporates several new features:

1. Two new chapters have been added: one, "Civil Rights," deals with our rights under the Canadian Bill of Rights; the other, "Family Law," is concerned with the law as it relates to marriage, divorce and children.
2. The context has been copiously illustrated with cases taken from the various law reports as well as with hypothetical examples designed to introduce and illustrate points of law. These cases are followed by questions intended to bring into focus the point of law concerned.
3. The new "consumer protection" laws have been included where they apply.
4. The assignments at the end of each unit include case problems and topics for discussion—many of them controversial in character—and projects for research and discovery.
5. A glossary of legal terms has been added at the back of the book.

Readers who are familiar with the earlier edition will notice that the order in which the topics are presented has been rearranged and that the original graphic illustrations have been redrawn and new ones, including photographic illustrations, added.

In view of the considerable increase in the content of the revised text, the chapter on Patents, Trade Marks and Copyrights—a very specialized field of law—has been deleted.

Although many variations in the law as it prevails in the different provinces have been noted, it is obvious that the size of this text limits the extent of these notations. Thus there are some areas where the reader may find it necessary to refer to the statutes of a particular province.

Finally, the authors wish to emphasize that a book of this sort which covers such a wide area of law permits only a very brief elementary treatment of the subjects covered. The text is not intended to be a substitute for professional counsel; rather, its function is to help the reader to recognize those problems where it is necessary to seek legal advice. To this end we trust this text will serve a useful purpose.

W. H. J.
T. G. Z.

CONTENTS

UNIT SEVEN
WORKING WITH AND ENDING LEGAL AGREEMENTS *147*

UNIT EIGHT
GOING TO WORK *167*

UNIT NINE
BUYING AND SELLING GOODS *201*

UNIT TEN
BORROWING, HIRING, OR STORING PROPERTY *245*

UNIT ELEVEN
SUBSTITUTES FOR MONEY *263*

UNIT TWELVE
THE LAW OF REAL PROPERTY *292*

UNIT ONE UNDERSTANDING OUR LEGAL SYSTEM

THE LAW

Much of our conduct is governed by rules. We accept many rules voluntarily, such as the dictates of good manners, the rules of a club, or the obligations of our religion. If we choose not to follow these rules, the worst penalty may be exclusion from a particular group or a decline in popularity.

Other rules which we observe do not, however, depend on individual acceptance. The State, representing the whole of society, has adopted rules to regulate our affairs, and enforces them. The rules and principles that are recognized by the courts and enforceable by the State may be described as *the law.*

JUSTICE

Opinions are sometimes expressed that a particular law is not just. The law, however, is what the State, representing society as a whole, views as constituting justice. To substitute an individual's opinion of justice for the law would have the effect of rendering our rules of law completely uncertain. If laws cease to represent the view of society as a whole they should be changed by society, *acting through properly constituted authority.*

Many of the rules and principles which make up our law have evolved through experience over many centuries, and can now be expected to remain relatively unchanged. Other parts of our law dealing with specific modern problems may be changed from time to time until a lasting solution is found.

Part 1

THE ORIGIN OF OUR LAW

HOW LAWS ORIGINATE

CASE 1

Lonely trappers far from urban areas need no law to regulate the use of their snowmobiles, but the recent surge in the use of snowmobiles in populated areas has created problems—noise, trespassing, accidents, etc. People are saying "There ought to be a law." As a result, municipalities are framing bylaws to regulate the use of these vehicles in urban centers, provincial legislatures are faced with making laws to control them on the highways, and the federal government is concerned with setting standards of manufacture.

(a) What will those who prepare laws for snowmobiles use as a a guide in creating new legislation?
(b) What does this situation tell you about why laws originate? What causes any law to come into being?

As soon as man began to live in groups, rules became necessary to govern his relations with his fellows. Even in the most primitive forms of society the rights of the individual (for example, ownership of land and goods) and the obligations to the group (for example, mutual defence and leadership) had to be defined. These laws were usually defined by a leader, or a ruler, sometimes with the assistance of an advisory council. As civilizations developed and society became more complex, more sophisticated systems of law were required. The Roman Empire presents a good example, for one of its outstanding features was its legal system. Roman laws were developed to meet the increasing needs of the Empire and were eventually reduced to writing in a logical and organized body of rules called the *Civil Code*.

The Roman Civil Code became the basis for most of the laws of continental Europe. These countries adopted codes in which the basic principles were drawn from the Roman law. Thus the jurisdictions which base their law on the Roman tradition are referred to as "civil law jurisdictions." In Canada, the Province of Quebec derives part of its law from the legal traditions of France which, in turn, were based on the Roman Civil Code. Much of the law of Quebec is to be found in the Quebec Civil Code.

Verdict Based On Roman Law

California Woman Must Return Engagement Ring

LOS ANGELES – Superior Judge Leo Freund reached back nearly 2,000 years to old Roman law – and found it good in California, 1947 – in holding that an engagement ring is not the woman's property until marriage . . . . The judge said Roman law held that an engagement ring was merely a symbol of troth – if the troth was broken the ring went back to the donor.

England did not adopt the Roman law. Whatever imprint the Romans left on Britain during their occupation of that country was swept away by the Anglo-Saxon invaders who brought with them their relatively simple Germanic laws and customs. The subsequent Norman conquest of Britain, in 1066, is generally regarded as the beginning of the development of a distinctive system of English law.

Canada, with the exception of Quebec, derives its legal system and most of its laws from England. To understand the Canadian legal system it is necessary to trace the development of the English law.

THE COMMON LAW

The Norman conquerors did not bring a new system of law with them to England, but they did bring the idea of a strong central government. Local communal courts were replaced by royal courts, which included a system of central courts at Westminster and travelling justices who heard cases throughout England.

There were at that time very few written laws, as we now know them. The judges, therefore, decided the cases on the basis of the *common* customs and usages of the people which for generations had been accepted as binding upon the members of the community. These customs, however, varied from community to community, and the travelling judges selected the best of what they found and adopted them as law. If there was no custom to guide them, the judges used their own initiative and, in effect, made new laws. Because of the travelling nature of the judiciary, the customs and usages that were adopted by the judges as law became uniform throughout England. As the Norman kings welded England into a united country, the royal courts began to apply uniform laws throughout the whole of England. This was the law common to all of England, or the "common law."

PRECEDENT

C—2

ERASED CHALK MARKS — YOUTH ACQUITTED

Court follows precedent

TORONTO – The court today acquitted a youth charged with erasing a police chalk mark from the tire of a car parked on the street outside his home.

The youth's lawyer pointed to an Ontario Court of Appeal decision which had ruled that a motorist might erase the police mark from his own car or, if he had the owner's permission, from another car.

The youth admitted that he had erased chalk marks from his own car and also from his neighbour's car parked outside their homes, but his lawyer argued that this act was not against the law because of the appeal court ruling.

(a) Why did the youth's lawyer claim that the erasing was legal?
(b) Of what use are previous court judgments to lawyers when they prepare a client's case?

As the royal judges decided cases by the application of old customs or the invention of new rules, there gradually developed a formal system whereby decisions in past cases were considered as having established authoritative principles of law that other judges *had to* follow in making decisions in similar cases — at least until the precedent-making decision had been changed by a higher court than that which had established it. This custom of standing by previous decisions is known as the *rule of precedent*. Over the years the common law has evolved, one step at a time, from the decisions on many cases and the rule of precedent.

COMPARISON BETWEEN CODE AND COMMON LAW

In contrast to the gradual evolution of the common law, the preparation of a code requires the writing out of a complete system of law (for example, the Quebec Civil Code) or of a branch of the law (for example, the Canadian Criminal Code). The code must then be adopted as law by the state, or province.

Where a code is in effect, for example the Quebec Civil Code, the judge in settling a dispute has the task of applying the appropriate principles of the code to that dispute. Again, in contrast, where the common law is in effect, for example, in the common law provinces of Canada, the judge applies to the dispute the principles of law established by the decisions made in similar cases in the past — that is, he follows the rule of precedent. In spite of the differences between the two systems, in many cases the results are very much the same.

EQUITY

As centuries passed, the common law grew in volume, but also became more rigid. Past decisions, when followed many years later, often produced unfair or inequitable results. As the common law lost its flexibility it was less able to deal with new situations for which there was no precedent. The king, however, remained the "fountainhead of justice," and the practice arose of appealing directly to him when plaintiff or defendant considered that the common law had failed to dispense justice. (A modern example of this type of appeal occurs in Canada today, when a person who is sentenced to death appeals to the federal cabinet for executive clemency).

As the volume of these appeals grew, the task of dealing with them fairly or *equitably* (that is, on their merits, without regard to legal doctrine) devolved upon the Chancellor, the King's secretary. In the early days the Chancellor was usually a member of the clergy, and his decisions often reflected a greater concern with conscience and morality than with the technical rules of law.

In time the hearings before the Chancellor became more formal, and a Court of Chancery developed. At first this court of equity was not concerned with past decisions, but eventually it began to follow its own precedents. As the volume of precedents grew, a new system of rules emerged, called *equity*.

In the nineteenth century, in both England and Canada, common law and equity were consolidated, and both of these bodies of law are now administered in a single court system. However, the significance of the principles of equity has not been lost, for if there is any conflict between the principles of common law and equity, equity prevails.

CASE LAW

Before the development of the printing press, and when only handwritten records were available, the term "unwritten law" was often applied to the common law because, to a large extent, the principles enunciated in previous cases existed only in the memories of legal practitioners and judges. With the advent of printing, the practice began of publishing judicial decisions. When the Court of Chancery was established, its decisions were published. The publication of judicial decisions continues, and law libraries contain thousands of volumes of past decisions. Some English law reports are over 600 years old. Not every judicial decision is published, but only those that deal with a new principle or a new application of an old principle. This accumulation of judicial decisions is generally referred to as *case law*. In this text, reference will be made to decided cases. Some of these are old, but the principles they established are still valid.

Many textbooks and digests have been prepared by experts to explain and summarize the case law in particular fields. These works are a convenient and invaluable aid in the search for, and interpretation of our law.

STATUTE LAW

A portion of one of Ontario's statutes

THE HIGHWAY TRAFFIC ACT Sec. 65 (*a*) 51

PART VIII

RULES OF THE ROAD

Direction of traffic by constable

62*a*. Where a constable or other police officer considers it reasonably necessary,

(*a*) to ensure orderly movement of traffic; or

(*b*) to prevent injury or damage to persons or property; or

(*c*) to permit proper action in an emergency,

he may direct traffic according to his discretion, notwithstanding the provisions of this Part, and every person shall obey his directions. 1960-61, c. 34, s. 7.

Right of way

63. Subject to sections 64 and 66, a driver or operator of a vehicle approaching an intersection shall yield the right of way to a vehicle that has entered the intersection from a different highway and, when two vehicles enter an intersection from different highways at approximately the same time, the driver or operator on the left shall yield the right of way to the vehicle on the right. R.S.O. 1960, c. 172, s. 63.

Stop at through highway

64. The driver or operator of a vehicle or car of an electric railway,

(*a*) upon approaching a stop sign at an intersection, shall bring the vehicle or car to a full stop at a clearly marked stop line or, if none, then immediately before entering the nearest crosswalk or, if none, then immediately before entering the intersection; and

(*b*) upon entering the intersection, shall yield the right of way to traffic in the intersection or approaching the intersection on another highway so closely that it constitutes an immediate hazard and having so yielded the right of way may proceed with caution and the traffic approaching the intersection on

When the settlers from the British Isles came to Canada, they brought the English law and the English legal system with them. Quebec, ceded to England by France in 1763, was allowed to keep the French civil law, but English criminal law was introduced.

In early colonial times, English law was essentially a system of case law. As society evolved, case law became inadequate, because new circumstances arose which case law did not cover. Also a faster moving economy required that laws be more readily ascertainable. As a result, new laws were made in the form of statutes passed by parliament or a legislature to meet the needs. And this has continued, the statutes being changed or repealed by the same authorities, according as those needs varied from time to time. For instance, in 1969 more than 100 amendments were made to the Criminal Code.

BILL 72 **1967**

An Act to amend The Highway Traffic Act

HER MAJESTY, by and with the advice and consent of the Legislative Assembly of the Province of Ontario, enacts as follows:

1. Subsection 5 of section 8 of *The Highway Traffic Act*, as re-enacted by section 3 of *The Highway Traffic Amendment Act, 1966*, is repealed and the following substituted therefor:

R.S.O. 1960, c. 172, s. 8, subs. 5 (1966, c. 64, s. 3), re-enacted

(5) A motorcycle while being driven on a highway shall have attached to and exposed on the back thereof a number plate furnished by the Department showing in plain figures the number of the permit of such motorcycle issued for the current year or any part thereof and so fixed that the number is plainly visible from the rear of the motorcycle.

Number plate on motorcycle

2. Subsection 13 of section 33 of *The Highway Traffic Act* is repealed and the following substituted therefor:

R.S.O. 1960, c. 172, s. 33, subs. 13, re-enacted

(13) A volunteer fire fighter under *The Fire Departments Act* may carry on the left front fender of his motor vehicle a lamp not exceeding 4 inches in diameter displaying an amber and a white flashing light showing the letters "V.F.F.", which lamp shall be illuminated only when such motor vehicle is proceeding to a fire or other emergency, and no other motor vehicle shall carry any such lamp.

Vehicles of volunteer fire fighters R.S.O. 1960, c. 145

3.—(1) Subsection 2 of section 35 of *The Highway Traffic*

R.S.O. 1960, c. 172, s. 35,

An amendment to an Ontario Statute repealing old laws and incorporating new ones

Some statutes are simply codifications of an existing body of case law. The benefit of the codification is that the law dealing with some particular matter is collected in a single statute and is thus more readily ascertainable; also, any obscurities in the case law are removed. The Sale of Goods Act and The Bills of Exchange Act are notable examples of the codification of case law.

C—3

CRIMINAL CODE CHANGED TO KEEP UP WITH THE TIMES

OTTAWA – Therapeutic abortions and the removal of all penalties for the advertising and sale of birth control methods became legal in Canada during August 1969 as more than 100 amendments to the Criminal Code took effect.

The amendments passed into law 20 months after being introduced in the Commons by Pierre Trudeau, then Justice Minister.

In addition to the existing ban on obscene phone calls, it is now a crime to harass anybody by repeatedly telephoning them. The Courts may now use suspended sentences and probation more liberally in the cases of offences that carry no minimum penalty.

A person may now be prevented for up to two years from owning a domestic animal or bird, if he has been convicted on two or more occasions of causing unnecessary pain, suffering or injury to an animal or bird.

Unless the accused has a lawful excuse, he may now be sent to prison for up to two years for possessing an instrument for breaking into a coin-operated device.

The six-month minimum prison term for mail theft has been removed, leaving the penalty to the court's discretion.

Justice Minister John Turner has previously announced that the matter of lotteries, firearms, the possession of automobile master keys, and driving while under the influence of alcohol will be dealt with in future amendments.

(a) What caused the federal government to amend the Criminal Code?
(b) Why would it have taken 20 months for the amendments to take effect?
(c) What current social issues may be reflected in the next round of Criminal Code amendments?

THE BRITISH NORTH AMERICA ACT

The British North America Act, passed by the British Parliament in 1867, created the Dominion of Canada, and divided the law-making authority between the provinces and the federal Parliament. The provincial legislatures have jurisdiction over local matters, for example, education, property, and civil rights. The federal government has jurisdiction over matters of national concern, for example, banking, trade and commerce, national defence, postal service. Canada is a federal union of provinces, each of which, through its legislature, can pass laws effective within its own boundaries. The federal Parliament passes laws for the entire country.

When the British North America Act was passed, the British Parliament retained the power to pass laws applying to Canada. In 1931, by the Statute of Westminster, the British Parliament surrendered the right to pass laws for Canada, unless specifically asked to do so. This last qualification is

Which level of government established these laws? Why is it desirable that all three levels of Canadian government pass pollution control legislation?

necessary so that the British North America Act itself can be amended from time to time. We have not yet been able to agree on a formula for amending the British North America Act in Canada.

APPLYING THE LAW

1. Your neighbour burns garbage in his back yard, creating offensive fumes. You wish to have the practice stopped. Would the relief you seek be under common law, equity, or statute law?
2. Judge X has his own personal opinion of how the case he is trying should be decided. Should he take this opinion into consideration?

DISCUSSION

1. Because of the nature of his job, the representative of a business firm is required to move his family from province to province. Each move creates difficulties in adjusting the children to a different provincial educational system. This man advocates that education come under federal jurisdiction. What difficulties would have to be overcome in order to make this possible? Do you agree with this man's opinion?
2. Sometimes laws are controversial, some people supporting them while others oppose them. What examples of such laws can you think of? What solution do you suggest to this problem?

Part 2
CRIMINAL AND CIVIL LAW

While law may be divided according to origin as common law, equity, and statute law, it may also be classified according to its nature and purpose. The two chief divisions on this basis are:

- Criminal law
- Civil law

CRIMINAL LAW

C — 4

A enters a restaurant and, while the cashier is otherwise occupied, opens the cash register, takes the money and runs.
B, while eating in a restaurant, slips the salt and pepper shakers into his pocket as souvenirs. He pays for the meal and leaves.
C, having finished his meal in a restaurant, receives an emergency telephone call. He rushes out of the restaurant without paying the bill.

Are any of these acts crimes? Why or why not?

C — 5

(i) X attends a Christmas party at his office and is persuaded against his better judgment to have several cocktails. On the way home X loses control of his car which mounts the curb and injures a pedestrian.

(ii) The Y Pharmaceutical Company produces a new drug called Mexin which is tested extensively and found safe. After several deaths, it is discovered through further tests that persons with a rare blood type react adversely to the drug.

Has either X or the Y company committed a crime? Explain.

The British North America Act assigns exclusive jurisdiction over criminal law to the federal Parliament. As a result, the criminal law is the same throughout Canada.

We have seen that in earlier days the main source of our criminal law was case law and that as time went on it became apparent that such an important branch of law should be clearer and easier to find. In the late nineteenth century a commission was appointed to sort out all the principles of criminal law contained in the case law, and to reduce them to a logical and organized system. The result was the *Canadian Criminal Code*, which was adopted by the federal Parliament in 1892, and came into force on July 1, 1893. Today, most of our criminal law is contained in the Canadian Criminal Code.

Punishment for common assault—Causing bodily harm by assault or otherwise.

231. (1) Every one who commits a common assault is guilty of

(*a*) an indictable offence and is liable to imprisonment for two years, or
(*b*) an offence punishable on summary conviction.

(2) Every one who unlawfully causes bodily harm to any person or commits an assault that causes bodily harm to any person is guilty of an indictable offence and is liable to imprisonment for two years.

Assault with intent—Other assaults.

232. (1) Every one who assaults a person with intent to commit an indictable offence is guilty of an indictable offence and is liable to imprisonment for five years.

(2) Every one who

(*a*) assaults a public officer or peace officer engaged in the execution of his duty, or a person acting in aid of such an officer;
(*b*) assaults a person with intent to resist or prevent the lawful arrest or detention of himself or another person; or
(*c*) assaults a person
(i) who is engaged in the lawful execution of a process against lands or goods or in making a lawful distress or seizure, or
(ii) with intent to rescue anything taken under a lawful process, distress or seizure,

is guilty of an indictable offence and is liable to imprisonment for two years.

KIDNAPPING AND ABDUCTION

Kidnapping—Forcible confinement—Non-resistance.

233. (1) Every one who kidnaps a person with intent

(*a*) to cause him to be confined or imprisoned against his will,

A portion of the Canadian Criminal code, from the Revised Statutes of Canada 1970 Chapter C-34 (Volume II)

Information Canada

NATURE OF A CRIME

A crime is a wrongful act, or the omission of an act, which is considered harmful to the state as a whole. The state prohibits those acts or omissions and imposes punishment on the offender. Punishment varies from small fines to terms of imprisonment and even death.

At common law it was generally considered that in order to constitute a crime the forbidden act or omission had to be committed with *mens rea* (a Latin term meaning a guilty mind). This requirement of mens rea, or criminal intent, continues to apply to such crimes as murder, robbery, and theft.

While we tend to think of criminal law as being concerned only with the classic examples of crime just given, the main purpose of criminal law

Windsor Ontario Police Department photo

Part of the collection of weapons taken from criminals by Windsor police

is the protection of society. In an earlier and comparatively simple society this purpose was considered accomplished when the law protected such fundamental rights as the ownership of property and the safety of the person. In this second half of the twentieth century, however, our more sophisticated society requires broader protection. Not only do we need protection against the traditional crimes of violence (assault, theft, robbery, etc.), but also against such things as pollution of the air and water, false advertising, and price fixing.

As a result of these increased needs, the areas covered by criminal law have continued to expand. In addition to new sections being added to the Criminal Code, important criminal law is to be found in other federal statutes; for example, the Combines Investigation Act, the Narcotics Control Act, and Official Secrets Act, just to name a few. In some of the new legislation the need to protect society is considered so essential that Parliament has omitted the requirement of proving *mens rea* in some of these new offences. The act or omission is prohibited absolutely, and the state of mind or intent of the offender is of no consequence.

PROCEDURE IN CRIMINAL PROSECUTIONS

At common law, crimes were divided into treasons, felonies and misdemeanors. Treasons included crimes against the security of the state; felonies included most of the other serious crimes, and usually involved the death penalty; misdemeanors included the less serious offences. The Criminal Code, however, eliminated those distinctions, and crimes are now divided into two classes:

- Offences punishable on summary conviction
- Indictable offences.

SUMMARY CONVICTION

Summary conviction cases are the less serious offences. Following arrest or summons to appear in court, the accused person is tried by a magistrate without a jury. These cases are heard in Magistrate's Court with a minimum of delay; hence the term *summary trial.* Examples of summary conviction cases are vagrancy, creating a disturbance, and many of the offences committed in the operation of an automobile.

INDICTABLE OFFENCES

Indictable offences are the graver crimes, and may be further classified according to the court in which they are tried, as follows:

Class A — The most serious crimes, such as treason and murder, must be tried in a Supreme Court with a jury.

Class B — The least serious group of the indictable offences, such as theft under $50 or conducting an illegal lottery, are tried by a magistrate.

Class C — For all the other indictable offences (which is the largest group) the accused may elect to be tried either

- by a magistrate,
- by a judge alone, or
- by a judge and jury

CANADA
PROVINCE OF ONTARIO
COUNTY OF
Essex

SUMMONS TO A PERSON CHARGED WITH AN OFFENCE
UNDER THE CRIMINAL CODE OR OTHER FEDERAL STATUTE

(Form 6)
(Secs. 441 and 700)

TO William Smithers
4270 University Ave., Windsor

WHEREAS YOU HAVE BEEN CHARGED before me that you on or about the 16th day of March 19 72, at the City of Windsor in the County of Essex

Did steal an automobile, the property of Riverview Auto Sales Ltd., of a value exceeding Fifty Dollars.

contrary to Section 280 Sub. (a)

THIS IS THEREFORE TO COMMAND YOU, in Her Majesty's name, to appear before the presiding Provincial Judge or before me on Mon. day, the 29th day of March next, at 10 o'clock in the Fore noon in the Provincial Courtroom Provincial Courts Building at City Hall Square, Windsor, Ontario or before any justice for the said County who is there, to answer to the said charge and to be dealt with according to law.

Dated this 18th day of March 19 72, at Windsor, Ontario

A Justice of the Peace in and for the said County (County or Province)

(D1123) (12/70)

Example of a Summons

Briefly, the procedure is as follows: The accused, after being summoned or arrested for an indictable offence, appears before a magistrate for arraignment, at which time the charge information is read to him. If the charge against him is in Class A, a date is fixed for a *preliminary hearing*. This is a hearing to determine whether there is sufficient evidence to put the accused on trial. If sufficient evidence is not found the magistrate will dismiss the charge. If the evidence is sufficient, he will commit the accused for trial at the next sitting of the Supreme Court.

If the charge is in Class B, the magistrate may proceed with the trial in the same way as if it were for a summary conviction offence.

If the charge falls in Class C, the accused is allowed to elect the method of trial. If he elects trial by magistrate, the trial may proceed without further delay. If the accused chooses either of the other two options, the magistrate holds a preliminary hearing. If the preliminary hearing discloses sufficient evidence, the accused is committed for trial either before a judge alone (which in most of the provinces means a County Court Judge), or before a judge and jury, according to the accused's choice. In some provinces "judge alone" may be either a County Court Judge or a Supreme Court Judge; in Quebec he is a Judge of the Sessions of the Peace. If the accused has elected trial by judge and jury, he will be tried at the next sitting of the County Court or the Supreme Court, depending on which will next be in session.

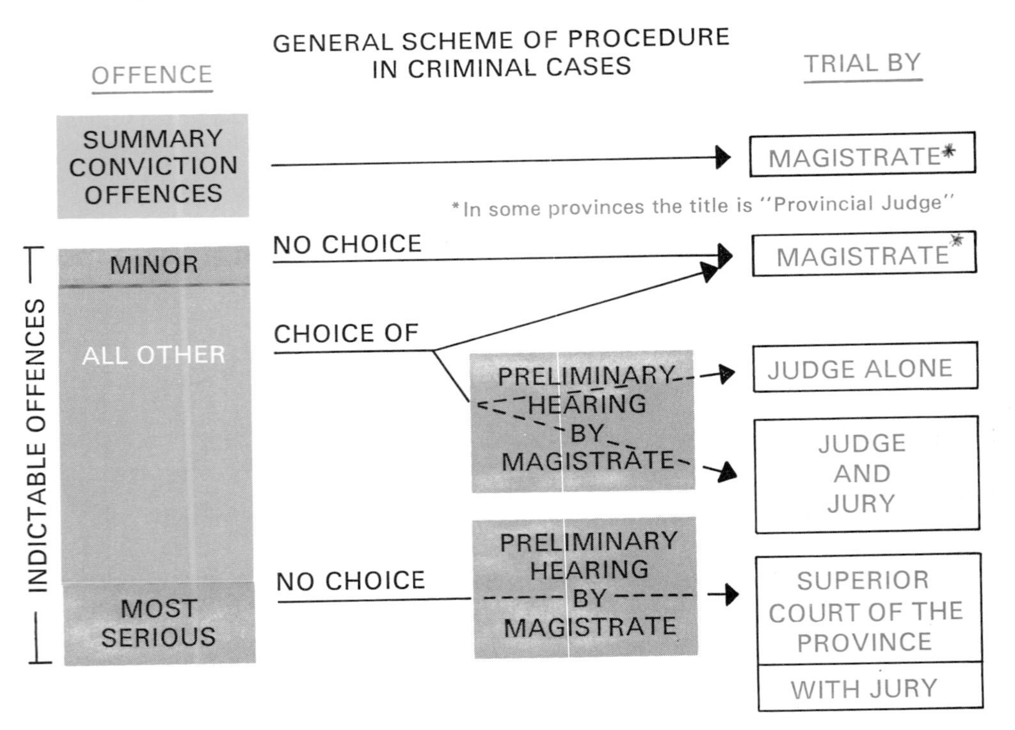

GUILTY OR NOT GUILTY

Once a person accused of a crime is before the court that has jurisdiction to try him, he will be asked if he pleads "guilty" or "not guilty." In summary conviction cases and in Class B of the indictable offences the plea is entered before the magistrate, but in cases within Class C the accused must first elect his court and method of trial. Usually, a person who is going to plead guilty will elect trial before the magistrate so that the matter can be dealt with immediately. Even if he elects trial by judge, or judge and jury, and a preliminary hearing is held, he may still plead guilty before the judge or court composed of judge and jury. In the most serious cases (Class A), a plea can be accepted only by a supreme court judge.

If a guilty plea is entered there is no necessity for a trial. The court, however, will require the prosecutor to disclose the facts upon which the charge was based. These facts are sometimes related by witnesses or sometimes read from a report by the Crown Attorney. Courts are careful to see that the facts justify the charge and also that an accused person has not pleaded guilty out of ignorance or fear.

If a court is not satisfied that a guilty plea is warranted, the guilty plea will be struck out and a plea of not guilty substituted for the accused so that a trial may be held and the issue of guilty or not guilty may be fully heard.

Courts are particularly careful in the case of young people who may plead guilty simply to avoid any further difficulty or publicity, when in fact they may not be guilty of the offence. For example, let us suppose that a young man takes a car without the owner's consent and then takes two of his friends for a ride. All three are apprehended and charged with theft. The two passengers feel that since they were in the car they are in the wrong and must plead guilty. A magistrate hearing the facts would strike out the guilty plea for the two friends. Subsequently, a trial would be held to determine whether or not the two did have anything to do with the theft.

In most cases, while an accused person awaits his trial he is at liberty; for instance, where the accused has come to court in response to a summons, he is free to go until the case is tried. If the accused has been arrested and then arraigned, he will still in many cases be released on his undertaking to return for trial, or upon his signing a *recognizance* (a document which contains his promise that he will appear in court at a certain time). In other cases the person arrested will be released on bail; however, in extreme cases the accused is kept in custody until tried.

While awaiting trial in those cases where an election of the method of trial is permitted, the accused is allowed to change his choice of trial court if he so desires.

In Ontario, Nova Scotia, Prince Edward Island, and Newfoundland, before an accused person who is to be tried by judge and jury is brought before a Court of General Sessions or a Supreme Court, the charge (Bill of Indictment) against him must be examined by a *Grand Jury*. This jury is chosen from a carefully selected list of jurymen, the number varying from seven in Ontario to twenty-three in Newfoundland.

The grand jury does not try the accused; it decides only if there is sufficient evidence to put the accused on trial. If, after hearing the witnesses in private, the grand jury thinks the accused should not be brought to trial on the charge as laid, it will bring in a *No Bill* verdict, and the accused will be discharged. If, on the other hand, the verdict is a *True Bill*, the case goes to trial. The grand jury simply repeats the work of the magistrate who conducted the preliminary hearing. For this reason the grand jury has been abolished in all of the provinces but the four mentioned above.

If the accused pleads "not guilty", the case is tried by the magistrate, judge alone, or judge and jury. In the case of a jury trial, the fate of the accused is in the hands of the *Petty Jury*, whose duty it is to render a verdict of "guilty" or "not guilty." (The Petty Jury is dealt with in some detail on page 31).

The fact that a person has been charged with a particular offence means only that he has been *accused* of a crime. Such a person is *presumed innocent* until his guilt is established beyond a reasonable doubt. It is part of our law that an accused is not called upon to demonstrate his innocence or justify his conduct. If, at the conclusion of the trial, a reasonable doubt exists as to whether a crime was committed, or, if one was committed, whether the accused person committed it, then the accused is entitled to a verdict of "not guilty."

The obligation resting on the prosecution to establish guilt beyond a reasonable doubt sometimes leads to the acquittal of persons who are strongly suspected of being guilty. It is, however, a part of Canadian legal tradition through English law that it is preferable that a guilty person should escape than that an innocent one should be convicted.

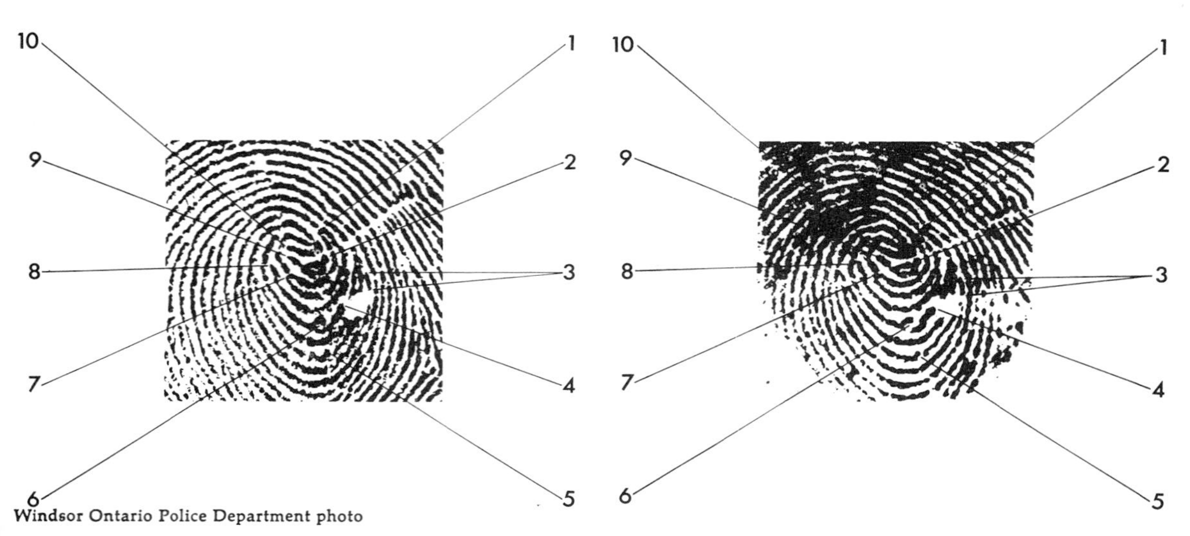

Windsor Ontario Police Department photo

How fingerprints are compared to prove the identity of a suspect. At Left is the inked thumb print of a man taken at police headquarters. At Right is a latent print developed on the door of a car, identified as being of the same thumb of that man. Points of similarity are shown: 1 and 7 Bifurcations. 2, 4, 5, 6, 8, 9 and 10 Ridge endings. 3 Short ridge.

DEFENCES

A person accused of a crime is, of course, entitled fully to defend himself. In the majority of cases the defence takes the form of a general denial, which is included in the plea, "not guilty." An accused person may also testify and call evidence of his own if he so wishes; or he may choose to remain silent, relying on the presumption of innocence and the possibility that the Crown's case will not be proved beyond a reasonable doubt. There are, however, some specific defences.

(1) *Insanity.*

C — 6

NOT GUILTY OF MURDER

CALGARY – Mrs. Joan Marvin was acquitted of non-capital murder yesterday by reason of insanity. A Supreme Court jury reached this decision following the presentation of medical evidence.

Mrs. Marvin had been charged with the shooting of her three school-age children.

The court found that Mrs. Marvin had a history of mental illness. At the time, according to the evidence, she was in a state of depression and was under a doctor's care.

(a) Why should insanity be reason for acquittal in a murder case?
(b) Would Mrs. Marvin be freed from custody after this trial?

Nineteenth century Toronto jail

John Ross Robertson Collection, Metropolitan Toronto Central Library

If at the time the accused committed an offence he was insane, he is entitled to an acquittal. An accused person who is insane is not, however, set free. He will be *remanded* (sent back into custody) to a hospital for the criminally insane until the authorities are convinced that he has recovered his sanity and is no longer a threat to society.

(2) *Self-defence.* The Criminal Code allows the use of force when a person finds it necessary in order to defend himself, his property, or anyone under his protection. The degree of force to be used, however, is only that which

appears "reasonably necessary under the circumstances." Unreasonable and unnecessary force, even when used in self-defence, may render the user guilty of assault or an offence of a more serious nature.

(3) *Double jeopardy.* It is often said that a person cannot be tried twice for the same offence, and, generally speaking, this is true—unless, of course, the first trial was defective and a court of appeal directs a retrial. With that exception, however, if a person has been tried and been either convicted or acquitted, he cannot be tried again for that offence.

(4) *Drunkenness.* Drunkenness of itself is not a defence to a criminal charge. In rare cases, the amount of drinking may have so impaired the mind of the accused as to have rendered the accused temporarily insane. Insanity, when proved, is a defence. If the offence is one that calls for proof of specific criminal intent, and it is shown that the drunken state of the accused rendered him incapable of such intent, drunkenness may constitute a defence.

PUNISHMENT

When an accused is found guilty, he is punished. The purpose of the punishment is to protect society by (1) deterring the accused and others from the commission of offences in the future, (2) reforming the offender, if possible, and (3) preventing the accused from doing further harm. The form of punishment varies according to the nature of the offence.

Suspended sentence. In some cases, especially those dealing with first offenders or young offenders, the court may suspend the passing of sentence for a specific period. Almost always the offender will be placed on *probation* during this time, which means that he must obey certain rules laid down by the probation officer, and must report to him regularly. If the offender exhibits good behaviour during this time, nothing further is done, but if he misbehaves during his probationary period, he may be recalled to the court where the conviction took place and be given the sentence for the original offence.

Fines. A fine is a money penalty that must be paid by the offender. There is usually an alternative penalty to the imposition of a fine, in the form of a prison term. But so that a person shall not be jailed simply because he does not have the means to pay the fine at the time of conviction, the courts are allowed to grant him a period of time in which to pay.

Suspension of driving privileges. When an accused is convicted of an offence that relates to the operation of a motor vehicle, part of the punishment may be the suspension of driving privileges for varying periods.

Imprisonment. For the more serious offences an accused may be imprisoned. If the term of imprisonment is less than three months, it will be served in a local or county jail. If the term is over three months but less than two years, the offender will be sent to a reformatory. When the sentence is two years or more, the term must be served in a federal penitentiary. In extreme cases, a persistent offender is prevented from committing further offences by being kept in prison indefinitely.

Photo: Miller Services Ltd.

In the local or county jails, because of the shortness of the individual terms of imprisonment no attempt is made to reform the prisoners. In the reformatories and penitentiaries an effort is made towards reform and rehabilitation by providing educational programs and training in the trades.

C — 7

PRISONERS TO GO OUT TO SCHOOL

Under a new program provided for in the 1968 Correctional Services Act prisoners may be allowed to leave their jail or reformatory for fifteen days (with an automatic renewal if he behaves) to take vocational training at school, or to continue their regular employment, or participate in rehabilitation programs. The prisoners are required to return to the jail or reformatory each night and on weekends.

Temporary absence for three days may also be granted a prisoner by his superintendent for medical or humanitarian reasons (for instance, a death in the prisoner's family,) or for reasons connected with his rehabilitation.

(a) Do you think this procedure is making life too "soft" for convicted criminals?
(b) Can a person who has committed a crime ever be fully rehabilitated?

Examples of training and counselling sessions offered inside Ontario reformatories. What change in attitude towards the convicted criminal is evident from these photographs?

Photo: Ontario Department of Correctional Services

After a substantial part of his sentence has been served in either the reformatory or the penitentiary, and if the authorities are of the opinion that a prisoner is a good candidate to resume his place in society as a law-abiding citizen, a prisoner may be *paroled* and allowed to return to society well before the expiration of his full term.

Death penalty. This extreme penalty has been abolished in Canada for all offences with the exception of (1) murder of police officers and prison guards while engaged in the execution of their duty, and (2) treason.

CIVIL LAW

The term "civil law" has two meanings, and care should be exercised to keep these meanings separate. In one sense the civil law means the system of law that exists in continental Europe and, to a large extent in Quebec, as contrasted with the common law or English law system. The term "civil law" is also used within the common law system to mean the law that governs the relationship between individuals, as distinct from the criminal law which governs the relationship between the state and an individual. Civil law, in this latter sense, is also known as *private law*, inasmuch as it deals largely with private rights and obligations. These include

- contractual rights
- property rights
- torts.

PROCEDURE IN CIVIL CASES

In criminal cases legal proceedings are initiated and conducted by public officials. An investigation is conducted by a police force and, in court, the case is handled by a Crown Attorney who is the state's representative for the prosecution of the accused. In contrast, a person who seeks to enforce his private legal rights must arrange these things himself. Generally, he will retain a lawyer to act on his behalf, choosing the appropriate court (depending upon the class and nature of the case), preparing the necessary papers and presenting his case for him.

THE WRIT

The first step in a private law suit or civil action is the issuance of a *Writ of Summons* by the Clerk or Registrar of the appropriate court.

The Writ is issued at the request of the plaintiff (the person wishing to sue) or by his lawyer acting for him. The court charges a small fee for this service. The writ includes a brief statement of the facts giving rise to the lawsuit, and commands the defendant (the person sued) to cause an *appearance* to be entered at the office of the Registrar or Clerk of the Court from which the writ was issued. The appearance commanded by the writ does not mean an appearance in person, but simply the filing of a document indicating that the defendant stands ready to defend himself against the plaintiff's action. If an appearance is not entered, the plaintiff wins his case by default.

If the defendant does file an appearance, both the plaintiff and the defendant exchange *pleadings*, which are documents outlining in detail the nature of the case each intends to present.

PLEADINGS AND EXAMINATION FOR DISCOVERY

After the service of the writ and the exchange of pleadings — but before the trial — both the plaintiff and the defendant have available to them procedures to ascertain the strengths and weaknesses of the other side's case. Either party may ask for an *examination for discovery*, which is an examination of the opposite party under oath presided over by a special examiner. Each side is entitled to inspect any documents dealing with the case or any property or goods that may have a bearing on the case which is in the possession of the other side. If either party alleges personal injury, the opposing side is entitled to have that person examined by a doctor. All these procedures are designed to promote as much as possible a full disclosure of the facts of the case before the trial. Frequently, as a result of these procedures, the parties agree to settle out of court, and withdraw the case. One of the advantages of a settlement out of court is that the court costs are minimized. In some cases court costs become quite high, especially when the loser is required to pay the other party's costs as well as his own.

Infants. In the case of an *infant* (a minor, See Part 11), a special procedure must be followed. An infant who wishes to sue for any reason other

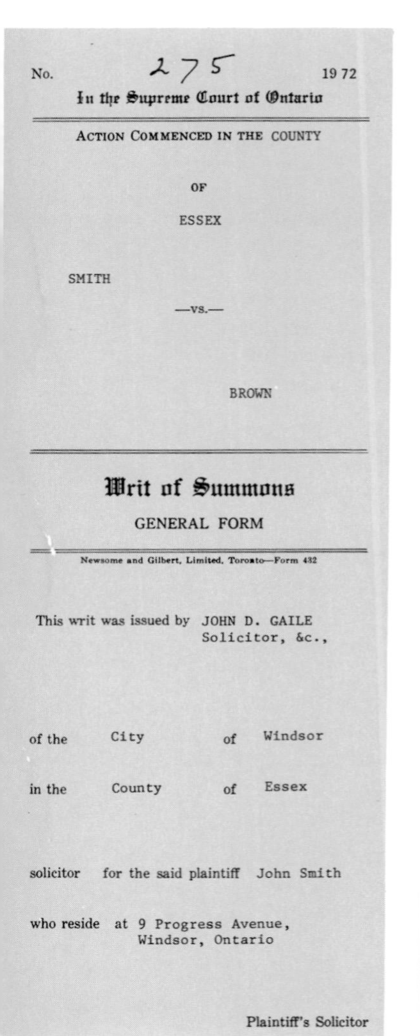

No. 275 1972

In the Supreme Court of Ontario

ACTION COMMENCED IN THE COUNTY

OF

ESSEX

SMITH

—vs.—

BROWN

Writ of Summons

GENERAL FORM

Newsome and Gilbert, Limited, Toronto—Form 432

This writ was issued by JOHN D. GAILE
Solicitor, &c.,

of the City of Windsor

in the County of Essex

solicitor for the said plaintiff John Smith

who reside at 9 Progress Avenue,
Windsor, Ontario

Plaintiff's Solicitor

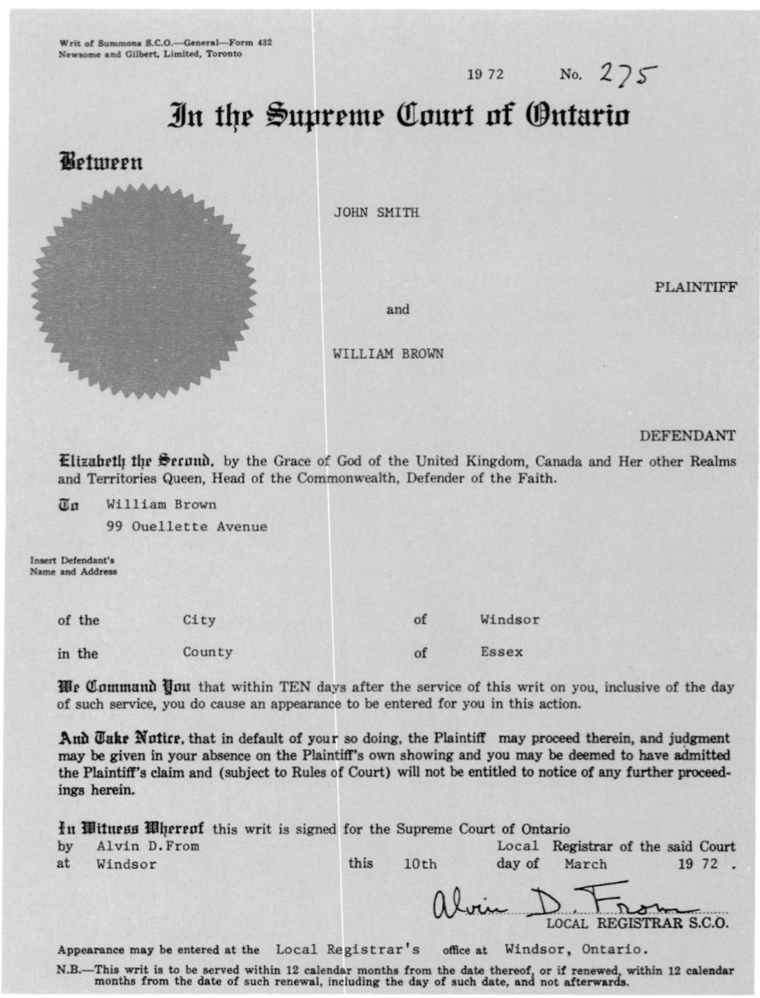

Writ of Summons S.C.O.—General—Form 432
Newsome and Gilbert, Limited, Toronto

1972 No. 275

In the Supreme Court of Ontario

Between

JOHN SMITH

PLAINTIFF

and

WILLIAM BROWN

DEFENDANT

Elizabeth the Second, by the Grace of God of the United Kingdom, Canada and Her other Realms and Territories Queen, Head of the Commonwealth, Defender of the Faith.

To William Brown
99 Ouellette Avenue

Insert Defendant's Name and Address

of the City of Windsor

in the County of Essex

We Command You that within TEN days after the service of this writ on you, inclusive of the day of such service, you do cause an appearance to be entered for you in this action.

And Take Notice, that in default of your so doing, the Plaintiff may proceed therein, and judgment may be given in your absence on the Plaintiff's own showing and you may be deemed to have admitted the Plaintiff's claim and (subject to Rules of Court) will not be entitled to notice of any further proceedings herein.

In Witness Whereof this writ is signed for the Supreme Court of Ontario
by Alvin D. From Local Registrar of the said Court
at Windsor this 10th day of March 1972.

Alvin D. From
LOCAL REGISTRAR S.C.O.

Appearance may be entered at the Local Registrar's office at Windsor, Ontario.

N.B.—This writ is to be served within 12 calendar months from the date thereof, or if renewed, within 12 calendar months from the date of such renewal, including the day of such date, and not afterwards.

Writ S.C.O.—General—p. 2—433

The Plaintiff's claim is For damages arising out of the negligent operation of a motor vehicle owned and operated by the defendant on or about the 2nd day of January 1972 at or near the intersection of Tecumseh Rd. and Chrysler Centre in the City of Windsor in the County of Essex and Province of Ontario.

than for the recovery of wages must sue through a "next friend." The case then proceeds in the name of the infant by the next friend who, generally speaking, is any responsible adult other than a married woman. The primary object of requiring that an infant sue through a next friend is to have someone before the court to answer for the propriety of the action. For example, the next friend will be liable for the costs of the action if it is unsuccessful. The prohibition against a married woman is based on the fact that, at least in earlier times, she had no money or property of her own with which to pay the costs of an unsuccessful lawsuit. This reason may not be valid today; nevertheless, the traditional rule remains in effect.

When an infant is sued, a similar procedure is followed. A lawsuit against an infant is not allowed to proceed until a guardian is appointed for him *for the purposes of the lawsuit*. This guardian for the purposes of the lawsuit is known as a guardian *ad litem*. Frequently, a parent or a relative will act as a guardian *ad litem*, but if this is not possible, the Official Guardian, a government official, discharges the function.

ENFORCEMENT OF JUDGMENT

At the conclusion of the trial, judgment will be given according to the rights of the litigants (parties to the case). The judgment may award a sum of money to one of the parties, or it may direct the restoration of property, or order the cessation of certain types of conduct.

The officials appointed to see that the orders of the court are carried out are the sheriff and the bailiff. The sheriff acts for the county, district, and superior courts, and the bailiff for the small debts courts. Their duties include the serving of summonses, attending at the sessions of their respective courts, and the sometimes unpleasant duty of enforcing court orders through the seizure and selling of property.

OTHER CLASSIFICATIONS OF LAW

There are other classes of law which are of a technical nature and, in view of the purpose of this text, need not be included here. The following three classes, however, are often referred to in the public press and are therefore defined:

- Military Law
- Martial Law
- International Law.

MILITARY LAW

This is administered by military authorities in military courts. Briefly, it deals with both administrative and disciplinary matters within the armed services. Military law in Canada receives its authority from the Militia Act. It should be noted that where civil and criminal offences are concerned, the civil and criminal courts take precedence over military tribunals.

MARTIAL LAW

In its proper sense, Martial law means "a suspension of the ordinary law and the temporary government of a country or parts thereof by military authorities." Such a situation will arise when ordinary law enforcement agencies are unable to maintain law and order. Martial law is then proclaimed and the military authorities take over until order is restored.

INTERNATIONAL LAW

International law consists merely of treaties between nations. It can only be truly called law when it can be administered and enforced by an international court. This, we should note, was intended to be one of the functions of the United Nations Organization.

APPLYING THE LAW

1. John Doe is arrested and charged with armed robbery, an indictable offence. What choice is he allowed by law with regard to his trial? What might influence him in making that choice?
2. A claims B owes him $25. B says the debt is only $20 and sends A his cheque for that amount. Do you suggest that A sue B for the balance or that he drop the matter?
3. A man sells his car for $150 to a person who agrees to pay for it within thirty days but fails to do so. The seller decides to sue him. Outline the legal procedure to be followed.

DISCUSSION AND PROJECTS

1. The main purpose of criminal law is the protection of society. From this point of view, discuss the effectiveness of each of the following forms of punishment: probation, fines, suspension of driving licences, imprisonment and the death penalty.
2. It is a part of Canadian legal tradition that it is preferable that ten guilty persons escape than that one innocent person be convicted. Do you agree with this view?
3. Prepare a written report for class or group presentation covering the following topics:
   (a) Bail for Arrested Persons
      - how the current system works in your province and community
      - how it might be improved there.

   (b) Prison, Reformatories and Rehabilitation
      - your province's past, present and future treatment of criminal offenders.

   (c) Juvenile Delinquents
      - what happens to them; the changes that have been proposed by the federal government concerning them.

   (d) Criminal Code
      - closer examination of what it contains; the latest group of proposed amendments being worked on by the Federal Government.

   (e) Drug Laws
      - present regulations; proposed changes; findings of the LeDain Royal Commission on Drugs.

Part 3
OUR JUDICIAL SYSTEM

Since so much of our law has been inherited from England, it is only natural that our judicial system (our system of courts) should be derived from the same source. Hence we find such names as the Court of Queen's Bench (Court of King's Bench when a king is monarch of the realm) and Court of Chancery still being used by some of the provinces.

The word *court* originally denoted only an enclosed space, and still survives in its architectural sense; for example, "courtyard" and "tennis court." At first the term meant the enclosed space where the king or one of his judges presided. Over the centuries, a special meaning of the word has evolved suggesting the presence of a presiding judge and officials in a place specially prepared for the purpose of hearing legal cases. Even today a judge can, in rare situations, convene his court in a hospital or private home.

At one time in England—in fact, for several centuries—one of the duties of the courts was to produce revenue for the royal treasury by the imposition of fines and fees. This duty may have impaired the true function of the courts. The gradual evolution of our laws and customs has now freed our courts from these burdens. Judges of the county, district, and superior courts are now appointed for life by the federal government. Magistrates (in some provinces called Provincial Judges) are appointed by the various provincial governments. These appointments are also of a permanent nature. The judiciary is therefore free to devote itself to the administration of our laws without fear or favour, as might be the case if their tenure depended upon the political party in power or some other consideration.

OUR COURTS

Both the federal government and the provincial governments set up courts. The provinces are responsible for the courts within their borders, while the federal government has sole jurisdiction over the Supreme Court of Canada and the Federal Court of Canada. While each province is responsible for its own judicial hierarchy and the nomenclature varies, the structure of the courts in the various provinces is roughly the same. Each province has a court of appeal which hears appeals from the trial courts of that province. With the exception of Quebec, the provinces divide their trial jurisdiction in three parts and distribute it between the highest court or Supreme Court; the County or District Court, which is a court of intermediate jurisdiction; and the lowest division which includes Magistrates' Courts and Small Debts Courts. Quebec has no intermediate division.

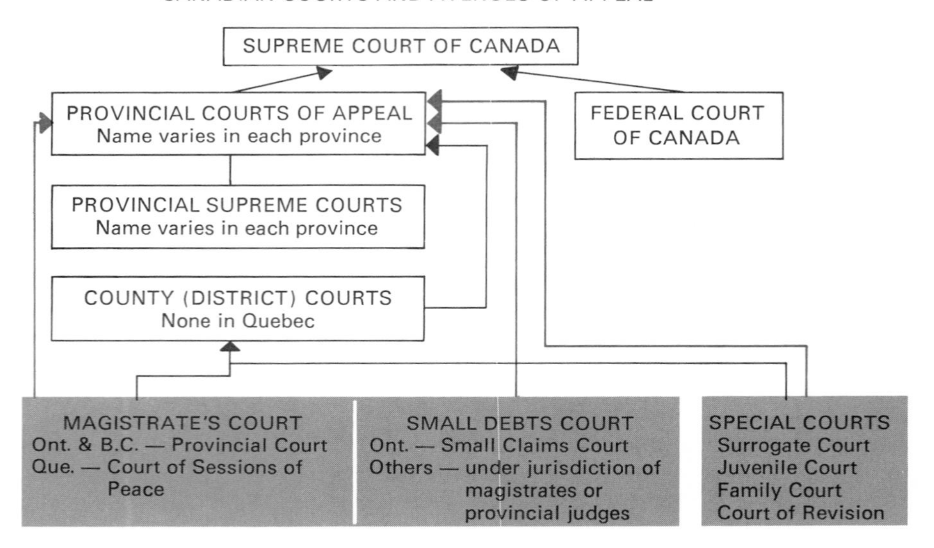

MAGISTRATE'S COURT

Magistrates' Courts are provided for in the Canadian Criminal Code, and are basically courts of criminal jurisdiction. Most of the provinces still use the designation "Magistrate's Court" as provided in the Criminal Code, but in British Columbia, Alberta and Ontario this court is now known as "Provincial Court." In the Province of Quebec the function of the magistrate's court is largely performed by the Court of Sessions of the Peace.

Although the Magistrate's Court is at the bottom of the judicial ladder of courts having criminal jurisdiction, it would be quite incorrect to describe this court as a minor court or one lacking in importance. All criminal cases begin in Magistrate's Court, and most criminal cases are also tried in Magistrate's Court. The lesser offences or the summary conviction offences as well as some of the less serious indictable offences are within the absolute jurisdiction of the magistrate. For offences beyond the magistrate's absolute jurisdiction (with the exception of the most serious crimes such as murder, rape and treason) the accused person may *elect* to be tried by a magistrate instead of going to a higher court, and many accused persons make this choice. Thus, as a result of the *absolute* jurisdiction and *consent* jurisdiction of the magistrates, most criminal cases are tried in Magistrate's Court. Even in those cases which are not tried in Magistrate's Court, and which are to be tried later by a higher court, it is the magistrate who must hold a preliminary hearing in order to ascertain whether or not there is enough evidence to hold the accused for trial by a higher court.

In addition to the trial of cases that may be properly described as criminal cases, the Magistrate's Court has been assigned jurisdiction to hear cases involving the violation of provincial statutes and municipal by-laws for which fines or other penalties are imposed. A person charged with the infraction of a provincial highway traffic law or a municipal by-law dealing with licenses will have his case heard by a magistrate. In sparsely populated areas, some of the lesser functions of Magistrate's Court are fulfilled by a Justice of the Peace, who is appointed by the province for that purpose.

Appeals from Magistrate's Court in cases involving indictable offences are heard by the Court of Appeal of the province. Appeals involving only summary conviction matters are heard by the County or District Court or, in some provinces, by a single judge of the Supreme Court.

"SMALL DEBTS" COURTS

These courts try disputes between individuals concerning claims for damages and debts where the amount of the claim is relatively small. Some provinces have separate courts to hear "small debts" claims; others have simply assigned jurisdiction in such cases to the Magistrate's Court.

The monetary limits of jurisdiction may be changed from time to time by provincial legislation, the tendency being to extend them upward to reflect the diminishing value of the dollar. The procedure followed in the small debts courts is rather informal and is based largely on the assumption that the litigants will handle their own cases without the assistance of lawyers. Court costs are quite low in order that those wishing a hearing may not be deterred by the expense.

COUNTY OR DISTRICT COURTS

All of the provinces except Quebec have an intermediate court. In Alberta, Saskatchewan, and Newfoundland, this court is known as a District Court. In Nova Scotia, New Brunswick, Manitoba and British Columbia, the name is County Court. Ontario uses the name County Court in Southern Ontario, and District Court in Northern Ontario.

In civil cases the County or District courts hear cases beyond the jurisdiction of the small debts courts, but also have their own monetary limits, ranging from $500 in Prince Edward Island to $10,000 in Nova Scotia. The monetary limits of the County or District Courts is further complicated by the fact that the limits are not absolute. In some circumstances the limits may be extended very considerably by the consent of the litigants. In 1971 Alberta removed entirely the monetary limit on its District Courts, which now exercise parallel jurisdiction in civil cases with the Supreme Court.

The County and District Courts also hear criminal cases involving indictable offences. If an accused elects to be tried by a higher court rather than by a magistrate, the trial may take place in the County or District Court, except when the offence is of the most serious type (murder, rape and treason), which by the rules of the Criminal Code must be heard in the provincial Supreme Court.

In addition to being trial courts, County and District Courts exercise a limited appeal function, hearing appeals from magistrates' decisions in summary conviction cases and, in some provinces, hearing appeals from the small debts jurisdiction of the magistrates.

SUPREME COURTS

At the top of the judicial ladder in each province there is a Supreme Court which has jurisdiction in both civil and criminal matters to hear cases that are beyond the jurisdiction of the lower courts. The names in the several provinces are as follows:

Alberta—Supreme Court of Alberta (Trial Division)
British Columbia—Supreme Court of British Columbia
Manitoba—Court of Queen's Bench for Manitoba
New Brunswick—Supreme Court of New Brunswick (Queen's Bench Division)
Newfoundland—Supreme Court of Judicature for Newfoundland
Nova Scotia—Supreme Court of Nova Scotia (Trial Division)
Ontario—High Court of Justice
Prince Edward Island—Supreme Court of Prince Edward Island
Quebec—Superior Court of Quebec (civil cases)
Court of Queen's Bench (criminal cases)
Saskatchewan—Court of Queen's Bench for Saskatchewan

Some of the above-mentioned courts are completely separate courts; others are only divisions of an over-all superior provincial court. For instance, in Ontario the High Court of Justice is a division of the Supreme Court of Ontario. Prince Edward Island, in addition to its Supreme Court, retains an extra division, the Court of Chancery, which is concerned with such matters as the estates of deceased persons, trusts, and the wardship of infants. In all of the other provinces the functions of the Court of Chancery is discharged by the Supreme Courts and County Courts.

COURTS OF APPEAL

Each province has a Court of Appeal which, with some exceptions, hears appeals from all the trial courts within that province. A panel of three or more judges presides over these courts, and the appeal is won or lost according to the decision of the majority of judges. The appeal courts of the provinces, as well as the trial courts, are not uniformly named. The nomenclature is as follows:

Alberta—Supreme Court of Alberta (Appeal Division)
British Columbia—Court of Appeal of British Columbia
Manitoba—Court of Appeal of Manitoba
New Brunswick—Supreme Court of New Brunswick (Appeal Division)
Newfoundland—Supreme Court of Judicature for Newfoundland
Nova Scotia—Supreme Court of Nova Scotia (Appeal Division)
Ontario—Ontario Court of Appeal
Prince Edward Island—Supreme Court of Prince Edward Island
Quebec—Court of Queen's Bench (Appeal Division)
Saskatchewan—Court of Appeal for Saskatchewan

THE SUPREME COURT OF CANADA

The Supreme Court of Canada is a court of appeal which hears appeals from the provincial courts of appeal and also from the Federal Court (formerly the Exchequer Court). The Supreme Court of Canada also has jurisdiction to deal with

Judges of the Supreme Court of Canada, Ottawa

National Film Board photo

matters referred to it by the federal government, particularly constitutional questions.

Not all cases may be appealed to the Supreme Court of Canada. In civil cases this court will deal with appeals from a provincial court of appeal where the amount in dispute exceeds $10,000. For appeals of civil cases involving a lesser amount special permission must be obtained. In criminal cases there may be an appeal to the Supreme Court of Canada if the accused has been sentenced to death, or if the offence was a serious one and a question of law is involved. In other criminal cases special permission must be given.

THE FEDERAL COURT OF CANADA

This court (formerly the Exchequer Court) deals with cases concerning taxation and other claims involving the federal government; for instance, a claim against the government for damage caused by an army truck, or disputes between the federal and the provincial governments. Cases involving trademarks, copyrights and patents also come before this court. In addition, the Federal Court has had conferred on it the power of an admiralty court to deal with lawsuits connected with navigation and shipping. It also has jurisdiction to hear appeals from federal boards, commissions or other tribunals. The Federal Court has its headquarters in Ottawa, but sittings are conducted from time to time at various other centers in Canada.

SPECIAL COURTS

The following courts are classed as special courts in the sense that their jurisdiction is limited to certain special matters:

1. *Surrogate Courts* deal with the probate of wills (officially proving them as authentic) and the administration of estates of persons dying intestate (without leaving a will). In New Brunswick and Nova Scotia this court is known

as the Probate Court. These courts are presided over by surrogate or probate court judges who, in most cases, are the county or district judges performing a different function with a different title.

British Columbia, Quebec, and Newfoundland do not have separate surrogate courts; the functions of this court are discharged by their superior courts — the Supreme Court of British Columbia, the Superior Court of Quebec, and the Supreme and District Courts of Newfoundland, respectively. In Prince Edward Island, the Supreme Court has an estates division.

2. *Juvenile Courts* are established under the authority of the Juvenile Delinquents Act of Canada. This court is administered by the province and, usually, is presided over by a magistrate or provincial judge. In some provinces the Juvenile Court sits as a separate division of the Magistrate's Court (or in some provinces, of the Provincial Court).

The Juvenile Court deals with children, not over the age of sixteen years, charged with offences under the Juvenile Delinquents Act. Although this court administers punishment when necessary, its chief purpose is to save the child from further delinquency. To this end, the court employs probation officers, and works through various social agencies such as the Children's Aid Society.

3. *Family Courts*, as the name suggests, deal with domestic relationships that have deteriorated to the point where the courts must take the matter in hand. This court is also, as a rule, presided over by a magistrate, and sits as a separate division of the Magistrate's Court (or Provincial Court). Most of the cases concern deserted wives and children and the failure of the husband and father to contribute to their support. In Quebec, this court is called the Social Welfare Court.

4. *Courts of Revision* function as boards of appeal in disputes concerning municipal assessments and voters' lists, and are not courts in the full sense of the word.

TRIALS

The primary function of our courts is to conduct *trials*, which are public hearings to determine guilt (or the lack of it) in criminal cases, or to resolve some issue in a civil case. Each side produces its evidence to establish its version of the facts, and presents its legal argument. In some cases the facts are not in dispute, and the whole contest revolves around the determination of a legal point. For example, A leases a piece of property to B for use as a race track for snowmobiles. The lease is to run for five years. Subsequently, the municipality in which the land is located passes a by-law prohibiting the use of snowmobiles in that municipality. The facts are clear. But what is the legal position of A and B? Is the lease ended, or must B continue to pay the rent?

In other cases the law is clear, and the trial proceeds on a question of fact. For example, two cars proceed toward an intersection on different roads. Traffic at the intersection is governed by an automatic signal light. A collision occurs and each motorist says that he had the green light. The law is clear that responsibility rests with the one who entered against the red light. But what are the facts?

In still other cases both issues are in dispute.

Trials are conducted on the basis of the adversary system; that is, each litigant (or his lawyer) presents evidence and offers arguments that favour his case. The court comes to a decision solely on the basis of the evidence offered. The court itself does not introduce any evidence nor does it undertake any investigation of the case.

NON-JURY TRIALS

Most civil cases are tried by a judge alone who hears the evidence and decides the issues of both fact and law in arriving at his decision. Years ago, jury trials were more common in civil cases, but the jury method of trial in civil cases has declined in popularity due to the fact that it is time consuming and expensive. The time expended in selecting a jury, instructing them as to their duties, and the extra time used to ensure that they understand evidence which may not be familiar to them can easily double the period required to try a case. In some civil cases there is no longer any right to a jury trial; in many others a jury trial is held only if one or other of the parties specifically requests it.

JURY TRIALS

The jury trial developed in England and is one of the more important products of the common law system. Despite the fact that the number of jury trials in civil cases has diminished, it still remains an important part of our legal system, and it is frequently reassuring to have the right to jury trial in a civil case if it is so desired.

In criminal cases jury trials are more common. As explained earlier, in some criminal cases the accused has a right to jury trial if he so elects. Furthermore, the most serious criminal cases, those of murder, for example, *must* be tried by jury. In criminal cases the number of jurors is fixed at twelve (six in Alberta) and the decision of the jury must be unanimous. In contrast, the number of jurors required for a civil case varies from province to province, ranging from five to twelve. The decision does not have to be unanimous; a substantial majority (for example, four out of five, or ten out of twelve) will suffice.

Every citizen is liable for jury duty except when his occupation excuses him. When people are summoned for jury duty, a relatively large number are required to attend at the court house at the opening of the court sittings. As a case begins, jurors' names are selected by lot from the entire group of potential jurors. The parties to the trial (prosecution and defence in criminal cases, or the plaintiff and defendant in civil cases) may challenge prospective jurors on the grounds that they are biased, and have them excluded from the jury. In addition, a certain number of jurors may be challenged peremptorily; that is, with no reason having to be given by either side.

Both civil and criminal jury trials proceed in much the same way. The evidence is presented and the jury, after hearing all the evidence and after being instructed by the judge with respect to the law applicable to the case, retires to decide on a verdict. After the decision is made, the foreman of the jury announces the verdict to the court. In the event that the jury disagrees and a decision cannot be reached, it is said to be a *hung jury*. That jury will then be discharged and a new jury will be empanelled. The case will then be tried all over again before the new jury.

APPEALS

It is part of our legal system that a person who believes that the decision of the

YOUTH WINS APPEAL

TORONTO – The Ontario Court of Appeal quashed the conviction of a 17-year old youth who had been convicted by a provincial judge in St. Catharines of exposing public view obscene writing on his trousers, contrary to the Criminal Code. The Appeal Court held that when the accused was arraigned before the provincial judge and given his choice as to the method of trial, it was clear that he did not understand the alternatives. It was recommended that the trial court should have taken steps to see that the youth received advice from either his parents or a lawyer.

The Court of Appeal directed that a new trial take place.

trial court has done him an injustice may take his case to a court of appeal. While our legal system is an excellent one, the people who administer it are human and subject to human error. The right of appeal is an important safeguard.

A decision in a particular case may be appealed on the grounds that there was a wrong decision on a question of law, or that a decision on a question of fact by a judge or jury was unreasonable and contrary to the evidence. In each province the appeal goes from any of the trial courts to the Court of Appeal for that province. This court proceeds to review the written record of the trial originally prepared by a court reporter. Except in the most unusual circumstances no new witnesses are examined nor is any new evidence heard. The Court of Appeal, if it finds that some error has been made, may either

- reverse the verdict entirely,
- vary the judgment (allow the main part of the judgment to stand, but vary some of the details, such as the sentence), or
- send the case back to trial court for a new trial.

APPLYING THE LAW

1. John, 15 years of age, and Bill, 18 years, have been caught in the act of stealing a car. They are both arrested and charged with theft. What is the difference in treatment prescribed by law because of the difference in age?

DISCUSSION AND PROJECTS

1. Consult an encyclopedia and bring in a report on
   (a) the origin and purpose of the John Howard Society
   (b) the forms of trial once used in early England, known as trial by ordeal, and trial by compurgation. (Sir Walter Scott's novel, *Ivanhoe*, contains an exciting story of trial by combat).
2. From your daily newspaper gather some examples of the kind of cases heard in Magistrate's (or Provincial) Court. If there is a courthouse in your area, arrange a visit.
3. Draw up a chart similar to the one on page 26 of the courts that exist in your province and show the avenues of appeal. Inside each box include not only the name of the court, but also its function.

UNIT TWO
RESPECTING THE LEGAL RIGHTS OF OTHERS

Part 4
THE LAW OF TORTS

The word *tort* is derived from the Latin "tortum" (wrong), which in turn has derived from "torquere" (to twist). It has come into our legal vocabulary through Old French "tort," meaning a wrong, and still retains that significance.

THE GENERAL NATURE OF TORTS

CASE 1

A 15-year-old newspaper carrier rang the doorbell of a house to collect from a person living downstairs, as he had done several times before. A man inside the house opened the door and hit the boy with a baseball bat, breaking the boy's wrist.
The man later stated that a gang of young people in the neighbourhood had terrorized his wife and he had thought the boy was one of them. He said he meant to hit the boy on the rear but hit his wrist by mistake.

(a) Should this case be classified as a crime?
(b) To constitute a criminal act, what type of facts might have to be evident in this case?
(c) What do you think should happen to the man? Should he be arrested by the police?

In law, *tort* has acquired a technical meaning. It means a *civil wrong* (other than a breach of contract or trust) for which the courts will award compensation to the victim for loss or damage suffered as a consequence of that wrong. In contrast, criminal law attempts to protect society by making the wrongdoer subject to punishment by the state, but does not concern itself with compensating the victim of the crime. A further distinction between crimes and torts is that the state has a duty to prosecute and punish those who commit crimes or break its laws. On the other hand, an individual who has suffered loss or damage because of another's wrongdoing is not duty bound to sue him for damages. Although he has a perfect right to do so, the exercise of this right is optional on his part.

Obviously, some forms of conduct constitute both a tort and a crime.

For example, A drives his car at a high rate of speed through an intersection against a red light. As a result he strikes another car and injures its occupants. A can be charged under the criminal code with dangerous driving or criminal negligence and can be punished. In addition to the criminal proceedings the occupants of the other car are entitled to sue A for damages (money) for their injuries, the damage to their car and any other losses they may suffer.

Not every type of interference with an individual's rights give rise to compensation. It must be recognized that when people live together in groups, a certain amount of interference is inevitable. There must be some balance between the necessary give and take of everyday living and the protection of individual rights. At the same time, there are types of loss for which compensation should be given and kinds of conduct that lead to the obligation to compensate. These constitute the subject matter of the law of torts.

INTENTIONAL TORTS

The wrongs first recognized by the law as a basis for awarding compensation were those that were *intentional*. As the various kinds of wrongful conduct were defined, they were labelled by the common law courts, and many of those well worn terms are still in use; for example, trespass, libel, slander, and assault.

INTENTIONAL INTERFERENCE WITH LAND

C—2

David Durant and his son Jeff rode their snowmobile onto a farmer's property. They went through a gate in the fence surrounding the property and did not see the following sign posted nearby.

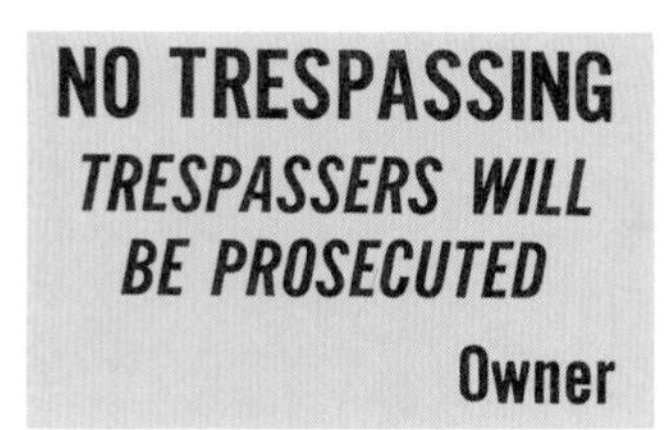

(a) What can the owner do about this invasion of his land? Does the sign mean that David and Jeff can be arrested?
(b) Why might this situation involve a tort?

The right to enjoy one's land without invasion or interference from another was one of the first rights recognized by society, and it remains an important right today. The law of torts prohibits entry onto another's land or property without permission or authority. If damage is done by one who enters wrongfully or trespasses, he will be obliged to compensate the owner for this damage. Even if no damage is caused, he may be liable to pay a nominal amount to the owner as damages for wrongful entry. If a trespasser does not leave upon request he may be forcibly ejected, but only reasonable force may be used.

INTENTIONAL INTERFERENCE WITH GOODS

As the law protected one's land from intentional interference, it soon recognized one's similar right with respect to goods. The person who intentionally damages another's goods will be obliged to pay for that damage. Those who take another's goods without permission or authority will be compelled either to pay for the goods or to return them. Similarly, a person who innocently obtains goods from someone who has taken them without permission is not entitled to keep them.

INTENTIONAL INTERFERENCE WITH THE PERSON

C—3

Conn sued David Spencer Limited for false imprisonment. Conn was shopping in the company's department store in Vancouver, B.C. He had made some purchases at the self-service department of the store and was waiting to make a purchase at the pastry counter when he was tapped on the shoulder by the house detective and accused of having stolen a cake of soap. He was asked to go upstairs to one of the offices. At first Conn refused, but rather than cause a scene he went upstairs where he was searched. It was found that the house detective had made a mistake and that Conn had stolen nothing. He was then allowed to go. At the trial the store officials argued that at no time had Conn been physically forced to go to the office, or forced to remain there. A British Columbia court held that Conn had agreed to go to prevent force from being used and to avoid creating a scene in a crowded store, but that he had nevertheless been "constrained in his freedom of action." Conn was allowed damages of $60.

(a) What does the phrase "constrained in his freedom of action" mean?
(b) Why would this action be classified as a tort?
(c) If Conn had not been asked to go upstairs but had simply been searched in the store, would his legal position have been different?

It is essential to a civilized society that one should not be threatened, beaten or confined. The term "assault" is used to describe both the actual striking of a person (or applying physical force to him) and a threat by act or gesture to strike a person (or to apply such force) when the threat is accompanied by the means of carrying it out. Also, if one is falsely arrested or imprisoned his liberty has been interfered with and he is entitled to be compensated.

DEFENCES TO INTENTIONAL INTERFERENCE WITH LAND, GOODS, OR THE PERSON

The rules set out above against interference with the land, goods or person of another are of a general nature; however, there are exceptional circumstances that provide a defence to a person who otherwise would be liable to compensate the victim of such interference.

Consent. One of the exceptions is consent. If a person consents to his goods being taken or his land invaded, he cannot claim that he has been wronged. Participants in sporting events involving physical contact cannot complain of having been assaulted; nor, generally, could anyone who voluntarily assumes a risk and suffers loss or damage thereby hold another party liable for his loss.

Self-defence. Self-defence is also a basis for justification of what would otherwise be considered a tortious act. A person defending himself, those under his protection, his goods or his land must, however, use only reasonable force to accomplish the defence.

Lawful Authority. Another exception is that the interference complained of has been performed under lawful authority. A parent has the right to administer reasonable disciplinary measures to his children; similarly, a teacher (who, by law, is considered as "standing in the place of a parent") may apply reasonable discipline to the students under his care. It is also by lawful authority that police officers and others connected with the administration of justice exercise the right, if they have a warrant, to enter premises, take possession of goods, or arrest and imprison those reasonably suspected of having committed a crime. It is also by lawful authority that, after trial and conviction, a person can be held in prison. If a person's liberty has been interfered with under lawful authority no right to compensation exists.

NUISANCE

C—4

Ontario Malleable Iron Co. Ltd. operated a foundry in Oshawa, Ontario. Russell Transport Ltd. bought land in the vicinity and used it as a marshalling yard for new automobiles which were to be transported to other places by truck. In 1951 it was discovered that the finish on the automobiles was being damaged by smoke and chemicals emitted by the foundry and that the property could no longer be used as a marshalling yard if this condition continued. The transport company sued for damages and also for an injunction (a court order) directing the foundry to stop emitting the smoke and chemicals. The Ontario High Court of Justice decided that it did not matter that the foundry was being conducted as skilfully as possible, or that the foundry had been there first. Damages were awarded and the injunction granted.

(a) What nuisance was being experienced by the transport company?
(b) What remedies were decided upon by the court?
(c) If the result of the injunction would be to close the foundry and thereby cause many people to lose their jobs, should this be taken into consideration?

C—5

The defendant had opened an isolation hospital in Vancouver, B.C., for the treatment of communicable diseases, 110 feet away from the plaintiff's home. The plaintiff sued, alleging the danger of diseases spreading from the defendant's property to his property. The British Columbia Supreme Court held that there must be an actual and real danger and not simply fear of danger. There was no evidence that the infection was air borne and would carry 110 feet. The plaintiff's case was dismissed.

(a) Against what nuisance was the plaintiff protesting?
(b) What is the difference between the nuisance described here and the one outlined in C—4?
(c) If there had been a real danger of infection, would the payment of money damages to cover the expense of selling one house and moving and buying another be an adequate remedy? (Consider the hospital a community necessity).

C—6

A man keeps two dogs in his back yard. The dogs are very noisy at night and disturb the neighbours.

(a) Why does this situation represent a tort?
(b) Have the neighbours any right of legal action?

In the law of torts, *nuisance* generally means the use of land in such a way that it interferes with the enjoyment and use of adjoining land. Since every landowner must put up with some interference from other landowners, the main question involves the "reasonable use of land." Nuisances can arise in a great many ways.

If the nuisance complained of has been authorized by statute law—for example, noise and fumes from a railway set up under the Railway Act—there is no legal redress for any resulting nuisance. In some cases the right to continue a nuisance may be acquired by *prescription*; for example, if a person uses another's land openly, undisputed, and without permission, as if it were a right, for more than twenty years, his right to the use cannot thereafter be denied. In this way a right to discharge rainwater from overhanging eaves onto adjoining land may be acquired. However, it is not likely that a prescriptive right can be acquired to commit nuisances by odour, noise or smoke, since it is essential that the twenty-year usage be uniform, that is, be carried on in the same way from year to year.

DEFAMATION

C—7

During an election campaign one candidate made charges of dishonesty against another, who then threatened legal action for damages for slander. The party who made the charges insisted they were true, but the plaintiff claimed that in any case his reputation had suffered.

(a) Has any violation of personal rights occurred?
(b) Does it matter if the statement made is true or false?
(c) Would any untrue statement about you represent a tort?

The law of torts affords a remedy for injury to reputation as a result of defamatory statements. A defamatory statement is one that lowers a person in the estimation of others. Usually such a statement is seen as being designed to bring the victim to "hatred, contempt, or ridicule." A defamatory statement may be either direct or indirect, or by cartoon, caricature, or by any other means in a published or written form. If the defamation is oral, it is described as *slander*; if it is written or printed or reduced to some permanent form, it constitutes *libel*. It is a complete answer for an action of libel or slander to demonstrate that the statements complained of are true, but it is not an adequate defence to say that one mistakenly believed them to be true.

PRIVILEGE

C—8

The plaintiff and a travelling company of actors appeared at the Royal Theatre in Plymouth, England, in a musical play written and composed by the plaintiff. The defendant newspaper published a highly critical review of the play, saying that it was "composed of nothing but nonsense of a not very humourous character." The review further stated that "among Mr. McQuire's company there is not one good actor or actress." The English Court of Appeal expressed the opinion that this was simply fair comment. Mr. McQuire had not been attacked in a manner unconnected with his authorship.

(a) Why is libel not present in this case?
(b) What kind of comment about McQuire would have constituted libel?

It is considered essential for the proper conduct of government and the administration of justice that the people who conduct these affairs be allowed, *but only in the course of their official duties,* to make statements which might prove to be untrue, without incurring liability for slander or libel. For example, the defence of *privilege* extends to statements made in the Parliament of Canada, the provincial legislatures, judicial proceedings—particularly in the courts—and between high officers of state.

There are other situations where, if a statement is made in the course of one's duty, a qualified privilege may exist. This means that the person who made the statement will not be held liable in either libel or slander unless the statement was made *maliciously*. For example, the news media are entitled to comment thoroughly upon matters of public interest such as politics, public affairs, music, painting, literature. The comments may indirectly involve reputations, but will not render those who make them liable for defamation unless the comments are made with deliberate intention to harm the persons concerned.

INTERFERENCE WITH ADVANTAGEOUS RELATIONSHIPS

C—9

Two football players were under contract to play for the Detroit Lions of the National Football League. Before their contracts expired they were signed to play for the Toronto Argonauts.

(a) Why would the Toronto Argonaut club be guilty of a tort?
(b) What remedy would you seek if you were the owner of the Detroit club?

If one person interferes with another's *advantageous relationships,* it is considered a tort, and the law awards compensation to the injured party. A wide variety of cases falls into this class of tort, as, for example, when one individual interferes with another's contractual relationship; or when a manufacturer or a seller of goods makes untrue statements about the goods of a rival firm and thus interferes with its "advantageous" business reputation. Action may also be brought by a parent against the person responsible for the seduction of his daughter, and a husband may sue the person responsible for enticing away his wife.

UNINTENTIONAL TORTS

C—10

A waterworks company installed a fire hydrant near Blyth's premises. The hydrant had been manufactured according to the best known system at that time, and had worked satisfactorily for twenty-five years. Due to an exceptionally severe frost in the year 1885 the fire hydrant was damaged and as a result Blyth's premises were flooded. He sued for damages. The English Exchequer Court in discussing Blyth's claim stated that "negligence is the omission to do something which a reasonable man, guided upon those considerations which ordinarily regulate the conduct of human affairs, would do, or doing something which a prudent and reasonable man ought not to do." Measured by this standard, the court held that the defendant (the waterworks company) had acted reasonably and was not guilty of negligence.

(a) Why did the court decide negligence was not present?
(b) When a company manufactures a product in accordance with the best standards of the time, but later finds that it is defective, what should it do? Why do automobile companies sometimes recall their products for changes?

C—11

Bill was the owner and manager of a hotel. Arthur, who lived 3 miles away, arrived at the hotel tavern at 5.15 one evening. Bill arrived on duty at 7 p.m. and later claimed that Arthur was sober at that time. Around 10 p.m. that evening Bill ejected Arthur from the hotel because he felt Arthur was in an intoxicated condition and unable to take care of himself. Bill knew that Arthur could only get home by going along a busy highway, on foot. On his way home Arthur was struck from behind by a car and suffered severe head injury and a broken leg. He had to spend 115 days in hospital and eventually his left leg was amputated two inches below the knee.

(a) Refer back to the definition of negligence contained in C — 10. Do you think it applies to Bill in this case?
(b) Would your answer in (a) apply to every situation where tavern owners eject patrons who have drunk too much?

The deliberate infliction of wrong as discussed under Intentional Torts above, is not common, but the infliction of harm through careless conduct or through negligence is extremely common. As evidence of this fact, one need only consider the injury and damage caused daily by the negligent operation of automobiles. The modern law of torts has been to a large extent concerned with the problem of compensation to victims of the negligence and carelessness of other people, that is the "unintentional" tort.

Negligence is considered to be conduct falling below what would be expected of a reasonable man of ordinary prudence in the same circumstances. The conduct may be an act or the omission of an act. However, a law that required the same standard of perfection from everyone would be impractical and unworkable;

thus, many of the problems that have arisen in this area of law have not yet been solved.

THE STANDARD OF THE "REASONABLE MAN"

The behaviour of individuals in an infinite variety of circumstances is so unpredictable that it is generally desirable to avoid specific rules; however, the legislatures have intervened to lay down rules in some areas of negligence; for example, the operation of motor vehicles, and the handling of dangerous substances such as gasoline, or dangerous machinery. But, generally speaking, the law of negligence simply imposes the standard of the *reasonable man*, and obliges the person whose conduct falls below that standard to pay for the consequences of his negligence.

This general standard of conduct applies to all fields of endeavour. For example, the surgeon in the operating room is obliged to perform an operation with the care and skill possessed by the ordinary competent surgeon. If he falls below that standard and injures or causes the death of his patient, he will be obliged to pay damages. On the other hand, if the patient suffers harm despite the "reasonable" care of the surgeon, there is no liability. Similarly, the operator of an air-hammer on a city street must use the care and skill of the ordinary competent air-hammer operator if he is to avoid liability for injuries to passers-by caused by his work.

THE PROBLEM OF DAMAGES

Another problem that has plagued the law of torts is the extent of damage for which the wrongdoer should be responsible.

C—12

> The defendant, Hay, had just gotten off a bus and was busy removing a basket from the floor of the bus when a motorcyclist passed on the other side of the bus and collided with an automobile about fifty feet ahead. Hay heard the crash but she did not see the impact. The motorcyclist was killed and, after his body was removed, Hay saw the blood on the road. As a result of what she heard and saw, she suffered nervous shock. There was no question about the fact that the motorcyclist was negligent in the manner in which he operated the motorcycle, but the question that confronted the House of Lords (England's final court of appeal) was how far liability should extend. The House of Lords dismissed Hay's case on the grounds that liability extends only to such persons as one can reasonably forsee being injured by the failure to exercise reasonable care.

(a) Why was Hay not awarded damages?
(b) If we assume that a person is negligent, is he to be responsible for all of the damage that follows as long as the "chain reaction" continues?
(c) Supposing that the bus had departed and that while Hay was standing at the curb the accident happened in front of her, would the result of the above case be any different?

Because of the general nature of the law of negligence specific examples of its application are almost endless, and many of the problems to which it applies cannot be dealt with in this text. However, it may be useful to mention the most common classes of negligence cases and some of the specific rules that apply to them.

AUTOMOBILE ACCIDENT CASES

C—13

Gordon lent his automobile to his friend Thompson, who while using it injured a pedestrian. The latter sued Gordon and Thompson.

(a) Why should Gordon also be held liable?
(b) If Thompson had borrowed Gordon's car without permission would Gordon still be liable?

Ontario Police Department photo

The most common cause for legal action on the grounds of negligence arises from automobile accidents. Court calendars are crowded with this type of case.

Each province has a Highway Traffic Act or similar statute which sets out in great detail specific rules for the operation of an automobile: speed limits, rules of the road, and so on. Generally speaking, violation of these rules will constitute negligence, but beyond compliance with them, the standard of the "reasonable man" continues to apply, and in some cases this standard may be more onerous than the statutory rules. As an example, a highway traffic statute may set a speed limit of 30 miles per hour, but to drive at even 20 miles per hour when the roads are glazed with ice may be an act of extreme carelessness or even recklessness. Thus, the driver, despite the fact that he is operating within the limits imposed by the Highway Traffic Act, may still be considered negligent.

In addition to laying down rules of the road, the various traffic acts have altered the relationship of the driver of a motor vehicle to some of the classes of people who may be injured by his negligence. For instance, the responsibility of the driver of a motor vehicle to his passengers is diminished unless the vehicle is being operated in the business of carrying passengers for compensation, such as a taxi or bus. Passengers who are travelling free are not entitled to compensation as a result of an automobile accident caused by their own driver unless that driver is guilty of *gross* negligence (a degree of negligence implying wilful and wanton misconduct). In British Columbia, ordinary negligence is now sufficient to incur liability.

On the other hand, if a motorist collides with something other than another motor vehicle, such as a pedestrian or a bicyclist, statute law requires that such motorist must prove that he was not negligent or he may be held liable. Ordinarily, a plaintiff must prove his claim, but in cases of the type just described the position of the parties has been reversed by legislation and the burden of proof shifted to the defendant.

The various traffic acts also provide that the owner of the motor vehicle as well as the driver shall be liable for any loss or damage caused by reason of negligence in the operation of such vehicle. If, however, the vehicle was in the possession of some person without the owner's consent, the owner will not be held liable for loss or damage caused by the driver. Consent need not be express; it may be implied. Occasionally, this point creates difficulty, particularly when the driver is a member of the owner's family.

MANUFACTURERS' LIABILITY FOR GOODS

C — 14 ✓

In 1932, the House of Lords in England dealt with a case involving a manufacturer of soft drinks. A bottle of ginger beer had been purchased from a retailer for a Miss Donahue by a friend of hers. The ginger beer was contained in a dark bottle and contained the decomposed remains of a snail. Donahue drank some of the ginger beer before she discovered its contents, after which she became ill. The House of Lords held the manufacturer liable on the grounds that he was negligent in the manufacture of the ginger beer, and that the consumption by the purchaser was foreseeable.

(a) How was the manufacturer negligent?
(b) If the ginger beer had been in a clear glass bottle would the manufacturer still be liable?

At one time the law of negligence was seldom applied to the maker of goods; the buyer and the seller were free to define their own standards by agreement. In modern society, however, the manufacturer seldom sells to the consumer. Manufacturers sell to wholesalers who, in turn, sell to retailers who, in their turn, sell to the consumer. As a result, the consumer is almost never a party to a contract with the manufacturer.

The principle in C — 14 has been extended from cases involving food and drink to many other commodities, and includes not only consumers of the product but also those who are injured by its use. Thus, the manufacturer of an automobile that goes out of control because of a defect of manufacture is responsible not only to the driver and the passengers but also to pedestrians and other motorists who suffer injury or loss because of that defect.

DANGEROUS PREMISES

C — 15

(a) Is the hostess liable for any costs incurred as a result of this accident?
(b) Would it make any difference if the person was a neighbour or someone who had come to the house to sell cosmetics?

C — 16

(i) Dominion Stores were sued by a customer, Such, who had slipped and fallen on an icy spot in the parking lot and claimed damages for injuries. He lost his case, and the Ontario Court of Appeal dismissed his appeal, on the grounds that Such knew that there was ice and snow in the parking lot, and that ice and snow in Canada is not an *unusual* situation. The Court ruled that considering both of these reasons, the ice in the parking lot did not constitute an unusual danger.

(ii) Campbell entered a branch of the Royal Bank in Manitoba on a snowy day, and slipped and fell where the floor was made slippery by the accumulated water resulting from snow tracked in by customers. The Manitoba Court of Appeal held that water on the floor of a bank on a snowy day in Manitoba was not an unusual danger, and dismissed the appeal. The case was then appealed to the Supreme Court of Canada. This Court decided that it was an unusual danger, and that the bank had failed to use reasonable care to prevent it. That court therefore gave judgment in favour of the appellant Campbell (the plaintiff in the original trial).

(a) Which of the following would you consider to be an unusual danger?
- a highly polished floor in a supermarket
- a highly polished floor in a dance hall
- dim lights in a coffee house
- a large hole in a parking lot covered with snow

- a deep ditch filled with snow in a ski area.

(b) The decisions were different in cases involving the above somewhat similar situations. Why?

The question of responsibility for injury caused by dangerous premises has given rise to a complicated pattern of rules. The duty of doing anything to make premises less dangerous falls upon the occupier of the premises. It may be that the owner is also the occupier, but the law places the responsibility on the party who is actually in occupation.

People who enter on to another's property are divided into three classes: (1) invitees, (2) licensees, and (3) trespassers.

An *invitee,* contrary to what might be expected, is not simply someone who is invited on to the property. An invitee is a business visitor, such as an employee, or a customer. The rule with respect to invitees is that the occupier has a duty to use reasonable care to prevent damage from unusual danger of which he (the occupier) knows or ought to know.

A *licensee* is a person who enters property or premises by permission of the occupier. This group includes those people who come on to the property for purposes other than business with the occupier. The occupier is not bound to make the premises safe for licensees, but is only required to warn him of concealed dangers of which the occupier knows.

C — 17

A boy, aged seven, was playing with other children in a playground in the Botanic Gardens of the City of Glasgow. The boy left the playground and entered a fenced area where he picked and ate some berries from a shrub named *Atropa Belladonna.* These berries were similar in appearance to grapes and were very tempting, but extremely poisonous. The boy fell ill and died. The father sued the City of Glasgow who defended on the grounds that the boy was a trespasser in the area where the shrub was growing and that no duty was owed to him. The House of Lords held that the defendant, the City, had presented a situation to children that was alluring and tempting; that it was therefore bound to take steps to prevent injury to children, and because of its failure to do so was held responsible.

(a) Should a city be responsible for any injury suffered by persons trespassing on its property? Why was the City of Glasgow liable in this case?

(b) Does the above case have any bearing on the backyard swimming pool?

A *trespasser* is a person who enters on another's property without permission; consequently, the occupier owes him no duty to make the premises safe. But an occupier will be liable if he does the trespasser any intentional harm.

Trespassing children present a different problem. The law recognizes that, occasionally, dangerous premises present an *allurement* to children; therefore, in some circumstances an owner will be liable to child trespassers when he would not be liable to an adult trespasser. What constitutes an allurement depends upon the circumstances in each case. If an allurement is considered to have existed, the occupier of the premises must be able to show that he had taken all reasonable precautions to prevent accidents which could reasonably have been foreseen; otherwise he may not be able to avoid liability. If circumstances rule out the presence of allurement, the child may be considered simply as a trespasser.

C — 18

If children are injured while playing in the sandpile, who should be liable — the city? the contractor? nobody, since the children should not have been playing there?

DEFENCES TO UNINTENTIONAL TORTS

In any action arising from an alleged unintentional tort it is obviously a defence to be able to deny any fact essential to the action (for example, to demonstrate the absence of negligence, or to show that the plaintiff was a trespasser). In addition to a general denial, however, there are certain specific defences available. Some of them are described below.

Act of God or Inevitable Accident. An inevitable accident may be described as one that is not avoidable by any precaution which a reasonable man would be expected to take, as, for example, if a moving vehicle is struck by lightning and the driver loses control and collides with a pedestrian on the sidewalk. In such circumstances there would be no liability.

Contributory Negligence. At common law, if the plaintiff as well as the defendant was found to be negligent, he could not recover from the defendant. The theory of the common law was that since both parties had broken the law, the law would not assist either one. This harsh doctrine has been abolished, and the defendant can no longer avoid all liability simply because negligence on the part of the plaintiff was a contributing factor in the case. *Contributory negligence,* however, remains a *partial* defence. If the plaintiff is also negligent, the court will apportion negligence between the parties in percentages so that the plaintiff will recover judgment only for that portion of his loss for which the defendant is held responsible. For example, assume that A and B are involved in an automobile accident. A's automobile is damaged to the extent of $500, while B's automobile is damaged to the extent of $1,000. Both are found to be negligent and responsibility is assessed at "fifty-fifty." B is therefore obliged to pay A $250, and A is obliged to pay B $500.

VOLUNTARY ASSUMPTION OF RISK

C — 19

(i) Murray, a six-year-old boy, was taken to see a hockey game at an arena, and was given a seat in the front row. In the course of the game, the boy was hit over the left eye by a flying puck, and the sight of that eye was seriously impaired as a result. The Court of Appeal in England dismissed the action on the grounds that a flying puck was an incidental risk of the game which was assumed by spectators.

(ii) Payne was a spectator sitting next to the boards at a hockey game in Maple Leaf Gardens who was injured when one player attacked another to take away his stick. Payne, who in the *mêlée* had been struck by the stick, sued and obtained judgment against the offending player. An Ontario court held that spectators at hockey games assumed the risk of accidents, but not the risk of injuries resulting directly from the improper conduct of the players.

(a) Accidents in similar settings resulted in different legal decisions in the above two cases. Why?

(b) What would be the legal position of a person injured by:
- a fly ball at a baseball game?
- a car that goes off the track and into the grandstand at a stock car race?
- a football player whose attempt to catch a pass carries him across the sideline and into the spectators?

(iii)

Toronto Telegram

(a) How does this stock car race compare with a hockey game in terms of voluntary risk by the spectators?

Voluntary assumption of risk as a defence to an action of negligence is much the same as the defence of consent in cases of intentional harm. In order for this defence to apply the victim must have had full knowledge of the risk to be encountered and must have had a choice as to whether or not he would assume the risk. In some cases, before a person is allowed to embark upon a dangerous activity he is asked to agree expressly to the acceptance of the risk. In other cases, despite the fact that nothing may have been said, the risk is considered to be apparent. The plaintiff is then considered to have accepted the risk by implication.

STRICT LIABILITY

In the case of both intentional torts and unintentional torts some sort of fault is present. In unintentional torts the degree of fault may be very slight but it is sufficient to give rise to the obligation to compensate the victim. Certain classes of activity, however, are regarded by the law as having so much potential for danger that the person who engages in them is responsible for any ensuing loss despite the absence of intention or of negligence. This is known as *strict liability*. Strict liability applies to such activities as the keeping of dangerous animals and engaging in dangerous activities.

DANGEROUS ANIMALS

C — 20

A person who kept a watchdog of a vicious nature allowed it to run loose in a closed yard. A gate was carelessly left open, and a delivery man was severely bitten. In the same neighbourhood a dog while being taken for a walk on leash suddenly bit a passer-by, causing him painful injury requiring medical treatment.

(a) Would the fact that one dog was "vicious" and the other supposedly gentle affect the liability of either dog owner?
(b) If the gate had been closed and the "vicious" dog had somehow jumped over the fence which should have confined him, would the owner still be liable?

If one keeps dangerous animals, he does so at his peril, for he will be responsible for any harm that the dangerous animal may do. Dangerous animals are divided into two classes: *wild animals,* such as lions and bears, which are normally dangerous despite the fact that some individual animal in particular may have been more or less tamed; and *domestic animals,* such as dogs and horses, which are known to possess dangerous propensities even though they are usually harmless.

A keeper of wild animals is responsible for the damage they do no matter how tame the keeper thought they were. On the other hand, a keeper of a domestic animal is liable only if he had reason to believe that it had become dangerous. Thus, the keeper of a dog which, for the first time, bites a passerby, may successfully defend himself by showing that he had no reason to suspect that the dog would ever bite a person. However, when the same dog again bites a passerby, he will no longer have this defence available to him, for he now knows of the dog's dangerous tendencies. Hence, the old maxim: "Every dog is entitled to one bite."

DANGEROUS ACTIVITIES

If a person uses his property in an unnatural way, such as storing water in a tank, or keeps natural gas, gasoline or explosives, and these materials either escape or explode, and cause damage, the keeper of these dangerous substances becomes liable despite the fact that all possible care was used in their storage.

LIABILITY IN TORT FOR THE ACTS OF OTHERS

Everyone is liable for his own tortious acts, but there are cases in which another person also may be held responsible for a wrongdoer's tortious acts, even though such other person may not have been guilty of either intentional or unintentional wrong. Some examples follow.

C — 21

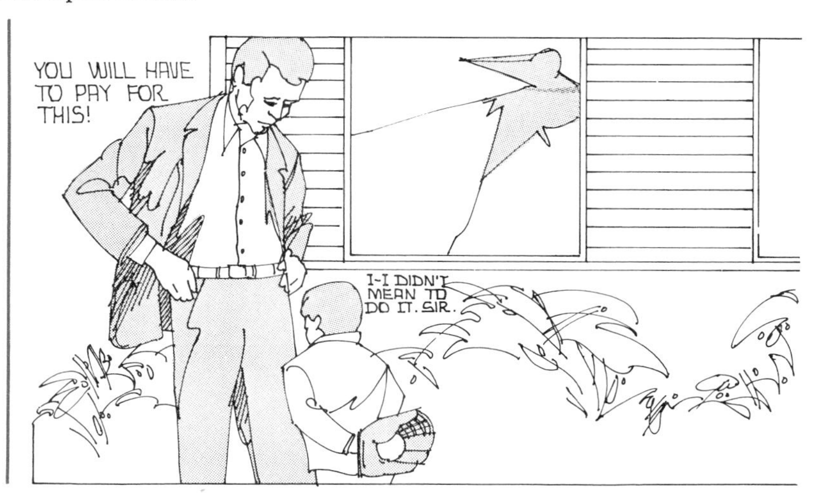

(a) Is the boy liable to pay for the damage?
(b) Would the boy's parents be liable?

C — 22

A boy while playing with an air-rifle injured another boy. Legal action was taken against the father of the boy responsible for the accident. In the course of the trial evidence was given that previous to the accident neighbours had complained to the father regarding the careless use of the air-rifle by his son.

(a) Should the father be held liable in this situation?
(b) If the neighbours had never complained to the father about the boy's use of the gun, would the father be liable?
(c) Would the boy's age affect your decisions in (a) or (b)?

PARENTS

Contrary to popular belief, parents are not responsible for the torts of their children simply because of the parental relationship. Parents of children who drive the family car become responsible not because they are parents but because they are owners of the vehicle. In other cases parents become liable for the tortious acts of their children because of their own negligence. For example, a parent who gives an air-rifle to his six-year-old boy may find himself responsible if the child uses it so as to cause injury or damage, not because he is responsible for the six-year-old boy's wrongful acts but because he, himself, was negligent in giving an air-rifle to such a young child. If the boy were fifteen years of age or more, the result of a claim might very well be different.

It must not be inferred from the above example that children are not liable for their torts. A child is liable for intentional torts if he is old enough to be capable of forming such an intention. A child can also be held responsible for negligence if he fails to show the degree of care to be reasonably expected from a child of his (or her) age. Children of seven years of age have in some instances been held responsible in tort. However, there is obviously no point in suing a child who is without independent means since a judgment against him could not be enforced.

EMPLOYERS

An employer is responsible for torts committed by his employee while the employee is acting within the scope of his employment (See Part 19). The employee is also liable, of course, but the injured party usually presses his claim against the employer because of the employer's presumably better financial position.

OWNERS OF MOTOR VEHICLES

By statute law the owner of a motor vehicle, as well as the driver, is responsible for any loss or damage sustained by any person by reason of negligence in the operation of such vehicle. If, however, the vehicle was in the possession of some person without the owner's consent, the owner will not be held liable.

PARTNERS

Partners are liable for any tort committed by other partners in the ordinary course of the partnership business.

REMEDIES FOR TORTS

C — 23

(i) In 1967 one of the U.S. astronauts died in a spacecraft fire. Subsequently the astronaut's widow sued the contractor employed by NASA for $10 million, charging the contractor with negligence.

(ii) A film company had plans to shoot a feature movie on a palatial estate in Rosedale, a well-established and affluent area of Toronto. They planned to use the estate's six acres of ground and 20-room mansion. Neighbours on the street applied to the court for an order (injunction) which prevented the film company from proceeding with their plans on that location. Their application claimed that noise from excessive traffic allegedly caused by the film company was a detriment to the street's residents.

(a) What are two ways to remedy the victims of torts?
(b) In general, when might each remedy be used? Could they both be used?

Once a court has determined the issue of responsibility, the next problem is the question of *remedy*. In most cases all the courts can do is to award a sum of money in order to compensate the victim. This money is described as *damages*.

DAMAGES

A sum of money is not always a perfect compensation. A person who has lost a limb, for instance, cannot be restored to his pre-accident condition. In such cases the courts attempt to do the best they can through monetary compensation.

Damages are awarded under various headings, and a victim may be awarded one or all of them.

Special damages are sometimes described as the bare out-of-pocket expenses of the victim. This would include such items as the cost of repairs to one's automobile, hospital and medical expenses, and lost wages.

General damages are an estimate in money to compensate for such things as pain and suffering, disability, disfigurement, and loss of earning power in the future.

Punitive or exemplary damages are damages given to the victim, and primarily meant to be a punishment to the wrongdoer. If a tortious act is committed in a high-handed and flagrant manner, this type of damages will be awarded. Punitive or exemplary damages are usually awarded only in cases involving intentional torts.

Nominal damages are damages of trifling amount awarded for the violation of a legal right when no real loss has been incurred.

INJUNCTIONS

In some cases, where the wrong is of a continuing nature, a court may order that the wrongful act be stopped. Such an order is known as an *injunction*. Most tortious acts occur as a single event, but some, especially those classed under the heading of *nuisance* are continuous, that is, they go on from day to day (for example, the emission of smoke or noxious fumes that cause injury or damage to persons or property). It is in this type of case that the court may grant an injunction and order the cessation of the wrong. Sometimes damages will be awarded in addition to the issue of an injunction.

Failure to comply with an injunction is considered *contempt of court* and may be punished by imprisonment.

SATISFYING JUDGMENTS FOR DAMAGES

Once a judgment awarding a sum of money is pronounced, the next problem is to effect collection. Frequently, the problem is difficult. A judgment given against a penniless defendant is almost worthless.

The defendant is primarily liable to pay the judgment, but in some cases enforcement procedures may have to be taken against him. The courts provide appropriate measures whereby the property or goods of a debtor may be seized and sold to satisfy a judgment. There are also procedures whereby the wages of a judgment debtor may be seized to satisfy a judgment. This is called a *garnishee* procedure. The various provinces have legislation protecting wages so that only a certain percentage may be garnisheed.

INSURANCE AGAINST LIABILITY FOR TORTS

Awards of damages for tort may vary from small amounts to many thousands of dollars. Many people have had to use all their savings and sell their property in order to pay a judgment debt. As a result it is a common practice for people to insure themselves against the possibility of having to pay judgments for tortious acts. For example, the occupier of a building or a house will likely insure himself against the possibility of injury to those who come upon his premises. The insurance company does not pay the injured person unless the insured party has been found liable to pay. The insurance company, however, will only pay amounts up to the value of the policy.

Similarly, those who operate automobiles insure themselves (or should do so) against public liability, so that if they injure someone and are found to be at fault, insurance funds will be provided to satisfy the judgment. In most cases the insurance policy is sufficient to pay the whole judgment. In some cases, however, the amount of the judgment is greater than the limits of the policy, and the defendant is personally obligated to make up the difference.

VICTIMS' INDEMNITY FUNDS

The large number of automobile accidents and the often large amount of damages involved brought into focus two particular situations. Many innocent persons who had suffered injury and loss were awarded judgments which were practically worthless because the guilty parties were not insured and had no personal resources with which to pay the judgment. Others were the victims of hit-and-run drivers who could not be sued because they could not be found. The volume of both types of cases was so great that it became a social problem. The various provinces have now set up *indemnity funds* for the benefit of:

- people with claims against uninsured motorists who are liable for damages arising out of automobile accidents, and who cannot satisfy the claims out of their own funds;
- victims of hit-and-run accidents. (In cases where neither the vehicle at fault nor the driver are identified the fund will pay only claims for bodily injury. Claims for property damage are not included).

The name given to the fund by the various provinces is not uniform; in Ontario it is the Motor Vehicle Accident Claims Fund; in the other provinces it may be Victims Indemnity Fund, Unsatisfied Judgment Fund, or Judgment Recovery Fund. But whatever the name, the purpose of the fund is the same.

When these funds were first established it was necessary to obtain a court judgment against the uninsured motorist and then exhaust all possible means of collection before recourse could be had to the fund. This procedure has been modified by most of the provinces. If the uninsured party does not deny liability, those in charge of administering the fund now usually have the power to adjust claims, settle the case, and pay the claim without recourse to the courts. But if the uninsured motorist does deny liability, it is necessary for the injured party to sue and obtain judgment against him. Then, if he does not pay the judgment, the claim may be presented to the fund and payment recovered.

In all the provinces, if the fund pays a claim or unsatisfied judgment, the uninsured motorist remains liable for the amount paid, and is obliged to reimburse the fund. His driver's license and owner's permit will be suspended and will not be reinstated until he makes satisfactory arrangements to repay the fund.

These indemnity funds are frequently confused with insurance, but they are significantly different. Insurance funds protect persons who might be found responsible in tort. The indemnity fund is created to protect the victims of tort.

VICTIMS OF CRIME

C — 24

(i) A Toronto man was assaulted and injured by an attacker and was subsequently awarded $1,500 for lost wages and $900 for medical and legal expenses.

(ii) A man in Kitchener, Ontario, was stabbed with a 17-inch file. He was awarded $4,384 for loss of wages, $3,500 for pain and suffering, and $200 for other sundry expenses.
Both of these cases are typical of the types of awards granted by the Ontario Law Enforcement Compensation Board.

(a) What seems to be the purpose of the Ontario Board?
(b) Why not just let crime victims sue for damages under tort?

For some years leading members of the legal profession have been suggesting that there should be a fund to compensate the victims of crime in the same manner as the various victims' indemnity funds connected with automobile accidents. The problems are similar. For example, a person who suffers a gunshot wound in the course of a bank robbery could sue the bank robbers in tort, but the likelihood of ever being able to collect anything is very small, just as the dependants of a murdered man have little chance of being able to recover compensation from the killer.

In response to these suggestions, in 1967 Saskatchewan passed the Criminal Injuries Compensation Act and created such a fund. In 1969 Ontario followed by passing the Law Enforcement Compensation Act, which provides for a lump sum payment up to a maximum of $10,000, or monthly payments of $500 a month, to victims of crime. One of the first cases to be dealt with under this legislation arose in Windsor, Ontario. A customs officer on duty at the Ambassador Bridge was shot by a motorist proceeding from Detroit, Michigan, to Windsor. The motorist was subsequently apprehended but an attempt to collect compensation from him would have been fruitless. Without this new Ontario law, the customs officer would have had to suffer his own loss; instead, it is being paid according to the terms of the Ontario Law Enforcement Compensation Act. Alberta and Manitoba have adopted similar plans and it is expected that in due course similar legislation will be adopted in the other provinces.

APPLYING THE LAW

1. A customer in a self-serve store was pushing a shopping cart along an aisle where soft drinks were on display. The customer was twelve feet away from a spot where three bottles of a certain beverage were resting on the floor when one of the bottles exploded without warning. A piece of glass from the bottle struck the customer's eye, causing serious and permanent injury. The customer sued the store claiming that the store was liable to him as an invitee. He also sued the company which supplied the bottled beverage on the grounds that the company was negligent in that it supplied the defective product which caused the injury. Both defendants denied being negligent.

   At the trial evidence was given that the bottle exploded from internal pressure and that the bottling company's method of inspection was inadequate to guard against weakened bottles being used.

   (a) What is the legal principle governing the liability of the store?
   (b) What is the legal principle governing the liability of the bottling company?
   (c) Do you think, from the facts given, that the store should be held liable? Why or why not?
   (d) Do you think the bottling company should be held liable? Why or why not?
   (e) Suppose the bottling company argued strongly that the bottle must have been weakened (cracked or broken) during its handling by the store. In view of the facts as given, how would you treat this argument?
2. Bob, who was 17 and licensed to drive, was driving his father's car at night, with his father's consent. At an intersection he collided with a bicyclist, who was seriously injured as a result.
   (a) Bob claims the accident was not his fault; instead, he says the bicyclist was careless. He has no witnesses to support his version of the accident, and the injured bicyclist denies being at fault. Where does the onus of proof lie?
   (b) If Bob is found liable, does any liability rest on Bob's father? Explain.
   (c) If both the bicyclist and Bob are found to be at fault, how will the damages be assessed?
3. A is injured in an automobile accident which is entirely B's fault. A suffers a badly fractured wrist which is rendered permanently immobile as a result of the accident. What might be an appropriate award of general damages if A is
   (a) a 22-year-old N.H.L. hockey player?
   (b) a 60-year-old night watchman?
   (c) a 40-year-old high school teacher?
4. A man broke into an abandoned house on Mr. Brindley's farm. When he opened a bedroom door, a shotgun, which was lashed to the bed, fired, the pellets ripping into the right ankle of the

prowler. The shotgun trap had been set by Mr. Brindley to protect his property while it was boarded up.

(a) Would the prowler still be guilty of breaking and entering?
(b) Is a trap which could kill or seriously wound a reasonable method of protecting property against trespassers or petty thieves?
(c) The prowler eventually sued the farmowner for $60,000 damages. Although he was a trespasser do you think he won?

DISCUSSION AND PROJECTS

1. The various industries that pollute our air with noxious fumes and our waters with poisonous effluent are, in most cases, legitimate public industries authorized by law to operate. Furthermore, they provide a livelihood for many people. And yet such pollution can definitely be classified as a public nuisance.
   Produce a report covering the following areas in terms of the laws and regulations which exist in your municipality to control these problems.
   (a) Anti-noise by-laws
   (b) Water pollution
   (c) Air pollution
   (d) Animal control
   Include your comments on the adequacy of the present laws concerning such public nuisances.
2. Obtain a copy of your provincial highway traffic act and report on its scope and general content. Include in your report some detail about points of traffic law that you feel the average driver may not know.
3. In connection with defamatory statements, why should any class of persons be protected by the right of "privilege"?
4. What determines the standard of the "reasonable man"? Would the standards set up for one person necessarily be the same as those set up for another person?
5. It is sometimes suggested that the law should be amended so as to make parents liable for damage to buildings (window-breaking and other vandalism) caused by their children. What is your point of view?
6. Some Canadian provinces are introducing "no fault" automobile insurance. Report on how this differs from the traditional form of car insurance. Also determine its possible benefits to the legal process of setting accident claims. Try to consult a lawyer, an insurance agent, and your provincial elected representative for information. If possible, obtain their opinions about this new form of car insurance.

UNIT THREE
CIVIL RIGHTS

Part 5
CIVIL RIGHTS AND CIVIL DISOBEDIENCE

CIVIL RIGHTS AND THE LAW

Since the end of the Second World War there has been increasing concern regarding the rights, freedoms, and liberties of people. A number of reasons have contributed to this concern. The colossal inhumanity of the war has no doubt made a great many people more conscious of the need to respect human dignity. Moreover, since the war the need for increased social services by the various governments led those governments to further intrude upon the lives of their citizens. Thirdly, the increase in affluence generally has led to the development of the principle that everyone is entitled to an equal opportunity to participate in this wealth.

In the late forties the legislatures of the provinces of Canada began to enact legislation dealing with discrimination. This legislation has increased and broadened over the years and now includes laws directed against discrimination in accommodation and employment. In 1960, after some considerable debate, the Federal Parliament passed the Canadian Bill of Rights, which declares and recognizes a list of human rights and fundamental freedoms. The Canadian Bill of Rights does not purport to change anything, but merely recognizes and declares rights in existence in Canada.

In some other countries, particularly the United States of America, certain rights of the citizens are entrenched in a written constitution and, as a result, are beyond the power of a state legislature or of the congress to change. It is true that the constitution itself can be amended, but the procedure requires a large degree of consent. On the other hand, the British legal tradition, which Canada inherits, is based on an unwritten constitution. Prominent legal writers of an earlier era expressed the view that the English law generally protected the freedoms and rights of British subjects, and no specific bill of rights or declaration of freedom was necessary. In more modern times it appeared that there were new rights that had to be specifically defined, and that a specific guarantee of old rights was required.

In Canada the rights that are set out in the various provincial statutes and the Canadian Bill of Rights are not entrenched in a constitution; they are simply statutes, and the legislature that enacted them can just as easily repeal them or change them. Many modern legal writers and public figures argue that a full and comprehensive Canadian Bill of Rights should be enshrined in a constitution and thus placed beyond the immediate power of the provincial legislatures and the federal parliament. One of the obstacles that stands in the way of the accomplishment of such a measure is the failure of the federal government and the provinces to agree on a method of amending the constitution we have. The British North America Act, which can be described as our constitution, is an English statute, and can be changed only by the English parliament. It is generally agreed that the constitution should be substantially updated and should be repatriated to Canada. However, the provinces and the federal government have not been able to agree on the mechanics of how to do this. Presumably, a bill of rights entrenched in a constitution will have to await this development.

THE CANADIAN BILL OF RIGHTS
8-9 ELIZABETH II

CHAPTER 44

An Act for the Recognition
and Protection of Human Rights
and Fundamental Freedoms.

[Assented to 10th August, 1960.]

The Parliament of Canada, affirming that the Canadian Nation is founded upon principles that acknowledge the supremacy of God, the dignity and worth of the human person and the position of the family in a society of free men and free institutions;

Affirming also that men and institutions remain free only when freedom is founded upon respect for moral and spiritual values and the rule of law;

And being desirous of enshrining these principles and the human rights and fundamental freedoms derived from them, in a Bill of Rights which shall reflect the respect of Parliament for its constitutional authority and which shall ensure the protection of these rights and freedoms in Canada:

THEREFORE Her Majesty, by and with the advice and consent of the Senate and House of Commons of Canada, enacts as follows:

PART I

BILL OF RIGHTS

1. It is hereby recognized and declared that in Canada there have existed and shall continue to exist without discrimination by reason of race, national origin, colour, religion or sex, the following human rights and fundamental freedoms, namely,

(a) the right of the individual to life, liberty, security of the person and enjoyment of property, and the right not to be deprived thereof except by due process of law;
(b) the right of the individual to equality before the law and the protection of the law;
(c) freedom of religion;
(d) freedom of speech;
(e) freedom of assembly and association; and
(f) freedom of the press.

From the Revised Statutes of Canada 1970, Appendix III, Canadian Bill of Rights (Appendices Volume)

Information Canada

THE CANADIAN BILL OF RIGHTS

The Canadian Bill of Rights was passed in 1960. As already stated, it only recognizes and declares certain rights which were regarded as existing prior to its enactment. However it serves the purpose of designating and bringing to the attention of all Canadians the rights they do possess, and affords a convenient catalogue of these rights. Part of the Bill of Rights is shown on the previous page.

The Rights listed in the Bill are dealt with in detail below, and you will notice that some of the cases used to illustrate the principles predate the enactment of the Bill of Rights, confirming that the Bill of Rights only declares rights which have long existed.

(A) *The right of the individual to life, liberty, security of the person and enjoyment of property, and the right not to be deprived thereof except by due process of law.*

Despite the very wide scope of the wording of this sub-section, much of the area appearing to be covered is within the jurisdiction of the various provincial governments; for example, property rights. This section of the Bill of Rights can only extend to those things that are within the jurisdiction of the Federal Parliament and includes the following:

1. *Freedom from arbitrary detention, imprisonment, or exile.*
2. *Freedom from the imposition of cruel and unusual treatment or punishment.*

Case 1

Michael Magda, a native of Roumania, was interned in Canada during the Second World War. He later became a Canadian citizen and sued the Federal Government asking damages for cruel and unusual treatment and punishment. The Supreme Court of Canada concluded that the treatment he had received was only the ordinary disciplinary and regulatory treatment of an internment camp, and dismissed the case.

(a) What right did Magda say had been violated?
(b) What might have constituted cruel and unusual punishment?

3. *A person who has been arrested or detained is entitled*
   - *to be informed promptly of the reason for his arrest or detention,*
   - *to retain and instruct counsel without delay, and*
   - *to the remedy of Habeas Corpus for the determination of the validity of his detention, and for his release if the detention is not lawful.*

A writ of *habeas corpus* (Latin for "have the body") is a centuries-old English law process for securing the liberty of the person. It is one of the special types of writ issued for the purpose of compelling inferior courts or officials to exercise their functions in accordance with the law, and to ensure that a person will not be unlawfully held in custody. Upon the application of the person imprisoned, or of his lawyer, a High Court judge commands the appearance of that person and inquires into the cause of his detention. If there is no legal justification for it, the party is ordered to be released. Simply being released on a writ of habeas corpus is not an acquittal, and such a person could be arrested at a later time when further evidence became available. This right prevents persons from being detained or imprisoned without a charge being laid. If a charge has been laid, the fact of the charge is, of course, a good answer to a writ of habeas corpus, and a release will not be ordered.

C — 2

(i) Fouché was taken into custody by immigration officers and subsequently ordered deported from Canada by the immigration department. Fouché applied to the Superior Court of Quebec for a writ of habeas corpus, arguing that her deportation was illegal. The Quebec Superior Court reviewed the case and found the deportation order was proper and that her detention by the immigration authorities was legal.

(ii) Two men were charged with armed robbery and arraigned before a magistrate. They elected trial by judge and jury. At the preliminary hearing the defence lawyer was not allowed fully to cross-examine some of the witnesses. At the conclusion of the preliminary hearing the magistrate committed the two accused for trial and they were held in jail to await that trial. An application was made to the Supreme Court of Ontario for habeas corpus on the grounds that the committal for trial was illegal. The commital was set aside. (The prosecution had the right to try again, however).

(a) In each of the above cases, what was the purpose of the habeas corpus proceedings?
(b) What must those who have a person in custody establish at a habeas corpus hearing?

4. *The right of a person giving evidence before a Court, Tribunal, Commission, or Board of other authority to have counsel and to be protected against self-incrimination.*

The right of an *accused* person to counsel has long been a part of our law. The Bill of Rights recognizes the right of a person arrested or detained to retain counsel without delay, and the right of a person *who gives evidence* to have counsel. This extends to a person who is only a witness and who is not charged with an offence. A witness' legal counsel may advise him as to his rights and the law concerning self-incrimination, etc. However, counsel for a witness will not ordinarily be allowed to take part in the trial.

It is not a part of our law that a witness may refuse to testify on the grounds that his answers may incriminate him, but if he asks for it, the law will protect him to the extent that his answers may not be used against him in a subsequent proceeding, except if he is charged with perjury. This section of the Bill of Rights recognizes and declares this principle, and provides that it shall not be withdrawn.

For example, let us suppose that X asks Y if he would like to buy a new transistor radio at a very low price, with "no questions asked." Y buys the radio and a few days later X is arrested and charged with theft of a number of radios. Y is *subpoenaed* (from Latin "under penalty of") as a witness at X's trial and is concerned about his own involvement. Y is entitled to

- retain a lawyer before he testifies in order that he may fully understand his own position;
- ask the protection of the court against self-incrimination.

Y will be obliged to answer the questions put to him at X's trial, but his answers cannot be used against him in the event that Y himself is charged.

Neither of the foregoing two rights *have* to be used; they are available to the person who testifies *if he wants them*. Most witnesses testify without ever needing or asking for counsel or protection against self-incrimination.

5. *The right to a fair hearing in accordance with the principles of fundamental justice.*

There are two principles involved in this sub-section. The first is that the judge or adjudicator be disinterested and unbiased. No one who has an interest in the result of the proceedings is qualified at law to adjudicate those proceedings. It is not important that the judge's interest would not influence his judgment. It has often been said that "not only must justice be done, but it must *appear* to be done." The second principle is that the parties must be given adequate notice and an opportunity to be heard.

6. *The right to be presumed innocent until proved guilty according to law; a fair and public hearing by an independant and impartial tribunal; and the right to reasonable bail.*

At common law everyone was presumed innocent until proved guilty, and this common law doctrine is carried into our modern criminal code. There are, however, some sections of the Criminal Code and some parts of other Federal legislation (the Narcotics Control Act, for instance) which diminish this presumption of innocence by casting upon the accused a burden of explanation. For example, one section of the Criminal Code reads: "Everyone who, *without lawful excuse, the proof of which lies upon him*, has in his possession any instrument for house-breaking, vault-breaking, or safe-breaking is guilty of an indictable offence and is liable to imprisonment for fourteen years." Since house-breaking instruments include such things as screwdrivers and other ordinary tools — even flexible plastic rulers have been used to spring door-locks in order to break into a house — the possession of such instruments in suspicious circumstances may place a person in an awkward position for which he must have an explanation. The emphasis, of course, is upon "lawful excuse," and it would be rare indeed for an innocent citizen not to be able to provide a satisfactory explanation for possession of such instruments. Nevertheless, the onus of proof lies upon the person in possession. Similar provisions apply to a person found in possession of counterfeit money.

It would appear that these specific sections of the Criminal Code are not affected by the Canadian Bill of Rights, since the Bill is only "declaratory" and does not change laws which were already in effect at the time of its enactment.

The right to a public hearing is not an unlimited right. The Criminal Code provides that a judge or magistrate may exclude the public from a trial if he is of the opinion that public morals, order or justice make it necessary.

C — 3

An accused who was charged with indecent exposure insisted on an open trial. The magistrate refused. The accused then applied to the Saskatchewan High Court for an order prohibiting the magistrate from proceeding with the trial. The court upheld the magistrate and dismissed the application on the grounds that the Canadian Bill of Rights, in providing for a public trial, did not reduce the power of a court under the Criminal Code to exclude the public in unusual circumstances.

(a) What basic right did the accused say was denied him?
(b) Should the public be excluded from the courtroom in any of the following:
(i) a trial dealing with the sale of secret plans to a foreign power?
(ii) an unusually gruesome murder case?
(iii) the trial of a member of a rebellious organization when all the members wish to attend?

In some cases, while an accused person awaits trial he may be held in custody unless bail is posted. If, however, the amount of bail were set at an extremely high amount, say, a million dollars, it is unlikely that anyone could post such bail. The Bill of Rights declares that bail should be reasonable — only such a sum as will ensure the return of the accused for trial, bearing in mind the seriousness of the offence.

7. *The right to the assistance of an interpreter in any proceeding in which a person is involved as a party or as a witness before a Court, Commission, Board or other Tribunal, if the person concerned does not understand or speak the language in which such proceedings are conducted.*

This provision in the Canadian Bill of Rights simply confirms an existing practice. It would appear that "understand" does not mean "understand perfectly"; thus, if a person understands reasonably well the proceedings which are being conducted an interpreter will not be deemed necessary.

(B) *The right of the individual to equality before the law, and the protection of the law.*

C — 4

Drybones, an Indian in the Northwest Territories, was found intoxicated off a Reserve and was charged with being "unlawfully intoxicated off a Reserve, contrary to Section 94(b) of the Indian Act." He was convicted by a Magistrate. The case was ultimately appealed to the Supreme Court of Canada. It was argued on behalf of the accused that, because of his race, he had been denied equality before the law with his fellow-Canadians. It was pointed out that it was an offence only for Indians to be intoxicated off the Reserve, and that the prohibition did not extend to all persons. The prosecution argued that the Canadian Bill of Rights was merely declaratory and did not change the effect of the Indian Act which was in effect long before the passage of the Canadian Bill of Rights. The Supreme Court held that enforcement of Section 94(b) would deny one of the rights declared and recognized in the Canadian Bill of Rights, and therefore Section 94(b) must be considered inoperative.

(a) What was the principal basis of Drybones' complaint?
(b) Do you know of any laws which necessarily apply to only a part of the population? Are those affected denied equality before the law?

Most of the matters to which this particular right applies comes under provincial jurisdiction, and it is in this area that progress towards equality has been made. All of the provinces except Newfoundland have enacted legislation dealing with fair accommodation and fair employment practices. Some of the provinces have consolidated their legislation on these matters into a single code known generally as the Human Rights Code. In Saskatchewan it is called the Saskatchewan Bill of Rights.

With respect to "accommodation," the various provincial statutes generally provide that everyone has a right to obtain accommodation facilities at any hotel, theatre, restaurant, etc., to which the public is customarily admitted, regardless of such person's race, creed, religion, colour, or ethnic or national origin. (In Quebec, the Quebec Hotels Act forbids discrimination in hotels, restaurants, and camping grounds.)

The provinces, except Newfoundland, through their various statutes also prohibit discrimination in employment by reason of race, creed, colour, or national origin. Discrimination in employment between men and women is also prohibited. Equal pay legislation (equal pay for equal work) or similar provisions have been passed in all the provinces except Quebec and Newfoundland.

While these statutes represent considerable progress, there is still much to be done to eliminate discrimination entirely, and the law has only begun to come to grips with the problems of discrimination in such areas as the sale of private housing and admission to private clubs.

In the final analysis, discrimination is only the outward manifestation of prejudices which exist in the minds of individuals. Even though discrimination may be checked by laws, prejudices cannot be eliminated by legislation.

(C) *Freedom of religion.*

The area of religious liberty which is protected is essentially freedom of religious thought and expression. Freedom of religion does not go so far as to allow conduct which violates our criminal law or legitimate measures for the protection of public morals, safety and health.

C — 5

Robertson and Rosetanni were convicted of operating a bowling alley on a Sunday, contrary to the Lord's Day Act, a Federal statute. They appealed to the Supreme Court of Canada on the grounds that to force them to observe Sunday interfered with their right of "religious freedom." The Court dismissed the appeal, holding that the Lord's Day Act was a part of the law of the land. The two accused were *free* to refrain from carrying on business on their own day of rest as well as on Sunday. While observing Sunday as a day of rest might be an inconvenience, it did not infringe upon their religious freedom.

(ii) An order was made committing a Doukhobour child to the custody of the Superintendent of Child Welfare because of truancy from school. The parents (who as Doukhobours held certain religious beliefs that prohibited sending their child to the public school) brought action against the superintendent alleging that the laws of British Columbia (school laws) impaired their freedom of religion. The British Columbia Court disagreed, stating that a religious sect was not entitled to legal protection which would give them the right to set up against the whole world rules of conduct which were peculiar to the religious beliefs of only that sect.

(a) How far does religious freedom extend?
(b) What type of law would interfere with the freedom of religion declared by the Bill of Rights?

(D) *Freedom of speech*

(F) *Freedom of the press*

These two topics will be dealt with together since they are variations of the same right. Freedom of speech and freedom of the press are, of course, not absolute freedoms, and are limited by the laws dealing with defamation, both civil and criminal, and also by the laws against obscenity and sedition.

C — 6

(i) In the 1930's the Province of Alberta passed an act entitled "An Act to Insure the Publication of Accurate News and Information." This empowered the government of Alberta to correct or amplify any statement appearing in a newspaper concerning any government activity, and oblige the newspaper to publish it. The Supreme Court of Canada found this Act unconstitutional and beyond the powers of the Province, on the grounds that it interfered with freedom of the press. Only the Parliament of Canada possessed the authority to legislate with respect to these rights.

(ii) Boucher, a farmer living in Saint Joseph de Beauce, Quebec, was convicted of uttering a seditious libel contained in a four-page religious pamphlet published by the Witnesses of Jehovah. The Supreme Court of Canada held that the strong language used in the pamphlet was not enough to sustain the charge; there had to be an *intention* to incite people to violence and to create public disorder or disturbance.
In connection with this case, Mr. Justice Rand said: "Freedom in thought and speech, and disagreement in ideas and beliefs on every conceivable subject are of the essence of our life. The clash

of critical discussion on political, social and religious subjects has too deeply become the stuff of daily experience to suggest that mere ill-will, as a product of controversy, can strike down the latter with illegality."

(a) Is freedom of the press and of speech unlimited?
(b) It is sometimes suggested that Canadian newspapers should not be allowed to fall into the hands of foreign owners. Also Canadian radio and television stations must broadcast a certain minimum of Canadian material. Do either of these concepts interfere with freedom of speech or of the press?

(E) *Freedom of assembly and association.*

Windsor Star Photo

Freedom of assembly and association are very closely associated with freedom of speech. The right to assemble is not an unlimited right and the Criminal Code contains provisions which limit it. Section 64 of the Code defines an "unlawful assembly" as an assembly of three or more persons who assemble for a common purpose and so conduct themselves as to cause others to fear that they will disturb the peace tumultuously, or that they will provoke others to disturb the peace tumultuously. Section 65 of the Code provides that an unlawful assembly that has begun to disturb the peace tumultuously is a *riot*. Persons taking part in a riot are liable to imprisonment for two years.

It is also provided that where twelve or more persons are unlawfully and riotously assembled together, an official shall read a proclamation commonly described as the "Riot Act," which is as follows:

Her Majesty the Queen charges and commands all persons being assembled immediately to disperse and peaceably to depart to their habitations or to their lawful business upon pain of being guilty of an offence for which upon conviction they may be sentenced to imprisonment for life. God Save the Queen.

CIVIL DISOBEDIENCE

It has become a common occurrence in recent times for persons who believe their civil rights are being denied them, to take some sort of dramatic action to attract attention to their protest against what they consider to be this denial. Often the manner of protest is itself an illegal act. In many cases this has been overlooked because the illegality attached to the protest was of small consequence; for example, the act of sitting in a restaurant after being asked to leave, or of parading without a permit. These acts are termed "acts of civil disobedience."

The Globe and Mail, Toronto

Those who support such actions argue that the laws broken thereby are trivial and that such conduct should be overlooked because of the magnitude of the injustice that is being attacked. In many cases not everyone will agree that the "magnitude" of the injustice justifies such actions. At the same time, one might find difficulty in disagreeing with this approach if, for instance, an unlicensed parade were held to call attention to the fact that political prisoners were being executed.

In recent times, however, protesters have increased the measure of disobedience to the point that, in some instances, the disobedience is serious and criminal. Destruction of property and assaults on persons constitute criminal activity and cannot be justified, even if done in furtherance of a good cause. There is no privilege that attaches to group behaviour. Violations of the criminal

Speech not delivered

Demonstrators in B.C. halt Turner's speech

VANCOUVER (CP) – About 30 demonstrators protesting against the federal Government's use of the War Measures Act in last October's terrorist kidnapping crises in Quebec heckled and shouted down Justice Minister John Turner on Saturday night at the University of British Columbia.

Mr. Turner was delivering a speech as part of the Vancouver Institute's weekly UBC lecture series. The topic of the speech he was prevented from making was Violence in Modern Society.

After the outburst, which included several scuffles between demonstrators and other persons in the audience, Mr. Turner told reporters he was very disturbed.

"They seem to have replaced logic with slogans . . . We've had disruption instead of dialogue," he said.

In the text of his speech, released to reporters later, he warned Canadians that "we'll have to face the threat of violence for some time in our society."

The Canadian Press

or civil law remain violations despite the fact that they may be committed by people congregated in large groups. Too often the group becomes a "mob," with all the connotations of that word. There should be no surprise that people who break the law in this manner are expected to pay the consequences of their acts and suffer punishment.

Civil rights and liberties belong to all of us, collectively and individually. Those who seek to enforce their own freedoms and liberties with such force as to take away from other people the same freedoms and liberties may ultimately defeat their own purposes. For example, those who attend public gatherings and, under the guise of their right to free speech and assembly, by shouting and demonstrating prevent the speaker from being heard have merely denied to another person the same right of free speech which they claim for themselves. In our society the enjoyment of civil rights and liberties implies an obligation to respect the rights and liberties of others, and to respect the lawful authority of the state which protects these rights. The law will not protect individuals who, under pretence of exercising their civil rights, take away from others the same rights and privileges.

THE WAR MEASURES ACT

When the country is under the threat of war or insurrection certain civil rights that exist under normal peaceful conditions may have to be suppressed, even if only temporarily, for the protection of the nation.

The War Measures Act provides that in time of war, invasion, insurrection, either real or apprehended, the Federal Cabinet may issue a proclamation that such a state exists. The cabinet may then exercise its powers under the Act to make orders and regulations which become law without being submitted to parliament for approval. These orders and regulations may cover a broad list of matters and include:

CHAPTER 288.

An Act to confer certain powers upon the Governor in Council in the event of War, Invasion, or Insurrection.

SHORT TITLE.

1. This Act may be cited as the *War Measures Act*. R.S., c. 206, s. 1. **Short title.**

EVIDENCE OF WAR.

2. The issue of a proclamation by Her Majesty, or under the authority of the Governor in Council shall be conclusive evidence that war, invasion, or insurrection, real or apprehended, exists and has existed for any period of time therein stated, and of its continuance, until by the issue of a further proclamation it is declared that the war, invasion or insurrection no longer exists. R.S., c. 206, s. 2. **Evidence of war, etc.**

POWERS OF THE GOVERNOR IN COUNCIL.

3. (1) The Governor in Council may do and authorize such acts and things, and make from time to time such orders and regulations, as he may by reason of the existence of real or apprehended war, invasion or insurrection deem necessary or advisable for the security, defence, peace, order and welfare of Canada; and for greater certainty, but not so as to restrict the generality of the foregoing terms, it is hereby declared that the powers of the Governor in Council shall extend to all matters coming within the classes of subjects hereinafter enumerated, that is to say: **Special powers of Governor in Council.**

(*a*) censorship and the control and suppression of publications, writings, maps, plans, photographs, communications and means of communication;

(*b*) arrest, detention, exclusion and deportation;

(*c*) control of the harbours, ports and territorial waters of Canada and the movements of vessels;

(*d*) transportation by land, air, or water and the control of the transport of persons and things;

(*e*) trading, exportation, importation, production and manufacture;

(*f*) appropriation, control, forfeiture and disposition of property and of the use thereof.

(2) All orders and regulations made under this section shall have the force of law, and shall be enforced in such manner and by such courts, officers and authorities as the

From the Revised Statutes of Canada 1970, Chapter W-2, War Measures Act (Volume VII)

Information Canada

- censorship and the control and suppression of publications and communications;
- arrests, detentions and deportations;
- appropriate control and forfeiture of property.

Orders and regulations made under the Act overrule the Bill of Rights.

C—7

Because of terrorist activities in the province of Quebec, the Federal cabinet in October, 1970, proclaimed the existence of a state of apprehended insurrection, and invoked the War Measures Act. Regulations were passed outlawing the F.L.Q. (Front de Libération du Québec) and giving the authorities the power to arrest and search without warrant, and to detain those arrested without laying a specific charge, and to deny bail.

(a) What rights that we ordinarily consider fundamental were taken away during the period that the War Measures Act was invoked?
(b) Should the government have such sweeping powers? When? Should there be safeguards?
(c) Are there certain rights which should never be taken away?

LEGAL AID

Increased concern for the rights of individuals has in turn led to an increased concern regarding the means to secure those rights. If a person is ignorant of his rights and is unable to pay a lawyer to assist him, he may not obtain the rights that belong to him unless he receives aid from some source.

Critics of our society have on occasion alleged that there is one law for the rich and another for the poor. In its literal sense this is not true; law is applied equally to all. However, if it means that the rich, by being able to afford the best legal assistance, are able to claim every right, every privilege, every defence that the law allows; and that those who cannot afford legal assistance frequently lose what is theirs through ignorance or default, then this criticism contains an element of validity.

To remedy this situation, *legal aid* schemes have been evolved whereby the services of a lawyer are furnished *free of charge* to those who need legal assistance and are unable to afford it.

By far the most comprehensive system exists in Ontario. A person without sufficient funds and in need of legal assistance, other than for trivial matters, may apply to a legal aid officer in his area. The need for legal service is evaluated as well as his ability to pay. The legal aid officer then determines whether or not the applicant can pay a part of or none of the legal expense. A legal aid certificate may then be issued to the applicant to cover the whole of the legal expense or the portion of it that the applicant himself cannot pay. The certificate enables the applicant to proceed to retain a lawyer of his choice. The legal aid plan pays lawyers 75% of their ordinary charges. The whole plan is administered by the Law Society of Upper Canada, and is financed by the Ontario government.

Many of the other provinces have shown great interest in the Ontario plan and are in the process of setting up similar plans of their own.

Lawyers themselves have often been in the forefront of the development of the legal aid schemes whether there is a partial payment of fees or no payment at all. Various provincial law societies as well as The Canadian Bar Association have contributed a great deal of time to the development of these schemes, and have been diligent in their efforts to insure that the rights guaranteed by our laws are available to all regardless of their ability to pay.

APPLYING THE LAW

1. Y is a member of a minority religious sect. Each Monday at sunset Y and about 50 other members of the sect gather in Y's backyard and, facing south, sit silently meditating. K, who lives in the next house south of Y is rather unnerved at the sight of 50 people all looking in his direction. He persuades the local council to pass a by-law prohibiting religious meetings in residential areas. Suppose Y wanted to enlarge his house into a temple. Would the Bill of Rights apply to either case?
2. A, the leader of the Everything for Everybody political party, attends a rally of the Primaeval Party and insists on getting on the platform with the Primaeval Party speaker. A attempts to give a speech and is arrested for causing a disturbance. A's defence is that he was only exercising his right to free speech. Is this a valid defence?
3. After convicting a young man of theft, a magistrate suspends sentence and places him on probation. A term of the probation is that he have his hair cut short and his beard shaved. Does the Bill of Rights affect this case?
4. A newspaper has changed the headings of two of its columns from "Help Wanted Male" to "Jobs Primarily for Men" and "Help Wanted Female" to "Jobs Primarily for Women." Is there any legal reason for doing this? Explain.

DISCUSSION AND PROJECTS

1. Provincial legislation in most provinces prohibits discrimination with respect to accommodation and employment. Discuss the opinion that "even though discrimination may be checked by laws, prejudices cannot be eliminated by legislation."
2. Does legal aid further the right of "equality before the law"? To what extent is legal aid available in your province? (Inquire at your local Court House.)
3. If your province has a Human Rights Code prepare a report for your group or class outlining how it complements the Canadian Bill of Rights.

UNIT FOUR
FAMILY LAW

Part 6
MARRIAGE, DIVORCE AND CHILDREN

THE MARRIAGE INSTITUTION

Poets and composers have often linked love and marriage, treating the latter as being the natural culmination of the former. Certainly, each may be defined in a variety of ways; at the same time, each is equally difficult to define comprehensively. To the man and woman involved, however, the marriage state in our social order represents the success of a courtship and their total commitment to each other.

As an institution, marriage has always had serious implications for society. Marriage is recognized as being necessary for the maintenance of the human species. Children may be born outside of marriage, but the helplessness of the human young and the need for prolonged care and training require the combination of mating and parenthood which constitutes marriage. In addition, marriage has customarily had a religious significance. While not always essential, a religious ceremony of some sort has generally accompanied or preceded the union from earliest times.

In the eyes of the law, marriage carries a host of legal implications, not only for the couple involved but also for the children and others who bear some relationship to either spouse and whose own status hinges on that marriage.

The institution of marriage, as it exists in Canada, is the result of a long evolution in which Greek, Roman, Hebrew and Christian traditions are the main elements. Prior to the rise of Christianity, in the Roman Empire marriage was achieved by the parties simply by living together with the intention of becoming husband and wife. When the Roman Empire was overrun by the Germanic tribes, the situation remained the same, and marriage could be freely initiated and terminated. During the Middle Ages, the civil authority took no steps whatever to regulate marriage, feeling that the matter was a religious issue, but for centuries even the Canon (or Church) law did not require any marriage formalities either. The Church, however, did feel that a matter of such religious significance should at least receive the blessing of the Church and, as a result, a custom developed whereby the couple intending to marry would, before entering upon their life together, meet the parish priest outside the Church door to receive his blessing. Eventually this attendance at the Church door was

prescribed as a religious duty; however, disregarding the duty did not invalidate the marriage.

In 1563, the Council of Trent (a council summoned by the Pope) made mandatory the celebration of the marriage before the parish priest and two witnesses. This, of course, had no effect in England which by this time had split away from the Church of Rome. In England, informal (or common-law) marriages were recognized until 1753. Such marriages were recognized in Scotland until 1939, and are still recognized in some of the States of America. The law in force in Canada is derived from the law of England, and for a valid marriage certain formalities are required, which vary according to the province.

While the Western world has always regarded as normal marriage involving only two persons, other cultures have recognized polygamous (more than one spouse) and polyandrous (more than one husband) unions. In Canada, monogamy (one spouse) is the only legal form of marriage. Our courts have defined marriage as a voluntary union of one man and one woman to the exclusion of all others.

LAWS AFFECTING MARRIAGE IN CANADA

Canada is a federal union and the law-making authority is divided between the federal government and the various provinces. Pursuant to the British North America Act, the federal government is given power to legislate with respect to marriage and divorce, except the "solemnization of marriage in the provinces."

Solemnization means performing the formalities which are part of the marriage ceremony. The provinces have jurisdiction to pass laws respecting the solemnization of marriage and also with respect to property and civil rights, which includes many of the collateral features of marriage such as ownership of property, right of support, and custody of children. Our laws, therefore, are derived partly from the federal government and partly from the provinces; and in the areas dealt with by the provinces, differences exist between the laws of one province and those of another.

REQUIREMENTS OF A VALID MARRIAGE IN CANADA

The requisites of a valid marriage in Canada are as follows:

1. *FREEDOM OF BOTH PARTIES TO MARRY*

Case 1

(i) During World War II Ruth is notified that her soldier-husband has been killed in action. Two years later Ruth marries Fred and two children are born of the marriage. When the war ends, Ruth's first husband is discovered in a prisoner-of-war camp.

(ii) Both Richard and Elizabeth were born and raised in Ontario. They marry and live in Hamilton. Elizabeth becomes disenchanted with the marriage and goes to Reno, Nevada. She stays there the required residence period and then divorces Richard. About a year after her return to Ontario she marries Arthur.

Is either of the second marriages in the above cases valid? Why or why not?

In its simplest terms this requirement means that neither party can have been a party to a prior marriage which has not been ended by death or by law. One who goes through a form of marriage when he is already validly married to someone else is guilty of *bigamy,* which is an indictable offence under the Criminal Code. The second marriage is, of course, void.

Presumption of death. There arise cases in which a person who wishes to marry honestly does not know whether he is free to marry or not. It can happen when a spouse disappears in circumstances that indicate that death was likely, but when that event cannot be conclusively established; for instance, a person is lost in a ship disaster from which no bodies are ever recovered; or a spouse just disappears and is never heard of again. Most provincial laws provide that in the first instance death may be declared in a very short time, and in the second instance, in seven years.

Once such declaration has been made, the surviving spouse is free to marry again. This is not to say, however, that the second marriage is necessarily valid. If it should subsequently be ascertained that the first spouse was, in fact, living at the time of the second marriage, the second marriage is invalid. The issuance of the license for the second marriage simply allows the parties to go through with the ceremony on the assumption that the first spouse is dead. In these circumstances the second marriage, if invalid, does not constitute the crime of bigamy, since the Criminal Code provides that no one will be guilty of bigamy who goes through a form of marriage believing in good faith and on reasonable grounds that the first spouse is dead or has not been heard of for seven years.

Divorced persons. A person who has previously married is free to marry again if the first marriage has terminated in divorce. At the same time, divorce decrees handed down in court are not final immediately and occasionally people have been known to "jump the gun." A waiting period of at least three months intervenes before the divorce becomes absolute. A second marriage taking place before the divorce becomes final will not be valid.

Foreign divorces. A divorce obtained in Canada is, of course, recognized in Canada; but the question of whether a foreign divorce will be recognized in Canada is a difficult and complex matter. Generally, the various provinces will recognize a divorce granted by the court of the husband's or wife's domicile. "Domicile" is understood in Canada to mean residence coupled with an intention to make that place one's permanent home. Therefore, persons who are ordinarily resident in Canada and who, in order to obtain a divorce, go to a jurisdiction where divorces are granted more freely, may, despite the fact that they satisfy all the residence qualifications required in that other jurisdiction, obtain a divorce that will not be recognized in Canada, and their subsequent marriage would be invalid.

2. THE MENTAL CAPACITY OF BOTH PARTNERS

C — 2

After graduation from University, Bill marries Mary whom he has known for many years. Within a few months of the marriage Mary begins to act strangely, and is later committed to a mental institution where she is likely to remain permanently.

(a) Would this marriage be valid?
(b) What additional circumstances might alter your opinion?

Generally speaking, in order to enter a valid marriage a person must be sane. At the time the marriage is performed both parties must be of sufficient mental capacity to understand the nature of the marriage contract and the duties and responsibilities it creates. Mental illness varies in type and severity, and it is only if a party is rendered incapable of understanding to the degree set out above that the validity of the marriage will be affected. The relevant time is, of course, the time of the ceremony itself. Subsequent mental disorders, while casting doubt upon the capacity of the person at the time of the marriage, are not sufficient. The person who alleges insanity in his or her spouse must prove it. Everyone is presumed sane until the contrary is established.

3. AFFINITY AND CONSANGUINITY

C — 3

When very young, Alan and his sister, Barbara, were left orphans through both parents being killed in an automobile accident. The children were adopted by different families. Many years later, Alan and Barbara meet and later marry. After the marriage it is discovered that they are in fact brother and sister.

Is the marriage valid? For what reason?

The parties to a valid marriage must not be related within the prohibited degrees of affinity (relationship by marriage) or consanguinity (relationship by blood). The early law on this subject is not at all clear, but the courts have consistently held that the prohibited degrees are those set out in Archbishop Parker's table of 1563. This table was printed in the Book of Common Prayer of the Church of England. The original table has been changed somewhat by parliament in that some of the prohibited degrees have been eliminated, notably the "deceased wife's sister" and the "deceased husband's brother." The situation as it now exists in Canada is as follows:

A man may not marry his	*A woman may not marry her*
Grandmother	Grandfather
Grandfather's wife	Grandmother's husband
Wife's grandmother	Husband's grandfather
Aunt	Uncle
Wife's aunt	Husband's uncle
Mother	Father
Stepmother	Stepfather
Wife's mother	Husband's father
Daughter	Son
Wife's daughter	Husband's son
Son's wife	Daughter's husband
Sister	Brother
Granddaughter	Grandson
Grandson's wife	Granddaughter's husband
Wife's granddaughter	Husband's grandson
Niece	Nephew
Nephew's wife	Niece's husband

It should be noted that these relationships include all such relationships whether of the whole or half blood, and whether legitimate or illegitimate.

4. MUTUAL FREE CONSENT TO THE MARRIAGE

Absence of true consent will render a marriage invalid. Ordinarily, "true consent" is presumed when two people go through the marriage ceremony or exchange their promises before a civil authority. When the parties are mutually competent and of full age, courts require very clear and persuasive evidence to find that true consent was absent.

In considering true consent as a factor in the marriage contract, care must be exercised not to confuse the concepts which apply to contracts generally. Many factors which destroy the consent necessary for a commercial contract will not necessarily have any effect on marriage, in particular the factors of mistake, misrepresentation and fraud, and duress.

Mistake

C — 4

The plaintiff, a young woman, came to Canada in 1964 from Sparta, Greece. Shortly afterwards she met the defendant, who was also a recent arrival from Greece, and they became engaged. In March of 1965 they appeared before a magistrate, and with the aid of an interpreter the marriage ceremony was performed.

The plaintiff later sued for annulment, and at the trial testified that she did not understand that the proceeding before the magistrate was a marriage ceremony; instead she thought it was only a solemn form of betrothal and that a church ceremony would be held later. The couple did not live together following the ceremony. The marriage was annulled on the ground that there was no real consent.

(a) What fact caused the court to annul the marriage?
(b) Would it have made any difference if the young woman had realized that the attendance before the magistrate was a civil marriage ceremony, but that in her conscience only a subsequent religious ceremony would make the marriage valid?

Mistake will render a marriage void in only two cases: Firstly, mistake as to the identity of the other party; for example, if a person went through a marriage ceemony at a masquerade party believing he was marrying one person but the unmasking revealed another. Secondly, mistake as to the nature of the ceremony to the extent that one of the parties does not realize that he or she is contracting marriage.

Mistakes other than the two types dealt with above will not invalidate a marriage. Mistake as to the chastity, financial worth, or religious affiliation of the other party is insufficient in the eyes of the law to destroy the reality of consent.

Misrepresentation and fraud

C — 5

Moss met a young woman and became engaged to her. She concealed from him the fact that she was already pregnant by another man. They married, and when Moss became aware of his wife's pregnancy she admitted the truth. Moss left his wife and sued for annulment of the marriage on the grounds of fraud. An English court held that the marriage was valid. The parties had realized the nature of the ceremony and had freely consented. The deceit extended only to the condition of the bride.

(a) What fraudulent act did Moss consider as the grounds for annulment?
(b) Why did the court disagree with the husband and rule the marriage valid?
(c) What types of misrepresentation or fraud do you think could render a marriage void?

Neither misrepresentation nor fraud by itself is sufficient to affect the validity of a marriage. If, however, these factors induce a mistake of the types previously discussed, then, of course, the marriage is void.

Duress

C — 6

In 1954, a 19-year-old boy and a 15-year-old girl went to Toronto where they stayed overnight at a hotel. Shortly thereafter both were found and detained by the police, the girl on a charge of being a juvenile delinquent, and the boy on a criminal charge. It was suggested that if they married the charges would not be proceeded with. Both families exerted great pressure on the girl, and after considerable protest she eventually agreed to go through with the marriage. The marriage was annulled a year later by an Ontario court on the basis that the pending charges, the girl's age, and the family pressure all operated to deprive her of her free will.

(a) What was there about this marriage that affected its validity?
(b) If the police had not suggested that charges might be laid, would the marriage have been annulled?

Duress means the use of force which induces fear. The force may be physical, but is not restricted to this only; it may also consist of threats, words, or acts which create fear or apprehension in the mind of the subject. Duress is a ground for declaring a marriage a nullity only if it can be shown that the person influenced by it was unable to act as a free agent.

What amounts to duress will, of course, vary depending on the age, character and mental capacity of the subject. Also important is the relationship between the person influenced and the person exerting the influence.

5. *SEXUAL COMPETENCE*

C—7

Although John and Irene have been married for five years they have no children. A medical examination reveals that Irene is incapable of bearing children. John, who desperately wants children, becomes very unhappy and dissatisfied with the marriage.

(a) Would Irene's medical condition make this marriage invalid?
(b) Should ability to have children be an essential element of a valid marriage?

Even in the eyes of the Ecclesiastical law a marriage was not final and indissoluble until the union had been consummated. According to law, a marriage is consummated as soon as the parties have had sexual intercourse after the marriage.

Because consummation is essential to the marriage, the ability of each party to perform the sex act is said to be an essential element in a valid marriage. A person who is incapable of performing the sex act is *impotent*, and impotence is a ground for annulment of a marriage. The inability to procreate children (sterility) is not an essential element in a valid marriage.

Impotence may be the result of a physical defect or caused by a nervous or mental condition. Non-consummation resulting simply from a refusal by one party is not in itself a ground for annulment. However, the refusal may be of such duration or be accompanied by such circumstances as to lead a court to draw the inference of impotence. The Divorce Act of 1968 has furnished an alternative by making non-consummation for a period of one year by reason of refusal, illness, or disability a ground for divorce.

6. THE PROPER AGE

At common law the age of consent to marry was 14 for males, and 12 for females. The provincial legislatures have all passed legislation dealing with the required age for marriage. Those who are over 18 in Alberta, Manitoba, New Brunswick, Ontario and Quebec; or over 19 in British Columbia, Newfoundland, Nova Scotia and Saskatchewan are free to marry. Prince Edward Island sets the ages at 21 for males and 18 for females.

If a person is below the ages outlined above, he may still marry if certain requirements are met. The provincial statutes vary, but generally persons below the above ages may marry with the consent of the parents, or pursuant to a judge's order if the consent of the parents is unreasonably withheld. Within this class the lower limit is set by most of the provinces at 16 (Ontario, 14), and marriages under this age will only be allowed to avoid the illegitimacy of an expected child.

7. STATUTORY FORMALITIES

C—8

A couple went through a ceremony of marriage in Ontario on March 3, 1949, according to the rites of the Jewish faith. The ceremony was performed by a cantor who was authorized by Ontario law to perform marriages, but no marriage license was issued. Following the marriage, the parties lived together until 1956, when the husband died. A dispute then arose between the surviving wife and the next-of-kin of the deceased husband as to the validity of the marriage. The next-of-kin took the position that the absence of the license rendered the marriage invalid. The widow argued that the license was a formality only, and that the essentials of a marriage were present. The Ontario Court of Appeal held that the marriage was valid. The Ontario Marriage Act required a license and even provided a penalty for proceeding without one, but since the parties intended to marry and had acted in good faith, the absence of the marriage license did not make the marriage itself invalid.

(a) What caused the dispute over whether the marriage was valid?
(b) Would the result have been the same if, unknown to the parties, the cantor was not authorized by Ontario law to perform marriages?

When the parties to a marriage go through a form of ceremony followed by cohabitation, a presumption arises that everything necessary to the validity of the ceremony occurred or was performed; and any person who asserts that there was a defect in the formal aspect of the marriage must prove it.

The various provincial statutes make provision for a number of formalities: for example, marriage licenses, the persons permitted to perform the ceremony, the conditions of the ceremony as to witnesses, hours, health certificates. Most of these requirements are merely formal procedures and will not render a marriage void or voidable unless the statute expressly or by clear implication so provides. Even the fact that a statute provides a penalty for failure to meet one of the requirements does not render the marriage invalid.

CONTRACTS TO MARRY

Does the engagement ring represent a contract of marriage?

People's Credit Jewellers

Marriage is usually preceded by a contract to marry or a period of engagement. This contract is governed by the same rules as relate to ordinary contracts. At the same time, because of their intimate quality, these contracts possess some special features.

FORM

There is no requirement that a contract to marry be in writing; an oral contract is enforceable. Obviously, a contract that is evidenced by some form of writing, such as letters, would be much easier to prove. If a party elects to sue on a broken promise to marry, the Ontario Evidence Act, R.S.O. 1960, Chapter 125, Section 13, provides as follows:

> *The Plaintiff in an action for breach of promise to marry shall not recover unless his or her testimony is corroborated by some other material evidence in support of the promise.*

Ordinarily, corroborative evidence is not difficult to obtain in cases of this type. For instance, the publication of banns in church, or the wearing of an engagement ring in public by the fiancée, would provide the necessary corroboration. It should be added that breach of promise cases are now very rare.

CAPACITY

C—9

Robert and Carol while in high school agree to marry as soon as Robert finishes school. Robert gives Carol a ring when they graduate from high school. They are both 17 years of age at the time.

(a) Is this agreement to marry legally binding?
(b) Suppose the engagement continues until Robert graduates from University four years later. Would the agreement be binding then?

The law dealing with the capacity of persons to enter a contract to marry is the same as that for contracts in general. The most frequent source of difficulty in contracts to marry arises from the fact that one or both of the parties are infants. A contract to marry made by a minor is voidable at his (or her) option; but at the same time, an adult party to a marriage contract may be held liable for damages if he fails to go through with the contract.

Another problem as to the status of the contract to marry arises when the infant reaches his majority during the currency of the contract. Contracts to marry which are voidable by a minor during his infancy are not enforceable against him after he reaches his majority unless he expressly ratifies them. This would usually involve some declaration by word or deed wherein the person who now has attained his majority adopts the contract made during his infancy. In Ontario, Nova Scotia, Prince Edward Island and Newfoundland this ratification is not binding unless it is in writing. In British Columbia no legal action can be brought on any such ratification, whether oral or written.

ILLEGALITY

A contract to marry by a person who is already married is considered contrary to public policy and therefore illegal. The reason for this policy is that so long as a marriage subsists each spouse is entitled to the cohabitation of the other, and the law will not approve any agreement which will impair that relationship and strike at the solidarity of the fundamental social unit.

UNOFFICIAL ENGAGEMENT

One of the features of modern life seems to be a substatus somewhat below engagement, which is termed "unofficial engagement." Such a relationship may be created by the exchange of such tokens as school pins. Whether this constitutes a contract to marry depends upon the state of mind of the parties. If it is their intention to be legally bound by the agreement, then obviously the agreement creates legal obligations. It would seem, generally, that the parties do not intend to be legally bound or to create any lasting obligations, and it is for this reason that the relationship is termed unofficial.

GIFTS MADE IN CONTEMPLATION OF MARRIAGE

C—10

A few days before their wedding is to take place, Richard and Patricia agree to called the whole thing off. Richard had given Patricia a very expensive engagement ring. Friends and relatives had sent many gifts.

(a) Can Patricia keep the ring?
(b) Is there any legal obligation to return the gifts?

A gift made in contemplation of marriage may be recovered from the party who broke the contract, but the party who is in breach may not recover any gifts he has given. Applying this rule, courts have held that a woman who has broken the marriage contract must return the engagement ring; conversely, a man who has broken the engagement is not entitled to the return of the ring. It appears that if a marriage fails to take place but neither party is at fault, then both persons must return their gifts. Gifts made in contemplation of marriage to the engaged couple by others (e.g., the ordinary wedding gift) are conditional upon the celebration of the marriage, and if the marriage does not take place must be returned to the donors.

PROPERTY RIGHTS UNDER MARRIAGE

At common law the husband and the wife were considered to be one person, and the husband represented that person. As a result, the property rights of married women were of little significance. That era has passed and today, by virtue of legislation in most of the provinces, married women are regarded as separate individuals with equal property rights.

A married woman may now own separate property free from the control of her husband. She may, of course, also own property jointly with her husband. In Quebec, however, community of property exists between husband and wife where there is no pre-marital agreement to the contrary, and the husband has exclusive power of administration and disposition.

THE HUSBAND'S RESPONSIBILITY FOR HIS WIFE'S DEBTS

C—11

Albert's wife has charge accounts at almost every store in town. Albert feels that his wife spends too much money foolishly. The wife feels that her husband is too stingy, and with gay abandon continues to use the charge accounts.

(a) Is Albert responsible for everything his wife buys?
(b) Can Albert do anything to lessen his responsibility?

The fact of marriage does not make the husband responsible for debts incurred by his wife. At the same time, when husband and wife are living together, the wife is presumed to have his authority to pledge his credit for such household or domestic items as a wife would ordinarily deal with. This authority, however, may be terminated. The husband may, for instance, expressly warn traders not to supply goods on credit to his wife; or the pledge of credit may be so excessive, having regard to the supply of goods already on hand or the size of the husband's income, that the wife's authority to make such a pledge would obviously be open to question.

Apart from this presumption of authority, a husband may expressly give his wife authority or hold her out as having authority. In such cases the husband will be responsible for the debts incurred by his wife. For example, a course of dealing whereby a wife buys customarily on credit and the husband pays the bill will constitute a "holding out" to that creditor that she has authority to continue to pledge her husband's credit.

OWNERSHIP OF PROPERTY ACQUIRED AFTER MARRIAGE

C—12

Kaakee purchased a house by making a down payment and giving back a mortgage for the balance of the purchase price. Kaakee took the property in his name alone. His wife alleged that it was understood that she was to be a co-owner. She stated that she contributed to the downpayment and subsequent mortgage payments out of funds acquired by taking in boarders. An Ontario Supreme Court judge held that the evidence did not establish a gift from husband to wife. The judge further held that the contribution of the wife did not arise from her separate income. The house was ruled to be the property of her husband.

(a) Why was the wife not considered a co-owner of the house?
(b) Would the result have been different if the wife had helped pay for the house out of her pay cheques from a part-time job?

After marriage the husband and the wife continue to be the separate owners of whatever assets each brought to the marriage. A somewhat more difficult problem arises in dealing with assets acquired after marriage. In cases where the husband produces the family income, assets subsequently acquired are the property of the husband. However, if the husband deposits money in a bank account in the name of himself and his wife jointly, or takes a deed to real property made to himself and his wife as joint tenants, there is a presumption of gift and intention to create joint ownership.

In cases where the wife has an income of her own, that income as well as the assets acquired by her in the use of her separate income is her separate property. Where both husband and wife have incomes and acquire assets together, the property becomes their joint property.

Dower. Apart from the above, a wife acquires certain rights to real property owned by her husband during their marriage, referred to in Eastern Canada as "dower rights" and in Western Canada as "homestead rights" (see Unit 12).

Inheritance. In the event of the death of one spouse the other usually inherits a substantial share of the property of the deceased. If the deceased spouse left no will, the survivor is entitled to a share prescribed by law. If the deceased left a will, the surviving spouse takes according to the will; but if the will makes no provision or an inadequate provision for the surviving spouse, an application may be made to the court to charge the estate with adequate provision. (See Unit 13).

The Use of the Matrimonial Home. The question of the right to occupy the matrimonial home, apart from the issue of ownership, sometimes presents a problem.

If the home is owned jointly, both husband and wife have a right to occupy the premises, a right that arises from joint ownership rather than from the married state. However, in rare cases a court will order one spouse to stay out of the home in order to protect the other.

In cases where the home is owned by only one spouse, the other, because of the marriage relationship, also has the right to occupy the premises, unless that right is forfeited by a marital offence such, for example, as desertion, cruelty, or adultery.

When and if the marital difficulty culminates in a separation agreement, judicial separation, or divorce, the question of occupation of the home will be resolved in that agreement or proceeding.

BREAK-UP OF THE MARRIAGE

C—13

Ron and Marion have been married for five years and their relationship has deteriorated to the point where conflict between them is constant and each is unhappy. Marion is told by her doctor that her health is failing as a result.

(a) What courses of action are open to Ron and Marion?
(b) If there are children of the marriage, what extra problems are there?

SEPARATION

In the event that a marriage fails, the parties may simply agree to live separately. As a part of such agreement, matters such as financial arrangements and the custody of children can be settled between them. Frequently, the understanding is reduced to writing and described as a separation agreement. There is no particular form to be followed since the agreement is simply a contract between the parties and is enforceable as such.

Since the separation agreement is based on the agreement of the parties, no particular grounds for the separation are required other than the fact that the parties agree to live separately.

If a separation occurs without an agreement, and one party deserts the other, the one who is deserted may take legal action for judicial separation or divorce. If that spouse is the wife, she may also claim for financial support.

In the common law provinces (other than Ontario) a husband or wife may sue to obtain a judicial separation. The judicial separation (ordered by a court instead of being privately agreed) is similar to the separation agreement in that it provides an arrangement whereby the parties agree to live apart; but the arrangement is in the form of a court order, not of a separation agreement. A judicial separation may be obtained on the grounds of adultery, cruelty, or desertion for two years or more without cause.

Prior to 1968 a great many of the marriages which failed resulted in either separation agreements or judicial separations. It is likely, however, that with the passage of the Divorce Act of 1968 and the wider grounds for divorce, the parties to marriages that have broken down will elect the remedy of divorce rather than the somewhat unsatisfactory remedy of separation, where rights are not clearly defined nor easily enforced yet the parties remain husband and wife.

ANNULMENT

As outlined in the first part of this Unit, there are certain requirements for a valid marriage. In the absence of these requirements the marriage will be defective, and as such may be void or voidable, depending on the type of defect.

A marriage is void, that is, absolutely invalid, where either of the parties

- was not free to marry for some reason; for example, a prior existing marriage;
- was mentally incompetent;
- did not consent freely to the marriage;
- had not attained the proper age.

In some instances a marriage may be void if the proper formalities essential to a valid marriage are not complied with; for example, a marriage between parties within the prohibited degrees of affinity or consanguinity is regarded as void in some provinces and voidable in others.

In the case of a marriage that is void, the marriage is invalid irrespective of any court order. In almost all cases, however, one of the parties to the void marriage will seek a *decree of nullity*, which formally declares the status of the parties.

In the case of a voidable marriage, the status of the marriage continues to exist unless it is declared non-existent by judicial decree. In some provinces, the fact that the parties are within the prohibited degrees of affinity or consanguinity will render a marriage voidable; the remaining ground which also renders a marriage voidable is impotency (see earlier in this Unit).

In view of the fact that the new Divorce Act makes non-consummation a ground for divorce, it is likely that in cases of sexual incompetence there will be little need to resort to the somewhat more difficult remedy of annulment. Annulment is procedurally more complicated than divorce, and non-consummation can be proved more easily than impotence.

DIVORCE

Prior to 1968 the grounds for divorce in Canada were very narrow. Generally speaking, a divorce could be obtained only when one of the parties to the marriage was guilty of adultery, rape, sodomy, or bestiality. In Quebec and Newfoundland, a divorce could not be obtained at all except by private act of the Federal Parliament.

In 1968, the Canadian Parliament passed the Divorce Act which reformed and broadened the whole law of divorce. Jurisdiction to hear divorce cases was assigned to the various provincial Superior Courts, except that cases arising in Newfoundland and Quebec may be heard in the Federal Court.

The basis of the law dealing with divorce, prior to the new Act, was the concept of a matrimonial offence. If one spouse committed a prohibited act (for example, adultery), the innocent party to the marriage could obtain a divorce. The concept of the matrimonial offence has been retained in the new Act, but has also been expanded. The Divorce Act now provides that husband or wife may petition for a divorce upon the grounds that the other spouse has

- committed adultery;
- been guilty of sodomy, bestiality, or rape, or engaged in a homosexual act;
- gone through a form of marriage with another person; or
- treated the petitioning spouse with physical or mental cruelty of such a kind as to render intolerable the continued cohabitation of the spouses.

In addition to the foregoing grounds, the Divorce Act has introduced a new concept into Canadian divorce law, namely the "break-down of the marriage" and the recognition of the fact that the marriage has already ended.

In recognition of this fact, the Divorce Act now provides that where a husband and wife are living apart, a petition may be presented for a divorce on the grounds that there has been a permanent breakdown of the marriage by reason of one or more of the following circumstances:

1. The respondent (the spouse against whom the petition is directed) has been in prison for a period of three years or more in the five-year period immediately preceding the presentation of the petition.
2. The respondent, immediately before the presentation of the petition, has been in prison for two years or more as a part of a sentence exceeding ten years.
3. The respondent for a period of three years or more immediately preceding the presentation of the petition has been addicted to alcohol or narcotics and there is no reasonable hope of rehabilitation.
4. The petitioner for a period of three years or more immediately preceding the presentation of the petition has had no knowledge or information of the whereabouts of the respondent, and has not been able to locate the respondent.
5. The marriage has not been consummated by reason of illness, disability or refusal of the respondent.
6. The husband and wife have been living separate and apart for a period of three years or more. If, however, the petitioner caused the separation by deserting the respondent, the period will be five years.

ALIMONY AND MAINTENANCE

C—14

TELEVISION STAR'S WIFE SEEKS $7,000 WEEKLY ALIMONY

NEW YORK – The wife of a prominent television personality is seeking $7,000 a week temporary alimony from her husband, it was disclosed yesterday in state Supreme Court in Manhattan. In arguments before the judge, the grounds on which she will seek a divorce or separation were described as cruel and inhuman treatment, abandonment and adultery.

(a) What would be the purpose of alimony?
(b) What might have determined the high amount being asked for by the wife?

Strictly speaking, the term *alimony* means payments ordered to be made by a husband to a wife during the existence of the marriage relationship; the term *maintenance* is the allowance ordered to be paid to a former wife after a divorce or annulment. In practice, however, the terms are used almost interchangeably, and even some legislation has mixed the terms.

Alimony may be claimed by a wife on the grounds of her husband's adultery, cruelty or desertion. A claim for alimony may be joined to a claim for judicial separation or, in the majority of the provinces, may be claimed independently. A claim for alimony and maintenance may also be made a part of an action for divorce. The grounds for divorce having been enlarged by the new Divorce Act, the grounds for the corollary relief of alimony and maintenance have also been broadened. Alimony may be claimed by the wife up to the time the divorce becomes final; thereafter, only maintenance may be claimed. It should also be noted that under the new Divorce Act a husband may claim alimony and maintenance from his wife.

The determination of the amount of either alimony or maintenance is frequently a difficult task. Regard is given to the station in life of the parties, the amount of property which each possesses, and to all the circumstances, such as illness, lack of employment, etc. As a general rule, courts have fixed the amount of alimony or maintenance at one-third of the husband's net income.

SUMMARY PROCEEDINGS

As an alternative to the foregoing claims for alimony and maintenance which are dealt with by the Superior Courts, Provincial statutes confer jurisdiction upon magistrates (or Provincial Judges) to order husbands to make periodic payments for the support of a deserted wife or children or, under some statutes, a "destitute wife." There are variations in the Provincial statutes, but generally a wife is "deserted" if the husband leaves her without justification or if the wife is obliged to live separately because of the husband's cruelty, adultery, or failure to supply her with food, clothing or other necessaries.

CHILDREN

MAINTENANCE

C—15

Eleanor and Jim have been married for six years. They have three children. Eleanor no longer has any affection for Jim and insists that he leave. Jim leaves the home and lives by himself.

(a) Is Jim obliged to support the children? Why?
(b) How long does this obligation last?

At common law there was no legal obligation resting on parents to support their children—only a moral obligation. However, beginning several centuries ago, a series of statutes imposed this obligation on the father. In 1968, the Federal Divorce Act imposed this duty on the mother as well. In divorce actions, therefore, a court may impose on either the husband or the wife the obligation to maintain the children of the marriage. A *child of the marriage* is defined as a child under the age of 16 years, or over 16 years if unable because of illness, disability or other cause to provide for himself. It has been held that full-time attendance in school constitutes "other cause" which renders a child unable to provide for himself.

Apart from divorce (which, as we have already said, comes under federal law) provincial statutes give courts the power when dealing with the custody of children to make orders obliging the father to maintain them. Provincial statutes also confer jurisdiction on magistrates to order a father to pay for the support of children he has deserted. A child is, generally speaking, considered deserted when the father does not provide for him, regardless of whatever justification there may have been for the husband to leave his wife. Generally, the obligation under provincial law to support children continues until the child reaches the age of 16.

CUSTODY

C—16

A young man and woman lived together in the Yorkville area of Toronto. When the woman became pregnant, they married, and in October of 1966 a baby was born. Both parents were users of marijuana, hashish and L.S.D. In March of 1967, the father was convicted of trafficking in drugs, some of the drugs having been hidden in the baby's crib. In 1968, the parents separated and a dispute arose over the custody of the child. An Ontario Supreme Court Judge found that neither parent was fit to have custody of the child. Custody was granted to the paternal grandmother with limited rights of access to each parent.

(a) What was the principal consideration in awarding the custody of the child to the grandmother?
(b) What other circumstances would justify children being given into the custody of someone other than the parents? If there are no near relatives to take the children, should they be taken by a public agency?

C—17

In 1906, a couple was divorced and, as a part of the divorce decree, custody of a daughter was awarded to the father. Three years later, the father planned to remarry. The daughter, who was now 16 years of age, was distressed at the thought of her father's remarriage and fled to her mother. The father then took legal proceedings against the mother to recover custody of the daughter. At the hearing, the daughter stated that she wished to stay with her mother. The English Court of Appeal discharged the original custody order and left the parties to their common law positions. The court stated "If the girl is minded to leave her father's house, it is plain that the father cannot reclaim her by . . . "[legal process].

(a) Why did the court allow the girl to stay with her mother?
(b) Should the wish of the child always be the governing factor when courts award custody?
(c) Could the welfare of a child be served by ignoring the child's wishes?

The Divorce Act provides that when a petition for divorce is presented, the court may make an order dealing with the maintenance and custody of the children of the marriage. Apart from divorce proceedings, provincial legislation also deals with the question of custody, and courts may make orders concerning the custody of children when the issue arises independently of divorce.

The paramount consideration in the issue of custody is the welfare of the child. Courts consider the wishes of the parents, their conduct, the children's ages, and other such factors, as well as the proposals of each parent for the maintenance and education of the children. Because the welfare of the children is the paramount consideration, even an agreement between the parents in a separation agreement or otherwise does not bind the court. Further, court orders dealing with custody are not final and may be varied as circumstances change. It should be added that, because of possible harmful emotional effects on the children, changes in custody are not often made.

If all other factors are equal, courts generally hold the mother is entitled to the custody of children during the period of nurture; that is, until the child reaches about seven years of age.

The parent who is deprived of custody is usually allowed a *right of access*; that is, a right to visit his children periodically. Generally, the custody of children is granted to one parent or the other, but may be granted to someone other than a parent if the welfare of the child so dictates.

As previously pointed out, under the Divorce Act "child" means a child under the age of 16, or over 16 if unable to provide for himself because of illness, disability or other cause. Pursuant to provincial law, courts have authority to deal with the custody of children up to the age of 16, and in some cases beyond that age.

However, as a general rule, courts will not deal with the custody of children who have reached the age of discretion (14 years for boys and 16 years for girls). At that point, it is presumed, the child will exercise his or her own judgment, and a court order to the contrary would be ineffective (other than in exceptional cases of illness or disability).

PARENTAL CONTROL

C—18

On reaching the age of 16, Ken stops having his hair cut, takes his guitar and heads for the big city seeking fame and fortune. His parents, who would have him stay in school and ultimately take over the family business, are extremely distressed.

(a) Can the parents force Ken to come home?
(b) Would it do any good even if they could?
(c) Is there any solution to the problem?

There is surprisingly little law on the right of a parent to control his child. The common law holds that a parent has the right to restrain and control his infant child and inflict punishment to a reasonable degree. Over two hundred years ago Sir William Blackstone, a famous English jurist (1723—1780), wrote: "He (a parent) may lawfully correct his child being under age, in a reasonable manner . . . the power of a father over the persons of his children ceases at the age of twenty-one."

In modern times, Blackstone's statement may continue to be valid in the sense that a parent is entitled to use reasonable force to discipline children in his custody. However, in most cases once a child reaches the age of 16, the parent's right to discipline becomes meaningless if the child refuses to live with the parent. The ability of a parent to control children over the age of 16 must depend basically on moral persuasion instead of legal rights.

(For the responsibility of a parent for the debts of his child, see Part 11. The right of a child to inherit from his parents is covered in Unit 13).

APPLYING THE LAW

1. Reggie and Susan met at a summer resort. After a courtship of only two weeks, they married. After the marriage, Susan was sadly disappointed: the large ranch and luxuriously furnished home Reggie had told her he owned turned out to be a shack on the edge of a swamp. The disillusioned Susan sought annulment of the marriage on the grounds of fraud and misrepresentation. How does the law apply?
2. The father of an intended bride gives his future son-in-law a new car just a week before the wedding is to take place. A few days later the couple quarrel and the young lady calls off the wedding. The young man leaves town. Can the father legally demand that the car be returned?
3. B wishes to emigrate to Canada. To improve her chances of being admitted, she arranges with A, a Canadian citizen, to go through a form of marriage. They obtain a license and go through the appropriate ceremony. After B is granted citizenship, they seek to have the marriage annulled on the grounds that neither party intended really to marry. How do you think the case would be decided?
4. L and M read in a newspaper that a minister has been exposed as an imposter, and that for twenty years he has masqueraded as the pastor of a church. This man had performed the wedding ceremony for L and M. Is the marriage valid?

DISCUSSION AND PROJECTS

1. "In cases where the husband produces the family income, assets subsequently acquired are the property of the husband." If the wife on her part works hard in taking care of her husband's home and his children, should she be able to claim a share of this property?
2. The age of sixteen marks a legal turning point in the life of a child. Discuss how this applies with respect to parental control and discipline, and parental responsibility for support and custody.
3. S and T have been married for ten years and have three children. The marriage breaks down and T, the husband, moves out of the marital home. T is steadily employed. What are T's obligations? What proceedings may S take if it becomes necessary?
4. What does the marriage legislation in your province require with respect to licenses and other formalities?
5. Find out if a marriage in Mexico or Reno, Nevada, is valid in Canada.
6. Have a report prepared which outlines the steps a woman would take if she wanted (a) a divorce (b) a separation. Consult a local lawyer and such reference books as *Law and Marriage*, Chapman (McGraw-Hill).

UNIT FIVE
CANADIAN CITIZENSHIP

Part 7
ACQUIRING AND LOSING CITIZENSHIP

THE CANADIAN CITIZENSHIP ACT

The Canadian Citizenship Act, passed by the Federal Parliament and effective from January 1, 1947, prescribes the conditions under which a person may become a Canadian citizen.

Substantial changes to the original Act have been made from time to time, particularly in 1952 and 1967. In this Unit, the law is described as of the time of this writing; however, it should be kept in mind that the law is still subject to change.

Canadian citizenship may be acquired by birth or by naturalization.

NATURAL-BORN CANADIANS

CASE 1

(i) Baby Jean is born in an Air Canada plane which is bringing his parents and his two-year-old brother, Pierre, all citizens of France, from Paris to Montreal.

(ii) Baby Edith is born in New York, U.S.A. The baby's father is a Canadian citizen, native of Winnipeg, who is taking post-graduate studies in that city. While in New York he married the mother, an American citizen.

(a) Are Baby Jean and Baby Edith Canadian citizens?
(b) Might the country in which each was born claim the child as a citizen?
(c) Is there such a thing as being a citizen of two countries?

A person born after the thirty-first day of December, 1946, is a natural-born Canadian if

(1) he (or she) was born in Canada or in a Canadian ship (including aircraft). This is so even though his father or mother or both may not have been Canadian citizens at the time of his birth.

(2) he was born elsewhere than in (1), above, and his father (or in the case of a child born out of wedlock, his mother) at the time of that person's birth was a Canadian citizen.

In the case of a person born "elsewhere than in Canada," the birth should be registered at a Canadian Consulate or with the Secretary of State of Canada within *two* years after its occurrence. In special cases the Minister of Immigration may authorize an extension of this period.

A person born elsewhere than in Canada and who, because his father was a Canadian citizen, qualifies as a natural-born Canadian, may have dual citizenship; that is, he may be a citizen of the country in which he was born—

Travellers at the Customs & Immigration shed in Vancouver Harbour, B.C.

National Film Board

simply because he was born there—as well as being a Canadian citizen because his father was a Canadian. However, after reaching the age of 21, *if he is still residing out of Canada*, within three years he must make up his mind whether or not he wishes to retain his Canadian citizenship. If he does so decide, he must within this three-year period file with the proper Canadian authority a *declaration of retention* of Canadian citizenship.

However, if such a person allowed this three-year period to lapse without filing the declaration, and so ceased to be a Canadian citizen, the Act provides that he may (for a fee) file an application for resumption of Canadian citizenship; and if his application is approved he will be granted a certificate of citizenship.

Where a natural-born Canadian who was born elsewhere than in Canada has since his birth returned to Canada and has his place of domicile permanently in Canada, there is no need to file a declaration of retention in order to retain his Canadian citizenship status.

CITIZENSHIP BY NATURALIZATION

C—2

Referring to Case 1(i) on page 92, suppose that Baby Jean's parents and brother were admitted to Canada for permanent residence.

(a) May they, if they wish, still retain their French citizenship?
(b) Is admittance to Canada for permanent residence sufficient to make them Canadian citizens?

An alien who has been admitted to Canada for permanent residence may apply for citizenship by *naturalization*. The procedure may be described in three steps:

- Filing the application
- A hearing before a judge
- Taking the Oath of Allegiance

The Application. The application forms may be obtained from and filed through the clerk of a court designated for that purpose by the Minister of Immigration.

A person applying for citizenship by naturalization is required to show that:

- He has attained the age of 21 years. (An exception to this rule is made in the case of a person who is the spouse of and who resides in Canada with, a Canadian citizen).
- He has resided in Canada for at least twelve of the eighteen months immediately preceding the date of his application.
- He has been lawfully admitted to Canada for permanent residence and has, since such admission, resided in Canada for at least five of the eight years immediately preceding the date of application. (Exceptions to this rule are made in the case of (1) a person who has served outside of Canada in the armed forces of Canada in a war in which Canada was engaged; (2) a person who has been lawfully admitted to Canada for permanent residence and is the wife of a Canadian citizen; and (3) a person who had a place of domicile in Canada for at least 20 years before January 1, 1947, and was not at that date under order of deportation).
- He is of good character and not under order of deportation. (Police records are a source of reference as to "good character.")
- He has an adequate knowledge of either the English or the French language; or (as exceptions to this rule), if he has not such adequate knowledge,

  (1) he was 40 years of age at the time of lawful admission to Canada for permanent residence and has resided continuously in Canada since for more than ten years; or

  (2) if he was less than 40 years of age at the time of lawful admission for permanent residence and has resided continuously in Canada since for more than twenty years; or

  (3) he is the spouse or the widow or widower of a Canadian citizen.
- He has an adequate knowledge of the responsibilities and privileges of Canadian citizenship and intends to comply with the oath of allegiance.
- He intends to have his place of domicile permanently in Canada.

Hearing Before a Judge

C—3

> An application for Canadian citizenship was rejected by a citizenship court on the grounds that the applicant did not meet the requirement of being a "person of good character." The court had found that the applicant had been convicted of shoplifting and thus had a criminal record. The applicant appealed to the Citizenship Court of Appeal. This court, after hearing the evidence, held that "after a person who has been convicted of a criminal offence has served any time of imprisonment that has been imposed on him . . . and after he has demonstrated by his subsequent course of conduct and way of life that he has rehabilitated himself in the eyes of right-thinking citizens, he is entitled to a finding that he is of good character. . . ."

(a) Why is a "criminal record" such a serious thing in deciding eligibility for citizenship?
(b) What did the judge take into account in connection with the criminal record?

Three months after the date of the application, the applicant will be advised to appear before a judge of a citizenship court for a hearing. At this hearing the judge will examine the applicant with regard to his application, and will make his recommendation accordingly. The application will then be sent to the Minister for his consideration.

If the citizenship court rejects the application, an appeal may be made to a Citizenship Appeal Court, consisting of one or more judges of the Federal Court of Canada.

Taking the Oath of Allegiance

In the presence of a judge and Royal Canadian Mounted Police constable, an immigrant takes the oath of allegiance before receiving Canadian citizenship.

Toronto Telegram

THE OATH: I . . . swear that I will be faithful and bear true allegiance to Her Majesty, Queen Elizabeth the Second, her Heirs and Successors according to law, and that I will faithfully observe the laws of Canada and fulfil my duties as a Canadian citizen. So help me God.

C—4

A citizenship court had refused an application for citizenship by the applicant and his wife on the grounds that, since the applicants had declared they did not believe in God, they could not comply with the oath of allegiance, which concludes with the words "So help me God." On appeal by the applicants, the appeal court found that the applicants were persons who had honest convictions and intellectual doubts which persuaded them to reject the idea of the existence of a Supreme Being; but that, nevertheless, they intended to comply with the obligations imposed by the oath of allegiance. The Court held that "lack of religious belief alone is not a ground upon which a citizenship court should decide against an application for citizenship," and that the applicants should not be required to take the oath of allegiance in its usual form, but should make an *affirmation* of allegiance in like terms.

(a) Do all natural-born Canadians believe in God?
(b) What was likely the original purpose of having the phrase "so help me God" in the oath of allegiance?
(c) According to this case under what conditions can an atheist become a Canadian citizen?

C—5

In the course of the processing of the appellants' applications for Canadian citizenship, a British Columbia citizenship court refused the applications because the applicants, on religious grounds, objected to serving in the armed forces of Canada and to voting in elections for public office. The Citizenship Appeal Court found that each of the appellants was willing to take the oath of allegiance, subject to their objections to military service and voting. The court held that the oath of allegiance does not expressly set out as a qualification for acquiring Canadian citizenship a willingness to serve in the armed forces of Canada, nor does it require an undertaking to do so; and that neither does the objection on religious grounds to voting disqualify an applicant from becoming a Canadian citizen.

(a) Does our law require that a citizen be willing to serve in the armed forces?
(b) Are natural-born Canadians free to vote in public elections or not to vote?
(c) What effect would the court's reasoning have on applications for citizenship in the above case?

If the Minister approves the application and the citizenship court judge's recommendations, he will grant and forward a certificate of citizenship to the clerk of the court, who then notifies the applicant to appear at a designated time before a judge to take the oath of allegiance. The certificate is not effective until the oath is taken, at which time the clerk will endorse on the certificate the date on which it was taken.

The foregoing cases indicate some of the difficulties occasionally encountered in connection with taking the oath of allegiance.

THE ACQUIRING OF CITIZENSHIP BY CHILDREN

C—6

Refer again to the case of Baby Jean, Case 1 (i), page 92.

(a) Is the citizenship status of the brother, Pierre, entirely dependent upon that of his parents?
(b) When parents become Canadian citizens does this automatically include their children?

The Minister may, in his discretion, grant a certificate of citizenship to a minor child of a naturalized Canadian citizen if the application is made by the responsible parent of the child or by a person authorized by the regulations, and the child has been lawfully admitted to Canada for permanent residence.

A child who is fourteen years of age or more must have an adequate knowledge of either the English or the French language, and must take the oath of allegiance.

THE ACQUIRING OF CITIZENSHIP BY WOMEN

C—7

With reference to Case 1(ii) on page 92, suppose that Baby Edith's family eventually returns to Winnipeg for permanent residence.

(a) Does the mother automatically become a Canadian citizen?
(b) Is the mother allowed to retain her United States citizenship and still reside in Canada?

Prior to the passing of the Canadian Citizenship Act, a woman, when she married, acquired the citizenship status of her husband. For example, if she was a Canadian before marriage and her husband an Italian alien, by marriage to him she lost her Canadian citizenship status and was considered to have acquired that of her husband. On the other hand, if she had been an Italian alien who married a Canadian citizen, she automatically acquired Canadian citizenship.

The Canadian Citizenship Act changed this situation so as to confer equal citizenship rights on men and women. The following rules now apply:

- A woman who is a Canadian citizen no longer loses her citizenship status simply because she marries an alien.
- An alien woman who marries a Canadian citizen after January 1, 1947, does not automatically become a Canadian citizen. She must make application and qualify in the manner described above under "Citizenship by Naturalization."
- An unmarried woman may acquire Canadian citizenship by the same procedure as does a man.
- An alien woman married to an alien may also acquire Canadian citizenship through the regular procedure, even though her husband remains an alien.

LOSS OF CANADIAN CITIZENSHIP

C—8

Suppose that Pierre, the child referred to in our first example, has been granted Canadian citizenship along with his parents. Now a grown man, Pierre becomes an active leader in a revolutionary group whose aim is to overthrow the government of Canada and to set up a totalitarian regime such as exists in communist countries. On the verge of arrest for his activities, Pierre has fled to a foreign country.

(a) Has Pierre voluntarily given up his Canadian citizenship?
(b) Can his Canadian citizenship status be taken away from him?

Under the original provisions of the Act a naturalized Canadian (with some exceptions) could lose his citizenship status merely by being out of Canada for a period of six (and later, ten) consecutive years, unless he had taken the necessary steps to retain it. This rule has now been repealed (1967). The amendment to the Act further provides that any person who had lost his citizenship by reason of such absence may, by filing a petition in accordance with the regulations, have his citizenship restored.

However, there are other reasons for which a naturalized citizen may lose his citizenship. The Governor-in-Council may, in his discretion, *revoke* the Canadian citizenship of any person *other than a natural-born Canadian* if he is satisfied that such person

(a) has obtained Canadian citizenship by fraudulent means; or

(b) when not under a disability since the passing of the Act has acquired the nationality or citizenship of a foreign country by any voluntary and formal act other than marriage; or has taken an oath of allegiance to a foreign country; or has renounced his Canadian citizenship.

The Act also provides that "where the responsible parent of a minor child ceases to be a Canadian citizen . . . , the Governor-in-Council may, in his discretion, direct that the said child shall cease to be a Canadian citizen if the said child is or thereupon becomes, under the law of any country other than Canada, a national or citizen of that country."

The citizenship status of a natural-born Canadian cannot be taken away from him. He loses it only when he, himself, renounces it. The renunciation is implied if he acquired the citizenship of another country.

APPLYING THE LAW

1. Betty, a citizen of the United States, married a Canadian. If Betty wishes to become a Canadian citizen, what exceptions to the regular conditions for naturalization are made in her case simply because she is now the wife of a Canadian citizen?
2. Recently some members of a revolutionary party in Quebec who had kidnapped a British Trade Commissioner were transported to Cuba (at their demand) in return for the release of the Commissioner. The kidnappers were natural-born Canadians. Have they by this action lost their Canadian citizenship?

DISCUSSION AND PROJECTS

1. Noting the decision in case C—5 on page 96, discuss whether or not a person may refuse to serve in the military forces of his country in time of war and still "bear true allegiance" to his country.
2. If possible, visit a session of the Citizenship Court and bring back to class a report of the proceedings.
3. Have one of your class or group obtain a blank set of forms of application for Canadian citizenship. Read and circulate these among your colleagues.

UNIT SIX
MAKING LEGAL AGREEMENTS

Part 8
THE NATURE OF A CONTRACT

Case 1

(i) You step into a taxi and say to the driver, "the Canadian National Railway Station." The driver does not reply but takes you directly to the station.

(ii) You have a date for a dance but at the last minute your date calls the whole thing off.

Which of the above situations involves a legally binding agreement?

A contract is an agreement *enforceable at law*. This definition is important because not all agreements are legally binding. The distinction lies in the fact that the court will recognize as contracts only those agreements under which the parties *intend* to assume legal rights and duties as opposed to engagements of a social character. For example, if a person agrees to take another to the theatre but fails to keep the appointment there is no ground for legal action, even though considerable inconvenience may have been caused to the second person, because this type of agreement is not recognized at law as a contract.

It is not always necessary that the intention be expressed in a formal way; the conduct of the parties may be sufficient. For example, a person enters a restaurant, orders the special dinner and eats it. Although no word has been said about the price there is an *implied* contract that the price will be paid.

Even if the intention to create a legal obligation is present, the agreement may still not be enforceable at law unless it complies with certain legal requirements involving (a) its form, or (b) the necessary elements of validity.

FORMS OF CONTRACT

All contracts are either specialty contracts or simple contracts.

SPECIALTY CONTRACTS

A *specialty* contract is one that must be "in writing and under seal." At one time, the seal consisted of the stamped impression of a distinguishing mark made in melted wax on the document. For a person who could not write his name, the seal constituted his signature. Often the design was on a ring which he wore.

Today, the tradition of using the stamped impression of a distinctive design is still followed by corporations and governmental bodies (your own school certificate may carry the seal of the school board that issued it), but usually a red sticker is now used instead of wax. For private individuals it is common practice, before the parties sign, to place small red stickers on the document. By signing opposite the red sticker the contracting party adopts it as his seal, and thus makes the contract a "specialty." If a red sticker is not available, the word "seal" written where the seal would be placed is sufficient. In most cases specialty contracts are witnessed. Some examples of contracts which must be in specialty form are deeds to property, mortgages, and long-term leases.

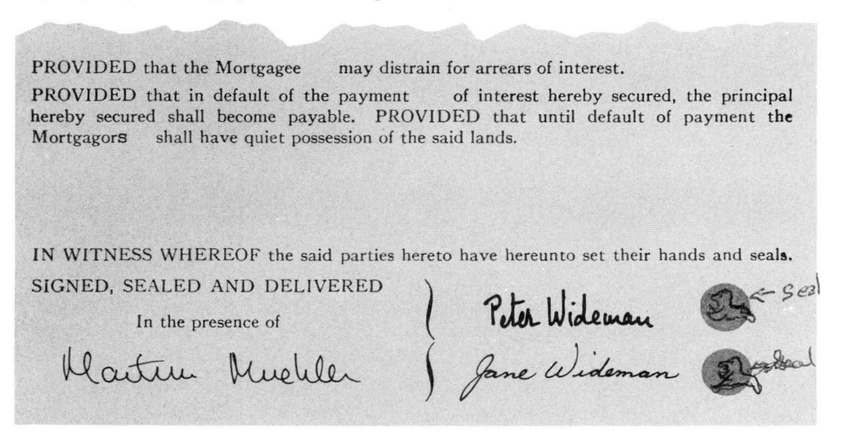
PROVIDED that the Mortgagee may distrain for arrears of interest.

PROVIDED that in default of the payment of interest hereby secured, the principal hereby secured shall become payable. PROVIDED that until default of payment the Mortgagors shall have quiet possession of the said lands.

IN WITNESS WHEREOF the said parties hereto have hereunto set their hands and seals.

SIGNED, SEALED AND DELIVERED

In the presence of

Martin Muehler

Peter Wideman

Jane Wideman

The formality of executing (signing and witnessing) a document under seal usually signifies to the courts that the parties have entered into the contract with due deliberation, solemnly promising to do or not to do something, and fully intending to carry out the promise.

SIMPLE CONTRACTS

C — 2

(i) A sends a letter to B offering car seat covers at a certain price. B replies by letter ordering a set of covers.

(ii) C notices an advertisement in his local newspaper in which D offers a used TV set for sale. C telephones D and gets information about the set — its make, condition, and price and says "I'll take it. I will call for it tomorrow." D agrees to hand it over on those terms.

(a) Would the two letters between A and B make a contract? Why?
(b) Do you think that a court would recognize the oral agreement between C and D?
(c) If you have had a job, has your agreement with your employer about duties, hours and wages been in writing? Would the form of that contract matter if your employer refused to pay the wages he owed you and you had to take him to court?

A *simple* contract is any contract not under seal. It may be in writing. In fact, the law requires some simple contracts to be in writing in order to be enforceable (See Statute of Frauds below); or it may be oral; or it may even be implied by conduct.

The advantage of a written contract is that it is evidence of the terms of the agreement. An oral contract may be impossible to enforce because of lack of proof of its terms.

C — 3

The owner of a hockey team in Nova Scotia engaged MacLean under an oral agreement to play hockey for him at a specified wage. Shortly afterwards the owner promised — again orally — to have formal written contracts drawn up by his lawyer providing for insurance against injuries to his players, and said that if a player became disabled he would be "looked after." Before any such contract had been drawn up, MacLean lost his right eye as a result of a playing injury. Following the injury, MacLean did not receive either wages or financial aid from the owner of the team. MacLean sued for damages for breach of contract, but was unsuccessful because: (a) according to the terms of his oral agreement with the owner, it was implied that wages were to be paid for playing time only; and (b) the promises regarding insurance and "looking after" were too vague, and were not enforceable since they were subject to the terms of a written contract that was never drawn up.

(a) If you had been the hockey player in this case, would you have insisted on a definite written contract before playing any game or would you have taken for granted that you would be "looked after"?
(b) How do you think it was "implied" that McLean was to be paid for playing time only?
(c) The court recognized that part of the oral agreement concerning wages but not that part concerning compensation for injuries. Why not?

THE STATUTE OF FRAUDS

C — 4

Is an oral agreement on this matter legally binding?

For centuries under English common law no distinction was made between the oral and the written contract. Eventually, because fraud and perjury were so often connected with the enforcing of old claims and various promises, a law was passed known as the Statute of Frauds (1677) which required that there must be written evidence of certain contracts if they were to be enforced by the courts. Similar provisions to those of the English statute were either re-enacted or adopted by the common law provinces of Canada. Accordingly, in Ontario and some of the other provinces the following classes of contracts must be supported by written evidence in order to be enforceable at law:

1. Any promise by an executor or administrator of an estate to pay debts of the estate out of his own pocket.

The executor or administrator of an estate is the person appointed to settle the affairs of a deceased person's estate — pay the debts, distribute the estate among the heirs, etc. Occasions may arise where the administrator or executor promises to pay the deceased's debt out of his own pocket. For example, a son who has been appointed as administrator may agree to pay a certain debt personally rather than from the proceeds of his father's estate, or perhaps the estate has no funds to pay the debt. Such a promise is not legally binding unless it is in writing.

2. A promise to pay for the debt, default, or wrongful conduct of another person.

The type of contract covered here is one in which a person promises to pay another's debt or obligation *if that person does not pay*. Such a contract is known as a *guarantee*. In contrast, a contract which assumes *direct responsibility* for another's debt (there is no condition to pay only if the debtor does not) is known as an *indemnity*. An indemnity does not have to be in writing to be enforceable (except in British Columbia). For an example, let us suppose that a young man is buying a motor cycle and that his father says to the dealer "Give him the bike; if he doesn't pay you, I will." This is a contract of guarantee which comes under the Statute of Frauds and is not enforceable at law unless it is in writing. However, if the father says "Give him the bike; I will see you paid," the contract is one of indemnity and not subject to the Statute of Frauds. You will notice that in the latter case the father's promise to pay is not contingent upon the condition whether or not the son pays. Furthermore, under a written guarantee the creditor is not entitled to take action against the father until he has first tried to collect from the son; under the indemnity, however, whether in writing or not, the father has accepted primary responsibility for the debt, and the creditor may look directly to him for payment.

3. Any agreement in consideration of marriage, except a mutual promise to marry.

Contracts in consideration of marriage include any promise to make a monetary settlement or transfer of property providing a certain marriage takes place. The promise may be made by either party or by a third party — a parent, guardian or other relative. For example, a young man promises to give his fiancée a yacht if she will marry him; or a father, in order to bring about his daughter's marriage promises his prospective son-in-law a share in his business if he will marry the daughter. This kind of contract is comparatively rare in Canada today, but at the time of the passing of the Statute of Frauds it was common enough in England to be singled out for inclusion in the statute.

4. Contracts for the sale of land or any interest in land.

A person is said to have an interest in land when he has rights or obligations connected with it; for example, a right of way or a mortgage on land.

5. Any agreement not to be performed within one year from the making thereof.

In 1954 England amended her Statute of Frauds so that of the five kinds of contracts listed above only two have been retained: contracts of guarantee (No. 2) and agreements for the sale of land (No. 4). At the time of this writing, of the common law provinces of Canada which had adopted the original English statute, only British Columbia has made a similar amendment to its act. British Columbia, however, included in its amendment contracts of indemnity as well as contracts of guarantee; therefore, in that province both contracts of guarantee and of indemnity must be supported by written evidence in order to be enforceable.

The Statute of Frauds of Prince Edward Island contains only one of the five classes of contracts listed above; namely, contracts of guarantee. Alberta, Saskatchewan, Manitoba and Newfoundland have no formal Statute of Frauds, but some of the provisions of the original English act have been given effect in other statutes.

FORM AND CONTENT OF THE WRITTEN MEMORANDUM

C — 5

Jones calls on Smith to settle the terms of a deal whereby Jones is to buy a piece of land from Smith. Smith is not at home, so Jones leaves a note as follows.

I will buy the house we
talked about last week.
Bill Jones

(a) If this is the only written memorandum on the deal do you think it would satisfy the requirements of the Statute of Frauds?

(b) What would be the minimum amount of information that would have to be contained in any written agreement?

The following rules apply to the form and content of the written memorandum:

1. The written memorandum need not be formal but it must contain the names of the parties to the contract and indicate its subject matter. The statute also provides that the memorandum of the contract must be signed by the party "to be charged" or his authorized agent. The party to be charged is the one who is subsequently sued. Since any party might be the one against whom action may have to be taken, it is prudent to have all parties sign. The memorandum may consist of letters or other papers that give sufficient evidence of the contract.

For example, when one of the parties to a contract who had not signed it wrote a letter acknowledging his obligation but stating also that he intended to repudiate it, the court held that the letter supplied the necessary evidence and that he was therefore liable on the contract.

2. When the parties have deliberately recorded their agreement in documentary form and it is evident that the written document was intended to embody the entire agreement between them, oral evidence that contradicts or varies this agreement is not admissible, except when the meaning of any particular part of the agreement is ambiguous or doubtful. The following case examples illustrate this rule:

C — 6

Wattie agreed in writing to sell to Lytton "pine and wood on Lot Number 13." The written memoranda, consisting of informal notes, did not specify the number of trees to be cut but it did specify the price. Subsequently, Wattie sued Lytton for damages for cutting an excessive number of trees. Wattie claimed that an oral agreement between them had specified that only 500 trees were to be cut. Lytton's defence was that this term was not contained in the written memoranda. The Ontario court which heard the case held that the price specified implied that there would be a limit to the number of trees to be cut, and that the written memoranda did not constitute the whole agreement intended by the parties. The oral evidence was therefore admitted and damages were assessed against Lytton.

(a) How could this court action, and the expense involved, have been avoided?
(b) How was Lytton trying to use the Statute of Frauds to give himself an unfair advantage?
(c) What are the circumstances which would suggest that there must have been some agreement about the number of trees to be cut?

C — 7

The defendant (a trucker) had made a written contract with the plaintiff (corn merchants in Toronto) to deliver stipulated quantities of corn to the plaintiff's customers. The trucker failed to deliver the quantities as agreed upon and was sued for breach of contract. The trucker claimed that according to an oral arrangement he had with the corn merchant, it was his intention (known to the merchant) to purchase the corn from local farmers. This he had found impossible to do because of the poor crop that year. However, corn was available elsewhere. An Ontario court held that when the written contract did not mention that local farmers were to be the source of supply, its terms could not be varied by an oral arrangement.

(a) What is the difference between the oral arrangements in C — 6 and C — 7?
(b) Why did the courts recognize one oral agreement, but not the other?

3. An oral agreement made after the written agreement for the purpose of changing the terms of the written agreement, or even of rescinding it, may be accepted as evidence.

C — 8

Finelli agreed in writing to construct a driveway for Dee. Subsequently, Dee orally cancelled the agreement, and Finelli's sales manager accepted the cancellation. However, while Dee was absent, Finelli constructed the driveway. Dee refused to pay, claiming the contract had been cancelled, but Finelli sued. An Ontario court ruled that a written contract could be rescinded by an oral agreement made *after* the written agreement for the purpose of cancelling it.

(a) Why was the oral agreement held to be binding?
(b) How does this case illustrate that an oral agreement can be just as binding as a written agreement?

THE EFFECT OF PART PERFORMANCE

C — 9

McManus orally agreed to sell Cooke a city lot and to build on it a house for him according to plans and specifications submitted by McManus. Building operations were commenced and inspection made by Cooke from time to time as the work progressed. Cooke later refused to carry out his part of the contract, claiming that since it was an oral contract for the sale of an interest in land, it was not enforceable. An English court, however, held that since there had been part performance by McManus to the knowledge and with the consent of Cooke, the contract was enforceable.

(a) What facts were proof that a contract for the sale of the land must have been made?
(b) In the circumstances, would it have been fair if the defendant could have repudiated his agreement simply because it did not satisfy the Statute of Frauds?

The lack of written evidence of a contract *concerning land* (or, in rare cases, goods) would not prevent enforcement if the plaintiff, relying on the oral contract, has already begun performance.

"His word is as good as his bond." It must not be thought that every person avails himself of legal technicalities to avoid his obligations. Most people accept their contracts as morally binding and carry out their agreements even though there may be loopholes for evading their obligations.

NECESSARY ELEMENTS OF VALIDITY

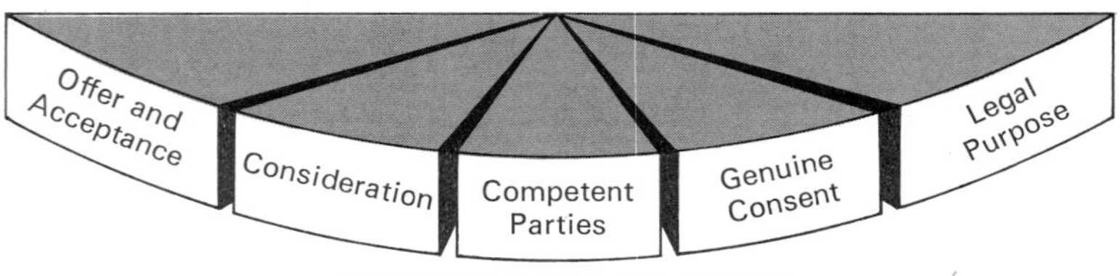

ESSENTIALS OF A CONTRACT

A contract is not valid unless certain requirements are met. In order to explain and illustrate these clearly, the remaining Parts in this Unit will deal with each requirement separately.

APPLYING THE LAW

1. Beggs is admiring one of Collard's paintings when Collard says "I think I might sell it some day if I can get $100 for it." Beggs says "Sold" and immediately offers $100 in cash.
   (a) Do you think Collard really intends his statement to be an offer?
   (b) Do you think Beggs really believes the statement is an offer?
   (c) Is there a contract? Why or why not?
2. Hardman telephones Bilker: "I received your cheque today. I know it is the amount stated in our written contract, but we agreed I was to get an extra $200." Bilker replies: "I don't recall any such agreement."
   (a) What difficulty would Hardman have in proving his claim?
   (b) If he can prove his claim, will the court enforce it?

DISCUSSION AND PROJECTS

1. Give some examples of contracts which are usually made orally.
2. Discuss the implications of the expression "His word is as good as his bond." Apply it to the case of *MacLean v. Kennedy* given on page 102.
3. Have each person in your group bring to class a specific example of a written agreement, specialty or other. Include such things as the following and examine the contract terms they contain: credit card, city parking lot ticket, theatre ticket, service station work order, dry cleaner's receipt.

Part 9
OFFER AND ACCEPTANCE

Toronto Star

At an ordinary auction sale an offer (or bid) is accepted when the auctioneer brings the hammer down or shouts "Sold."

In order to be valid the offer and the acceptance must comply with the following rules:

1. The offer must be definite and seriously intended. For example, let us suppose that B is having trouble with his new motorcycle. In exasperation he exclaims "I would sell the thing for $10." C, who overhears the remark, says "Sold." This, however, does not make a contract, because B does not seriously intend his statement to be an offer.

On this point of "intention" it should be noted that, at law, advertisements, price circulars, and the like are not generally considered as offers. Rather, such announcements are interpreted legally as invitations to the public to make offers. Ordinarily, therefore, when a purchaser answers an advertisement for the sale of goods, he is not "accepting" the advertisement; he is merely making an offer to buy which the seller may or may not accept. To constitute an offer, the words of the advertisement must be capable of application to specific persons, and must be distinguishable from mere invitations to transact business.

2. In simple contracts both the offer and the acceptance must be *communicated* by one party to the other by a written or an oral statement, or implied by conduct. For example, a person who has found a lost article learns, before he returns it, that a reward has been offered for its return. When he returns the article, he may legally claim the reward. His acceptance consists of the performance of the condition required by the offer, namely, the returning of the article. On the other hand, if the finder had returned the article in ignorance of the fact that the owner had offered a reward, he has no legal contractual claim to this reward. He cannot be said to have accepted an offer of which he did not know; thus, there could be no contract.

Similarly, an offer containing such a condition as "Unless I hear from you to the contrary, I shall consider the contract closed," is not deemed accepted if the one to whom it is made fails to make a reply. At the same time, there is no obligation to communicate your refusal to buy goods delivered to you unasked, or to return them. It is sufficient if you hold the goods ready to give to the owner if he calls for them. However, if you use the goods, your conduct may constitute acceptance.

C — 10

McSweeney suffered injuries from gas fumes that escaped from a gas burner installed by the employees of a gas company and sued for damages, claiming negligence on the part of the employees. The company's defence was that their contract with McSweeney contained a clause which provided that the company (the defendant) would not be liable for damages to persons or property resulting from the "use or pressure or escape of gas, whether accidental or otherwise." This clause was printed on the bottom half of a card, the top half of which McSweeney signed as an application for gas service. According to the evidence given at the trial, the rules on the bottom half of the application card were never called to McSweeney's attention and he was not aware of their content. The company admitted that it was not their practice to draw the customer's attention to these clauses. The court held that the company was liable for damages caused by the negligence of their employees, and that the rules on the card limiting the liability of the company could become binding only if they were reasonably brought to the attention of the customer, which in this case had not been done.

(a) Does the decision in this case mean that customers have no responsibility to read the documents they sign?
(b) In view of the decision in this case, what would you suggest that the gas company do about future applications for gas service?

There are some situations in which it is not easy to determine whether or not the offer has been communicated within the meaning of the law. For example, many people buy railroad tickets or accept parking receipts without taking the trouble to read them carefully. Sometimes important conditions are in very small print or are on the back of the ticket. Likewise, in certain documents a clause may be inserted inconspicuously in a corner or at the bottom.

The general rule which applies is that when such contracts are entered into without objection by the offeree, his act amounts to an acceptance, and he is bound by the contract even though he may not have informed himself of its contents. At the same time, the courts have held that where certain printed conditions on a ticket or similar document are so obscure as to escape the attention of the person accepting it, he is not bound by such conditions. Sufficient prominence must be given to these conditions to indicate that they are a part of the general contract.

3. An offer may lapse and can no longer be accepted if: (a) either the offeror or the offeree dies before acceptance; or (b) the offer is not accepted within the time specified or, when no time is specified, within a reasonable time.

What is a reasonable time depends upon the particular circumstances in each case. For instance, in the case of an offer to sell a commodity that is subject to day-to-day fluctuations in value, a reasonable time to accept would be less than in the case of a commodity that is not subject to such frequent changes. The urgency indicated in the offer would also have to be taken into account.

4. The offer must be accepted in the manner stipulated or indicated in the offer.

If the offeror — no matter how his offer is made — indicates specifically that the acceptance is to be made by mail or by telegram, he is not necessarily bound by an acceptance made in any other manner. Also, if an offer made by mail does not suggest a different mode of acceptance, it implies that the acceptance should be by mail. Similarly, in the case of an offer by telegram that does not stipulate the manner of acceptance, it is implied that the acceptance shall be by telegram.

C — 11

A written agreement for group medical services between the plaintiff, Loft, and the defendant, Physicians' Services Inc. (operating in Ontario), provided that any notice to Physicians' Services Inc., "may be given by registered letter." Loft gave notice to enrol a new-born child and sent the notice by ordinary mail. The defendant declared that the letter had not been received. They further claimed that the notice was not effective because it was not sent by registered mail, as indicated by the conditions of the contract. The court held that the word "may" in the contract was of a permissive nature; therefore, the letter mailed by ordinary post was permitted by the contract. Also, since the mail was indicated in the contract as the proper means of acceptance, the notice was binding as soon as posted.

(a) If the word "must" had been used instead of "may," how might the case have been decided?
(b) Since mail was the means of acceptance asked for, why should the acceptance become effective as soon as it was mailed?
(c) If Loft had telegraphed his reply to Physicians' Services Inc., when would the contract have become legally binding?

An important point to remember is that when the offer either expressly or by implication requires that the acceptance is to be made by mail, *the contract is closed as soon as the letter of acceptance is placed in the mail,* and both parties are bound even though there may be a delay in delivery by the postal authorities, or even if the letter is lost in the mail. Similarly, when the offeror requires the acceptance to be made by telegram, the contract is closed as soon as the message is delivered to the telegraph company. The date and hour stamped upon the envelope or upon the telegram would indicate the time at which the contract became binding.

When the method of acceptance is neither expressed nor implied in the offer, the acceptance may be made by any efficient mode; for example, by mail, telegram, or telephone; but, in such cases, *the acceptance is not effective until it is actually received.*

Where the method of communicating the acceptance is instantaneous, such as by telephone or teletype, the message of acceptance must be *actually received* by the offeror before it is legally effective. For example, suppose A is telephoning B, offering to buy B's car. The line goes dead and the conversation is cut off so that A does not hear B's reply accepting the offer. There is no acceptance at that moment; the acceptance was not actually received.

5. The acceptance must be unconditional; if otherwise, the condition must be treated as a counter offer which requires acceptance to make a contract.

C—12

Wrench had offered to sell a farm to Hyde for £1,000. Hyde's reply was that he would give £950. Wrench refused. Later, Hyde said he would accept the original offer of £1,000. Wrench now refused to sell at all, and Hyde sued. The court held that Hyde's counter offer of £950 had the effect of terminating the original offer, and that Hyde's subsequent "acceptance" of the original offer was not an acceptance but rather another offer that Wrench could choose to accept or reject.

(a) What is a counter-offer?
(b) What is the legal effect of a counter-offer?
(c) If Wrench had said "O.K., I'll take £950," would that have been an offer or an acceptance?

A refusal of an offer, of course, causes the offer to terminate, and it cannot thereafter be accepted unless it is repeated. However, a mere inquiry as to whether the terms of the offer can be changed is not considered a counter offer or a refusal.

6. An offer may be revoked (withdrawn) at any time before it is accepted. To be legally effective, the revocation must *reach* the person to whom the offer was made before that person's acceptance has become effective.

C — 13

Byrne made an offer by mail on October 1, requiring an acceptance by cable. The offer was received by Tienhoven on October 11, and a cable of acceptance was sent immediately. On October 8, Byrne had mailed a letter revoking the offer. However, it was not received until after October 11, the date on which the acceptance had been cabled. In a court action on the matter, the decision given was that the revocation was not legally effective because it had not been *received* before the acceptance was made.

(a) Tienhoven's acceptance was binding as soon as cabled; the offeror's revocation was not effective until actually received. Why the difference?
(b) If a person decides to withdraw his offer, why should he use the quickest possible means of communication?

APPLYING THE LAW

1. Is the portion in small print an effective part of the contract?
2. Bondy offered to sell his car to Trudelle for $3,000. The down payment was to be $1,000; the balance was to be paid at $500 a month. Trudelle accepted the $3,000 price but declared he could not pay more than $500 down. Is there a contract at this point? Why or why not?
3. Davis, who wanted a thoroughbred labrador dog, travelled 100 miles to Blueridge Kennels to look at a litter of pups which the owner was offering at $150 each. Davis did not make up his

mind at the time but told the owner he liked one particular puppy and would make up his mind in a day or so. Five days later Davis mailed a letter to the owner saying that he would take the puppy he had liked at the price asked.

(a) According to the facts given, does the kennel owner have to keep the puppy Davis had liked until Davis had made up his mind?

(b) Would you say that Davis has accepted the offer within a reasonable time?

DISCUSSION AND PROJECTS

1. Ordinarily a sale advertisement in a newspaper is legally only an invitation to the public to make an offer. Is this rule allowed as an excuse for false advertising? Prepare a report outlining the controls for this type of advertising.
2. If the owner who has offered a reward for the return of a lost article refuses to give the finder the reward, what is the finder's legal position? May he turn the article to his own use? May he simply retain it in safekeeping until the owner agrees to give the reward? Must he surrender the article to the owner? Is there any other course open? Consult your local paper and examine the wording of lost-and-found ads for legal obligations.
3. Make a list of the kinds of contracts you know of which are implied by conduct.

Part 10
CONSIDERATION

C—14

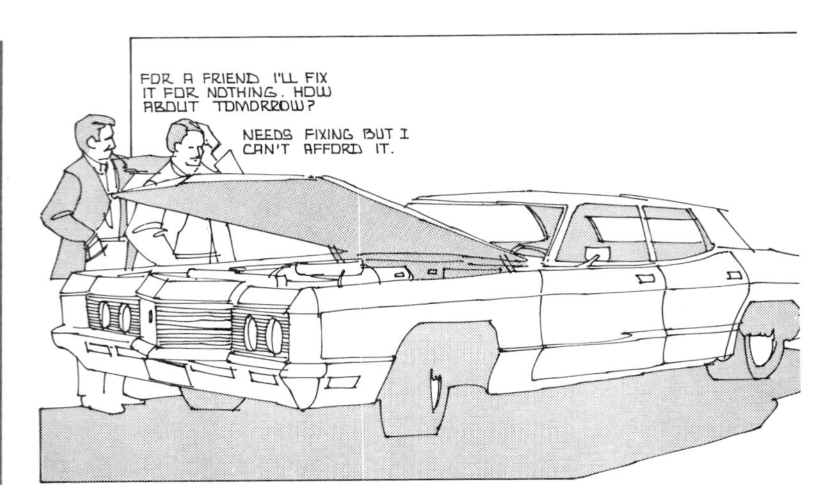

If the "fixer" changes his mind, will he be breaking a contract?

A simple contract requires consideration to make it valid. A promise to do something for nothing is not enforceable at law. Consideration consists of the values exchanged by the parties to a contract, and is that which induces them to be bound. It has been defined as "some right, interest, profit or benefit accruing to one party, or some forebearance, detriment, loss or responsibility given, suffered or undertaken by another."

Until the fifteenth century, the English common law courts recognized only one kind of executory contract, the formal written contract bearing the seal of the signatory. At that time, only two other classes of actions on contracts were allowed at common law: claims for non-payment of money due for goods supplied or work done or money lent, and claims for the recovery of goods kept back by the defendant from the plaintiff. Apart from these exceptions, courts of law would not concern themselves with the intentions of those who had not made their contract in solemn form and under seal.

At the same time the Court of Chancery, which administered the law of equity, recognized contracts that were not under seal as long as there was evidence of genuine intention of the parties thereto. Such evidence could be found in the fact that *consideration* was present in the contract.

As a result of the influence of the law of equity, the common law courts also came to recognize consideration as a basis for the enforcing of simple contracts, and today it is an established principle that all simple contracts require consideration to support them. However, tradition is still followed in that contracts under seal are enforceable without consideration being shown; the solemnity of the form of the contract is accepted as evidence of the genuine intention of the parties.

CONTRACTS NOT UNDER SEAL

C — 15

McGregor's cow had strayed onto the highway (in Ontario) and was struck by Garden's car while Garden was driving. The car suffered some damage. McGregor must have feared some liability in the case, for without any demand or suggestion on Garden's part he intimated that he would pay for the repairs to the automobile. Later, he denied liability, and Garden sued. The Ontario Court of Appeal held that McGregor's promise was unenforceable on the grounds that Garden gave no consideration for McGregor's promise. According to the evidence given, Garden had not suggested that he intended to sue, nor had he intimated that he would refrain from suing because of McGregor's promise to pay for the repairs; thus, there was no compromise of a disputed claim.

(a) Why did McGregor make the promise to repair the car?
(b) Why is McGregor's promise a "gratuitous" promise?
(c) What is meant by saying that Garden gave no consideration for McGregor's promise?
(d) What is a "compromise of a disputed claim"? What kind of compromise might McGregor and Garden have made?

If a person promises his services *gratuitously* (free of charge), he cannot be legally bound on his promise, unless the promise is made under seal. It must be remembered, however, that if such person undertakes to do work gratuitously, and by carelessness or negligence causes loss to the person for whom the work is performed, he will be liable *in tort* for damages. The liability in such cases is based on the person's negligence, not on his contract.

Similarly, a promise to pay a person to do what that person was already legally bound to do would not be enforceable. For example, suppose that a contractor under contract to build a house finds that he has underestimated the cost, and that he tells the owner he will have to abandon the project unless he gets more money. Faced with this prospect, the owner promises to pay him an additional $500 to complete the work. Actually, the contractor is giving no consideration for the promise of the additional money, for under his contract he is already bound to complete the house at the original price. Therefore, a legal action to enforce payment of the extra $500 would fail.

By common law, an agreement to settle a debt by paying a lesser amount than the original claim is not enforceable unless consideration can be shown for the reduction; for example, payment of the debt before it is legally due, or a compromise settlement made in order to avoid litigation. However, in British Columbia, Alberta, Saskatchewan, Manitoba and Ontario, statute law* provides that a part payment *accepted and received* by a creditor — not merely promised to him — in full satisfaction of a debt, though *without any new consideration*, extinguishes the debt.

CHARITABLE SUBSCRIPTIONS

Subscriptions (or pledges, as they are sometimes called) to charitable organizations are generally unenforceable unless specific consideration can be shown for the promised subscription.

C — 16

A university in Nova Scotia solicited funds for maintaining and improving its operations, and for the construction of new buildings. Boutilier, who had promised a donation, died while in default on his promise. The university submitted a claim against the deceased's estate, and eventually sued to recover the amount subscribed. The case was finally decided in the Supreme Court of Canada, which ruled that in view of the total subscribed in the campaign (over $2,000,000), "it was difficult to believe that the university in doing the work and making the increased expenditure, did so in reliance upon the deceased's subscription." In other words, there was no specific consideration given or undertaken in return for the promised subscription. Therefore, the appeal to enforce the claim was not allowed.

(a) For what purposes was the fund to be used by the university?
(b) Would you say that Boutilier's subscription was specifically for one of these purposes or simply a gift to the University?
(c) Why did the court rule that there was no consideration for Boutilier's promise?

However, a pledge to give money for a specific purpose, for example, the erection of a particular building, is binding if, in reliance on the pledge, the promisee has begun work and incurred expenditures on the specific project.

C — 17

Subscriptions were solicited for the erection and equipping of a building (in Manitoba) for the Y.M.C.A. In reliance on the subscriptions received, the building was begun. One of the subscribers, Nicholson, defaulted on his pledge and was sued. His defence was "lack of consideration." The Manitoba Court of Appeal upheld the trial court's decision that the contract was binding. Beginning the work and incurring liabilities on the specific project for which the pledge had been given furnished sufficient consideration for the promised subscription.

*B.C., *Laws Declaratory Act*; Alta., *Judicature Act*; Sask., *Queen's Bench Act*; Man. & Ont., *Mercantile Law Amendment Act.*

(a) Was Nicholson getting any personal benefit in return for his subscription? Do you think this is what he meant by "lack of consideration?"
(b) On what grounds did the court rule that there was consideration given for the pledge?

It is interesting to note that the Statute of Frauds of Prince Edward Island provides that subscriptions to a public utility, place of worship, school house, bridge or road is enforceable if in writing regardless of whether consideration is present or not.

ADEQUACY OF CONSIDERATION

C — 18

Paisley agreed to sell Fleming his stamp collection for $3,000. Before paying for the stamps Fleming discovered that he should only have agreed to pay $2,000 since the stamps were not worth what he had thought when he made the contract. Fleming refused to pay the $3,000, but Paisley sued and won his case.

(a) What was the consideration for each party?
(b) In what way did Fleming feel he was not receiving adequate consideration?
(c) Why do you think Paisley won his case?

Consideration must be of some value in the eyes of the law, but it need not be adequate.

It is not for the court to determine whether or not the consideration which has been agreed upon is adequate; it is sufficient if it is present. Different people set different values upon the same things. For example, an ardent stamp collector will agree to pay a large sum merely for the pleasure of possessing some rare stamp. Another person may place little value on the same small piece of paper. Usually, therefore, the court concerns itself only with determining whether or not consideration is present in the contract and, unless fraud is alleged, does not consider the adequacy of the consideration.

The value of the consideration involved must be capable of being estimated in money. In this respect, it has been held that friendship, gratitude, natural love and affection are not valuable consideration and will not make a promise legally binding. For example, a promise to do something in return for natural affection would not be enforceable. If, however, the promise has been performed, the parties may not be restored to their original position. This means that if a gift has been made from motives of friendship or affection, it cannot thereafter be recovered on the grounds that no consideration was received in return when it was given.

PAST CONSIDERATION

C — 19

Eastwood, the plaintiff, had been the guardian and agent of a Mrs. Kenyon while she was a minor, and had borrowed money on his own promissory note in order to finance his ward's needs.

He did this voluntarily. When his ward came of age, she promised to reimburse him. After her marriage, her husband (Kenyon) also promised to pay the note. When he failed to pay, Eastwood sued. Eastwood claimed that Kenyon was under a moral obligation to keep his promise, but the court ruled that Kenyon's promise was gratuitous in that he received no consideration from Eastwood in return. Kenyon had made the promise out of a sense of moral duty, but for a consideration which was wholly *past*. Therefore, Kenyon's promise was not enforceable at law.

(a) Was the promise made by Mrs. Kenyon binding upon her? Why or why not?
(b) Why was Mr. Kenyon's promise considered gratuitous?

A promise to do something in return for past benefits already received is said to be given for "past consideration" and is not legally enforceable. Promises of this nature are really gratuitous.

ILLEGAL CONSIDERATION

Consideration must be legal. It is obvious that the courts would not enforce a contract where the consideration constituted a violation of the law or was contrary to public policy; for example, a promise to bribe a public official, or an agreement to give false evidence at a trial, or a contract to instal an electric service knowing it to be in violation of a municipal bylaw.

APPLYING THE LAW

1. Assume that A is making some repairs to his car in his driveway. A's next-door neighbour, B, who is a motor mechanic by trade, comes over and after looking at the car says "Here, let me do this." Thereupon B makes the repairs, in the course of which he uses some of his own tools and a few used parts from his own garage. There is no mention of payment for the job. A assumes his neighbour is doing the job simply as a favour.
   (a) From the facts given, could B later legally claim payment for the job?
   (b) Assume that after the job has been completed A says "Thank you very much. When I get my bonus at the end of the month, I'll see that you get $10." Is A's promise legally enforceable?
   (c) Suppose that A's car is afterwards involved in an accident and that the cause of the accident is found to be B's carelessness in doing the work. B's defence is "Well, I wasn't getting paid for the job anyway." Could any legal liability rest on B? Why or why not?
2. A debtor owes his creditor $1,000, well overdue. The creditor agrees to take $750 in full settlement. In some provinces the legal position of the parties when the $750 is accepted and re-

ceived is quite different from what it would be if only the promise existed, that is, if no money had yet been paid.
(a) Which provinces have this law?
(b) What is the difference in legal position?

DISCUSSION AND PROJECTS

1. Discuss the liability of those who promise substantial subscriptions to (a) church building programs; (b) annual community fund drives. Obtain a pledge card and examine its wording.
2. "Strong moral obligations are not necessarily legal obligations." Discuss this statement. (See *Eastwood v. Kenyon*, C — 19, page 117.) Do you know of any instances where the persons concerned carried out their moral obligations although they were not legally bound to do so, for instance stores accepting returned damaged merchandise.

Part 11
LEGAL CAPACITY TO MAKE BINDING CONTRACTS

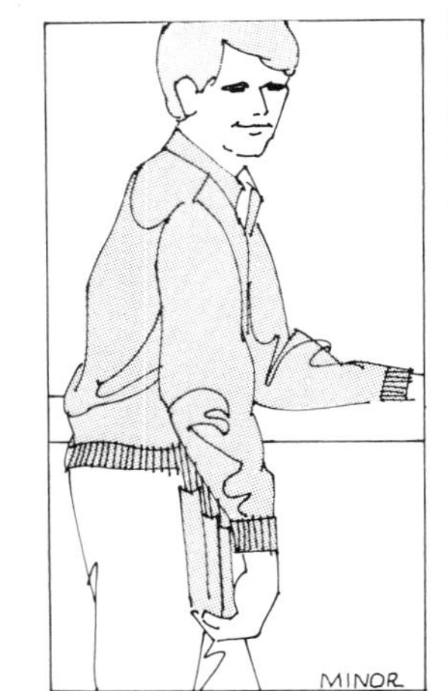

Can either of these persons be held to the contract he makes?

Generally speaking, the law regards a sane, sober adult as capable of managing his own affairs and therefore able to make contracts of a binding nature. However, some persons are regarded as less than fully capable, and their ability to make contracts is restricted for their own protection. The major classes of persons who enjoy this protection are as follows.

- *Minors.* At common law persons under the age of 21 years were minors and were referred to in legal terminology as *infants*. Recently, most of the provinces have reduced the age at which a minor reaches his majority. In British Columbia, Nova Scotia, Newfoundland and Saskatchewan, a person reaches his majority at the age of 19; in Ontario, Alberta, Manitoba and Quebec, at the age of 18. In those provinces where the age has not been changed, the age of majority continues to be 21 years.
- *Insane persons.*
- *Intoxicated persons.*

The principle that underlies the law regarding the above classes is that others should not be allowed to take advantage of them. Frequently, the contracts that they enter into are *voidable*, which means that the person to be protected may elect to treat the contract as either binding or not binding, as he wishes. This permits the person entitled to be protected to enforce the contract if it is to his advantage, or to decline to go through with it if it is not. In each class, however, there are some exceptions to the general rule; therefore each class will be treated separately.

MINORS

The law dealing with the responsibility of a minor (or infant) for the agreements he makes may be best considered by dividing the subject into types of contracts:

- Valid contracts
- Void contracts
- Voidable contracts
- Obligation to pay for necessaries supplied.

VALID CONTRACTS

There exists at common law a small class of transactions in which the infant may make a binding contract. These are contracts of apprenticeship and contracts of service for the infant's benefit. This type of contract is no longer very common, but it is still recognized as binding at law.

C—20

Doyle, who was a minor, applied for a license as a boxer and agreed to abide by the rules of the British Boxing Board. He was issued a license. One of the rules of the British Boxing Board provided that the boxer's money for a bout would be withheld if he committed a foul. In a boxing match at the White City Stadium Doyle committed a foul and his pay was withheld. He sued the Stadium and the British Boxing Board, claiming that the contract was not binding on him because he was a minor. An English court held that he was bound on the contract, on the grounds that infants can make contracts binding on themselves for apprenticeship and service, provided that these contracts are for the infant's benefit.

(a) What is the legal meaning of "infant"?
(b) In what way was the boxing match a contract for Doyle's benefit?
(c) What occupations accept apprentices today? How would this decision apply to those situations?

VOID CONTRACTS

There is another comparatively small class of contracts involving minors, which the common law regards as *void* (that is, empty of any effect). These are contracts that are clearly prejudicial to the infant, or to his detriment.

C—21

Beatty, a minor residing in Ontario, was engaged in selling stock of the Colorado River Irrigation Company. He sold some stock to Beam, and in order to ensure that Beam would suffer no loss, gave him his personal guarantee in the sum of $1,100 whereby he promised to make up any loss that Beam suffered as a result of buying the stock. Several years later, the stock turned out to be worthless, and Beam sued Beatty to enforce payment of the guarantee. Beatty's defence was that the guarantee was so onerous and so clearly to his detriment that it was void. The trial judge held that the contract was voidable only, and had been ratified by Beatty after he reached the age of majority. Beatty appealed this decision, and the Ontario Court of Appeal agreed with Beatty that the guarantee imposed on him a penalty that was clearly to his detriment and was absolutely void from the beginning; therefore, it could not be ratified. Accordingly, the decision of the trial court was reversed.

(a) Was "his personal bond" a contract?
(b) What does "ratified" mean?
(c) On what grounds did the trial court consider that Beatty had ratified the contract?
(d) Why did the appeal court rule the contract void from the beginning?

C—22

The plaintiff, Butterfield, who was a minor, was struck and injured by a car driven by Sibbit and owned by the Nipissing Electric Company. About a month later, and before Butterfield reached his majority, he accepted a certain sum of money in payment of his claim, and signed a release (a statement releasing the defendant from any further liability). Subsequently, it appeared that the sum was not adequate, and Butterfield sued for damages. The defendants argued that Butterfield had released his claims when he accepted the money and signed the release. Butterfield's answer was that he was a minor when he signed the release. An Ontario court held that the settlement was to the infant's detriment and, therefore, void; consequently, Butterfield was not barred from suing for damages. However, the amount of money that he originally received was deducted from the total judgment subsequently awarded.

(a) Why should one be cautious in signing releases?
(b) Why in this case was the release held to be void?
(c) If an adult signs a release in consideration of an adequate settlement, would a court rule the release void?
(d) What is similar about cases C-21 and C-22?

VOIDABLE CONTRACTS

The majority of contracts entered into by infants fall into the *voidable* class. These are contracts which one of the parties has the option of treating as either binding or not binding; that is, he may either accept the contract or avoid it. A minor's voidable contracts in turn must be divided into two classes:

- Contracts which are binding on the infant unless he takes some step to repudiate the contract during his infancy or within a reasonable time after reaching his majority.

- Contracts which are not binding on the infant unless ratified after he reaches his majority.

Contracts Which are Binding Unless Repudiated. This class of contract includes those involving the acquisition of an interest in property of a permanent nature with continuing obligations attached to it; for example, leases or purchases of shares in a company.

C—23

The heirs to an estate sold a piece of land to Hilliard. The deed by which Hilliard obtained the land was signed by several persons, one of whom, Dillon, was still a minor when this event occurred. Years later, at the age of 35, Dillon repudiated her part in giving the deed, claiming that she was a minor at the time of signing, and was not bound by her signature. The Ontario High Court held that while she could have repudiated her signature on the deed while she was a minor or within a reasonable time after she reached her majority, a "reasonable" time had long expired in the intervening years. As a result, the signature could not now be repudiated, and the contract was binding.

(a) How was Dillon trying to take advantage of the law?
(b) What did she hope to achieve by doing so?
(c) What do you think might have been a reasonable time within which to repudiate the agreement?

Contracts Which Are Not Binding Unless Ratified. This class of contract includes all of the voidable contracts other than those that deal with permanent property and the obligations attached to it (see above). This is a very large class for it includes the common types of contract made by infants, such as the purchase of clothing and other personal items, bicycles, and automobiles. The distinguishing feature of this class of contract is that the contract is still not binding upon the person (who made it during infancy) after reaching the age of majority unless he *ratifies* it—that is, does something to confirm it.

In Ontario, New Brunswick, Nova Scotia, Prince Edward Island and Newfoundland even the ratification is not binding unless it is in writing. In British Columbia a ratification, either oral or written, is of no effect.

C—24

Montgomery, an infant, subscribed to a correspondence course offered by an accounting society, promising to pay a tuition fee of $165. A few months later, but before Montgomery reached his majority, the society obtained a series of post-dated cheques from him. Some of the cheques were cashed after Montgomery attained his majority, but there was still a balance owing on the fee, which Montgomery now refused to pay. An Ontario court dismissed the society's claim for the balance because the contract had been made while Montgomery was a minor, and was not valid until ratified. The court further held that the cashing of the post-dated cheques by the society after Montgomery reached majority did not constitute ratification by Montgomery. However, if the post-dated cheques had been given by Montgomery after he had reached majority, this would have constituted ratification.

(a) What are post-dated cheques?
(b) Why did the court not order the refund of the money Montgomery had paid?
(c) Why was Montgomery permitted to repudiate payment of the balance owing?
(d) If Montgomery had given cheques after he had reached his majority, what decision would the court have made?

The Effect of Avoidance. The fact that a minor or infant elects to repudiate or avoid his contracts in either of the classes of voidable contracts discussed above means that he is not obliged to perform the contract to any further extent, but it does *not* imply that he is able to recover money already paid or property transferred. The avoidance of repudiation does not necessarily have a retroactive effect. However, in cases where the infant has received no benefit whatever under the contract, he is able to recover the money that he advanced or the property he transferred. On the other hand, in cases where he has received some benefit, whatever the infant has already paid will not be refunded.

C—25

In an English case the plaintiff, Tulip Steinberg, an infant, applied for and was allotted 500 shares in the defendant company, Scala (Leeds) Ltd. The price was £1 each. Two shillings per share was payable immediately; the balance was to be paid by instalments from time to time. After Miss Steinberg had paid £250, she chose to avoid the contract. She sued, asking not only to be relieved from the burden of paying the additional £250, but also for a refund of the £250 already paid. The English court of Appeal agreed that she was entitled to avoid the contract and was not obliged to pay the balance. The Court, however, added that since she had received some benefit she was not entitled to a recovery of the money already paid. She had received shares and could have sold them; therefore, some benefit had accrued to her under the contract. In electing to avoid the contract she was obliged to give back the shares, and although she was freed from the obligation to pay the balance of £250, she lost the £250 already paid.

(a) Why was Tulip entitled to repudiate the paying of the balance of the contract?
(b) What was the court's reasoning in ruling that Tulip had received some benefit from the contract?
(c) Why was she not permitted to recover the money already paid?

OBLIGATION TO PAY FOR NECESSARIES

C—26

Richard, 17 years of age, lives away from home and is supporting himself but is temporarily out of work and out of money. His dentist, boarding house keeper, and the store where he buys clothes are reluctant to supply Richard's needs on credit because as a minor he cannot be held liable on his contracts.

(a) Does the law of contracts work for Richard's protection in this case?
(b) For the benefit of a minor like Richard, should there be some exceptions to his right to repudiate contracts?

Apart from the law of contracts, an infant may be responsible to pay *some* amount for goods and services *supplied to him*, if the goods and services are "necessaries." Necessaries include board, lodging, medical attention, clothing, and education. But to be considered a necessary, each of these must be (1) suitable to the infant's circumstances or "station in life", and (2) needed at the time of the purchase. Items that might be a luxury to a person of one station in life could be considered a necessary in the case of a person of a different social standing.

C—27

Nash sold to Inman eleven rather flashy sports coats. Inman, a minor, was a freshman attending Trinity College in England. His father, an English architect, testified that the boy was already well equipped with clothes. The English court, in making its decision, stated that "an infant, like a lunatic, is incapable of making a contract of purchase in the strict sense of the word, but if a man supplies the needs of an infant or a lunatic by supplying to him necessaries, the law will imply an obligation to repay him for services so rendered, and will enforce the obligation against the estate of the lunatic or infant." However, since Inman in this case was already well equipped with clothes, the eleven sports jackets were *not considered necessaries*, and Nash's claim was dismissed.

(a) Because a person "wants" something does not necessarily mean he "needs" it. How does the court determine what things are necessaries and what things are not?
(b) A minor may agree to buy something which we would all agree is a necessary. In what circumstances could a minor repudiate such an agreement?
(c) Could the seller take advantage of the fact that a minor must pay for necessaries supplied by charging him more than the usual price?
(d) Why would the courts consider infants to be similar to lunatics in the area of making contracts.

The claim for payment for the supplying of necessaries is, in strict terms, not a claim in contract. Therefore the amount to be awarded to the person who supplies the necessaries is not necessarily the amount agreed upon. The court will look at the value of the services or merchandise supplied, and award a *fair* amount so that the plaintiff will receive adequate compensation. If the necessaries have not been actually supplied to the infant, but there has been only an agreement to supply, the court does not hold the infant to the agreement. The obligation to pay for necessaries is confined to those things that have already been supplied.

FRAUDULENT MISREPRESENTATION OF AGE

C—28

Broad, a minor, was the father of an illegimate child. In place of other legal proceedings that could have been taken, an agreement was prepared and signed by Broad whereby he agreed to support the child. In signing the agreement he represented that he had reached his majority. Later, he refused to pay, and was sued on the agreement. He then revealed that he was a minor. An Ontario Court held that the fact that Broad had lied about his age made no difference; as an infant he was incapable of binding himself in contract, and was free to avoid it on the grounds of infancy.

(a) How did Broad take advantage of the law?
(b) Does this case mean that a minor can lie about his age, saying that he is "of age," so that a merchant will enter a contract with him, and then later repudiate the contract?

The position of a person claiming against an infant is not improved by the fact that the infant lied about his age. The theory of the law is that an infant is not capable of binding himself in contract. His capacity cannot be altered by a misrepresentation about his age.

PARENTS' LIABILITY FOR DEBTS OF MINORS

C—29

Casey Jr., 16 years of age, and living at home, buys a small radio for $50. Junior pays $10 down and contracts to pay the balance in monthly payments of $10 each. Junior expects to earn this money from his paper route, but unfortunately, the employees of the paper go on strike. For Junior this means no income and, consequently, no payment.

(a) Is there any legal obligation on the part of Casey Senior to pay his son's debt?
(b) If the father pays, what is the possibility concerning future debts incurred by Junior?

The Criminal Code, as well as provincial statutes, obliges fathers to support their children up to the age of sixteen years. In the event that this duty is not discharged, the Code provides a penalty; however, this does not mean that the parent is liable for debts incurred by his child. A parent is no more liable for goods supplied to his child than anyone else is.

In some circumstances, however, the child may pledge his parent's credit by acting in the capacity of an agent of his parent. The agency relationship may arise in two ways: *expressly*, for example a parent may indicate to a storekeeper that his child has his permission to purchase items on credit (in which case, of course, the parent is responsible); and *by implication*, for example a child may from time to time make purchases from a merchant on his parent's account, followed by regular payments of those accounts by the parent. This course of conduct on the part of the parent suggests to the merchant that the child has his parent's authority to pledge his credit, and, consequently, the parent becomes liable.

THE TRADESMAN'S LEGAL POSITION WHEN DEALING WITH A MINOR

C—30

What would be the legal position

(a) if the boy had not completed paying for the rod?
(b) if the rod had been fully paid for?

The position of the merchant in dealing with an infant is a difficult one, and he does so at his own risk. In most of the cases where the infant repudiates his agreement the merchant is unable to recover the price of the goods. His only recourse is to get back the goods the infant has obtained from him, *in whatever condition they may be, or what is left of them.* On the other hand, since it is only the infant who has the privilege of avoiding his contract, an adult is bound on a contract with a minor just as much as he would be with another adult.

INSANE PERSONS AND INTOXICATED PERSONS

C—31

(i) In a British Columbia case, the defendant, Falk, had given Hardman an option to buy a farm, but when Hardman offered Falk the purchase price it was declined. Hardman then sued to obtain the farm upon payment of the $50,000 purchase price. The defence for Falk was insanity. Falk, was, in fact, insane at the time he agreed to the option but neither Hardman nor the lawyer who handled most of the dealings knew that. Because of Hardman's lack of knowledge of Falk's insanity, the British Columbia Court of Appeal held that the contract was binding upon Falk, and ordered the transaction completed.

(ii) In this case, which took place in Ontario, the plantiffs, Chait & Leon, agreed to buy Harding's tailoring business for $1,000. Later, Harding refused to go through with the transaction, claiming that he was drunk at the time he made the agreement. The Ontario Supreme Court found that at the time the transaction was made, Harding was in a helpless condition and, further, that this condition was known to one of the plaintiffs. As a result, Harding was allowed to avoid his transaction and the lawsuit was dismissed.

Compare the decisions in these cases. Why was one contract enforced and the other set aside?

The contracts of those who are insane or intoxicated are voidable if it is established that:

1. The condition of intoxication or insanity made the person incapable of understanding what he was doing, and
2. The other contracting party knew of the condition.

Apart from contract, persons who are intoxicated or insane are obligated to pay for necessaries supplied to them. The principles that apply are the same as those governing the supply of necessaries to infants.

If an intoxicated or insane person elects to avoid a contract, he must repudiate it within a reasonable time after recovering from his incapacity and ascertaining what he has done. The contract may not be repudiated if after recovering from his incapacity the insane or intoxicated person accepts benefits from the contract.

C—32

This case was finally settled in the Supreme Court of Canada. In September Ross agreed to sell a large quantity of wheat to Bawlf Grain Co. Ltd. At the time the sale was made Ross was incapable due to intoxication, and this fact was known to the company's agent. However, throughout October Ross knew of the contract but did nothing to repudiate it. Subsequently the price of wheat went up, and in early November Ross refused to go through with the contract. The Supreme Court of Canada held the contract binding on the grounds that Ross had delayed an unreasonable time in the exercise of his right to repudiate the agreement, and that the company had suffered by the delay.

(a) Why do you think Ross repudiated his contract?
(b) What do you think would be a reasonable time in which to repudiate the agreement?

OTHER PARTIES HAVING LIMITED POWERS

In addition to minors, insane persons and intoxicated persons there are two other classes whose legal capacity to make contracts is restricted: (1) corporations; (2) enemy aliens.

CORPORATIONS

A corporation is an artificial person created by law with the power to make contracts in its own name in the same way as a natural person. There are many types of corporation, ranging from municipal corporations (towns, cities, etc.) to commercial and industrial corporations both large and small. There are also Crown corporations created by governments to handle special matters; for example, the Canadian Broadcasting Corporation. Many organizations, including universities and charitable institutions, find the corporate form a convenient method of owning property and handling their affairs.

The ability of a corporation to make a contract is sometimes limited by the statute under which it was incorporated. In some cases the statute may be one of general application under which many companies are incorporated; in others it may be a special statute which deals only with the incorporation of a specific company. Banks and railway companies, for instance, are incorporated under special statutes.

ENEMY ALIENS

Aliens (those who are not Canadian citizens) enjoy the same capacity to make contracts in Canada as do Canadian citizens. In time of war, however, contracts with *enemy* aliens are declared illegal and void. Contracts with enemy aliens already existing at the time war is declared are suspended during hostilities, but may be reinstated after peace has been restored.

MARRIED WOMEN'S CONTRACTS

Under English common law the rights of a married woman were narrowly restricted and she could not make a valid contract in her own name. Today, however, in all the common law provinces of Canada the common law has been greatly modified by statute, so that a married woman has the same legal capacity to make contracts as an unmarried woman or a man. She may hold separate property, real and personal, in her own name; make contracts; sue and be sued on contracts made in her own name. Her property is free from the control of her husband and may not be seized for his debts. She may dispose of her property by sale without her husband's signature or consent, and she may also dispose of it by will.

In Quebec, *except where the parties make a marriage settlement providing for separate property rights*, the personal properties of husband and wife become common property upon marriage. While the property is jointly owned, the husband has power to administer the whole. The wife cannot bind herself by contract without his consent. At the husband's death the wife acquires half the common property, the other half being disposed of as the deceased husband's estate.

APPLYING THE LAW

1. A, 17 years of age and employed full time, purchases a motorcycle from B. At the time, A falsely represents himself to be of legal age. A makes a down payment and contracts to pay the balance in three months. A week later A brings back the machine in a badly battered condition saying he has changed his mind about buying it. When B objects, A reveals his true age and claims his minority status gives him the right to repudiate the contract. He also demands the return of his down payment. Assuming the motorcycle is not a necessary, how does the law apply to A's liability? (Consider the misrepresentation of age, the fact that A is fully employed, and the badly battered condition of the motorcycle).
2. G, a college student and a minor, rents a room for a full semester at $60 a month. Two months later he has an opportunity to move to less expensive lodgings and, his rent being paid up to date, he leaves without giving notice. The landlord thinks he can hold G liable for damages for breaking the rental contract. How does the law apply?
3. A man goes into a camera shop and selects and pays for an expensive camera. He is noticeably under the influence of liquor at the time. Three days later he brings the camera back and asks for the return of his money, claiming that he was so drunk at the time he bought the camera he didn't know what he was doing. The seller claims that although the man's actions showed that he had been drinking, he certainly knew what he was doing. How does the law apply?

DISCUSSION AND PROJECTS

1. Should parents be liable for all or any debts incurred by their children? Arrange for your class or group to survey some merchants in your neighbourhood and report on how they handle transactions with minors.
2. Compare the law's treatment of the contracts of minors and those of mental incompetents. Which are treated more favourably? Should this be so?

Part 12
GENUINENESS OF CONSENT

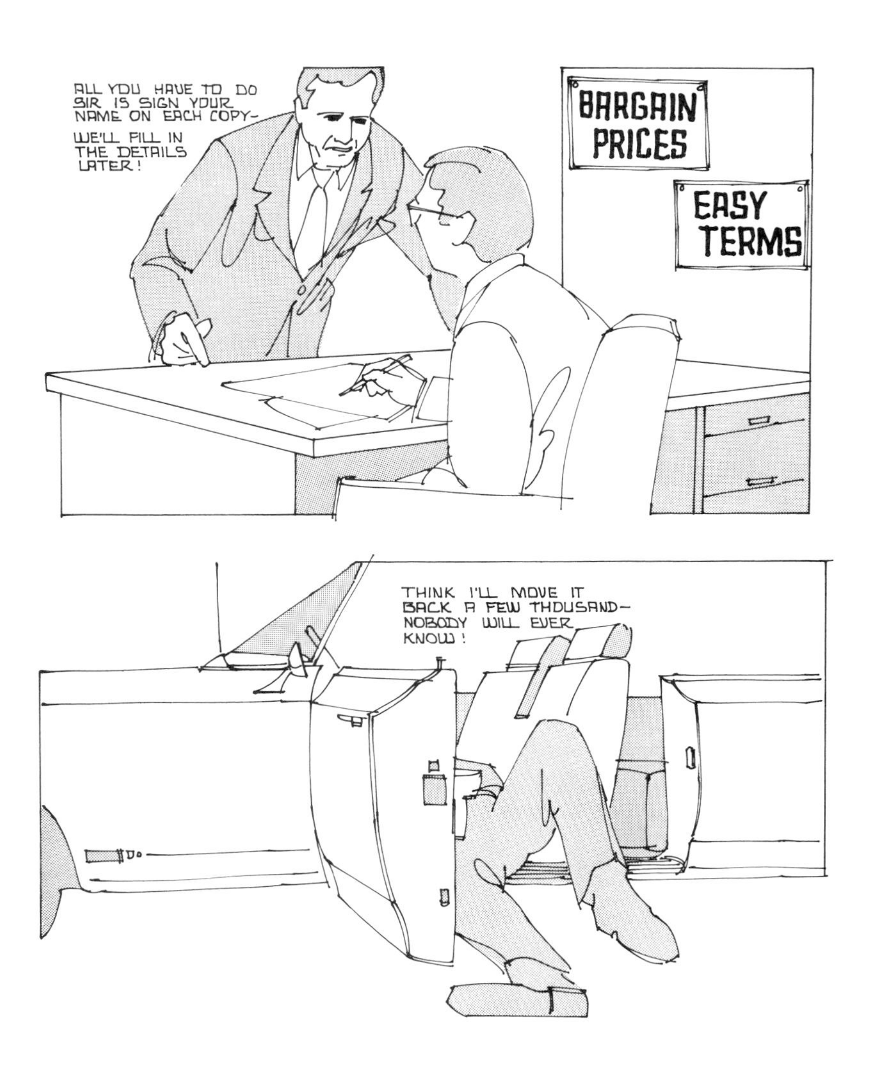

The consent of the contracting parties is not genuine if it has been obtained through misrepresentation, either innocent or fraudulent, or by means of undue influence or duress. In some circumstances there is no real consent if both parties are genuinely mistaken about some fundamental condition of the contract when making it. In each of these circumstances the law recognizes that the injured party is entitled to some redress. However, an individual who has made a bad bargain because of his own mistaken judgment or because of his own ignorance or carelessness cannot, at common law, expect any redress.

MISREPRESENTATION

Misrepresentation is a false statement of a *material* fact. A material fact is one that induces (or brings about) the contract. If a person makes a false statement of a material fact without intention to deceive and in the honest belief that it is true, the misrepresentation is said to be *innocent*; if it is made with intention to deceive and either deliberately or with reckless disregard of the truth, it is considered *fraud*.

REMEDIES FOR INNOCENT MISREPRESENTATION

C—33

Dorsch, a Saskatchewan farmer, signed a contract that he thought was an assignment of part of his royalty rights from an oil company. In fact he was assigning all his own rights and would receive no royalties at all himself. The contract was in such complicated terms that Dorsch did not pretend to read it, but depended upon the explanation given by the company's agent who himself had such difficulty interpreting it that, in fact, he misrepresented its terms. When Dorsch later learned the true import of the contract he took action to have it set aside on the grounds of misrepresentation. The court found that there was misrepresentation, although unintentional, and ruled that the contract should be rescinded.

(a) What would be royalty rights?
(b) What was misrepresented in this case?
(c) In what way was Dorsch's consent not genuine?
(d) Why was the farmer entitled only to rescind the contract and not to collect damages as well for any loss he suffered?

The general remedy for innocent misrepresentation is *rescission* of the contract; that is to have it rescinded or set aside. If possible, the parties will be put back in the same position as they were before the contract was made. There should be no undue delay in taking action for rescission, or the right may be lost.

C—34

Cobb purchased an English car from McKinley Motors Ltd. which they represented as a 1963 model car. As part of the deal, Cobb traded in another car. Although Cobb had stipulated that he wanted a 1963 model, and thought that was what he was getting, he later learned, after having driven the car 9,000 miles, that the

car had been imported in 1961. Cobb sued for rescission of the contract, or in the alternative, for damages.
At the trial, evidence was given that the model of the car in question had not been changed for some years, and it was the practice of dealers, sanctioned by the manufacturer, to refer to it as the "current year's" model. The court held that the dealer was not guilty of wilful intention to deceive but that he was guilty of innocent misrepresentation. However, since the car traded in had already been resold, and the new car had been driven 9,000 miles, it was impossible to put the parties back to their original positions as at the time the contract was made. Rescission was not granted, but damages were awarded for breach of contract, the breach being that the dealer had guaranteed that the car was a 1963 model, which it was not.

(a) Why did this situation lack genuineness of consent?
(b) Why would the model year be a material fact?
(c) What would have had to be done to put the parties back to their original position?
(d) Were the damages awarded to punish the party guilty of misrepresentation or to compensate Cobb for the actual loss sustained?

Sometimes it is impossible to grant rescission of the contract; for example, if the contract is one for the sale of goods and the goods have been resold to an innocent third party, such third party does not have to give back the goods. When rescission is impossible, but the misrepresentation has become a term of the contract, the injured party may have the right to sue for damages for breach of a term of the contract.

REMEDIES FOR FRAUD

C — 35

F & B Transport bought from White Truck Sales a used truck which the latter had fraudulently represented as a 1958 model when in fact it was a 1956 model. After using the truck for nine months and spending considerable amounts for repairs, F & B Transport discovered the true age of the truck and took action to have the contract rescinded. On the evidence presented, a Manitoba court found White guilty of fraud, and ruled that F & B was entitled to rescission of the contract and also to damages. Therefore F & B had to return the truck, and White had to refund the price paid plus finance charges and amounts spent on repairs, less an allowance for the use of the truck.

(a) What fraud was present in this case?
(b) Why was the buyer of the truck entitled to damages as well as rescission of the contract?
(c) What is different between the facts of this case and those of C — 34 (Cobb v. McKinlay Motors) which would cause a different judgment?

As already explained, the difference between fraud and innocent misrepresentation is that fraudulent misrepresentation is intentional; thus fraud contains the element of tort. Consequently there is a difference in the remedy allowed. In the case of fraud the injured party is entitled to enter a claim for rescission of the contract, or damages, or both. As in the case of innocent misrepresentation, if a defrauded party wishes to avail himself of his legal remedies he must do so without undue delay.

UNDUE INFLUENCE

C—36

In the course of administering a deceased person's estate, an executor, Morley, brought legal action against Loughnan, in whose house the deceased had lived for a number of years. The action was to recover money paid to Loughnan by the deceased during the period he had lived in that house. Judgment was given in favour of Morley based on the fact revealed by the evidence that Loughnan had taken possession, so to speak, of the whole life of the deceased, and the gifts were not the result of the deceased's own free will, but the effect of that influence and domination.

(a) How can one person take "possession" of another person's life? How could this affect contracts?
(b) What difficulties would there be in proving that undue influence had been exercised in this case?
(c) What other situations can you think of where you could assume that one of the parties might be in a position of strong influence over the other?

Undue influence is the improper use of any power exercised over the mind of a contracting party so that consent is not voluntary. Such a contract is voidable at the option of the injured party, but legal action must be taken without undue delay, for undue delay may imply affirmation of the contract.

In most cases, the person who takes action to avoid a contract on the grounds of undue influence must prove his charge or he cannot succeed. In certain situations, however, special relationships exist under which it is reasonable to believe that one person was dominated by another; for example, if a contract is made by a child with a parent, a ward with his guardian, a patient with his doctor, a client with his solicitor, or any person with his spiritual advisor. If such child, ward, patient, client or other person brings an action at law to avoid the contract on the grounds of undue influence, the court *presumes* that such relationships call for proof by the party so charged that he did not take undue advantage of his position. Unless such proof is forthcoming, the contract may be set aside. For instance, a young woman living with her stepmother made an agreement to share her property with her stepsisters. Later, she sought to have the contract set aside, charging undue influence on the part of her stepmother. When the charge could not be disproved the court set aside the contract.

The same rule applies to contracts where one of the parties is uneducated and inexperienced, and the other party is a person of knowledge and experience, or where one party is in urgent need and is thereby induced to sacrifice future advantages.

Generally, the presumption of undue influence does not apply to the relationship of husband and wife. Where a wife enters into a contract for her husband's benefit, such as guaranteeing his debts, and later seeks to avoid the contract on the grounds that she entered into it through either fear of, or affection for him, the contract may be set aside *only* if she can prove that she acted under undue influence. However, if she acted upon legal advice that was not independent, (for instance, if her legal advisor also acted for her husband and the creditor in the same transaction), that would be strong evidence to support a claim of undue influence.

C—37

Mrs. Harper was co-signer with Mr. Harper on promissory notes given as security for her husband's debts to McMurchy. On default, the creditor sued both husband and wife. The wife in her defence contended that she had had no independent legal advice on the transaction, and that she had been subject to undue influence by her husband, and to great pressures on the part of McMurchy. After considering the evidence a Manitoba court held that the wife had failed to establish either undue influence or duress, and had not satisfied the onus on her to prove either. The fact that she did not have independent legal advice was not of itself proof of undue influence.

(a) What is meant by not having independent legal advice? How could such advice have helped the wife?
(b) If a wife charges undue influence on the part of her husband, does she have to prove the charge, or will the charge hold unless her husband can disprove it?

C—38

A wife who was a confirmed invalid had guaranteed her husband's debts to a bank. Later, in settling her estate, the guarantees were repudiated on the grounds of undue influence. The final decision was that she had acted under undue influence and that her contracts made under that influence could be set aside. Undue influence was established from the evidence that she had "acted in passive obedience to her husband's directions," and also from the fact that the solicitor who had advised her was also the solicitor for the bank and for her husband.

(a) In what way was the wife in this case at a disadvantage when entering the contract to guarantee her husband's debts?
(b) Why was the decision in this case different from that in C—37?

DURESS

Duress is some unlawful pressure imposed upon a person which compels him to enter into an agreement—if it can be so called—against his will. It may consist of actual or threatened violence or imprisonment directed against a party to the contract or against his wife, parent or child. It must be inflicted or threatened by the other party to the contract or by an agent acting for him and with his knowledge. However, whether or not the threat or constraint amounts to duress depends upon the circumstances in each particular case.

Duress, when proved, renders the contract voidable at the option of the injured party. If action is taken, it must be done as soon as the party is freed from the duress.

MISTAKE

C — 39

A farmer had contracted for the purchase of a piece of land, an essential condition being that the land include a tobacco-growing quota of 14 acres which the seller had previously been allotted by the Tobacco Marketing Board. Both the seller and the buyer thought that it was a quota of 14 acres which was being transferred, but a subsequent survey showed that both were mistaken and that it was only 10.95 acres. The buyer then refused to pay the full price and the seller refused to proceed further with the transaction. In a legal action which followed the court held that when both parties had contracted under a false assumption regarding an essential term of the contract the agreement was void.

(a) What was the fact about which both parties were mistaken and what effect did this have on the contract?
(b) Why was this fact considered an essential term of the contract?

When both parties are genuinely mistaken about the existence of the subject matter of a contract the agreement may be declared void. The classic example of this rule is an English case (Couterie v. Hastie, 1852) in which the parties had contracted for the sale of a cargo of corn that was being shipped from Greece to England. Unknown to either party, the corn had already been sold by the ship's master, who had disposed of it after it became overheated in order to avoid a total loss. The purchaser was sued for the price. The court held that the contract was void, on the grounds that at the time the contract was made both parties were mistaken as to the very existence of the subject matter of the agreement. More than a hundred years later, as you saw in C — 39, the same rule was invoked in Ontario.

C — 40

The Commonwealth Disposals Commission had advertised for tenders for the salvaging of a shipwrecked tanker located on a reef known as Jourmand Reef. The tender of McRae, a salvage firm, was accepted by Commonwealth, and McRae at considerable expense prepared for the salvaging of the ship. The salvage firm then found that there was no such tanker and no reef known as Jourmand Reef in the area indicated by Commonwealth. The salvage firm then sued for damages to recover the expense of fitting out the expedition. In defence the Commission claimed mutual mistake as to the existence of the subject matter of the contract. The court of appeal found that the defendants had been reckless and irresponsible in advertising for tenders for the salvage of the tanker, and should have known that any tenderer would be assuming that the Commission would be at least warranting its existence. The court therefore held that the contract was not void for mistake, and allowed McRae damages.

(a) In what respect is this case similar to case C — 39?
(b) In what does it differ?

A claim to avoid a contract on the grounds of mutual or common mistake may not be allowed if the mistake is one which, in the circumstances, has some irresponsibility attached to it.

CAVEAT EMPTOR

C — 41

(a) Would the seller's non-disclosure of facts, as shown in the drawing, make the contract invalid?
(b) Suppose that the buyer were indeed aware of the new highway project but knew too that a hotel chain was also interested in the property (something the seller did not know). Would that make the buyer guilty of misrepresentation or fraud?

As has already been pointed out, an individual may not avoid his contract simply because he has made a poor bargain as a result of his own error or bad judgment. This is the old rule of *caveat emptor* (let the buyer beware). The rule implies that the seller is not obligated to disclose defects which the buyer could discover for himself. It is the buyer's responsibility to examine the subject matter and interpret the terms of the contract, and to make his own decision.

At the same time, if by keeping silent the seller's shrewdness amounts to deceit, the buyer may obtain redress. For example, in a transaction for the purchase of a horse the buyer thought the seller was selling him a sound animal—and the seller knew what the buyer was thinking. Shortly after the purchase, the buyer discovered that the horse was blind. He also learned that it had been subject to periodic spells of blindness and that this defect was known to the seller, who had sold the horse at a time when the animal appeared to have normal sight. The purchaser then sued to have the contract set aside. The seller's defence was the rule of caveat emptor. An expert's opinion, given at the trial, was that the defect could not have been detected at the time of the sale even by a qualified veterinarian. The court held that the seller was guilty of deceit and allowed rescission of the contract.

A contract will not be enforceable if it enables one person to profit knowingly from another's clerical mistake embodied in the contract. For instance, if by mistake a bookkeeper credited your account with a payment of $100 instead of the $10 you had paid, or sent you a bill for a lesser amount than you really owed, you could not take advantage of what you knew to be a clerical mistake.

Today the strict application of the *caveat emptor* rule has been modified by "consumer protection" legislation (see also Part 21) enacted in all the common law provinces. This legislation provides that a householder who has signed a contract with a house-to-house salesman may, within a specified period, have the contract set aside. The "cooling off" period varies from two days in Ontario to ten days in Newfoundland. Thus, the law provides a "loophole" for the householder who has made a contract with an itinerant salesman and later regrets having bound himself on such an agreement.

APPLYING THE LAW

1. A needs to borrow money for business purposes. A's bank agrees to lend him the money if A can get someone to guarantee the loan. A's wife, who has inherited property and money, agrees to guarantee her husband's loan. Before concluding the transaction, the bank gives A's wife a copy of the contract of guarantee and instructs her to take it to her own lawyer (not her husband's lawyer) and sign it only after discussing it with her lawyer. She is then to return the document to the bank. Explain the purpose of this formality.
2. Suppose that A has an old painting in his possession which he believes is a genuine Krieghoff canvas, and that he offers it to B as such for $2,000. B accepts A's opinion and buys the painting at that price. What are the rights and liabilities of A and B if
   (a) the painting is found not to be a genuine Krieghoff?
   (b) the painting is genuine and found to be worth a great deal more than the $2,000 B paid for it?
3. Suppose that in the above case A knew that the picture was not a genuine Krieghoff, but deliberately and fraudulently misrepresented it as such to B, and that B bought it because of that misrepresentation. How would you decide the case?

DISCUSSION AND PROJECTS

1. Discuss the legal effect of shrewdness as distinct from deceit in business transactions. Provide some examples. Where does one draw the line between the two?
2. Consumer protection legislation appears to have shifted the emphasis from "caveat emptor" to "caveat vendor." Investigate your province's consumer legislation and determine if this is so. As part of this project invite a government representative working in Consumer Affairs, or someone from your local Better Business Bureau, to speak with your class.

Part 13
ILLEGAL CONTRACTS

A contract is illegal if its object is contrary to established law or against public policy. (By "public policy" is meant a policy in the best interests of the public).

Obviously a contract to commit a crime or to perform a tortious act is illegal and void. Other classes of illegal contracts are not so obvious. Some of these are considered below.

C — 42

(i) Mennell has a bet with Pringle that the Toronto Maple Leafs will win the Stanley Cup. Mennell loses the bet but refuses to pay.

(ii) A car dealer announces that he intends to open for regular business on Sundays as well as on weekdays. On the first Sunday of business four people agree to purchase cars.

(iii) A department store advises its charge customers that 3% will be charged each month as interest and carrying charges on all overdue balances. This is equivalent to 36% per annum.

(iv) Tony buys out Dean's barber shop business in Vancouver. One of the terms of their written agreement is that Dean shall not open a barber shop ever again in that city. Dean later feels that the condition was unreasonable.

(v) Marie, an only child, is left a large inheritance by her uncle on the condition that she forfeit the inheritance if she ever marries.

(vi) X promises to pay Y $10,000 if he will destroy certain evidence required in a criminal case against X.

In which of these situations would a court not enforce the related contract because it was illegal?

BETS AND WAGERS

C—43

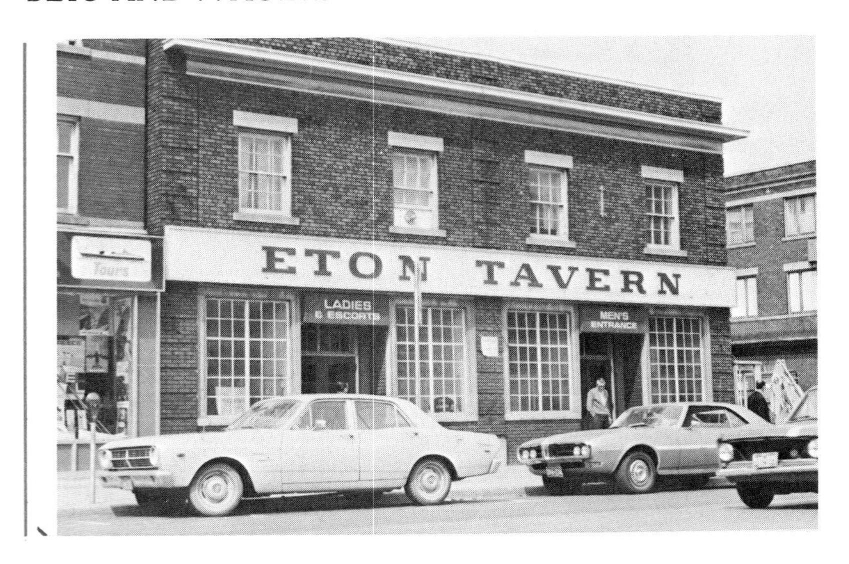

Would a contract be legal if made while inside the tavern?

Operating a common betting house is illegal according to the Criminal Code. Consequently, a person placing a bet with such an operator could not use the court to collect his winnings. An exception is the pari-mutuel system of betting allowed at horse races while the races are in actual progress.

On the other hand, the making of bets or wagers between individuals is not forbidden by statute but, generally, the law will not aid in enforcing the paying of a bet. However, the Ontario Gaming Act provides that if more than $40 is paid on a game or pastime (but not on any other kind of wager), the loser may recover his money by court action. The court will also aid in recovering money from a stakeholder before it is paid out to the winner and thus prevent what the law considers an immoral act. We may note in passing that the Criminal Code provides that "Everyone who, with intent to defraud any person, cheats while playing a game or in holding the stakes for a game or in betting is guilty of an indictable offence and is liable to imprisonment for two years."

CONTRACTS MADE ON SUNDAY

The Lord's Day Act, a federal statute, makes it unlawful for any person to carry on or transact any business of his ordinary calling on Sunday, except works of necessity or of mercy. It is this exception that makes it legal for such businesses as drug stores, restaurants, and transportation agencies to operate on Sunday. It follows, therefore, that any contract made with regard to any act that is unlawful under the Lord's Day Act is also illegal and void.

The Act gives the provinces the right to modify its provisions. A province may also delegate this power to its municipalities. As a result, the manner in which the Lord's Day Act is observed may vary from province to province and also among the municipalities within a province.

ILLEGAL RATES OF INTEREST

C — 44

If the loan is accepted, can this rate of interest be collected at law?

The maximum rates of interest which may be charged by banks and money-lending companies, including the well known "finance" companies, is regulated by statute law. These rates are subject to change but at the time of writing the maximum rate a finance company can charge is 2% per month on loans up to $300. On loans over that amount the rate is less.

Consumer protection legislation also covers the area of money lending. The law is particularly concerned with the cost of borrowing when the loan is to be repaid in instalments of principal and interest lumped together as one sum. It now requires that the loan agreement disclose to the borrower the *full* cost of the borrowing, both as an annual percentage rate and as a total amount, in dollars and cents. Similarly, when goods are purchased on a time-payment plan the law requires that the cost of credit (the carrying charges) be fully disclosed both as a total in dollars and cents and also as an annual percentage rate.

C—45

(i) In order to obtain a much needed loan, Morehouse gave a five-year mortgage on his property for $4,050 with interest at 7% per annum. The principal sum included a bonus of $1,550 to the lender and $130 in fees, so that the borrower received only $2,370 and yet had to pay back $4,050 with interest as well. Subsequently Morehouse (the borrower) sought relief under the provisions of the Ontario Unconscionable Transactions Relief Act. The court, after considering the cost of the loan in relation to the risk involved, the urgent need of the borrower, and whether or not there had been fair dealing so that the borrower fully understood the terms of the agreement, found the cost of the loan was unconscionable and excessive in the circumstances, and granted relief in the amount of $800.

(ii) Lavoie, who had borrowed money on a mortgage repayable in three months with interest equivalent to about 30% per annum, defaulted on his contract and was sued. He then sought relief on the grounds that the transaction was unconscionable. The court refused his plea because (a) he had been under no pressure to seek the loan, not being in any financial distress, (b) Miller (the lender) had assumed more than an ordinary risk, and (c) the court had no power to relieve him from the consequences of his own folly in securing such a loan when apparently there was no need for it.

(a) What is an "unconscionable" rate of interest?
(b) Why did the courts deny relief to Lavoie in the second case but allow some relief for Morehouse in the first case?

In the case of one individual borrowing from another there is no statutory rate of interest, but the court will not enforce the paying of an *unconscionable* rate. The question of what is an unconscionable rate is determined by the circumstances in each particular case. It has been held that a fair test is the question "Could the loan have been secured for less?" All the provinces have enacted legislation which provides that where the court finds the cost of the loan excessive, harsh and unconscionable, it may set aside or revise the contract or order refund of any excess paid by the debtor.

CONTRACTS IN RESTRAINT OF TRADE

C—46

Harasimo sold her beauty parlour business to Cope under an agreement whereby Harasimo promised not to engage in the same business within a radius of 25 miles of the premises sold. The agreement also provided that in the event of a breach of this promise, Harasimo would pay Cope $2,500 as damages. Four years later Harasimo opened a beauty parlour not far from Cope's place of business. As a result, the number of Cope's customers decreased to the point where the business had to be closed. Cope sued for the damages provided by the contract. Harasimo's defence was that the contract imposed an unreasonable restraint of trade. A British Columbia court held that the restrictive agreement was not unreasonable considering the nature of the hairdressing business, and allowed the claim for damages.

(a) What did Harasimo mean by "the contract imposed an unreasonable restraint of trade"?
(b) Why did Cope have to close shop?
(c) Why in particular was the "nature of the hairdressing business" considered by the court in this case?

C—47

An agreement between Giannone, the buyer of a hotel business in the city of Calgary, and the company that sold it to him contained a promise by each of the shareholders of that company not to engage in the hotel business within 15 miles of Calgary. Subsequently, some of the shareholders bought a piece of land about one and a half miles away, intending to replace an old hotel on the site with a new one. Giannone took legal action for breach of contract, but the court held that the restriction set out in the contract was unreasonable and not necessary for the protection of the buyer's business; therefore, the restriction could not be enforced.

What was the reasoning behind the court's decision that the restriction was unreasonable?

The general rule for this class of contract is that the restraint of trade imposed by contract must not be greater than is reasonably necessary for the protection of both parties, and in no case against *public policy*. By public policy we mean a policy in the best interests of the public.

With respect to contracts between employers and employees which restrict the employee's right to take employment *after* he leaves his employer's service, the courts have generally taken the position that a person's freedom to make a living must be protected.

C—48

Taylor had resigned from the defendant company and was later employed by a competitor of his former employer. Taylor then approached his former employer with regard to making his pension payable at age 65. The trustees of the company's pension plan rejected his request on the grounds that a clause in the plan allowed them, at their discretion, to discontinue pension benefits of employees who took employment with a competitor company. Taylor sued. The court held that the clause in the pension plan was void in that it imposed an unreasonable restraint on the right of their former employee to take employment.

(a) What was the restrictive clause in the pension contract?
(b) Do you think Taylor would have taken a job with another employer if he knew this would cause him to forfeit his pension rights?
(c) Why was the restrictive clause in the pension plan ruled void?

Agreements between dealers in commodities, made with the purpose of maintaining price control or otherwise restraining trade, are not only illegal as being against public policy but are also indictable offences. The Combines Investigation Act, a federal statute, provides penalties of heavy fines and/or imprisonment for any person or corporation who "conspires, combines, agrees or arranges with any other person or with a railway, steamship or transportation company":

1. To limit unduly the facilities for transporting, producing, manufacturing, supplying, or the storing of goods.

2. To prevent or lessen unduly the manufacture of goods.

3. To prevent or lessen unduly competition in the manufacture, production or dealing in goods.

4. To fix a common price or resale price or a common rental or a common cost of storage or transportation or to unduly increase the price, rental or cost.

5. Generally, to restrain trade or injure commerce.

C—49

Howard Smith Paper Mills, manufacturers of paper, were found guilty of a violation of the Combines Investigation Act but appealed the decision of the Ontario trial court on the grounds that the alleged illegal agreement was not detrimental to the public. The appeal was dismissed, the appeal court holding that once it is established that there is an agreement to lessen competition to the extent that the parties to the agreement are not subject to the influence of competition, injury to the public interest is conclusively presumed.

(a) In what ways might manufacturers agree to lessen competition among themselves?
(b) In what way could an agreement to lessen competition be detrimental to the public?
(c) In what way is keen competition between manufacturers beneficial to the public?
(d) Put the appeal court's judgment in your own words.

Any six persons, Canadian citizens, resident in Canada, twenty-one years of age, who are of the opinion that a combine exists, may apply in writing to the Combines Commissioner for an investigation, and it is the duty of the proper authority to deal with all such applications and to investigate the business.

CONTRACTS IN RESTRAINT OF MARRIAGE

C—50

MODEL ASKS RIGHT TO WED

TORONTO – Beautiful Martha Saunders, a honey-haired model whose pretty face and figure have been seen on many a magazine cover, is suing her agent, Harry Beard, for the right to get married without paying a $10,000 penalty.

But Beard insists he won't permit her to get married to Kit Moore, also a model, unless she pays off.

"I spent two and a half years building her up," Beard explained, "and I'm not going to lose that time and money."

Martha's mother, Mrs. Elizabeth Saunders signed a six-year contract containing a marriage-penalty clause with Beard in 1967, and the model ratified it when she became of age.

Her attorney contends such a clause is "against public policy."

Beard insists "she is the tops in my 10 years as an agent for models and I will oppose any action to nullify the clause."

(a) Is the restraint of marriage in this contract reasonable?
(b) Why would the model's attorney claim that the contract is "against public policy"?

Contracts in general restraint of marriage are held to be against public policy and are therefore void; for example, a contract not to marry anyone but a particular person, or an agreement not to marry at all. Any contract in *partial* restraint of marriage would be valid, provided the restraint is not unreasonable. The validity of such contracts depends upon the reasonableness of the restriction; therefore each case must be judged on its own particular merits.

CONTRACTS WHICH INJURE THE STATE OR OBSTRUCT JUSTICE

Under this broad category the law seeks to prevent certain types of agreement. Examples include the following:

- Agreements to trade with the enemy, or to injure the state in its relations with other states.
- Agreements tending to injure the public service. The law will not uphold an agreement whereby a public official agrees to restrict his freedom of action, or an agreement whereby a person agrees to use his influence to procure some benefit from government.
- Agreements which tend to pervert the course of justice; for example, an agreement to stifle a prosecution, or a collusive arrangement to obtain a divorce.

APPLYING THE LAW

1. Several doctors formed a medical partnership under an agreement which prevented retiring partners from practising surgery within ten miles of the place of partnership for ten years. Subsequently, one of the doctors retired but resumed private practice in breach of his contract. The other parties to the partnership sought an injunction to stop this breach of contract. There was evidence that at the time the partnership contract was made the population of the town in which the partners had their practice was not very great and there was a considerable number of surgeons available.
   (a) Do you think the injunction should be granted? On what grounds?
   (b) If the retired doctor's new practice cuts into the earnings of the partnership, might the partners recover money damages?
   (c) What bearing on the case would the number of surgeons available in proportion to the town's population have?
   (d) In connection with the action for breach of contract, should the ratio of doctors to population be considered as at the time the contract was made or when the breach of contract occurred?
2. In the following cases what additional facts might make one suspect that a violation of the Combines Investigation Act was being committed?
   (a) Three paving companies submit tenders on a substantial paving job.
   (b) An increase in the price of gasoline by three big oil companies.
   (c) The freight rates charged by several trucking companies are sharply increased.

DISCUSSION AND PROJECTS

1. What are the regulations in your municipality governing (a) bingo games? (b) lotteries?
2. Find out the maximum rate of interest a finance company may charge on loans over $300.
3. How do combines among business firms come to the attention of the authorities? Find some recent examples of industries being charged under the Combines Investigation Act.

UNIT SEVEN
WORKING WITH AND ENDING LEGAL AGREEMENTS

Part 14

ASSIGNMENT OF CONTRACT

Occasions may arise when a party to a contract may wish to assign (transfer) to another his rights or obligations under it. Generally speaking, a person may readily assign his *rights* under a contract, but he may not assign his obligations without the consent of the other party to his contract.

ASSIGNMENT OF RIGHTS

CASE 1

Johnson contracted with Dayus Roofing Co. to reshingle the roof of his house. The price was to be paid in equal monthly instalments. Before the first payment became due, Johnson received notice from a finance company that the payment contract had been assigned to them and that payments were to be made at a local bank as they came due.

(a) Had Dayus assigned a right or a liability?
(b) Could Johnson have refused to pay the finance company?
(c) If the finance company had instructed Johnson to make his payments by post office money order and to mail them by registered mail to the company's head office in Toronto, would such conditions have been binding on Johnson?
(d) If the reshingled roof began to leak because of defective work, to whom would Johnson look for repairs?
(e) If Johnson defaults on his payments, who will be entitled to take action against him, Dayus or the finance company?

A creditor (the one who is owed) may assign his right to receive money or goods *without* the consent of the debtor (the one who owes). The following conditions apply:

1. The assignment must be in writing.

2. The assignee (the person to whom the rights are assigned) must give the debtor written notice of the assignment; otherwise payment by the debtor to the original creditor would be valid.

3. The assignment must not increase the debtor's burden or diminish his rights and remedies.

4. The assignee acquires the same rights subject to the same defences as the original creditor had.

If the above conditions have been met, the assignee may bring action directly against the debtor if the debtor defaults on his agreement.

It is a common practice for vendors who have sold goods under a conditional sales contract requiring payment in instalments to assign the contract to a finance company in consideration of an immediate lump-sum payment from that finance company, who will collect the instalment payments as they become due. When such assignments are made, it is important to observe the rule that the debtor must be notified.

C—2

McKenna bought a water softener and, as part of the contract, had signed a promissory note for $520. The original contract was assigned to the Industrial Acceptance Corporation, and McKenna received written notice of this assignment. Later, the Industrial Acceptance Corporation reassigned the contract to Allux Ltd., who did not notify McKenna as required by the Conveyancing and Law of Property Act of Ontario. Later, McKenna defaulted on the contract, and Allux Ltd. sued. When the court learned that McKenna had not been notified of the reassignment, the case was dismissed.

(a) Does the dismissal of this case wipe out McKenna's debt?
(b) What do you think Allux Ltd. should do now to try and collect its money?

The decision on the above case does not mean that McKenna was no longer liable for the debt; it simply means that the second assignee (Allux Ltd.) was not able to recover from McKenna because legal notice had not been given. The second assignee may now give the proper notice and claim again, or look to the assignor (in this case the Industrial Acceptance Corporation) for redress, who in turn must took to McKenna.

ASSIGNMENT OF OBLIGATIONS

A debtor may not assign his obligation to pay his debt unless the creditor consents. Nor may a person who has obligated himself to do some work in which his special skill or personal ability is the important factor in the agreement legally delegate the performance of the work to another. For example, an artist does not have the legal right to delegate to another artist a contract to paint a portrait. Where the work does not depend upon the personal qualifications of the performer, a contract to perform work or duties may be delegated to another, but the original promisor remains liable for proper performance. An example of this principle is the practice of sub-contracting jobs in which the fundamental requirement is the performance of work according to specifications rather than that it be done by any particular person.

ASSIGNMENT OF BOOK DEBTS

By "book debts" we mean debts owed to some business proprietor by his customers and carried in his books as accounts receivable. In order to maintain his credit, the proprietor may find it necessary to assign the book debts to some other person or agency as security for a loan or to pay his own debts. This type of transaction is governed by statute law, which is quite similar in all the provinces. The main features of the law are as follows:

1. The assignment must be in writing and be accompanied by the *affidavit* of an attesting witness. This affidavit is a signed statement by a witness that he knew the assignor and saw the assignment signed. Such statements are sworn before a *notary public*, a person appointed by the province to take statements under oath.

2. There must be a further affidavit of the assignee that the assignment is *bona fide*, that it was made in good faith, and for good consideration and not for the purpose of enabling the assignee to hold the debts or accounts out of reach of the creditors of the assignor.

3. The assignment, together with the affidavits, must be *registered* (filed in the official Registry Office) within the specified number of days prescribed by the law of the province concerned.

ASSIGNMENT BY PROCESS OF LAW

In the following cases assignment is a legal requirement:

- According to bankruptcy law in Canada, when an insolvent debtor has been declared bankrupt, all his contracts are assigned to the trustee appointed by the creditors.
- When a person dies, his rights and liabilities are automatically assigned to the executor or administrator of his estate.

APPLYING THE LAW

1. A building contractor sub-contracted the electrical work required for a building he had agreed to construct. Is this a true assignment? How does the law apply to the practice of sub-contracting work?
2. What is the legal reasoning behind the rule that without permission a creditor may assign his right to receive money but a debtor may not assign his obligation to pay it?

DISCUSSION AND PROJECTS

1. (a) What transactions do you know of by which the creditor assigns the debtor's contract to a finance company?
   (b) Visit a local car dealer or furniture store and find out what assignment takes place with the financing contracts they offer to their customers.
2. Have someone in your group find out where your nearest registry office is; visit it and determine the way assignments and accompanying affidavits are recorded and filed.
3. Obtain from a local lawyer a sample of a sworn affadavit and examine its form and purpose.

Part 15

LIMITATION OF ACTIONS

C—3

Our legal system specifies a time limit for taking action against a party who has defaulted on his contract.
(a) Why do you think such a time limit exists?
(b) Why do you think this person waited seven years before wanting to sue?

A person who is entitled to take legal action against another is required by law to begin that action within a prescribed period or he loses his right to do so. The need for this legal limitation arises from the fact that, as time passes, old claims may be difficult or even impossible to settle because evidence has been lost or forgotten and witnesses are no longer available.

The effect of the law is that if court action is not taken to collect a debt or enforce a claim within the required time, the right to sue is *barred* and the debt is said to be *outlawed*. Note particularly that it is only the right to sue that is barred; the debt is not extinguished, even though the creditor may not be able to use the courts to enforce his claim.

Each province has a general *limitations* statute which prescribes the limitation period for taking legal action on certain matters. For simple contracts and ordinary claims, the law of limitations is fairly uniform over the provinces.

SIMPLE CONTRACT CLAIMS

Simple contract debts, as for example, promissory notes, trade accounts, claims for wages, interest and rent, are outlawed after six years in all the provinces except Quebec, where the period is five years. The following rules apply to such claims:

1. Each item of a trade account is considered a separate debt. The six-year term counts from the date that the term of credit on each particular purchase expired. For instance, if on January 15, 1972, A buys a carpet from Ingram Furniture, and on March 12, 1972, he buys a chair, both items will be on his charge account, but under the law each is a separate debt and the six-year limitation period runs separately for each.

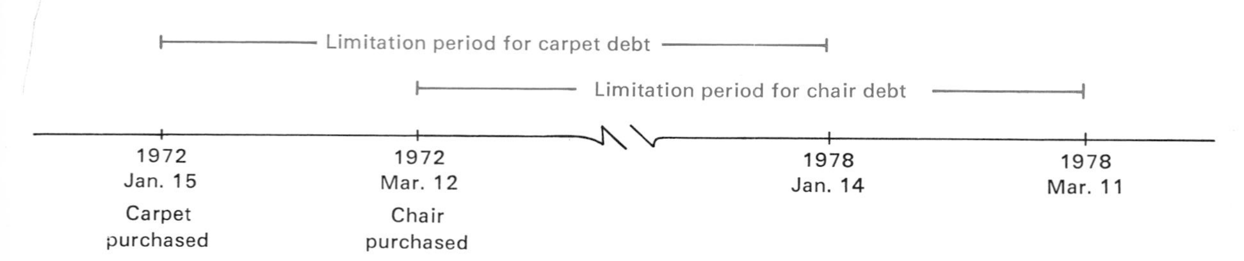

2. The six-year period begins to run at the time the plaintiff was first entitled to bring action on the contract. For example, on January 4, 1972, A borrows $500 from B, to be paid back on March 31, 1972. The limitation period begins to run on March 31, the date on which the payment becomes due.

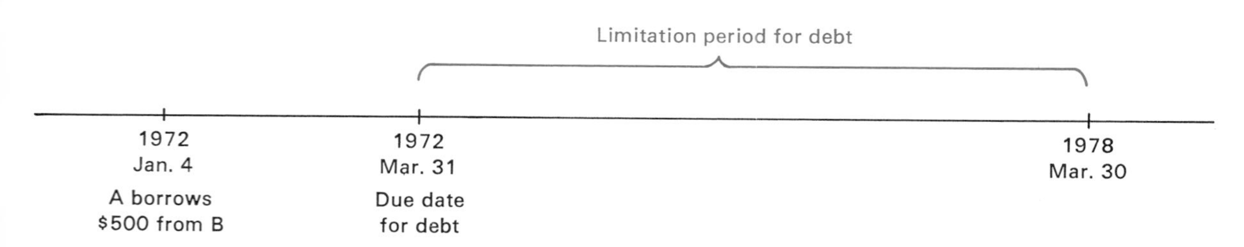

3. A part payment, or a written promise to pay, or even a written acknowledgment of a debt will form a new starting point for the limitation period unless the payment or acknowledgment is made conditionally so that a promise of further payment is not implied. For example, the period of limitations on a debt due January 15, 1972, is scheduled to run for six years from that date. But if a part payment of the debt or an unconditional written acknowledgment of that debt is made on June 15, 1972 (or on any date within the six-year period), the

period of limitation starts afresh from that date. Thus such part payments and/or written acknowledgments could keep the period of limitation running indefinitely.

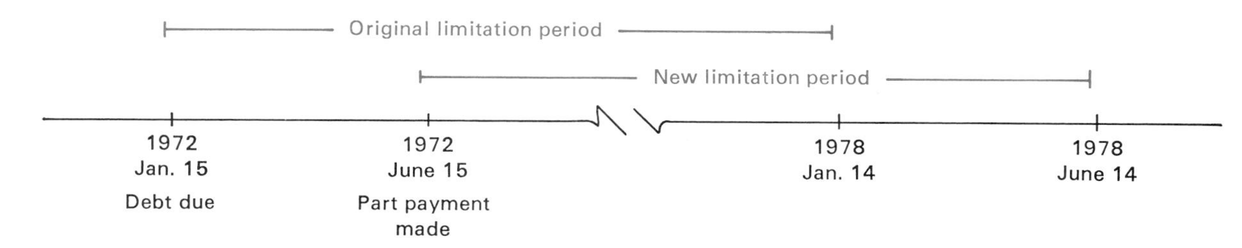

(In Alberta, Saskatchewan, Manitoba and New Brunswick a written acknowledgment or part payment renews the period of limitation, regardless of whether a promise to pay is implied by it, and even if it is accompanied by a refusal to pay more.)

4. If the debtor has disappeared on the date on which the creditor is first entitled to bring action on the debt, the operation of the statute is suspended until the debtor's return, at which time the period starts afresh. In such case the creditor is said to have been under a *disability*; however, if the creditor could have taken legal action *before* the debtor disappeared, the disappearance would not affect the running of the limitation period. As an example, if A owes B a debt due on March 15, 1972, this is the earliest date on which B is entitled to take legal action if A does not pay. Suppose that on April 15, 1972, A disappears. Since B was entitled to take legal action on the debt at any time from March 15 to April 15, but had negelected to do so, the limitation period is not affected; it still runs from March 15. However, if A had disappeared on February 15, a month before B was entitled to bring legal action against A, the limitation period would be suspended during A's absence (creditor's disability) and would begin to run afresh on A's return.

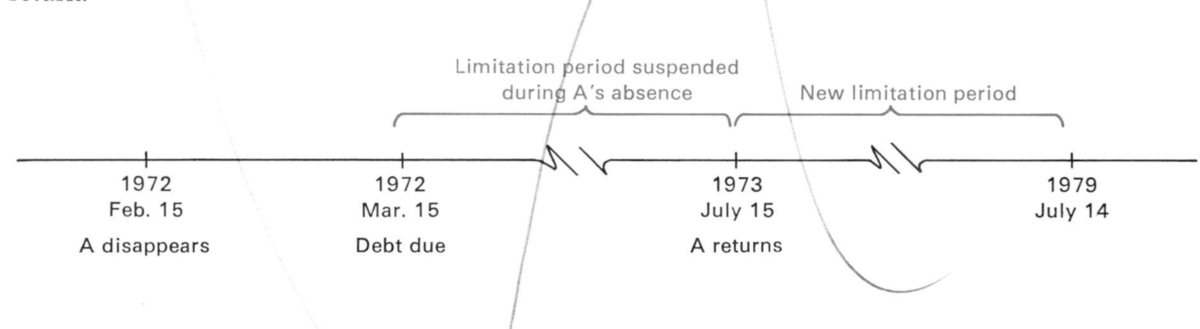

If the creditor is under the disability of infancy or mental incompetency, the limitation period is suspended until he reaches majority or is mentally sound. (There are some provincial variations with regard to disabilities.)

In addition to the "general" limitation statutes, many other statutes prescribe specific periods for the taking of legal action on the matters with which they are concerned. These periods vary from a few days in some cases to years in other cases, depending on the type of action and the province within which it takes place.

C—4

Water from the town's municipal sewage and drainage system accumulated on the adjoining properties of J and P, making the land unusable and constituting a nuisance. P took legal action against the town, claiming damages and basing her action on the town's breach of contract to construct a drainage ditch across her property. J had not contracted with the town for a drainage ditch, so he framed his action in tort, claiming damages for the years 1959 and 1960 solely on the basis of the nuisance committed.

The trial judge allowed damages to both parties, but on appeal by the town, the appeal court held that J's claim in tort for the year 1959 must fail because of a section of the Town Act of Saskatchewan which provided that an action of this type (claim for nuisance) had to be brought within three months of the time the damage was sustained. By the time J's claim was made (June 2, 1960,) the three-month limitation period for 1959 claims had elapsed and that claim was barred. However, his claim for damages for 1960 had not been barred and was allowed. The appeal court therefore disallowed the damages awarded to J for the year 1959.

In the case of P, however, since the claim was for a breach of contract for which the limitation period was six years, the Town Act did not apply, and the claim had not been barred by the passing of time. The appeal court therefore upheld the trial judge's ruling and allowed damages to P.

What lesson is there in the above case for people who have a cause of legal action?

SPECIALTY CONTRACT CLAIMS

Specialty contracts (contracts under seal) are outlawed in most of the provinces in twenty years. In Alberta, Saskatchewan, and Manitoba, the time is six years; in Quebec, thirty.

REAL PROPERTY CLAIMS

Claims in connection with real property may be for the right of possession of the land or the right to receive money payments. These rights may arise by will, inheritance, or by deeds, mortgages, or other agreements. The limitations prescribed vary according to the province and also to the nature of the claim. The presentation of these variations is beyond the scope of this text. Where limitation of legal action concerning real property claims is in question, competent legal advice should be sought without delay.

REVIVING OF OUTLAWED DEBTS

C—5

> Ten years ago K was unemployed and unable to pay his rent. Finally, he vacated the premises while owing rent for several months. Because of K's financial circumstances at the time, the landlord did not take any legal action about the overdue rent, and eventually lost track of K. Now K is in good circumstances having inherited a substantial sum of money.

(a) What is the legal effect of the passing of the ten years?
(b) Should K consider that he no longer owes for the rent?
(c) What circumstances might have arisen during the ten-year period which would give the landlord a legal right to collect?

A simple contract that has been actually outlawed may be revived and a new time-limit put into operation as a result of the following:

- A part payment by the debtor applying to the outlawed debt.
- A written promise to pay the debt, or an unconditional written acknowledgment that can be interpreted as promising payment.

In each case the starting point of the new time-limit is the date on which the promise is written or the payment is made.

APPLICATION OF PAYMENTS

When a debtor makes a partial payment of his indebtedness to a creditor, the rules as to the application of the payment are:

1. The debtor may apply it to a particular debt or debts at the time of payment.

2. If the debtor owes money on separate debts and does not indicate how the payment is to be applied, the creditor may apply it as he chooses. He may even apply it to a debt that has been outlawed; however, in this case the *unpaid balance of the outlawed debt would not be revived*, since the creditor's action does not imply a promise by the *debtor* to pay that particular debt and thus revive it.

3. If there is a running account, it is presumed that the payments are applied to the debts in order of date. But if the amount paid is the exact amount of a particular debt, it is presumed that the payment is in discharge of that debt.

4. If the debtor applies a payment to a particular debt, and the creditor does not agree to its being so applied, the creditor may refuse to accept the payment and may take action to enforce what he believes to be his legal rights.

APPLYING THE LAW

1. Over a period of the last ten years A has incurred debts with B, several of which are still unpaid, including one debt which is now outlawed by the expiration of the limitation period. A now pays B some money without indicating to what particular debts he wishes it applied. What are B's rights with respect to the manner he applies the payment?
2. H has owed J $350 for eight years. During that period the two parties met occasionally and each time H orally promised he would pay the debt as soon as possible. Finally, after eight years, J sends a letter to H threatening legal action. Shortly afterwards H sends a letter to J saying he believes the debt is outlawed and he does not intend to make any payment on it.
   (a) Did the oral promises have any effect on the running of the limitation period?
   (b) What is the effect of the letter from H?

DISCUSSION

1. A garage operator felt that he was covered as far as the outlawing of his customers' debts was concerned when he mailed statements to them regularly. What do you think of his point of view?
2. "No gentleman ever takes advantage under the Statute of Limitations." Discuss the implications of this statement.

Part 16

BREACH OF CONTRACT

C—6

Fitch, a carpenter, agreed to repair a house for Mr. Fuller. When the job was finished, Mr. Fuller discovered some work not according to their agreement, in particular that the three upstairs bedrooms were painted pink instead of beige. He refused to pay, claiming breach of contract.

Fleming orders 1,000 tons of coal to be delivered August 1. On July 1 he wires the local dealer that he will not accept shipment.

(a) Which of these two situations do you feel represents the most serious breach of contract?

(b) Could the injured party refuse to honour his part of the contract in each case?

A breach of contract may be of a minor nature, it may involve a fundamental condition, or it may be a breach of the contract as a whole. The remedy available to the injured party varies according to the nature of the default.

COMPLETE BREACH OF CONTRACT

C—7

Christner had contracted with Mason & Risch Ltd. for an upright piano of a certain style to be built for $850. When the piano was completed, Mason and Risch offered to deliver the piano as agreed upon, but Christner, who now found that he could not obtain certain funds he had expected to get, refused to accept delivery. The firm then brought an action for the full price, but was allowed only $391 as damages. Christner appealed the amount of damages, but the Ontario Court of Appeal held that the proper amount of damages would be the actual loss sustained by the injured party. Assuming that Mason & Risch would have to pay an agent a commission for reselling the piano and also incur other expenses in connection with the breach of contract, the appeal court assessed the actual loss sustained by them to be $325 instead of $391. The damages were therefore reduced to that amount.

(a) Why did the trial court not allow Mason & Risch the full price of the piano? Why did it assess the damages at $391?
(b) Why did the appeal court reduce the damages from $391 to $325?

When one party refuses to perform any part of his contract—a complete breach of contract—the other party is discharged from his obligation. If he suffers loss because of the breach, he may be entitled to damages. Damages are usually assessed at the actual financial loss sustained by the injured party.

SUBSTANTIAL PERFORMANCE

C—8

In this case, settled in the Nova Scotia courts, the plaintiffs, Downie and Hatt, had constructed a house for the defendant Norman, but Norman refused to pay the final instalment of the contract price. He contended that the house had not been constructed in a workmanlike manner and that the materials used were not of a proper quality. The trial judge found that the work had been "substantially" performed. He noted that while there were defects and omissions, these were not sufficient to keep the builder from recovering the balance of the contract price (with a deduction for the correction of the defects.) Norman appealed this decision, but the Court of Appeal upheld the trial judge's decision, although increasing the deduction for defects.

(a) Do you think Norman was unreasonable in refusing to pay the final instalment?
(b) Why could not Norman have asked for all his money back?
(c) What is the difficult thing to decide in cases such as this?

Where the contract has been *substantially* performed, but there is a default of a minor nature, the injured party is *not* discharged from his obligation entirely. He is entitled only to damages to compensate him for any pecuniary loss suffered by reason of the default.

LIQUIDATED DAMAGES

Sometimes a contract will include among its terms one which provides that, should one party commit a breach of contract, he will pay the other a specified sum as damages. Damages of this type are called *liquidated damages*, meaning that the parties have agreed upon a fixed amount as damages in the event of breach of contract. Such terms are enforceable provided the amount of damages specified is not so great as to constitute a penalty as well as compensation.

C—9

In this British Columbia case an agreement between the purchasers and vendors of a house contained a clause that read in part: ". . . and unless the balance of the cash payment is paid and a formal agreement entered into within the time mentioned to pay

the balance, the owner may, at his option, cancel the agreement, and in such event the amount paid by the purchaser shall be absolutely forfeited to the owner as liquidated damages."
The only payment made on this agreement was a deposit of one dollar. Subsequently, the purchaser refused to make any further payments. At this point the vendors had two alternative courses of action: they could sue to enforce the agreement, or they could, as provided in the contract, cancel the agreement and retain the amount paid as liquidated damages. In fact, they sold the house to another party at a lower price and then sued the first purchasers to recover the difference in price. The court held that by reselling the house to another party they had adopted the second alternative; that is, they had elected to cancel the agreement and keep the amount paid. Thus, their only right now was to keep the one dollar deposit as liquidated damages.

(a) When there is an option for damages in the event of breach of contract, should the amount be specifically stated or not?
(b) Do you think the vendors really understood the terms of the contract? Would it have made any difference to the court's decision if they had claimed they did not understand the terms?

In the above case the liquidated damages were insignificant, being only one dollar. If the payments had been greater, the purchasing party might have hesitated to forfeit them. In most cases liquidated damages are stated at an amount that will compensate the injured party and at the same time serve as a deterrent against breach of contract.

MITIGATION OF LOSS

The party sustaining the loss must take reasonable steps to avoid unnecessary loss. The court will not award damages for loss which the injured party could reasonably have avoided. This rule is particularly significant in the case of a refusal by a purchaser to accept delivery of perishable goods. The seller should not delay in disposing of the goods at the best price he can get. If he still suffers loss, he may then sue for damages to cover his actual loss.

SPECIFIC PERFORMANCE

C—10

Grimes gives Scott a written offer to purchase Scott's farm for $20,000. Scott signs an acceptance of the offer which provides that Grimes has 15 days in which to close the deal. On the closing date Grimes is ready to complete the transaction, but Scott, who in the meantime has changed his mind, refuses to give up the property. Scott, however, offers Grimes a sum of money to compensate him for the breach of contract, but Grimes says he doesn't want money damages. He wants *specific performance*, that is, the transfer of the farm to him exactly as the contract provides.

(a) Why might Grimes not be satisfied with money damages?
(b) On what grounds might a court order specific performance?
(c) If the positions of the parties were reversed, that is if the purchaser refused to buy but the seller demanded specific performance, would the court's decision be the same?

When damages would not be an adequate remedy, specific performance will be enforced if the case is such that the court can compel the defaulting party to perform the contract, or else perform it for him. Generally, contracts for

Sometimes money compensation is not sufficient where property has unique features.

the sale of land can be specifically enforced. If the purchaser is in default, he can usually be compelled to carry out his contract, that is to take the property and pay the price. Similarly, if the seller is in default, he can usually be compelled to take the price and give up the property. However, the injured party has the option of suing for damages instead of entering a claim for specific performance.

The same principle applies if the contract is one for a sale of goods of peculiar value, such as rare antiques which are irreplaceable, and when money damages would not be an adequate remedy. Ordinarily, however, the remedy for breach of contract for the sale of goods is money damages.

PERSONAL SERVICES

A contract for personal services cannot be specifically enforced. The employee can not be compelled to serve a particular employer, nor an employer be compelled to keep a particular employee in his service. An exception to the latter circumstance is found in labour legislation which provides that where an employer has a collective bargaining contract with a union, if he wrongfully discharges an employee who is a member of that union, he may be compelled to reinstate the employee and reimburse him for loss of wages.

Although a contract for personal services cannot be specifically enforced, in some circumstances an employer can obtain an *injunction* (a court order) to prohibit the employee from taking employment with a competitor-employer. However, the courts are increasingly reluctant to grant this remedy, because it might deprive an individual of an opportunity to earn a living.

C—11

D, a professional football player, made a contract with the Detroit Lions' Club which gave the club the option of renewing the contract for a further term. By the contract, D also agreed not to play for any other club during the term of the contract. Before the term expired, D entered into a contract with the Toronto Argonauts but, also before the term expired, the Detroit Club notified D that it was exercising its option of requiring his services for another term. When the club learned that D had joined the Argonauts, they took legal action to obtain an injunction restraining D from playing for that team, and, if that was not granted, then for damages for breach of contract. Since the season covered by the broken contract had already expired before the action came to trial, the injunction could not be granted, but D was held liable for damages for breach of contract.

(a) What was the breach of contract committed by the football player?
(b) What was the purpose of the proposed injunction?
(c) If an injunction had been granted, might the football player have been out of a job?

APPLYING THE LAW

1. A workman made extensive renovations to a house. After he had completed the work, the householder claimed it was inferior workmanship, and refused to pay any part of the price. The workman offered to reduce his price, but the householder still refused to pay anything. How does the law apply?
2. Although both the purchaser and the vendor had signed an agreement for the sale of a piece of lake-front property in a summer resort area, the seller changed his mind and absolutely refused to give up the property. The vendor was wealthy and offered the buyer any reasonable amount of money he asked for in order to cancel the agreement. How does the law apply?

DISCUSSION

1. Discuss the reasons for not enforcing specific performance in the case of contracts for personal services, as for example hockey players' contracts.
2. The cancellation of contracts such as sales orders and shipments is one of the common features of our business life. How may liability for breach of contract be avoided in these cases?

Part 17
DISCHARGE OF CONTRACT

DISCHARGE BY PERFORMANCE

Where both parties to a contract perform their obligations according to the terms of the contract, the contract is said to be discharged, or, in other words, both parties have discharged their duties under their contract and can also be said to be discharged from it.

For example, A agrees to paint B's house for a specified price. A does the work according to his contract and B pays the price in cash. The contract is discharged by both parties.

Sometimes only one of the parties carries out his agreement, while the other fails in some respect.

For example, A agrees to paint B's house for a specified price. A does the work according to his contract and B offers him his cheque in payment. A, having once received a bad cheque, refuses to take B's cheque. B says "You can take my cheque or nothing." A is discharged from his contract, but B is not because B's cheque is not *legal tender*.

LEGAL TENDER

Legal tender in Canada consists of

- Bank of Canada notes.
- Gold coin of Canada, Great Britain and the United States.
- Canadian silver coins—but only up to the amount of $10.
- Canadian copper coins—but only up to the value of twenty-five cents.

To be strictly legal, the payment offered must be the exact amount of the debt. We have become so accustomed to the practice of giving a bank note which is more than the debt and receiving the "change" that this point of law appears to have little practical significance. Nevertheless, it is law and could be invoked. For example, if you offered a $50 bank note to a bus driver to pay for a single fare, he would be within his legal rights to refuse it, not because it was in-

Various expedients were resorted to as media of exchange to meet local needs before legal tender was standardized throughout Canada.

Wooden tally and brass tokens representing beaver pelts were issued by the Hudson's Bay Company.

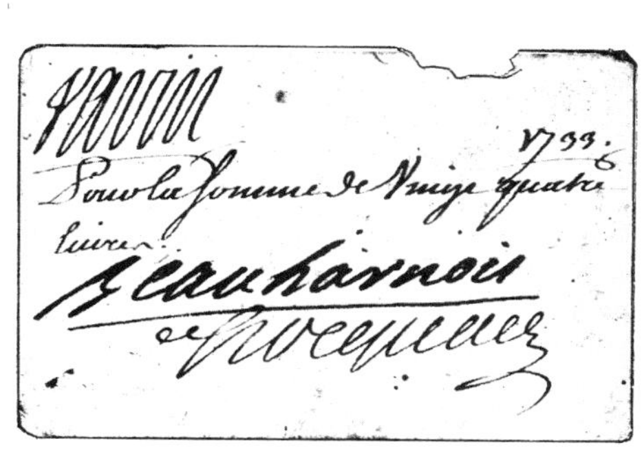

Playing cards countersigned by the French Governor and Intendant were used to pay the garrison troops while awaiting arrival of supplies. This card could be exchanged for 24 livres when the ship with money arrived.

Canadian Imperial Bank of Commerce

nvenient or impossible for him to change it, but because it was not the exact nount of the fare and, therefore, not legal tender.

Notwithstanding that the practice of using cheques has become so ell established that it is the method used for the greater part of all money payents today, cheques are not legal tender at law. In certain circumstances this fact ould not be overlooked. For example, a tenant mailed his cheque to his landlord payment of his rent. The landlord refused to accept the cheque and returned it. the time the tenant got around to offering legal tender, the rent was overdue to e extent that the landlord took advantage of the terms of the lease whereby he uld, and did, terminate the lease.

The creditor's refusal to accept legal tender does not discharge e debtor from his debt.

For example, A agrees to pave B's driveway. When the job is done, B ers A $200 in cash. A claims the price agreed upon was $225 and refuses to take e $200. If A then brings legal action against B, B may deposit the $200 with the urt and if the court finds in his favour, he may plead that having legally tendered yment he is not liable for interest on the debt accruing after the date the tender s made, or for the costs of the action.

When there is a dispute about a contract, one of the parties may try settle the matter out of court by making a compromise proposal. To prevent this oposal from being presented in court as evidence of his admission of liability, the event his attempt to settle fails, the proposal should be in writing and rded somewhat as follows: "Without prejudice, I make the following offer . . ." e phrase *without prejudice* means without admission of liability. A statement so de can not be admitted as evidence in a court action.

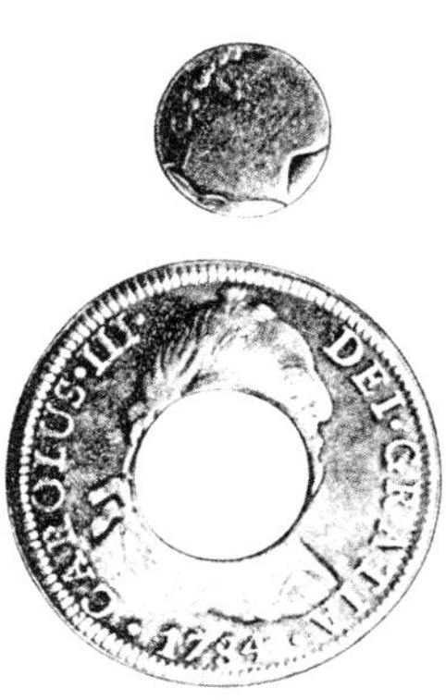

Prince Edward Island's Holey Dollar was devised in order to discourage people from taking currency off the Island to areas where the exchange rate was higher. The punched out disc was used as a shilling while the outer ring retained the 5-shilling Halifax currency value.

Canadian Imperial Bank of Commerce

DISCHARGE BY MUTUAL AGREEMENT

The contract itself may contain provisions for its own cancellation under certain conditions. As an example, fire insurance policies usually contain a clause to the effect that if a house is left vacant for more than a specified time and fire loss occurs during that vacancy, the policy is not effective.

A contract may also be discharged by the parties making another agreement to release each other from previous obligations.

DISCHARGE BY IMPOSSIBILITY OF PERFORMANCE

C—12

Would the trucker be discharged from his contract on a plea of impossibility of performance?

At one time, under English common law, if a party found it impossible, because of subsequent events, to perform according to his agreement, this fact did not legally free him from his obligation. It was held, generally, that the circumstances which might make performance impossible should have been anticipated and covered by appropriate conditions in the contract. If such conditions were not provided for, it was presumed that the promisor had voluntarily assumed the risks involved.

That very harsh doctrine has been modified over the years, and the courts now recognize the principle that an *implied* term may be read into some contracts that subsequently become impossible to perform; namely, a presumption that both parties intended from the beginning (although the intention was not expressed) that if certain conditions essential to the performance of the contract ceased to exist, the contract would be discharged. The three kinds of contracts described below come under this rule.

1. When the subject matter of the contract becomes unfit or is destroyed.

The Windsor Star

C—13

The owner of a music hall agreed to rent it to Taylor for the purpose of giving a series of concerts. Before the concerts began, the hall was destroyed by fire. Taylor then sued the owner of the hall for damages to compensate him for losses suffered from the cancellation of the concerts. The court held that the contract was not binding, because it had been discharged by "impossibility of performance."

What similar events, if any, have occurred in your community that would cause impossibility of performance?

2. Where incapacitating illness makes impossible the performance of a contract for personal services.

C—14

Mrs. Davidson, an eminent pianist, promised to perform at a concert arranged by Robinson at some considerable expense. Illness prevented her from performing as promised, and Robinson sued for damages to recover his expenses. The court held that the contract was discharged by impossibility of performance resulting from incapacitating illness.

Give other examples of cancelled performances where the contract might be discharged through impossibility of performance.

3. Where a change in the law, subsequent to the making of the contract, makes the contract illegal. For example, early in World War II so much steel was needed for war purposes that the Canadian government restricted its use in certain building projects, particularly where construction could be carried on with substitute materials. Contracts specifying the use of steel, made before the restrictions came into effect, were discharged because, under the new law, they were illegal.

In an attempt to remedy some of the inequities arising from the discharge of contracts because of impossibility of performance (or *frustration of the contract*, as it is also called), England in 1943 passed the Frustrated Contracts Act. Following that example, most of the provinces of Canada have enacted similar legislation. Generally speaking, these acts contain provisions for a reasonably just settlement between the parties when their contract becomes "frustrated" because of impossibility of performance.

APPLYING THE LAW

1. Dawson claims Ellis owes him $40, but Ellis disputes the amount as being too much. One day Ellis brings a sack of 4,000 pennies and dumps them on Dawson's desk saying, "Here's your money." What do you suggest that Dawson do—refuse the pennies and demand legal tender, or accept the payment? Why?
2. Riley arranges with McCurdy, an electrician, to instal some electrical services in Riley's house. When McCurdy arrives on the appointed day at Riley's house with his tools and materials, Riley refuses to let him begin work because he and his family are leaving at once on vacation. Riley says "Come back in two weeks." McCurdy does not show up after two weeks nor the week after that. When Riley asks him why he hasn't come to do the work, McCurdy says he is too busy and doesn't know when he will be able to do the work, if at all. Has there been a breach of contract by either party or by both parties? Explain.

DISCUSSION

1. A caterer agrees to provide dinner for a gathering of 500 people. During the afternoon on which the food is to be prepared, a severe electrical storm occurs and the power is shut off. The caterer, having electrical appliances, is unable to do any cooking. Just before the dinner is to begin, electrical power is restored.
   (a) Should the caterer have anticipated such a possibility and provided for it in his contract?
   (b) When electrical power was unavailable, should the caterer have made arrangements to have the dinner prepared by someone at some place with gas appliances?
   (c) Would you excuse performance by the caterer on the grounds of impossibility of performance?

UNIT EIGHT
GOING TO WORK

TRAINEE ASSISTANT
FOR
THEATRE ORGANIZATION
Some typing. Pleasant personality. Ambitious. Willing to travel. Ability to meet people. Well groomed. Must have genuine interest in theatre business. References. Bondable. Apply in own handwriting to:
BOX Z586
THE DAILY NEWS

BOOKKEEPER — TYPIST
ESTABLISHED FIRM REQUIRES EXPERIENCED BOOKKEEPER CAPABLE OF MAINTAINING COMPLETE SET OF RECORDS.
- TYPING REQUIRED
- WILL PAY ACCORDING TO ABILITY

Reply in own writing to:
BOX 351 CITIZEN REVIEW

AUTOMOTIVE
PARTS SALES PERSON
WITH JOBBER EXPERIENCE
To Call upon
- GARAGE
- SERVICE STATION
- FLEET ACCOUNTS

— ESTABLISHED IN WINDSOR FOR PROVINCE WIDE JOBBER
Salary plus commission
Call 987-6543

In which of these situations might the employee make contracts on behalf of his employer?

The relationship of employer and employee may arise in two ways:

- Under a contract of agency as between *principal* and *agent.*
- Under a contract of employment as between what has been traditionally known as *master* and *servant.*

DISTINCTION BETWEEN AN AGENT AND A SERVANT

The general distinction between an employee who is an agent and one who is classed as a servant is that an agent is authorized to make contracts for his employer (his principal) with third parties, while a person who is acting in the capacity of a servant does not have such authority. The distinction is largely one of function, for it is possible for the same person to act in either capacity for the same employer. For instance, the owner of a small service garage may employ a mechanic who works under the owner's direct supervision and control, and does not enter into contracts for his employer with other people. Under these conditions the mechanic is classed as a servant. However, if the owner goes on vacation and leaves the mechanic in charge of the business while he is away, the mechanic will presumably have to enter into contracts (for example the ordering of parts and agreements to make repairs) for which his employer will be responsible, and in such transactions the mechanic will be acting as an agent.

INDEPENDENT CONTRACTOR

It is important not to confuse the status of agent or servant with that of *independent contractor*. Generally, a person who employs a contractor to do a particular work does not supervise or control the details of the operation beyond requiring that the work be performed according to the terms and specifications of the contract. For example, suppose you engage a painting contractor to paint your house for an agreed price, the quality, colour and number of coats of paint, and any other conditions being expressly specified. Ordinarily, the contractor will select and provide his own equipment and materials, and will direct and control his own employees without interference or direction from you, other than your checking that the work is being done according to the contract.

In some cases it is not easy to determine whether the party concerned is an independent contractor, a servant, or an agent. The distinction is important because, generally speaking, a person engaging an independent contractor may not be held liable by third parties for damages due to the contractor's negligence or other wrongdoing; neither is he liable to the contractor for injuries suffered by the contractor or his workmen in carrying out the contract. Both of these responsibilities may, however, rest on the employer with respect to his agent or his servant.

CASE 1

Trucking

MAN WITH TRUCK FOR
Delivery, or moving, small or big
And yard clean-up. Call 542-1021

(a) If you employ this man to clean up your yard, what would determine whether he is employed as a servant or as an independent contractor?
(b) What difference could it make to you legally, whichever he is?

C—2

The owners of a building in Manitoba had had it constructed by a reputable firm of contractors who, in this particular case, did part of the construction in the winter months when temperatures fell well below zero. The following summer a wall of the building collapsed on adjoining business property causing considerable interruption in business activities and, consequently, some loss. The party whose business was thus disrupted claimed damages from the owners on the grounds of negligence. The court found that the collapse of the wall was due to faulty construction during winter conditions, and held that the construction firm was an independent contractor and not an agent or servant of the owners. Therefore, the claim against the owners on the grounds of negligence failed; the damage was entirely due to the negligence of the contracting firm or its workmen, and any liability rested upon them.

(a) What facts would determine whether or not the construction firm was an independent contractor?
(b) What bearing on the case does the contractor's reputation have?

Part 18
PRINCIPAL AND AGENT

Agency is a relationship established by contract whereby one person, known as the *principal*, employs and authorizes another person, called the *agent*, to represent him in business transactions with third parties. Many examples come to mind: sales agents, purchasing agents, insurance agents, real estate agents, etc. In fact, agency is one of the essential features of modern business. Corporations, for instance, can function only through their agents, the officers and employees of the company.

C—3

(a) Would a minor be *legally* competent to represent his employer in business affairs?
(b) What is the law respecting a deal like this?

Any person capable of entering into a contract in his own behalf may authorize an agent to contract in his name. Thus a minor may be appointed as an agent and the contracts he makes for his principal will be as binding as if the principal had made them personally. At the same time, although a minor may appoint an adult as his agent he is not bound by the contracts made by such agent unless the minor could have been bound had he made the contracts himself.

ESTABLISHING THE AGENCY RELATIONSHIP

The relationship of principal and agent may be established in several ways: it may be by express appointment; or by implied authority; or by ratification; or, in some cases, simply by necessity.

EXPRESS APPOINTMENT

An agent is appointed by contract. It is not essential that such contract be in writing, unless it is so required by statute, as is the case for contracts that are to run for more than one year. In many situations the appointment may be quite informal; for example, A tells his neighbour, B, he is going to look at some firewood advertised for sale and, if satisfactory, buy a cord. B says: "If you like it order a cord for me." B and A are now principal and agent respectively.

Although a particular agency contract may not be required by law to be in writing, it is advisable to have a written contract which sets forth the terms of the agency. In some provinces an agreement to pay a commission to a real estate agent is not enforceable unless it is in writing.

If an agent is to be required to make contracts under seal for his principal he must receive his authority under seal. The appointment is known as *Power of Attorney*, and this should always be given if the agent is to have authority to perform such acts as signing notes, accepting drafts and issuing cheques in the name of the principal.

Know all Men by these Presents that

THELMA EVANS, sister of the undersigned

Fill in here the name, business and address of the Attorney.

of 800 Sussex Street

Essex, Ontario

has been made, constituted and appointed, and is by these presents made, constituted and appointed the true and lawful Attorney of the undersigned

ELIZABETH EVANS, spinster

Fill in here the name, business and address of the ~~Company~~ Principal

of 12 Peter Street

Essex, Ontario

for and in the name of the undersigned to endorse all or any Bills of Exchange, Orders, Drafts and Cheques for deposit; to draw and sign all Cheques, Orders and Drafts for payment of money; and to receive all paid cheques and other

Attorney hereunder shall be binding on the undersigned.

In witness whereof these presents have been executed by the undersigned at Essex the 10th day of February one thousand nine hundred and seventy-two

Witness:-

Margaret McFadden

Elizabeth Evans

[SEAL]

[SEAL]

[SEAL]

[SEAL]

Example of a Power of Attorney

AGENT BY APPARENT AUTHORITY

When, in making a contract for his principal, an agent exceeds his real authority or errs in exercising his authority, the principal, nevertheless, is bound if the third party can reasonably assume that the agent was acting within the *apparent* scope of his authority.

C—4

G insured his car with the plaintiff company through an insurance agent, F. The agent, who used the company's application form, asked G the questions on the form and filled in the answers himself. One of the questions requested details of any accidents in which the applicant had been involved. G described two rather minor accidents, the costs of which he had paid out of his own pocket. The agent assured G that it was not necessary to put this information on the application form, and entered "nil" opposite the question. The policy was issued and delivered to G by F. Some time later, when G presented a claim, the company informed him that, because of his withholding information concerning previous accidents, they were denying liability on his claim and were returning his premium. Later, the company entered an action against G seeking to have the insurance policy annulled. The company claimed that (1) the misrepresentation of facts in the application made the policy void and (2) F was not their agent since he had not been *expressly* authorized to issue or sign policies in their name. G's defence was that he assumed F was the company's agent and that F had the authority which he exercised in determining how the questions on the application form should be answered. The court's decision (confirmed later on appeal) was that G had acted in good faith and that F also had acted in good faith, notwithstanding his error. Further, since F had been furnished with the company's application forms and had been allowed to collect premiums, issue receipts and deliver policies, it could be presumed that F was acting within the scope of his apparent authority as the company's agent. The company was therefore bound on the insurance contract made by their agent, F.

(a) If you had been applying for the insurance, would you have permitted the agent to fill in the application form?
(b) Why did the agent not record the two minor accidents on the application form?
(c) What did the company mean by asserting that F had not been *expressly* authorized to issue or sign policies in their name?
(d) What facts show that F acted within his apparent authority as an agent of the company?

At the same time, if the third party knows or has reason to suspect that the agent is exceeding his authority, he should check immediately with the principal concerning the matter; otherwise he may find that the principal may legally repudiate the contract made by the agent.

C—5

A clerk named Burgess was employed by the Canadian Government Elevators and was authorized to take money or cheques in exchange for warehouse receipts and to make deposits to the credit of the Receiver General in the Royal Bank. From time to time, Burgess remitted by draft to the Receiver General the money that had been deposited. A rubber stamp bearing the words "Deposit to Credit of Receiver General, Canadian Government Elevator Account" was supplied to Burgess for the purpose of endorsing cheques for deposit.

Subsequently, one of the cheques received by Burgess and made payable to "Dominion Government Elevator Company" was endorsed by Burgess as follows: "Canadian Government Elevator per F. S. Burgess," (the words Canadian Government Elevator being impressed by a rubber stamp). B then cashed this cheque at the Royal Bank, and took the proceeds for himself.

In an action by the government against the bank to recover the stolen money, on the grounds of negligence on the part of the bank teller, the court held that the bank was liable. The bank teller should have noted that Burgess had signed as agent and that there was a discrepancy between the name of the payee as written on the cheque and the endorsement, and this should have been sufficient reason to put the teller upon his guard and to enquire as to the agent's authority to cash the cheque. Simply because a person has authority to receive cash and to make deposits in the course of his employment, it does not follow that the same person has authority to cash cheques payable to his employer.

(a) Did Burgess have authority to cash cheques made payable to Canadian Government Elevators?
(b) How did the rubber stamp used for endorsing cheques for deposit differ from the rubber stamp used for endorsing the cheque that Burgess cashed?
(c) What was there about the endorsement used by Burgess in cashing the cheque that indicated that Burgess was acting as an agent of the Elevator company?

AGENT BY ESTOPPEL

C—6

A newly-arrived immigrant woman required hospital treatment. On admittance to the hospital she gave the name of a friend (without the friend's permission) as one who would be responsible for the bill. When the bill was presented to the friend, he paid it without informing the hospital of the circumstances. Some time later, the woman was again hospitalized, and again without authority named the friend as security. This time, however, the friend refused to pay, explaining that he had paid the first time only to keep the woman "out of trouble." The hospital sued and the court held that he must pay. Having paid the previous bill without objection or explanation, he was *estopped* from denying liability on similar bills incurred later with the same party.

(a) What is meant by the term "estopped"?
(b) If the man had refused to pay the first bill, could the hospital have held him liable on it?
(c) If the man had paid the first bill but at the same time had informed the hospital of the circumstances, could he have been held liable on the second bill?

If a person has no real authority at all to act as an agent, but the person for whom he presumes to act allows a third party to believe that the relationship of principal and agent exists, the principal is estopped (prevented) from denying liability on contracts made by the agent with the third party. This principle of law is called *estoppel.*

C—7

Davis was the owner of a farm in Saskatchewan which he leased to a tenant, Mudge, on shares. The tenant was to have half the crop and the use of the farm machinery, which he was to keep in good repair. The tenant had certain repairs made by Agnew, who kept a stock of parts in his store. On one occasion the tenant was in the store selecting some repair parts when Davis saw him and came in and paid for the repairs. On a later occasion Davis was with the tenant when repairs were contracted for. Subsequently, after the tenant had left the country, Davis refused to pay the account for repairs, claiming that the tenant had no authority to pledge his credit. The court held that Davis by his conduct had held out the tenant as his agent and was now *estopped* from denying liability.

(a) What was the particular conduct which prevented Davis from avoiding liability for the repairs?
(b) How could Davis have avoided such liability?

A HUSBAND'S LIABILITY FOR HIS WIFE'S DEBTS

At common law, a wife, living with her husband, is *presumed* to have authority to pledge her husband's credit for household necessaries which are in keeping with their social standing. However, the husband may avoid liability if he can prove that he had provided the wife with sufficient funds to make it unnecessary for her to pledge his credit; or that he had forbidden her to pledge his credit at all—even though the creditor was not aware of this circumstance. On the other hand, if the husband has honoured any charges to his credit made by his wife in the past, then he is estopped from denying liability for similar charges made subsequently with the same creditors, unless and until he advises the creditors directly that he will not accept responsibility for such charges. Similarly, if a man pays debts incurred by his childen without his express authority, he will be liable for their future debts to the same creditors unless he notifies those creditors otherwise.

When husband and wife are separated and living apart, the law *presumes* that the wife no longer has any implied authority to pledge her husband's credit; to make the husband liable in such case, the onus would be on the creditor to establish that the wife still retained her authority, and that the goods or services contracted for were suitable necessaries.

AGENT BY RATIFICATION

C—8

Without authority from her husband and without his knowledge, Mrs. W. signed a conditional sale agreement for the purchase of a piano. She signed both her own name and that of her husband. The piano was delivered while Mr. W was absent, and when he learned about it he protested to his wife but did not say anything to the sellers. The wife, who earned some money from keeping boarders, made some payments but most of the cheques were signed by Mr. W. According to the evidence, some of these cheques had been made out by the wife and handed to the husband for signing; others were drawn by the husband himself.

When payments fell in arrears, the piano company wrote letters to the husband threatening legal action, and on one occasion called on the husband to collect and were paid $20 on account. The company then brought action against both Mr. and Mrs. W. The trial court held Mrs. W liable, but dismissed the case against Mr. W. The plaintiffs thereupon appealed the decision with respect to Mr. W, and the appeal court held Mr. W liable on the grounds that he had full knowledge of all the material circumstances (Mrs. W had admitted that she had told her husband everything about the purchase, including the fact that she had signed his name to the contract and on the down-payment cheque) and that he did not at any time until shortly before court action was brought make any protest to the piano company or repudiate his liability. The court held that Mr. W had ratified the contract made by his wife to which she had signed his name, and was therefore liable on the contract.

(a) What does "ratified" mean?
(b) On what facts did the court rule that Mr. W had ratified the contract made by his wife?
(c) How could Mr. W have avoided liability in this case?
(d) If Mr. W had avoided liability, what do you think would have been the legal position of his wife?

If an agent has neither actual nor apparent authority to make contracts in a principal's name, the principal is not bound by such unauthorized act. However, the principal may subsequently *ratify* the contract and make it as binding as if it had been done with his express authority. Furthermore, the ratification relates back to the date of the contract and makes it effective as of that date.

A contract made without authority cannot be adopted by ratification unless (1) the party for whom the agent acts was in existence at the time and could legally make the same contract, and (2) the agent acted in the capacity of an agent. Also, if the named principal does ratify the contract he must ratify it as a whole; he cannot accept only that part which is beneficial to him and reject the other part; also he must ratify it within a reasonable time.

If the named principal does not ratify the contract, the person who acted without authority as his agent becomes personally liable to the third party for any loss suffered because of his unauthorized act. (See Liability of Principal and Agent to Third Parties, page 178).

AGENT BY NECESSITY

C—9

In the village of Semans a woman was struck down by an automobile in the early morning hours and suffered a broken leg. She was taken to the office of a doctor who was also the village medical health officer. The doctor put a temporary cast on the leg and took the woman to a private hospital in a neighbouring town. The woman, having no financial resources, could not pay; and the hospital sent the bill to the village of Semans. The Semans village council refused payment, claiming that the doctor had exceeded his authority, and that only the village council could have authorized hospital charges for an indigent person. The court, however, held that under the circumstances the doctor had acted in the capacity of an "agent by necessity" of the village council, and that the council was bound to honour the contract he had made.

(a) What is an indigent person?
(b) Was the village council correct in asserting that only the council had the *actual* authority to authorize hospital charges for an indigent person?
(c) Why would the hospital assume that the village council would accept responsibility for the bill?

Certain circumstances may make it necessary that a person act in another's name without express authority. For instance, when a husband deserts his wife leaving her unprovided for she may contract in his name for necessaries in keeping with her station in life. She is recognized as her husband's *agent by necessity.*

It has also been held that an agency by necessity may arise in connection with the care of animals. For example, in an old English case, a railway company incurred the expense of stabling and caring for a horse after it had taken the horse to its destination but there was no one there to take delivery. Although the railway company had no express authority to incur such expense, the court held that it was, as an agent by necessity, entitled to be indemnified by the owner.

The situations in which the principle of agency by necessity is recognized at law are few, and would appear to be confined to those cases where a real state of emergency creates the necessity.

THE AGENT'S LEGAL OBLIGATION TO HIS PRINCIPAL

C—10

(i) Hawkins, a real estate agent, is engaged by Little to sell Little's house. Hawkins also secretly acts as an agent for Wilson in buying Little's house. He receives a commission from both parties.

(ii) Harney is a purchasing agent for a building supply firm. A sales agent for a manufacturer of roofing materials manages to secure a substantial order for roof shingles from Harney (for Harney's employers) by arranging (unknown to Harney's employers) to have Harney's own summer cottage reshingled free of charge.

(iii) A vegetable processing plant authorizes its representative to rent farms for the growing of sweet corn. The representative is expected to make the best deal he can considering the productivity of the farm and the rental cost. This representative, without his employer's knowledge or consent, rents his own farm to his firm at the maximum rate although the farm is below average in productivity. To avoid his name appearing in the deal, he uses the name of the tenant who occupies a residence on the farm.

(a) Are the agents in the above examples carrying out their legal duty to act for their employer in the "utmost good faith"?
(b) In each case indicate wherein the agent's act is detrimental to his principal's interest.

An agent must act for his principal in the utmost good faith, and must not allow his personal interests to conflict with this duty. Thus, certain rules apply to this relationship unless the express terms of the agency contract specify otherwise.

1. An agent is bound to perform his work with reasonable skill and diligence. If an agent is employed as one claiming special skill, unless such skill is shown, he may be liable for damages to his principal for loss sustained thereby.

2. An agent may not sell his own goods to his principal without the principal's assent even though the goods may be exactly what the principal has ordered him to buy.

3. The agent must at any time be prepared to give a complete account of all moneys entrusted to him.

4. If at any time the agent makes a secret profit out of his employment, the principal may claim such profit.

5. An agent may not accept commissions from both the buyer and the seller, and where double commissions are accepted, the principal may recover for himself the commission paid by the third party or repudiate the entire contract with the third party. Such conduct is also grounds for dismissal of the agent. Incidentally, the Criminal Code (Sec. 368) provides a penalty of two years' imprisonment for an agent who "corruptly" accepts a "bribe" for doing or forbearing to do any act relating to the affairs or business of his principal. The same penalty is incurred by the person offering the bribe.

6. Unless the agency contract expressly or by implication provides otherwise, the agent may not delegate his duties to another party.

7. If the agent acts beyond his actual authority he may be liable to his principal for loss suffered by the principal through such unauthorized act.

C—11

Mrs. Ella, who owned land in an Ontario township, was approached by Pearlman, who informed her that he was a real estate agent and would like to act as her agent for the sale of her property. Later, Pearlman introduced her to a purchaser who bought the land as trustee for a company to be formed, and Pearlman received his commission accordingly. Subsequently, Mrs.

Ella learned that Pearlman had acquired an interest in the land he had induced her to sell, and she sued for the return of the commission given to Pearlman and the profits made by him from the land. From the evidence the court found that from the beginning the real intent of Pearlman was to acquire the lands for the purpose of reselling at a profit, and that at all times Pearlman was, in fact, a purchaser. Further, at no time was his interest disclosed to Mrs. Ella prior to the closing of the transaction. The court held that Pearlman was clearly in breach of his duty to exercise the utmost good faith and to make full disclosure of his interest in the property respecting which he was an agent for Mrs. Ella. Mrs. Ella was given judgment to recover the full commission paid and any profits made by Pearlman on the resale of the land.

(a) In what way did Pearlman, the agent, not act in good faith for his principal, Mrs. Ella?
(b) If, before selling the land, Pearlman had informed Mrs. Ella of what was eventually to be done with the property, would the court's decision have been different?

THE AGENT'S RIGHTS AS AGAINST HIS PRINCIPAL

In certain circumstances the agent is entitled to his commission even though the principal refuses to carry out his part of the contract entered into on his behalf by his agent. Each case, however, is decided according to the facts of the agency contract and no general rule can be applied.

An agent is entitled to be indemnified for any loss or liability incurred by him in the performance of his duty under the agency contract. If, however, the loss can be attributed to the default of the agent himself, he loses his right to indemnity.

LIABILITY OF PRINCIPAL AND AGENT TO THIRD PARTIES

The principal is bound on a contract with third parties when the agent acts within the actual or apparent limits of his authority. Thus a principal cannot free himself from liability for his agent's acts by privately limiting or revoking authority which he has allowed his agent to assume publicly.

C—12

Edgecombe, a merchant in New Brunswick had employed S of Montreal as his agent to purchase ladies wear, and from time to time the agent had made purchases for Edgecombe from the O.K. Ladies Garment Company which were paid for in due course. Subsequently, Edgecombe wrote the agent asking if he could arrange with the company to have a shipment of 50 coats sent on consignment. (Goods shipped on consignment remain the property of the consignor, unsold goods being returned to him). S, the agent, did not inform the company of the instructions in the letter, but ordered the 50 coats to be shipped as a regular sale.
Edgecombe, after selling eight of the coats, and thinking he was

selling on consignment, returned the other 42. The company refused to accept them, claiming the purchase price, and denying that the coats had been shipped on consignment and that the agent had ordered them on consignment. Edgecombe refused to pay and the company sued.
In his evidence the agent admitted that since he had never before obtained goods for Edgecombe on consignment he had ignored the instructions for this particular shipment. The court held that from the company's viewpoint the agent was acting within his apparent authority, and that this apparent authority could not be curtailed by private communications between principal and agent of which the company did not know. If the principal desires to limit or change the authority which he has allowed his agent to assume in transactions with a third party, he must notify that third party of such limitations or changes; otherwise, he will be bound by contracts made by his agent within his apparent authority. On those grounds the court held that Edgecombe must honour the contract made by S, the agent.

(a) Why did the agent ignore his principal's instructions about the shipment on consignment?
(b) Should the company (the sellers) have anticipated such an order and checked more closely with the agent?
(c) Why did the court rule that from the seller's point of view the agent was acting within his apparent authority?
(d) How could Edgecombe have avoided such a situation?

If an agent does not disclose that he is an agent acting for a principal, and the third party later learns of the existence of the principal, both the agent and the principal are liable, and the third party may elect which he shall sue—but he cannot sue both.

C—13

Hal H. Paradise Ltd. contracted with Kozma to supply carpets and other furnishings for a building which Kozma and his company were to construct. At the time, Paradise believed that Kozma was acting in the capacity of an independent contractor, whereas, in fact, he was acting as an agent for the defendants, owners of the building to be constructed. Kozma had been expressly authorized in writing to order work and purchase materials in the name of the owners for the building. Shortly after Paradise had procured the materials and stored them, they were notified that because of financial reasons the agreement to construct the building had been terminated and that the order for the furnishings was to be cancelled. It was now that Paradise first became aware that Kozma had been acting as an agent and not as an independent contractor. Paradise was able to return the materials to their suppliers, but at a loss. In addition, they had paid storage charges and had to forego the profit expected on the transaction. They therefore sued for damages for breach of contract, electing to sue the undisclosed principal, the owners of the building, instead of K. The court held that the owners were liable as an undisclosed principal, and allowed the plaintiffs damages to cover the actual loss and expenses incurred, and also the unrealized profit.

(a) Why did the plaintiffs elect to sue the owner of the building instead of Kozma?
(b) What did the court include in the assessment of damages?

If an agent performs any unauthorized act not within the scope of his apparent authority, and the principal does not ratify such act, neither the principal nor the agent can be held liable *on the contract*. The principal avoids liability because the agent acted without authority or beyond the scope of his apparent authority; and the agent is not liable on the contract because the third party contracted only through him as an agent, and not with him as a principal. The agent, however, is liable to the third party for any loss suffered by the third party as a result of the agent's *breach of warranty of authority*.

C—14

Sanford was one of the three executors of an estate. On behalf of the executors, but without their authority, he entered into an agreement with Maneer to sell him property which was part of the estate. The offer of purchase was accepted and a cheque for $250 received. Later, when the co-executors would not ratify Sanford's act, Sanford returned the agreement and the cheque to Maneer. Maneer then sued Sanford for breach of warranty of authority. The court held that Sanford was personally liable for misrepresentation of authority, and allowed Maneer to recover damages for loss of his bargain as well as for his expenses incurred in the transaction.

(a) In what way did Sanford misrepresent his authority?
(b) Do you think Sanford was guilty of dishonesty?

The principal is liable to third parties for the fraudulent acts or torts of his agent committed in the ordinary course of his employment. When the third party discovers the fraud, he may void the contract or affirm it or look to the principal for damages. If fraud or tort is committed by acts beyond the scope of the agent's employment, the agent only is liable.

C—15

Mrs. Lloyd, a widow, went to a real estate firm for the purpose of consulting them about her property. The managing clerk of the firm, professing to act for the firm, induced her to give him instructions to sell the property, and got her to sign documents (which she did not read) which, in effect, were conveyances of the property to himself. He then disposed of the property and pocketed the proceeds. On discovering the clerk's dishonesty, the widow sued the real estate firm to recover her property. The court held that the managing clerk was acting within the apparent scope of his authority when he committed the fraud, and that the firm, as his principal, became responsible for that fraud.

(a) Mrs. Lloyd (the plaintiff) did not read the documents she signed. Was this negligence on her part? Why or why not?
(b) Why was his employer responsible for the clerk's fraud?

TERMINATION OF AN AGENCY

C—16

> Three years ago, T, an agent of a life insurance company, sold J a life insurance policy. Today J receives a letter from the insurance company advising him that T is no longer in their employ. J suspects that T has been dismissed, but he wonders why the company has sent him the letter.

What do you think is the reason?

When an agency contract does not provide otherwise, it is implied that either party may terminate it simply by notifying the other party. As previously stated, a principal cannot limit privately the authority which he has allowed his agent to assume publicly. If circumstances arise which justify the principal in revoking the contract with his agent, he (the principal) should notify third parties who knew of the agency relationship; otherwise he may be held liable for the subsequent acts of his agent. Consider the recorded case of an agent who was authorized "to receive, borrow and pay money" for his principal, and who borrowed an amount in the name of the principal after he had left his employment. The lender was able nevertheless to recover from the principal on the grounds that he had not been made aware that the agent's authority had been terminated.

As a general rule, the death, disability or bankruptcy of a principal puts an end to an agent's contract; for if the principal can no longer act for himself, his agent cannot act for him. A special exception is an executor or trustee appointed to administer the affairs of an estate after the principal is deceased.

SPECIAL CLASSES OF AGENT

Up to this point we have outlined only the general law of agency as it has been established by common law. At the same time, there are certain special agencies which, because they offer services to the public at large, are subject to special legislation. The statutes are provincial in character and, having the same purpose, are similar in their main features. These agencies include real estate brokers, stock brokers, commission agents, insurance agencies, employment agencies, collection agencies, solicitors, conveyancers (those who prepare documents for the conveying of title to property) and common carriers (shippers and railways).

One of the chief purposes of these statutes is to regulate the operations of the agencies so that the interests of their clients are protected. An important provision in each case is that the agency must be *registered* and *licensed*. In some cases the agent must be *bonded*, (have his honesty guaranteed by an insurance company).

As a rule, these agencies must file regular reports of their operations; they are also subject to inspection and investigation by the provincial authorities. It is therefore important that any person intending to engage in an agency of a specialized class should ascertain if it comes under statute law; and, if so, he should make himself familiar with the statutory regulations as they apply in his province.

PARTNERS AS AGENTS

Under the Partnership Act of the various provinces, "every partner is an agent of the firm and his other partners for the purpose of the business of the partnership." A peculiarity of the partnership agency is that every partner is both a principal and an agent. As agent he may bind the firm and at the same time be jointly liable with his co-partners for the firm's obligations on the contract.

THE AGENT'S SIGNATURE

An agent who signs a contract on behalf of a principal should clearly indicate the capacity in which he signs. By signing "Capital Motor Company, per R. Ross, Manager," the agency relationship becomes apparent. If he signs simply as "R. Ross, Agent for Capital Motors," he may possibly find himself personally liable.

C—17

The defendants, the president and the secretary of Highland Grove Farms Limited, both signed a cheque without indicating that they occupied any position as officers or officials of any company, although there was stamped on the cheque below the signatures the words "Highland Grove Farms Limited." The cheque was made payable to Alliston Creamery for goods supplied to the Highland Grove Farms. The cheque was not honoured when presented for payment, and Alliston Creamery then sued the defendants whose signatures appeared on the cheque. The court held that the defendants were liable on the grounds that a person who puts his name to a bill of exchange makes himself personally liable *unless it is apparent upon the face of the bill* that he signs as "a mere scribe for another party." In this case there was nothing on the face of the cheque to indicate that the defendants were officials of the Highland Grove Farms, or that they were signing in any other capacity than their own.

How could the cheque have been signed so that it would be clear that Highland Grove Farms Limited was the drawer of the cheque, and that the two signatories were officers of the company acting as its agents?

C—18

In a similar case in the same year, the cheque in question was one that obviously had been printed for the company's use. The company name appeared at the top in large letters, and again was printed at the bottom of the cheque, with a line below it obviously designed for the signature of an authorized person. On this line the defendant's name had been written. The court held that these facts made the cheque appear to be a company cheque with the signatory only an authorized agent for the company and not a person acting as a principal in the transaction.

APPLYING THE LAW

1.

What is the law respecting a deal like this?

2. A doctor coming upon the scene of an automobile accident gave first-aid treatment to the injured parties and called an ambulance. Since the injured parties had not asked for any services, were they later liable to pay for the ambulance? Explain.
3. A clerk, employed by the A.B. Company, orders a desk for the company's office and has it charged to the company's account. The desk is delivered and the bill is paid by the company. Later, the clerk orders a typewriter and has it charged to the company also, but without the company's knowledge. When the typewriter is delivered, the clerk conceals it and later sells it privately. When the bill arrives, the employer refuses to pay, claiming he had not authorized the purchase. How does the law apply (a) to the employer? (b) to the clerk?

DISCUSSION AND PROJECTS

1. Discuss the conditions under which a wife is presumed to have authority to pledge her husband's credit, and also those conditions where such authority cannot be presumed.
2. Compare the agent's legal obligations to his principal with his principal's obligations to him. Is the legal situation one-sided? Justify your position.
3. Consult a bank official to find out what procedures the bank would require in the case of a very old woman who, realizing she needs help in doing her banking transactions such as making deposits and withdrawing money, wishes her niece to do these things for her.
4. Find out how theatrical agents work for actors, or how a similar agent works for recording artists and musical groups. What are the agents' functions, and how are they paid? Have someone interview such an agent, or invite one to meet your class.

Part 19
MASTER AND SERVANT

The modern term for "master and servant" is employer and employee. The older designation symbolizes a period when employment approximated what today we call domestic service, the servant usually being a member of his master's household. It was during this period that a great deal of our common law concerning master and servant was established and, as a result, the case law on this subject uses the older term.

The term is still useful and will likely persist, for it serves to distinguish this particular relationship from other relationships of employer and employee; for example, principal and agent, and employer and independent contractor.

These distinctions have already been referred to in the introduction to this Unit; nevertheless, they will bear repeating, for in many court actions the decision has hung upon the interpretation of the exact relationship between employer and employee.

- The status of "servant" does not entitle him to represent his master in making contracts with third parties; if he is able to do so, it is because he is also an agent, and this aspect of his job is governed by the law of principal and agent.

- A servant is distinguished from an independent contractor in that a master has the power to direct not only what work the servant is to do, but also the manner in which he shall do it. An independent contractor is not subject to direct control in this manner.

The line of distinction is not always clearly drawn. As a result it has been the cause of much litigation, particularly when third parties have tried to recover from the employer on the grounds that he was legally a "master."

C—19

The defendants in this case were a fuel company and the truck driver who delivered sawdust-fuel for the company. The sawdust was delivered by a truck with a blower attachment which blew the sawdust through a hose into a bin in the home of McDonald. The intake of the blower was quite close to the exhaust pipe of the truck and, in the course of delivery exhaust fumes were carried into the house, resulting in some members of the family suffering from carbonmonoxide poisoning and being hospitalized. One of the victims, an elderly woman, when overcome by the gas fell and broke her hip. The injured parties sued both the fuel company and the truck driver. The company denied responsibility, contending that the truck driver, who owned his own truck and was paid a unit price for deliveries, was an independent contractor and, as such, was solely responsible for what had occurred.

From the evidence, the court found that (1) the truck driver worked practically full time for the company and reported to the company's office each morning to receive instructions for the pick-up and delivery of sawdust; (2) although the truck driver owned and maintained his truck and was paid a unit price for deliveries, the truck bore the company's name on its sides and was painted by the company. On the basis of these facts and other circumstances of the case, the court held that the truck driver carried out his duties *under the direct control and direction of the company*; therefore, he was a servant rather than an independent contractor. Consequently, the company, as his master, was liable for loss or damage caused by the negligence of their servant.

(a) On what grounds did the court rule that the truck driver was acting in the legal capacity of a servant and not of an independent contractor?
(b) Why was the company held liable for damages in this case?

THE EMPLOYMENT CONTRACT

At one time conditions of work, remuneration, rights and duties, and other such matters were either determined by the master and the servant themselves or were implied by common law rules. Today, the traditional character of the relationship of master and servant has been changed by an ever increasing volume of statute law which, in many circumstances, supersedes or modifies common law rules and imposes on the employer many obligations with respect to the welfare and protection of his employee. This body of law, generally known as *labour legislation*, applies for the most part only to the larger industrial and commercial undertakings. There are, therefore, some classes of employment that are still subject to common law rules.

COLLECTIVE BARGAINING

Toronto Star

Collective bargaining is the process of establishing conditions of employment by negotiations between an employer and a trade union. The individual employee has little or nothing to do with the actual drawing up of the *collective agreement* (the employment contract). This is done by a bargaining committee authorized by the union to act for its members collectively. Once the collective agreement has been accepted, the individual member is bound by its terms whether he personally agrees with them or not. Although the individual member has surrendered some personal freedom of contract, the practice of collective bargaining has doubtless done far more for him than he could ever have accomplished by himself.

The right to bargain collectively has been established by statute law. The legislation concerning it usually goes under the title of Labour Relations Act or Trade Unions Act, each province having its own particular act. The federal government has a Labour Relations Act that covers those areas coming under federal jurisdiction. The main features of these statutes are fairly uniform throughout the provinces. Briefly, these are:

- Every employee has the right to be a member of a trade union and to participate in its activities. An employer may not discriminate against an employee because he is a member of a trade union.
- No employer shall interfere with the formation of a trade union or contribute financial support to it.
- Where a trade union has been certificated for the purpose of making a collective agreement with the employer, it is *compulsory* that the employer deal with such trade union.
- The collective agreement must contain provisions for the settlement of disputes without work stoppage.
- The employer has the right to suspend or discharge an employee for sufficient cause, but certain procedures that are usually incorporated into the collective agreement must be followed. If an employee is wrongfully dismissed, the employer may be compelled to reinstate him and compensate him for loss of wages.
- Both the employer and the trade union are subject to penalties for refusing or neglecting to comply with the regulations.

Although non-union employees usually make their own employment contracts individually, most of the provinces have passed legislation under one title or another which provides that upon the petition of representatives of employees and employers of any particular trade or industry in any particular area or zone, the Minister of Labour may convene a conference to investigate and consider the conditions of labour and/or wage rates which exist therein, and to negotiate with respect to such conditions or rates as they apply to that area. This legislation makes it possible for employees in certain occupations who are not organized into unions to take advantage of the principle of collective bargaining; for example, gas station employees in certain localities have taken advantage of this procedure to establish hours of work for their particular zone.

WORKING CONDITIONS

Each of the provinces has legislation in force that prohibits child labour, provides for specific safety and health measures, sets up minimum scales of wages in some classes of employment, regulates the maximum hours of work, provides for vacations with pay and, as already noted, legalizes collective bargaining. Most important is the fact that the law provides for systems of inspection to ensure that regulations are being observed and standards maintained.

There is some variation in these laws from province to province, and generally they apply only to industrial and manufacturing concerns. Again, certain classes of employees may not come under some particular statute; for instance, the laws governing hours of work and vacations with pay do not apply to professional people, farm employees, domestic servants and those employed in charitable institutions. But we must remember that this body of law is amended from time to time to meet the needs of society, the tendency being to bring more and more of our activities under government regulation.

ANTI-DISCRIMINATION LAWS

In most provinces it is provided by statute law that an employer may not discriminate against an employee by reason of his race, colour, or religion. Exempted from this rule are domestic servants, and religious, educational or social organizations, and employers employing fewer than a stated number of employees (in Ontario, five). Some provinces have made it law that a woman receive *equal pay for equal work*; that is, the same rate of pay as a man receives for doing the same kind of work. Similar federal legislation exists with respect to employees coming under federal jurisdiction.

THE MASTER'S LIABILITY FOR INJURIES SUFFERED BY HIS SERVANT

C—20

Archie and Bill work next to each other in a factory. They often exchange banter and occasionally engage in what they consider harmless pranks. One day Archie throws a dirty rag at Bill while Bill is working at his machine. In dodging the rag Bill's hand becomes caught in the machine and is badly injured.

(a) Is Bill engaged in his employment when the accident occurs?
(b) Does the accident arise out of his employment?
(c) Do you think the employer should be held liable for the injury suffered by Bill? Is Archie liable?
(d) Does the employer incur liability because he has a prankster in his employ?

Under the old common law, the lot of an employee injured on the job was not a happy one. The employer was obliged to compensate the employee only if it could be shown that the employer himself was negligent (1) in the provision of a safe place or system of work, or (2) in the selection of competent fellow employees. The common law also inferred that when the employee took service he assumed (unless he specifically contracted otherwise) the ordinary risks incident to the work carried on upon the employer's premises. Also, the servant could not hold the master liable for injuries caused by the negligence of a fellow servant, unless it could be shown that the master was negligent in that he knowingly employed an incompetent fellow servant.

This state of the law still survives in some of the common law provinces with respect to farm labourers, and domestic and menial servants.

C—21

Reister hired Cummings to assist him in harvesting his crop. The harvesting involved the use of a combine, and a grain loader mounted on a truck operated by Anderson. Cummings was instructed by Reister in the operation of the combine, but not in the operation of the grain loader. Nor did Anderson give Cummings any instructions in its use.

In the course of the work, Cummings was instructed by Reister to assist Anderson in the unloading of the truck at Reister's barn. While unloading, Anderson left Cummings alone in the truck box, with the machine still running, while he climbed into the barn loft to investigate the cause of some trouble with the unloading. Cummings claimed that Anderson, in adjusting the spout of the loader, drew it close to Cumming's side where it came into contract with his hand, severing two fingers. Reister and Ander-

son contended that Cummings suffered the accident as a result of his own negligence.
From the evidence the court found that Reister and Anderson were negligent in not warning Cummings of the dangerous character of a machine with which he had had no previous experience, and that Anderson was further negligent in leaving the machine running while Cummings was left alone with it. The court held that Cummings was also negligent in standing too near the loader and in allowing his left hand to be near enough to the machine to get caught. The degrees of fault were therefore set at 50% for Cummings and 50% for the defendants. Damages in the case were assessed at $3,248.60 of which Cummings, being 50% at fault, was given judgment against the defendants for $1,624.30.

(a) Why was Reister held liable?
(b) Why was Anderson held liable?
(c) Why was Cummings held partly responsible for his own injury?
(d) If Cummings had been given instruction in the use of the grain loader and warned about its dangerous features, might the accident have happened anyway? In that case would Reister and Anderson have been liable? Why or why not?

It has been held that the employer is not liable—except where statute law intervenes—when an employee is injured in an accident which is the result of something unforeseen, which had never happened before, and in connection with which the employer was not guilty of negligence.

C—22

Renner, employed by the defendants, operated from time to time a compressed-air spray apparatus. The air was pumped into the tank by hand. At the time of the accident, Renner was using the apparatus to spray whitewash. In the course of the work, the nozzle became clogged, and in the process of making it work the hose became loosened from the tank. Renner's face was sprayed with the whitewash liquid with the result that his eye was injured so seriously that it had to be removed. Renner sued, claiming that the defendants had not maintained their appliance in proper and safe condition, and that they had failed in their duty to inspect the spraying apparatus regularly. The defendants denied any negligence, contending that the sprayer had been operated satisfactorily by Renner for some time, and that they had no reason to anticipate that such an accident would happen.
The court found that Renner had used the apparatus for over a year in several operations (including spraying whitewash) and that he was more familiar with the appliance than were the defendants. Any loosening of the hose would have been just as apparent to Renner as it would have been to the defendants. Further, there was some reason to believe that the hose had come loose not as a result of air-pressure or defect, but as a result of Renner's putting undue tension on the hose when trying to find out what the trouble was when the spray had stopped. The trial judge exonerated the defendants from all charges of negligence,

on the grounds that they had no knowledge of the danger nor did he think they ought to have known. Moreover, he was of the opinion that Renner had had the same means of knowing of the danger that the defendants had, and consequently, could not recover. He therefore dismissed the action. On appeal to the Saskatchewan Court of Appeal, the appeal was also dismissed.

(a) Why were the defendants (the employers) not held liable for the accident?
(b) How does this case differ from C—21?

Gradually, over the years, the position of the employee has been improved by statutory requirements concerned with the safety and health of employees at work, culminating in the Workmen's Compensation Act, which set up a new basis for compensating injured employees.

Workmen's Compensation. Under the old common law the employee could recover damages for injuries suffered in the course of his employment *only* if he could prove that the employer was *personally* negligent. The result was often lengthy and costly litigation and consequent hardship to the employee. The Workmen's Compensation Act, passed in England in 1906, and within a few years enacted (with provincial variations) in all the provinces of Canada, has tremenduously improved the position of the employee injured in the course of his employment. It has eliminated costly litigation, ensured compensation for accidents, and secured promptness and certainty of payment without unduly burdening the employer, and at no direct cost to the employee. The most important provisions of the legislation are:

- A fund is provided and maintained by assessments against employers. No contributions are required from the employee.
- An employee, covered by the plan, who is injured in the course of his work, presents his claim immediately to the Workmen's Compensation Board. Claims are handled promptly and paid by the Board, thus avoiding possible costly and lengthy litigation through the courts.
- The injured employee is compensated for all medical expenses and for a substantial proportion of his loss of earnings.
- Where the employee is fatally injured, the widow and/or dependents receive benefits.
- The question of who is negligent does not affect the employee's right to compensation. If he was injured "on the job," he is eligible for benefits under the plan, no matter who was at fault. The only exception to this rule occurs when the accident is caused solely by the workman's wilful misconduct. Even this exception does not apply if the accident results in serious disablement or death.

Chiefly because of difficulties of administration, the benefits of the workmen's compensation plan as outlined above apply *only* to certain classifications of employment. Each province has set up its own particular schedules of coverage. Generally, all include the larger industrial and commercial enterprises; for example construction, manufacturing, transportation, mining, lumbering. A business must have not fewer than a specified number of employees in order to be eligible for coverage under the plan. The provinces keep the matter of coverage and benefits under constant review, and from time to time new classifications of employees are admitted and benefits are improved.

Employers' Liability Under the Act. Most of the provinces have added a second part to the Workmen's Compensation Act. This part applies to employees excluded for one reason or another from the benefits of the regular compensation plan. It provides that such employees are entitled *to recover from their employer* when personal injury is suffered by the employee by reason of defective machinery, unsafe conditions or systems of work, and dangerous premises used in the employer's business; or by negligence of the employer, or of any person in his service acting within the scope of his employment. Also, by simply continuing in his employment with knowledge of a danger involved, an employee is no longer deemed to have assumed the risk of injury, although the employee is expected to bring such danger to the attention of an employer who does not know of it. Nor is contributory negligence on the part of the employee a bar to recovering damages from his employer on a proportionate basis.

Although the employees to whom this second part of the Workmen's Compensation Act applies have been given a substantially improved position, their rights to recover from the employer can be enforced only by action through the courts.

Domestic and menial servants and, in some provinces, farm labourers, are excluded entirely from the provisions of the Act and, as we have already noted, the rights of these employees in the event of injury on the job are still subject to common law rules.

C—23

Neilsen was employed as a farm labourer on Redel's farm, and had been directed by Redel to feed bundles of clover through a feed cutter. The machine was old and had no self-feeder, the original one being beyond repair and obsolete. The machine could handle certain kinds of feed without being fed by hand, but not clover bundles, which had to be fed into the machine by hand.

Neilsen had warned his employer that the machine was not working well and that something should be done about it; nevertheless, the employer instructed Neilsen to use the machine—although under his supervision—and allowed him to continue feeding the bundles into the cutter by hand. In the course of this work, Neilsen's left arm was caught in the machine and cut off about three inches below the elbow.

Neilsen sued his employer, Redel, for damages, claiming that he had failed in his duty to provide safe conditions of work. Redel contended that Neilsen knew of the danger and that the injury was due to Neilsen's own negligence.

The court held that Redel had failed to provide safe and proper appliances and equipment, and that he had not fulfilled his duty to take reasonable care for the safety of his employee. The court therefore awarded damages to Neilsen. On appeal, this decision was affirmed.

(a) Who knew that the machine was not working properly?

(b) The employer argued that if Neilsen had been more careful there would not have been an accident. How did the court answer this argument?

(c) Why was Neilsen not covered by workmen's compensation?

The employer does not fulfil his obligation to provide a safe system of work simply by employing an independent contractor to whom he delegates the performance of the work.

C—24

Borgstrom had hired L to supply and operate a portable wood-sawing outfit to saw his wood. Borgstrom also employed Marshment to assist in the operation. At one interval in the course of the work, the saw was permitted to run free at such excessive speed that the fly-wheel on the apparatus burst and a section of it severely injured Marshment's leg. Marshment sued his employer Borgstrom claiming the injury was due to Borgstrom's failure to provide proper equipment and a safe system of work, and to select properly skilled persons to supervise the work. Borgstrom argued that he had hired L as an independent contractor to furnish and operate the equipment, and denied any personal responsibility for the accident.

The trial court found that the method of operating the saw was a defective system, and held that Borgstrom could not avoid liability, simply because he had hired an independent contractor to supply and operate the machinery. The employer was therefore held liable for damages.

This decision was reversed by the Court of Appeal of Ontario, but upon further appeal to the Supreme Court of Canada the judgment of the trial judge was restored.

(a) Who was in charge of the sawing operation at the time Marshment was hurt?
(b) Why was Borgstrom held liable for the injury?
(c) Why was Marshment not covered by workmen's compensation?
(d) Which of the court decisions about this case would have provided a precedent for similar cases occurring later?

Fatally Injured Employees. Under the old common law rules, only the injured party could enter an action for damages. Thus, if an employee died as the result of an accident, no one else could sue the employer, and the dependants of the fatally injured employee had no recourse against the employer. This situation has been remedied by the Fatal Accidents Act, which has been adopted in each province. This act provides that the dependants of a person (including an employee) whose death has been caused by another's negligence, may take legal action to recover damages for loss which they have suffered thereby. (If the employee is covered by workmen's compensation, no action can be taken under the Fatal Accidents Act; the dependants receive compensation under the provisions of the Workmen's Compensation Act).

THE MASTER'S LIABILITY TO THIRD PARTIES FOR ACTS HIS SERVANT

C—25

Riley, was employed by Finnegan as a waiter in Finnegan's hotel. One day, when Finnegan was absent from the hotel, S, a customer, became objectionable and quarrelsome in the ladies' beverage

room. As a result of an altercation between S and Riley, S sued both Riley and Finnegan for damages for assault, and recovered judgment against both (Finnegan was held liable for his servant's tort). Finnegan paid the judgment and costs, and later brought action against Riley for indemnification, claiming that the assault committed by Riley was unauthorized and contrary to his instructions. Riley's defence was that he was only carrying out his duty according to his interpretation of his instructions.
The Ontario Court of Appeal held that the employee, Riley, had been clearly guilty of an assault upon S. The court also held that Finnegan, the employer, who was not present at the time of the assault, had not given any instructions, either personally or through any agent, that would have justified Riley in committing such an assault. The court therefore held that Riley must indemnify Finnegan, his employer, for the judgment Finnegan had paid.

(a) If Finnegan, the employer, was not on the scene when the assault occurred, why was he liable to S?
(b) Does it make any difference to the employee's liability to S whether Riley was carrying out his employer's instructions or not?
(c) If Riley had been carrying out his employer's instructions, do you think Riley would have had to indemnify Finnegan?

Windsor Ontario Police Department photo

When an employee through carelessness causes injury or loss to third parties, the employee incurs personal liability for his tort, since it is he who has caused the injury or loss. At the same time, it is a common law rule that if the negligent act occurs while the employee is carrying out duties that are in the course of his employment, the employer is also liable. The injured party may elect which of them he will sue, or he may sue both together. If the employer pays the damages, he is entitled to be indemnified by the employee.

If the unlawful or negligent act is committed in circumstances in which the employee is not acting within the scope of his employment, the employer is not liable and action may be taken only against the employee.

C—26

Wallace, an engineer employed by Viking Sprinkler Company, was frequently sent out of town on his company's business. Wallace used his own car, and was paid for its use on the basis of what the rail fare would be to the place visited. When returning from Peterborough after completing work for his company, he caused an accident.

The plaintiff, Hoar, sued both Wallace and his employer, and obtained judgment against both. The employer appealed the decision against himself on the grounds that at the time the accident occurred, his employee was not acting within the scope of his employment. The Ontario Court of Appeal found that Wallace, having completed his work, was free to return home as he pleased without any control or direction from his employer as to route, mode or time of transportation, and that at the time of the accident he was not engaged in the course of his employment. On these grounds the court (with one judge dissenting) allowed the appeal.

(a) Why in this case did the court not hold the employer liable for the damage and loss caused by their servant Wallace?
(b) If the company (the employer) is not liable, who is?
(c) Would the court's decision have been different if Wallace had been driving a company car?

If, in the above case, the automobile had been owned by the employer, the outcome of the case might have been different. The Highway Traffic Acts of the various provinces provide that full responsibility for damages due to the negligent operating of a motor vehicle on a highway rests on the owner as well as on the driver. Thus, if an employee in operating his employer's truck or other motor vehicle *on a highway* causes damage or injury through negligence or recklessness, the employer-owner as well as the employee-driver is liable, whether or not the act was done within the actual scope of the employee's work. The owner is not liable, however, if the vehicle is in the possession of the driver without the owner's consent. Also, if the accident occurs when the vehicle is elsewhere than on a public highway, the Highway Traffic Act does not apply, and the liability of the employer-owner is then subject to the law of master and servant.

C—27

Raitar Transport employed James Roach as a chauffeur to operate their truck. In the course of his work, Roach was liable to be called out to drive the truck at any hour in an emergency, and had access to the truck at all times. At the same time, Roach had instructions that he was not to drive the truck without permission or outside of working hours. On one occasion, however, Roach, who had been drinking, took the truck without permission and contrary to instructions, and at about 1:00 a.m. on a Sunday was the cause of an accident in which Clayton was injured. Clayton sued both the driver and the owner of the truck. The owner, in defence, argued that Roach was driving the truck on a day outside the period of his employment, and at a time he could not be said to be their chauffeur.

After considering all the evidence, the court found that Roach was the company's chauffeur, in that he was in possession of the vehicle with their consent, even though at the time he was disregarding his employers' instructions. The court held that under the Highway Traffic Act the owners of the vehicle were absolutely liable for the negligent operation of the vehicle by their chauffeur.

(a) On what grounds did the court decide that the driver was in possession of the truck with the owner's consent?
(b) If the company had to pay for the damage, would the driver be free from legal liability in the matter?

TERMINATING THE CONTRACT OF EMPLOYMENT

A contract of employment may be terminated through its own terms, as, for example, when the specified term of employment has expired or the work agreed upon has been completed. It may also be discharged, as in the case of other contracts, by mutual agreement or by impossibility of performance.

Where the contract of service is for an indefinite period, it may be terminated by giving notice. Certain circumstances, however, may justify terminating a contract without notice.

TERMINATION WITH NOTICE

C—28

Carson, a university student, had been hired by the Dairy and Poultry Pool for general, unskilled maintenance work at a monthly salary to be paid twice monthly. There was no specified period of employment agreed upon and no agreement regarding the period of notice to be given for either quitting or dismissal. After being employed for a short time, Carson was given one week's notice of dismissal. Carson protested that this was not sufficient, and demanded either two week's notice or two weeks' pay in lieu of notice. The employer, instead, offered him one week's pay in lieu of notice. Carson refused this offer and sued for damages for wrongful dismissal.

The court held that under the circumstances one week's notice was reasonable, considering the character of the employment, the length of service of the employee, and the availability of similar employment, having regard to the age, experience and qualifications of the employee.

(a) Why do you think Carson believed he was entitled to two weeks' notice?
(b) On what grounds did the court rule that one week's notice was reasonable?

The common law rule as to time of notice is that either party is entitled to reasonable notice. What is "reasonable" must be decided with reference to each particular case, having regard to all the circumstances. Unless conditions of employment imply otherwise, hiring at an hourly, daily, weekly or monthly rate generally—but not always—implies that a similar period of notice is reasonable, even though wages are paid at different intervals. Usually, when employment is at an annual rate, three to six month's notice is considered reasonable, but in some cases it may be more.

Instead of giving notice, the employer may dismiss an employee immediately by paying him wages for the period of notice to which he is entitled. The employee may not, however, quit without notice by offering a similar amount to his employer.

TERMINATION WITHOUT NOTICE

C—29

Doeing had been employed as a taxicab driver by Wagner, who operated a taxicab business. At the time of the hiring, nothing was said about the term of employment. Wagner followed the practice of paying all his taxicab drivers each Saturday night on a weekly basis for a term commencing on Sunday and terminating on the following Saturday. After a few weeks of employment, Doeing quit his job on a Wednesday night without notice. Wagner refused to pay him wages for the period from Sunday to Wednesday unless Doeing completed the week's service.

Doeing entered a claim in Magistrate's Court to recover wages for the period in dispute, and won a judgment in his favour. Wagner appealed the decision to the Saskatchewan District Court and this court found that Doeing had quit his employment without lawful excuse or proper notice, and (reversing the decision of the magistrate's court) held that he was not entitled to any payment following the end of the last period for which wages were due and payable.

(a) In what way was Doeing guilty of breach of contract?
(b) What were the consequences?

An employer may dismiss an employee without notice *with wages to the date of dismissal* for dishonesty, incompetency, misconduct, negligence, or absenting himself without permission. The employee may also quit without notice and is entitled to wages to the date of quitting if the employer tries to enforce unreasonable orders or fails to maintain safe machinery and appliances with which to work. If the employee quits *between pay periods* without notice and without lawful excuse, the employer is liable for wages only up to the end of the last period for which wages were due and payable.

If an employee is wrongfully dismissed, the employer is liable for damages for breach of contract. Generally, the amount of damages includes wages for the required time of notice less what the employee has earned during this particular period at other work, or what he might have earned if he had made reasonably diligent efforts to obtain work, plus reasonable expenses incurred in the obtaining of new employment.

C—30

Woods was employed as a clerk-typist at the Miramichi hospital. She had been hired for an indefinite period at a monthly salary paid on a monthly basis, and had been in the employ of the hospital for a number of years. Through no fault of her own, Woods failed to appear for work on a day when she was needed for important work. When she returned to work she and the administrator quarrelled about the matter of the absence. During the argument Woods defied the administrator to fire her, whereupon she was abruptly dismissed. She then sued for damages for wrongful dismissal. The court found she was wrongfully dismissed, without justifiable cause and without notice, and held that four month's notice would have been reasonable. The court therefore gave judgment for four month's wages in lieu of notice. On appeal, the New Brunswick Court of Appeal upheld the decision with regard to wrongful dismissal but the Appeal Court reduced the judgment for damages to one month's wages, on the grounds that new employment would not be difficult to obtain for a person of the plaintiff's qualifications, and that one month's notice would have been reasonable and sufficient.

(a) For what reasons may an employee be dismissed without notice? Is an argument with "the boss" sufficient reason?
(b) What things did the appeal court take into consideration when determining what would be reasonable notice?

An employee has a duty to his employer to be faithful and honest, and is under an implied obligation not to use for his own purposes or to disclose to others, either during his employment or after he leaves that employment, any special information or knowledge of secret processes he acquires during his employment.

C—31

For four or five months preceding his resignation, Hawkins, while receiving his salary regularly, had been making arrangements, without his employer's knowledge, to take employment with a competitor of his employer. During that period, Hawkins also extracted information from his employer's files which would be useful to him in his new employment. When his plan was discovered, Hawkins immediately resigned.
The employer then sued Hawkins to recover the salary paid to him for the five month's prior to his resignation. The court found that Hawkins had failed in his duty to be faithful and honest in his dealings with his employer, and that for the latter part of his

employment he had not given full and satisfactory service. The court held Hawkins liable to compensate his employer for breach of duty, but assessed the damages at about one-third of the employer's claim.

(a) On what grounds did the employer sue Hawkins for his last five months' salary?
(b) In what way was Hawkins' scheme dishonest?

Under common law an agreement for personal services cannot be specifically enforced. Therefore, the employee cannot compel the employer to take him back, nor can the employer compel the employee to return to his employ, the only remedy being to recover damages for breach of contract. But as we have seen, this common law rule has been superseded to some extent by statute law relating to collective bargaining agreements.

RECOVERY OF WAGES

A claim for wages is a civil matter that would ordinarily be processed through the civil courts. However, the schedule of sittings of the civil courts would cause a delay in settlement which in many cases would be a hardship to the employee. To avoid this hardship, legislation exists in most provinces which provides that actions to recover wages may be heard in magistrate's court, which sits daily.

UNEMPLOYMENT INSURANCE

This legislation was passed by the federal parliament and applies to all Canada. It is entirely outside the jurisdiction of the provinces.

The Act includes all general industrial undertakings. Occupations which by their nature or location would raise difficult problems of administration are excepted from the regulations.

Where the Act applies, it is compulsory that the employer and the employee make regular contributions to the fund according to the statutory schedule. The federal government also contributes to the fund and bears the cost of administration.

The Act provides for the payment of benefits to unemployed persons who are qualified according to the regulations. Employees may be disqualified from receiving benefits for the following reasons:

- Loss of work due to misconduct.
- Voluntarily leaving the job without justifiable cause.
- A labour dispute in which the employee is directly involved.
- Unwillingness to accept suitable employment.

The Unemployment Insurance Commission has established courts of referees to handle claims that cannot be adjusted through the regular offices.

APPLYING THE LAW

1.

This illustration depicts a nasty accident. What would be the workman's legal rights to compensation for injuries, in each of the following circumstances:

(a) The two painters were independent contractors doing the work on a contract basis.

(b) The two painters were employed by a contractor in the painting and decorating business who regularly employed a force of 20 to 30 workmen.

(c) The two painters had been employed at an hourly rate by the owner of the house, who supplied paint, ladders, etc., and who directed and controlled their work.

2. Assuming that the victim of the accident in this illustration is not a trespasser, explain the liability of (a) the employer; (b) the employee.

3. Pete, a delivery-truck driver, on his way back from making a delivery, stopped at a shopping center on a personal errand. When parking the truck in the parking lot Pete damaged a car. Explain the liability of both Pete and his employer for the damage to the car.
4. Bennett, who is employed by a large construction firm, is seriously injured while at work in an accident which is clearly the fault of another workman. Bennett will be hospitalized for months and may never again be able to resume his old job.
   (a) Is Bennett's employment one which is usually covered by workmen's compensation?
   (b) What difference does it make whether Bennett is covered by workmen's compensation or not?

DISCUSSION AND PROJECTS

1. Under the headings given below discuss how the lot of the worker as it existed under the old common law rules has been bettered by modern legislation:
   (a) Contracts between labour unions and employers.
   (b) Conditions of work (safety, health, etc.).
   (c) Compensation for injuries suffered in the course of employment.
2. Can discrimination in the field of industry and business be eliminated by legislation? Find out from your provincial Department of Labour what legislation exists for that purpose.
3. Consult the Canada Year Book for information on the amount paid out in your province for workmen's compensation.
4. Have one of your class or group obtain a Department of Labour explanatory pamphlet and a set of application forms for workmen's compensation. Circulate these among you for careful reading.
5. (Optional). Has one of your family or acquaintance ever received workmen's compensation? If so, you may care to tell your colleagues what you know of the circumstances—the nature of the accident, the amount of benefit received and the steps required to qualify.

UNIT NINE
BUYING AND SELLING GOODS

Part 20
ABSOLUTE SALES OF PERSONAL PROPERTY

THE SALE OF GOODS ACT

Up to the end of the nineteenth century our law concerning sales of goods was found in the voluminous body of case law (mostly English) which had accumulated over the years. By that time the common law rules for this type of contract had been well established. At the same time the growth of commerce and industry had created an obvious and increasing need to organize the law concerning sales of goods into a logical and simplified pattern. To meet this need, in 1893 England passed the Sale of Goods Act, which was a codification of the existing common law rules on the sale of goods and personal property.

Within a few years all the common law provinces of Canada had adopted the English Act almost word for word. Other parts of the British Empire also adopted the Act so that we can now find it in force in many parts of the world. In the United States the Uniform Sales Act, which has been adopted by most of the states and which came into effect shortly after the turn of the twentieth century, was closely patterned after the English codification. In Quebec, sales are governed by the Quebec Civil Code. On some points of law concerning the sale of goods, the Civil Code agrees with the English law, but on many points it is different.

In this Unit we shall attempt to present the law only as it applies in the common law provinces.

NATURE OF A SALE OF GOODS

The Sale of Goods Act defines a contract for the sale of goods as an agreement whereby the seller transfers or agrees to transfer to the buyer the ownership of the goods for a money consideration called the price.

The following examples illustrate the difference between a sale and other contracts related to the exchange of goods.

Example 1: A sells his car to B for $1,000 cash and transfers the owner's permit accordingly. This is a transfer of the ownership of goods for a money consideration and is a sale which comes under the Sale of Goods Act.

Example 2: In answer to a newspaper advertisement reading, "Will trade car, value $1,000, for hard-top camper or small trailer," X accepts Y's sports-car in exchange for a camper-trailer. Such a transaction does not constitute a sale since the goods are not exchanged for a money consideration. An exchange of goods for other goods is known as *barter*, and does not come under the Sale of Goods Act.

Example 3: Novelties Limited sends a shipment of Christmas toys to Thompson Hardware. The arrangement is that Thompson Hardware does not purchase the goods—they are still owned by Novelties Limited—but sells them on a commission basis, and at the end of the season will return the unsold goods to Novelties Limited.

This type of transaction is known as selling *on consignment*. Since the ownership of the goods is not transferred from the seller to the buyer, it is not a sale in terms of the Sale of Goods Act.

Under the Act, the term *goods* means personal chattels—tangible, moveable things, but not shares of stock, or bonds, or negotiable instruments, or money. Real property, which includes all rights or interests in lands, and buildings and other things which are attached to the land, does not come under the Sale of Goods Act.

Contracts for *work and labour* must also be distinguished from contracts of sale. Generally, where a person agrees to make an article for sale to another, the maker supplying the materials, the agreement is a contract of sale. However, if the materials are merely incidental to the whole contract, the contract may be considered substantially as one of work and labour, and not subject to the provisions of the Sale of Goods Act; for example, where in a contract for repairs to a car, the repairer may supply some new parts. The distinction is often very difficult to determine.

REQUIREMENT OF A WRITTEN MEMORANDUM

CASE 1

Winfield entered into an oral agreement to sell his motor boat to Stewart, the boat being left at Winfield's mooring location at Stewart's request. On one or more occasions Stewart took out pleasure parties in the boat. Two months later, Stewart attempted to repudiate his agreement and Winfield sued.

Stewart set up as a defence the fact that the agreement was not in writing. The court, however, held that the act of using the boat as Stewart had done was sufficient acceptance under the Sale of Goods Act and that no memorandum in writing was now required. Judgment was given in favour of Winfield.

(a) What did Stewart do which the court considered implied that he had accepted the boat?
(b) If Stewart had never used the boat do you think the decision would have been different?

The original English Sale of Goods Act included a section taken from the English Statute of Frauds. The Canadian provinces adopted the same provisions.

The section concerned provides that a contract for the sale of goods of a certain value (Ontario, New Brunswick and Nova Scotia have specified $40 or more; Prince Edward Island, $30 or more; and the other provinces, $50 or more) is not enforceable at law unless one of the following conditions has been met:

- Some note or memorandum of the contract has been made in writing and signed by the party to be charged or his agent, or
- Part or all of the goods have been accepted by the buyer, or
- The goods have been wholly or partly paid for or some consideration has been given to bind the bargain.

In 1954 the English Sale of Goods Act was amended by deleting this particular section. Of the Canadian provinces, only British Columbia (at the time of this writing) has made the same amendment.

We may here refer back to the description of a contract of *work and labour*, and point out again that such contracts do not come under the Sale of Goods Act. For that reason, the section we have just quoted above does not apply to contracts of work and labour, and a memorandum in writing is not required to make such a contract enforceable.

DELIVERY, ACCEPTANCE AND PAYMENT

C—2

A, wishing to sell his piano, places the following advertisement in his local newspaper.

FOR SALE. Upright piano in excellent condition. $250. Call 555-5555.

B makes a hurried call at A's residence to look at the piano, accepts it and gives A a deposit of $5 to bind the bargain. At the time, nothing is said about who is to pay the cost of delivery (a piano mover may charge up to $20 for moving it), nor is there any agreement about when and how the full payment is to be made.

(a) May B take for granted that A will look after the delivery?
(b) May B assume that he will be allowed to pay for the piano over a period of time?

One important fact is here emphasized: the Sale of Goods Act has not removed the right of the contracting parties to make their own conditions of sale. This is clearly indicated by the wording of the clauses of the Act, which usually begin by "Unless otherwise agreed" or "In the absence of an express or implied agreement to the contrary" or some other words to that effect. However, where the parties do not make their own conditions, the rules of the Sale of Goods Act apply.

DELIVERY

The Sale of Goods Act provides that in the absence of an express or implied contract to the contrary, the seller does not have to send the goods to the buyer. The buyer takes delivery at the seller's place of business or at the place where the goods are when the sale is made and any delivery expense is to be borne by the buyer.

In cases where the seller agrees to send the goods to the buyer, two types of contracts are common: f.o.b., and c.i.f.

f.o.b. contracts. The letters f.o.b. stand for "free on board." For example, a car is advertised as follows:

PINTO, $2,180* F.O.B. Oakville. *Manufacturer's suggested retail price.

This means that the seller agrees to bear whatever cost of transportation is necessary to place the goods into the hands of a transportation agency at Oakville. Unless agreed otherwise, the buyer accepts the goods at that point and becomes the owner. From that point on any risk of loss to the goods is to be borne by the buyer—subject, of course, to any liability for the loss on the part of the transportation agency.

c.i.f. contracts. The letters c.i.f. stand for "cost, insurance and freight." Under a c.i.f. contract the seller ships the goods and charges the buyer for the price of the goods plus freight to the point of destination, and the cost of insuring the goods during transit. The insurance policy is made in favour of the buyer and is forwarded to him. Unless agreed otherwise, the risk attached to the goods passes to the buyer at the time shipment is made.

ACCEPTANCE

C—3

Belick and Naiman agreed to buy from Goodwin Tanners a certain number of hides described by the sellers as being of No. 1 and No. 2 grades, delivery to be taken at the premises of Canada Packers where the hides were then stored. The buyers did not make arrangements to inspect the hides at Canada Packers, since they had never had any previous dealings with that firm and did not know if inspection facilities were available there or if, in fact, they would be permitted to inspect the goods there.

As soon as the hides had been taken to the buyer's premises they were inspected. The buyers then found that the greater part of the hides were of a lower grade than that described by the sellers, and notified the sellers by telephone that they were not accepting the hides. Next day they confirmed this telephone call by letter in which they requested the sellers to "pick up the hides as soon as possible." The sellers made no reply to this letter, and the buyers then took the hides to the seller's place of business. The sellers, however, refused to take them back.

Subsequently, the sellers sued for the price of the hides claiming that as a result of the buyers' taking delivery of the hides at Canada Packers, the buyers had accepted the hides so as to make the contract binding, and property in the goods having passed to the buyers, they could not now repudiate the contract. On the other hand the buyers contended that there was no agreement that they would not have a reasonable opportunity of examining the hides before accepting them, and that when they did examine them, the hides were not according to the description agreed to in the contract.

The Ontario Court of Appeal held that according to the Sale of Goods Act, (1) the buyers were entitled to a reasonable opportunity of examining the hides to ascertain if they were according to the contract and, in the circumstances, were justified in taking the hides to their own premises for inspection; (2) the contract of sale implied a condition that the hides would correspond with the description—which they did not; and (3) a breach of the implied condition gave the buyers a right to refuse to accept the hides. The buyers were also allowed their counterclaim for the expense incurred in transporting the hides to the sellers premises and back.

(a) The sellers argued that by taking the hides from Canada Packers premises and transporting them to their own premises, the buyers had accepted the hides. What was the court's answer to that argument?
(b) If the buyers had examined the hides at Canada Packers and then transported them to their own premises, what decision would you expect?

C—4

G. A. Grier and Sons agreed to purchase the whole output of the Alkins Bros. sawmill for the sawing season of 1920, delivery to be taken at Callendar. Grier & Sons did not examine the lumber at Callendar although they had a reasonable opportunity to do so. Grier then resold some of the lumber and had it shipped from Callendar to dealers in Toronto and Montreal, but these latter complained of its quality. Grier & Sons then attempted to reject the lumber contending that they were not bound to pay for it because of its very poor quality.

The Ontario Court of Appeal (affirming the decision of the trial court) held that by failing to exercise their right to examine the lumber at Callendar (at which time the defects could have been easily discovered), Grier had waived any right to reject the lumber later; and further, that the act of reselling the lumber and having it transported to other places constituted an acceptance of the contract. Therefore there was an acceptance of the lumber by G. A. Grier & Sons in accordance with the provisions of the Sale of Goods Act, and a waiver of any right to reject it—but without prejudice to Grier's right to damages for breach of warranty of quality.

(a) Why did the buyers, after reselling the lumber, try to reject it?
(b) Why did the court rule that the buyers could not reject the lumber?
(c) What other remedy was open to the buyers?

There is an acceptance of goods according to the Sale of Goods Act if the buyer receives the goods and/or does any act in relation to the goods which would infer that the ownership had passed from seller to buyer. At the same time, the buyer is entitled to a reasonable opportunity to examine the goods to see if they are according to the contract, and he may reject them if they are not.

PAYMENT

C—5

Northern Fuel Co. took delivery of a shipment of 146 cords of wood from McCutcheon. According to the company, no contract in respect of either quantity or price had been made for the wood, but Northern accepted the shipment following a custom of paying the dealer the market price less the amount of freight paid by the buyer on taking delivery. Northern fuel disposed of the wood and offered McCutcheon $3.65 per cord less the freight cost. McCutcheon refused this offer and sued for a higher price. The company then paid the amount of their offer into court pending the outcome of the action.

The trial court ruled that McCutcheon was entitled to recover only the amount paid into court, whereupon McCutcheon appealed that decision. The Manitoba Court of Appeal applied the principle that where no specific price has been agreed upon, the reasonable market price should be paid. Evidence was produced to show that at the time the wood was received a reasonable market price was $4.50 a cord less freight, and judgment was given in favour of McCutcheon accordingly.

(a) What was the point of dispute in this case?
(b) Why did the company pay the amount of their offer into court?
(c) What rule of law did the court invoke to settle the case?

The Sale of Goods Act provides that, in the absence of an agreement expressing or implying a different intention, payment is to be made at the time the goods are delivered. If the contract fails to fix a price, it is implied that the buyer will pay what is reasonable.

DEPOSIT ON PURCHASES

C—6

Stevenson contracted with Colonial Homes Ltd. for the purchase of a prefabricated cottage, and made a down payment of $1,000 according to a clause in the printed contract which read:

> *"Payment to be made as follows: $1.000 as down payment and the balance of funds . . . $1,206.00 . . . as follows: . . . ."*

The clause shown above was in printed form except for the insertion in handwriting of the amount of the balance, and was followed by Stevenson's signature. Subsequently, a dispute arose between Stevenson and the company about the inclusion of ceilings in the cottage. As a result, Stevenson refused to take delivery, and claimed a refund of the down payment subject to any right of the defendant for damages for breach of contract. The company argued that it was entitled to retain the whole $1,000 as a deposit which had been forfeited by the buyer for breach of contract; and as proof that the payment was given as a deposit, pointed to printed words "Deposit Rec'd" in a box on the printed form headed "For Head Office Use Only."

The Ontario Court of Appeal found that in refusing to take delivery Stevenson was in breach of contract. They also found that the blanks in the box marked "For Head Office Use Only" were not filled in at the time the contract was signed by the buyer, and that he had no other intention than that the $1,000 was to be a down payment as indicated in the contract above his signature. The court therefore held that the payment was a part payment and not just a deposit, and that Stevenson was entitled to its reurn *subject* to the company's claim for damages for breach of contract.

(a) Why did Stevenson refuse to take delivery of the prefabricated cottage?
(b) In view of the reason for (a), above, why do you think the court ruled that refusal to take delivery was a breach of contract?
(c) Why did the court consider the $1,000 as a down payment rather than a deposit?
(d) Suppose the contract contained a clause which read: "In the event of default on this contract, it is agreed that any and all payments made by the purchaser shall be forfeited to the seller as liquidated damages." How might the case have been decided?

Whether or not a deposit made on a contract of sale can be considered a down payment, or—in the event of the buyer's default—liquidated damages, depends upon the intention of the parties to the contract. If it is intended as security for the performance of the contract, on default by the buyer the deposit is forfeited to the seller as liquidated damages; if it is intended to be a down payment, the seller would be entitled to keep only so much of it as to cover the damages to which he is entitled. On the other hand, if the seller defaults so that the buyer is entitled to repudiate the contract, the buyer has a right to recover his deposit.

TRANSFER OF OWNERSHIP AND RISK OF LOSS

C—7

FOR SALE. Fabulous 19" Zenith Color TV with UHF, $338. Terms. Phone 111-222

McAdam answers the above advertisement, goes to see the TV

and accepts it at the price offered. Terms of payment are arranged but no money is paid at that time. The seller agrees to deliver the TV the next day.

(a) According to the facts as given, who has title to the TV at this point?
(b) If the TV were stolen before delivery, would McAdam be still liable to pay for it?

As a general rule, the risk of loss in connection with personal property rests on the owner. Therefore, in a transaction where goods are to be transferred from one person to another by sale, it is important to be able to determine when ownership or "title" to the goods passes from seller to buyer.

Where the intention of the parties has been clearly expressed or implied on this point, such intention will govern. When, however, the intention is not clear, the rules of the Sale of Goods Act prevail. The rules make a distinction between specific goods and unascertained or future goods.

Specific goods, also called ascertained good, are articles which have been identified and set aside for the buyer; for example, where a buyer selects certain planks from a pile of lumber and has them set aside for him.

Unascertained goods are articles not yet specifically selected by or for the buyer and set aside for him; for example, where a buyer orders a quantity of lumber out of a pile but has not yet selected any particular pieces. Future goods are goods not yet in existence but which are to be manufactured, produced, or acquired at a future time.

TITLE TO SPECIFIC OR ASCERTAINED GOODS

1. When a contract for the sale of goods in a deliverable state contains no conditions to the contrary, the ownership of the goods passes *at the time the contract is made*. It is immaterial whether or not delivery or payment is to take place at some future date.

C—8

Beardmore purchased a quantity of tan bark from Craig. At the time the contract was signed, the bark was lying in the bush some 14 miles from the railway siding where it was to be delivered for shipment by rail to the buyers. The bark had already been measured and classified where it lay in the bush, ready for delivery to the railway; and a payment on account had been made by Beardmore. Subsequently, a large portion of the bark was drawn to the railway siding and some of it was loaded on cars while the rest remained in the yard because the railway company refused to ship any more bark to Beardmore for the reason that Beardmore's railway siding was filled with cars which they were unable to unload.

About a month later all the tan bark which remained in the yard, not loaded into cars, was destroyed by fire. The buyers refused to pay for the bark which had been burned. Craig sued, claiming that the title to the bark had passed to Beardmore at the time the contract was made. Beardmore contended that title to the

bark did not pass until it had been loaded on the cars which, in the case of the bark that had been destroyed, had not been done.
The court found that there was no intention, expressed or implied, on the part of either party to indicate that the ownership had not passed at the time the contract was made. The bark had already been measured, classified, and accepted by the buyers when it was still in the bush ready for delivery, and the court held that "where there is an unconditional contract for the sale of specific goods in a deliverable state, the property in the goods passes to the buyer when the contract is made; and it is immaterial whether the time of payment or the time of delivery or both be postponed." Judgment was therefore given for the sellers and the buyers were required to pay for the bark which had been destroyed.

(a) Whose fault was it that some of the bark had to remain in the railway yard?
(b) Why did the court rule that the purchasers owned the bark that was destroyed?
(c) If the contract had stated the price of the bark was f.o.b. Railway Siding (the siding from which the bark was to be shipped by railway to the purchaser,) what do you think the decision would have been?

2. If the seller has to do anything to put the goods into a deliverable state, or if anything has to be done to ascertain the price, such as weighing or measuring the goods, title to the goods does not pass until such work or act is done and the buyer is notified of it.

C—9

McDill agreed to buy certain specific pieces of furniture from Hillson. Because the furniture was chipped and scratched, the agreement was that Hillson would have the furniture French-polished before delivery. However, this could not be done right away as the polisher was on strike. McDill paid a deposit and some time later paid the balance of the price even though the goods were not yet ready for delivery. Before the polishing was done, the furniture in question was destroyed by fire. McDill sued for the return of the purchase price, but Hillson refused, claiming that the payment of the price by McDill had completed the sale so that title and ownership to the goods had passed to him. The polishing, he claimed, was a collateral agreement and not part of the contract of sale.
The Manitoba Court of Appeal found that at the time the contract was made the goods were not in a deliverable state, and that there was nothing express or implied in the terms of the contract to indicate that the parties intended the title to the furniture to pass before it was polished. Further, the payment of the purchase price did not of itself pass title to the goods unless it was the intention of the parties that it should do so, and clearly this was not inferred by the circumstances in this case. On these grounds the court held that McDill was entitled to the return of his money.

(a) On what grounds did Hillson, the seller, claim that McDill, the purchaser, owned the furniture?
(b) On what grounds did the court deny Hillson's claim?

3. When goods are delivered to the buyer on approval or trial, the ownership does not pass to the buyer until he expresses his approval to the seller, or does some act which indicates his intention of adopting the transaction, such as retaining the goods an unreasonable time or beyond the time fixed by the agreement. Unless it is otherwise agreed, loss of or damage to the goods while in the buyer's possession does not make the buyer liable to pay for the goods unless the loss or damage was due to the fault of the buyer.

C—10

Laurin forwarded a quantity of stamps to Ginn on the understanding that Ginn would return them if not satisfactory. While in Ginn's possession the stamps were stolen. Subsequently, Ginn was asked to pay for the stamps, but refused. Laurin then sued for the price. The court held that Ginn had not kept the stamps beyond a reasonable time, and that the stamps were stolen through no fault of his. Ownership of the stamps had not passed to Ginn and since the stamps were Laurin's property at the time they were stolen, Laurin must bear the loss.

(a) At the time the stamps were stolen, who owned them?
(b) Had Ginn given any guarantee for the safety of the stamps?
(c) If it was evident that the stamps were stolen because of Ginn's negligence, how would that affect Ginn's liability?

TITLE TO UNASCERTAINED AND FUTURE GOODS

Examples of unascertained goods are "so many tons of coal out of a pile," or "so many gallons of oil out of a tank." They may also be articles ordered by the buyer out of a number of identical articles carried in stock by the seller. An example of future goods could be a quantity of automobile parts to be manufactured; or next season's apples from a certain orchard.

The rule with respect to unascertained and future goods is that the title to the goods does not pass to the buyer until the goods have been definitely identified or selected, and "appropriated" to the buyer; that is, either set aside for the buyer so that the seller is no longer able to substitute other goods for delivery, or delivered to the buyer, or to a carrier for him. In other words, the title to unascertained goods does not pass until the goods have become specific and ascertained.

C—11

In October of 1957 Marsh bought certain nursery stock from Caradoc Nurseries Ltd. Delivery was not made until April of 1958, at which time the buyer refused to accept delivery, claiming that the contract called for delivery in the fall of '57. The seller sued for the price.

The trial court found that the contract was for spring delivery, and gave judgment to the nursery for the price.

Marsh appealed this decision, and the question was raised whether or not, under the contract, the property to the goods had passed to the buyer. The Ontario Court of Appeal, affirming the judgment of the trial court, held that "the plaintiff's (the nursery company's) appropriation (of the goods to the defendant) was not final when the goods were selected, nor when loaded for delivery and being carried to the buyer's house. The plaintiff could have recalled the goods at any time before they were tendered for delivery, but when they were tendered, the appropriation became unconditional." The title to the goods had therefore passed to Marsh, and the company was entitled to recover the price.

(a) What was the question to be decided by the Court of Appeal?
(b) What does "appropriated to the buyer" mean?
(c) At what point in the transaction had the goods become appropriated to the buyer?

C—12

Danforth Wine Co. entered into a contract with Orr for a specific number of tons of No. 1 grapes. At the time of the contract, the grapes were still on the vines, not having matured, and at that time were of No. 1 quality. Delivery was to be made between the dates of October 7 and Ocober 18. On October 7, and before the grapes were picked, the grapes were damaged by a severe frost. Nevertheless, Orr picked a quantity of grapes and tendered them to the company at New Toronto. The company refused to accept the grapes because of their damaged condition. Orr then sued for the price.

The question to be determined by the court was whether or not the property to the grapes had passed to the company at the time of the making of the contract. The Ontario Court of Appeal ruled that there had not been a transfer of the ownership of the grapes at the time the contract was executed, and that the grapes were still the property of Orr and at his risk when the frost occurred. The court based its decision on the following facts: (1) The contract was not for the whole crop, but only for a specified quantity which could not be ascertained until the grapes were severed from the vines. (2) Before delivery, certain things had to be done by the seller—picking, packing and weighing, etc.,—and the grapes to be delivered could not be ascertained and appropriated to the buyer until this had been done. (3) According to the Sale of Goods Act, the goods are at the seller's risk—in the absence of an agreement otherwise—until the property to the goods passes to the buyer, and if there is a sale by description of unascertained goods, no property to the goods is transferred to the buyer until the goods are ascertained and unconditionally appropriated to the contract. The court therefore held that Orr could not recover the price.

(a) Why were the grapes ordered by the wine company still unascertained goods while they were on the vines?
(b) Why did the buyer refuse to accept the grapes?

CONDITIONS AND WARRANTIES

"Conditions" and "Warranties" are simply terms of a contract. A condition is a term so essential to the contract that failure to fulfil the condition amounts virtually to non-performance of the whole agreement. A warranty is not such an essential term, and failure to observe it does not nullify the main purpose of the contract.

C—13

(i) Marshall needs a utility trailer that will carry heavy loads. He buys one guaranteed to have a load capacity of 1,500 pounds. The first time Marshall uses the trailer he intends to transport fifteen 80-pound bags of fertilizer to a customer. However, when ten sacks have been placed in the trailer, he notices that the frame begins to give way. Marshall then realizes that the load capacity of the trailer is far less than that guaranteed.

(ii) Jessop buys an Electro dehumidifier. Attached to the appliance is a small brochure of instructions which also contains the following:

> *Electro guarantees to the original owner free service on any defect that develops in normal use within one year from date of purchase. . . .*

After being used for three months the dehumidifier suddenly fails to function.

(a) In which of the foregoing cases is the guarantee a "condition"? In which is it a "warranty"?
(b) What would be the buyer's remedy in each case?

Although it is not always easy to distinguish between terms which are conditions and those which are merely warranties, the distinction is important. Breach of condition entitles the injured party to repudiate the entire contract and possibly to sue for damages as well; breach of warranty entitles the injured party to sue only for damages but not to repudiate the entire contract.

According to the Sale of Goods Act, if the buyer has accepted and kept the goods for an unreasonable time, or used the goods in such a way as to indicate that he intended to keep them, "the breach of any condition to be fulfilled by the seller can be treated only as a warranty, and not as a ground for rejecting the goods and treating the contract as repudiated—unless there is a term of the contract express or implied to that effect."

C—14

Diamond bought a thoroughbred race horse at an auction sale, but because of a mistake on the part of both buyer and seller, the horse sold (although a thoroughbred animal) was not of the lineage and breeding the buyer thought it was. Some time later the buyer tried to rescind the contract on the grounds of mutual mistake, but the seller claimed the contract was binding.

The court held that the mistake was not such as to render the contract void, not being as to the subject matter of the contract but only as to some quality of the subject matter. This quality, however, was sufficiently fundamental to be considered as a condition, and the contract could have been rescinded on that ground if action had been taken as soon as the mistake was discovered. However, Diamond had retained the horse beyond a reasonable time before advising the seller he was rejecting it, so he must be deemed to have accepted it. Therefore his remedy was limited to a claim for damages for breach of warranty.

(a) What was the breach of condition that resulted in this lawsuit?
(b) Why did the court treat the condition as a warranty?
(c) By treating the breach of contract in this way, what was the difference in the remedy allowed?

Of course, where conditions and warranties are carefully spelled out in the contract, the intentions of the parties will prevail. But in the absence of definite and specific terms, the Sale of Goods Act provides that certain implied conditions and warranties apply regarding:

- The seller's right to sell the goods
- Sales by description or sample
- Quality and fitness of the goods for use

SELLER'S TITLE

C—15

LADY, DID YOU BUY A PERSIAN RUG FROM A PEDDLER LAST WEEK?
YES. WHY DO YOU ASK?

If the rug was "stolen goods," what do you think would be the lady's legal position?

Unless a different intention is shown in the contract, there is an implied condition that the seller owns the goods and has the right to sell them. Hence, if a buyer learns that goods he has bargained for do not belong to the seller, he may repudiate the agreement without making himself liable for breach of contract. If the buyer has suffered loss as a result, he may also sue the seller for damages.

There is also an implied warranty that the buyer will have quiet possession of the goods without interference from any person who has a better title to them. Thus, if a person buys goods believing they are the property of the seller, but later has to surrender them to the rightful owner, the buyer has a right of action for damages against the seller for breach of warranty of title.

C—16

On November 28, 1950, Smith purchased a used car from Goral, a car dealer, on the instalment plan. The dealer had purchased the car from Jolley on November 20, 1950, making full payment at the time. A few months after the sale to Smith, the Royal Canadian Mounted Police seized the car from him because no customs duty had been paid when someone imported it from the United States on October 30, 1950. Apparently, neither of the three parties knew that the car had been illegally imported into Canada until it was seized. Smith was unable to find the true owner, and there was some reason to believe that the car had been stolen before being imported, although this had not been proved. The car dealer refused to refund to Smith the amount he had paid on the contract, and Smith sued.
The contract of sale provided that "the car is free of liens and encumbrances." The car dealer argued that no warranty of title

was given, and that "liens and encumbrances" did not include the Crown's right to seize the car and declare it forfeit under the Customs Act. The court held that the circumstances of the contract did not deny the existence of the implied condition under the Sale of Goods Act that the seller has a good title to the goods; or the implied warranty that the buyer shall have and enjoy quiet possession of the goods; and the implied warranty that the goods shall be free from any charge or encumbrance in favour of a third party not known to the buyer at the time the contract is made. On these grounds Smith was entitled to recover his money from the car dealer. The dealer, on the same grounds would be entitled to recover from Jolley.

(a) Why could the car dealer not give good title to the car to Smith?
(b) What remedy did the court grant Smith?
(c) If the car dealer recovers from Jolley, from whom does Jolley recover?

A purchaser of stolen goods can acquire no better title to the goods than was possessed by the seller; thus a person who buys stolen goods cannot own them even if he has paid for them, and the true owner (if he can prove his ownership) is entitled to recover his goods from such buyer. The buyer, of course, has the right to recover his money from the person who sold him the goods illegally.

C—17

Wales, a second-hand car dealer, purchased a car from Thomas who, by trickery, had stolen it from Roberts. Wales, however, had no knowledge of this and purchased the car in good faith. A few days later, Roberts, accompanied by police, called at the dealer's premises and demanded the return of the car. Eventually, Roberts had to sue for its return.

Wales contended that the thief must first be convicted before Roberts had the right to take legal action for repossession, but the Supreme Court of British Columbia held that this was not the law. The court held that Wales had no better title to the stolen car than had the thief; therefore Roberts was given judgment to recover the car.

(a) Why was Roberts able to recover the car?
(b) How would the car dealer recover the money he paid for the car?

The same rule does not apply to stolen money or negotiable instruments. Stolen money, when in the hands of an *innocent holder for value*, cannot be recovered from him by the person from whom it was stolen. So, too, in the case of a completed negotiable instrument which has been stolen, an innocent holder for value acquires good title.

SALES BY DESCRIPTION OR SAMPLE

If a buyer orders goods on the basis of the seller's description (for example, as contained in a letter, advertisement or catalogue), the Sale of Goods Act provides that "there is an implied condition that the goods will correspond with the description, and if the sale is by sample as well as by description, it is not sufficient that the bulk of the goods corresponds with the sample if the goods do not also correspond with the description."

Similarly, in the case of a contract for the sale of goods by sample, "there is an implied condition (a) that the bulk will correspond with the sample in quality; (b) that the buyer will have a reasonable opportunity of comparing the bulk with the sample; and (c) that the goods will be free from any defect rendering them unmerchantable that would not be apparent on reasonable examination of the sample."

Thus, if goods are ordered by description or sample or both, and they do not correspond with the description or sample, the goods may be rejected without making the buyer liable for breach of contract.

C—18

A merchant ordered two hundred raincoats from a manufacturer "to be confirmed upon receipt of sample." Further correspondence established that the coats were to be made with silk piping. A sample coat was supplied and accepted. When the first hundred coats arrived, the buyer refused to accept them because they were not according to sample. The sellers sued for damages for breach of contract. The court held that the buyers had a right to reject the coats since they were not according to sample. Furthermore, it was no answer on the part of the sellers to claim that the coats supplied were of better quality than the sample. The buyers had a right to reject goods which were not according to their order and which did not answer their requirements.

If the buyers had the right to reject the coats, was the breach of contract one of a condition or of a warranty?

C—19

Thompson bought some rugs from Schooley who described them as "Oriental rugs." Later, Thompson discovered them to be cheap imitations. Thompson then sued to recover the difference in price between the actual value and the price paid.
The Ontario Court of Appeal found that the sale was, in fact, a sale by description and that the goods did not comply with the description. Thompson, therefore, could treat the breach of contract as a condition and have the contract rescinded, or treat the condition as a warranty and sue for the difference in value as damages. On these grounds Thompson was given judgment for the difference in value.

If Thompson had chosen to treat the breach of contract as a breach of condition, what remedy would the court have allowed?

We should note again that if the goods have been accepted and received so that it is too late to reject the goods, the buyer has only a right to sue for damages for breach of warranty.

QUALITY OR FITNESS OF THE GOODS FOR USE

Under the old common law there was no implied condition or warranty respecting the quality of the goods sold or their fitness for use. The rule of *caveat emptor* (let the buyer beware) prevailed. If the buyer wished to protect himself, an express warranty had to be obtained from the seller.

The Sale of Goods Act has modified the doctrine of caveat emptor by providing that in the absence of express or implied intentions otherwise, certain implied conditions and warranties apply. Section 15(1) of the Ontario Act states that:

> *Where the buyer, expressly or by implication, makes known to the seller the particular purpose for which the goods are required so as to show that the buyer relies on the seller's skill and judgment, and the goods are of a description that it is in the course of the seller's business to supply (whether he is the manufacturer or not), there is an implied condition that the goods will be reasonably fit for such purpose.*

Often the key question to be determined is whether the buyer has made known to the seller the particular purpose for which the goods are required "so as to show that the buyer relies on the seller's skill and judgment."

C—20

(i) Buckley, in response to a Lever Bros. advertisement, sent fifty cents and two labels from packages of soap made by the defendant, for which she received

> "the prettiest, most practical apron you ever saw . . . made of sturdy koroseal . . . complete with a dozen brightly coloured plastic clothespins of exclusive design."

Buckley had used the clothespins for only the third time when, in the act of securing clothing to the clothesline, one of the plastic clothespins broke and shattered in such a way that a splinter from the pin entered her eye. As a result, she lost the sight of this eye. She sued for damages claiming that the injury was due to a breach of the implied warranties as set out in the Sale of Goods Act. Lever gave evidence that this was the only complaint made by a person being injured by the breaking of one of the clothespins during the course of a total of about 500,000,000 pins manufactured. Lever also questioned Buckley's claim that she relied on the seller's skill and judgment.

From the evidence offered, the Ontario High Court found (1) that the clothespin which shattered was substantially new and in the same condition it had been when delivered; but that it had proved not to be fit for the purpose for which it was intended to be used; (2) that Lever Bros. Ltd., by offering the clothespins for sale under the scheme as advertised, made it a part of their business to supply clothespins; and (3) that the buyer had done nothing to indicate she was buying the goods on the basis of her own skill and judgment. As a result of their findings, the court held that she was entitled to succeed and gave judgment in her favour of $6,689.32.

(ii) Jannison bought a steam shovel from a dealer in that type of machinery. The particular purpose for which the shovel was to be used was made known to the seller who then recommended a certain type of shovel. Jannison, however, after looking over the dealer's literature on shovels, decided to buy a heavier type than the seller had recommended. When this shovel was delivered, it proved to be too heavy for the soft ground and particular location where he wished to use it. The machine was therefore practically useless for Jannison's purpose. Jannison refused to complete payment on the machine, and the seller sued.
The court held that the evidence showed that the buyer had selected the machine relying on his own skill and judgment. In these circumstances there was no implied warranty on the part of the seller that the shovel would work under conditions in which Jannison intended to use it. He, therefore, was held liable to pay the price.

(a) In this case and the preceding one, upon what claim did the plaintiff base his or her case?
(b) Why was the court's decision different in the two cases?

In many cases the specific purpose for which the goods are to be used is obvious from the nature of the goods themselves; for example, clothing and food. In such cases it is not necessary that the purchaser expressly make known to the seller that he is buying the food to eat or the clothing to wear; his purpose is sufficiently implied by the fact that he is buying them.

In some cases both the retailer and the manufacturer may be held liable to the purchaser, the retailer for breach of an implied condition or warranty under the Sale of Goods Act, and the manufacturer in tort for negligence.

C—21

Grant suffered from a skin disorder, dermatitis, caused by some chemical substance in the underwear which he had purchased from John Martin & Co. Ltd. Grant sued both the vendor and the manufacturer for damages.
The court held that Grant could recover against both. The manufacturer was liable in tort for negligence in the manufacturer of products that reach the consumer when these products have hidden defects unknown to the consumer. The retailer was liable in contract for breach of warranty that the goods shall be reasonably fit for the purpose for which they were sold, and shall be of merchantable quality.

Might there be difficulty sometimes in determining whether or not the goods are "reasonably fit" for the purpose for which they were purchased?

If a person buys goods asking for them under their patent or trade name, there is no implied warranty on the part of the seller that the goods will be fit for any particular purpose unless the circumstances show that the buyer was relying on the skill and judgment of the seller in buying the article. Usually, when goods are bought under a trade name, the buyer is relying on his own judgment. At the same time, if the buyer is injured by using the goods, he may be able to hold the manufacturer liable in tort.

C—22

O'Fallon purchased from a retailer a certain brand of hair dye. She selected the dye herself, asking for it by its trade name, and without relying on the retailer's "skill and judgment." As a result of using the dye, she suffered severe inflammation of the scalp, neck and face so that she required the services of a physician. She also lost time at work.

She then sued the retailer, the wholesaler and the manufacturer together for compensation for injuries and loss of work. Expert evidence given at the trial showed that the dye was dangerous and should not have been used without a previous test; and that the injury could have been avoided by more detailed instructions on the package. The court dismissed the action against the retailer on the grounds that the article was sold under its trade name. In these circumstances, according to the Sale of Goods Act, there was no implied condition on the part of the retailer that the goods were fit for any particular purpose. However, the court held both the manufacturer and the wholesaler liable in tort for damages to the woman for failing to provide a proper warning on the container. An appeal against this decision by the manufacturer and the wholesaler was dismissed.

Compare the decision in this case with that in C—21. Why were the decisions different?

When buying goods *by description* from a seller who deals in goods of that description (whether he is the manufacturer or not), it is obvious that the buyer is relying upon the seller to select the specific goods ordered. In such circumstances there is an implied condition that the goods sold shall be of *merchantable quality*. This rule does not apply, when the buyer examines the goods, with respect to defects which the examination ought to have revealed, but it does apply with regard to defects which it is not reasonable to expect that the buyer should have discovered.

C—23

Chomyn purchased from the American Fur Co. a fur coat which turned out to be very unsatisfactory, because the skins of which the coat was made frequently ripped apart at places where they were sewn together. After using the coat for over two seasons, during which time the coat was taken in for repairs several times, Chomyn finally sued the seller claiming that the coat was valueless; that it had been bought "by description," but was not of merchantable quality.

From the evidence given, a Saskatchewan District Court found that the coat had, in fact, developed rips in the skins due to faulty sewing at the factory, and was not of "merchantable quality." However, neither the buyer nor the seller could have discovered the defects at the time of the sale without taking out the lining;

and it was not reasonable to expect that the buyer's examination should have gone as far as that. Notwithstanding that the coat was not of merchantable quality, it was not "valueless," as Chomyn had claimed, since it had been worn two seasons and part of a third. For this reason, the court held that it was too late to rescind the contract, but that the buyer was entitled to damages. The fact that the defects were the fault of the manufacturer did not relieve the seller of liability.

(a) What is meant by describing the coat as not being of merchantable quality?
(b) Why did the court not order that the coat be returned to the seller and that the purchaser's money be refunded?

Regulation of Food and Drug Products. At this point it is appropriate to draw attention to the fact that a number of statutes have been passed by the federal government to protect the consumer by providing regulations and a system of inspection of the manufacture and distribution of certain products. The Food and Drugs Act is the best known example, but federal regulations also apply to canned goods, meats, poultry, milk, fruit, vegetables and honey to ensure that they are prepared and distributed under proper and sanitary conditions. Several provinces have passed similar legislation for the same purpose.

Disclaimer Clauses. It is not unusual for a contract to contain terms by which the seller disclaims liability for implied conditions or warranties. These disclaimers may become effective if they are inserted into the contract with the knowledge of the buyer, and he, nevertheless, accepts the contract. By such disclaimers it is sometimes possible for the seller to avoid liabilities which otherwise he would have to assume. At the same time, disclaiming liability for *implied* warranties and conditions does not avoid liability for conditions and warranties *expressly* stated in the contract, and a clause which would disclaim liability for any type of condition, the voiding of which would amount to a fundamental breach of the contract, would not be binding.

C — 24

Lightburn bought from a car agency a small car made in England and imported by the agency. Before buying, Lightburn discussed with the agency the qualities of the car, describing what he wanted and indicating that he was relying upon their recommendations that the car would be reasonably fit for the purposes he had described. He used the car eight months, accumulating about 8,000 miles, but the car had to be taken in to the agency for repairs seventeen times during that period and, generally, proved to be so unreliable that he never felt that he could depend upon it from one day to the next. Finally, the car stalled on the highway on a snowy night when Lightburn's family were travelling with him in the car.

The next morning he gave the car back to the agency and asked for the return of his money. The agency refused, and Lightburn brought action claiming that he bought the car depending upon the seller's skill and judgment, and that the general defectiveness of the car amounted to such a fundamental breach of contract as to entitle him to rescission of the contract. The car agency contended that Lightburn's use of the car for eight months constituted acceptance of the car and that it was now too late for rescission. They further pointed out that the contract contained certain warranties as to defective parts and also *an exempting clause* which stated. "This warranty is expressly in lieu of all other obligations or liabilities on the part of the Vendor except such obligations or liabilities as the Vendor may assume by its Owner Service Policy or other separate written instrument." The car agency argued that this clause exempted them from a claim for rescission of the contract.

The Supreme Court of British Columbia ruled that the law on exempting clauses and, generally, on the doctrine of fundamental breach of contract was that "where defects are so numerous that, taken *en masse*, they destroy the workable character of the thing sold, this may amount to a fundamental and total breach of the contract so as to disentitle the defendant from taking refuge behind an exclusionary clause upon which, if the defects were considered singly, he might rely." Further, "it is now settled that exempting clauses of this kind (the kind in the contract), no matter how widely they are expressed, only avail the party when he is carrying out his contract in its essential respects. . . . They do not avail him when he is guilty of a breach which goes to the root of the contract."

The Court held that in this case there was, in fact, a fundamental breach of contract so that the car agency could not rely on the exempting clause. Lightburn was therefore entitled to rescission of the contract.

(a) On what grounds did Lightburn sue for rescission of the contract?
(b) What were the car agency's two points of defence?
(c) Why did the court rule the contract could be rescinded?

Since the above case was decided, the law (in three provinces, so far) has been changed. In the case of *retail* or *consumer* sales in British Columbia, Manitoba and Ontario, new mandatory provisions render *void* any term in a contract which disclaims, negatives or diminishes any of the implied warranties or conditions prescribed by the Sale of Goods Act.

RIGHTS AND REMEDIES OF THE UNPAID SELLER

The unpaid seller has the following rights and remedies:

- Reservation of the right of disposal.
- A lien on the goods—if they are still in his possession.
- The right of stoppage in transit.
- The right of resale (subject to certain limitations).
- The right to sue for the price or for damages for breach of contract.

RESERVATION OF THE RIGHT OF DISPOSAL

By reserving control over the goods until certain conditions are fulfilled, the seller virtually remains the owner of the goods. For example, if goods are sent c.o.d. (cash on delivery), the seller retains ownership and may recover possession of the goods if the price is not paid at the time of delivery. Similarly, if goods are shipped under an order bill of lading, with sight draft for the price attached, the conditions are that the buyer may not get possession of the goods until the draft is paid.

RIGHT OF LIEN

Where no credit is allowed on a sale and the goods are still in the possession of the seller, he may exercise his right of lien; that is, he may retain possession of the goods until they are paid for. As already explained, if no credit terms have been arranged, payment and delivery are concurrent events.

The seller loses his right of lien once the goods have been delivered to a carrier for transportation to the buyer, unless, of course, the seller has still reserved his right of disposal.

RIGHT OF STOPPAGE IN TRANSIT

If after shipping goods to a buyer the unpaid seller learns that the buyer is insolvent, the seller has the right to notify the carrier not to deliver the goods to the buyer. The seller may then retake possession of the goods even though title had already passed to the buyer when the goods were delivered to the carrier.

However, once the buyer or his agent has obtained possession of the goods, the seller loses his right of stoppage in transit, and his only recourse is to seek payment of the price. Should possession have been obtained by the buyer because the carrier disregarded the seller's stoppage order, the carrier becomes liable for damages.

If the seller stops delivery of the goods wrongfully, and the buyer proves his solvency, the buyer is entitled not only to delivery of the goods, but also to be indemnified for any loss caused by having delivery withheld.

RIGHT OF RESALE

When an unpaid seller has exercised his right of lien, he may resell the goods only if (1) the goods are of a perishable nature, in which case he should make reasonable efforts to resell in order to minimize loss; and (2) notice has been served on the buyer of the intention to resell the goods, and the buyer does not redeem the goods within a reasonable time. For example, a buyer having refused to accept a large portion of a shipment of fish, the seller sold the rejected goods as soon as possible at the best price available, and sued the buyer for the difference between the contract price and the price obtained from the resale. The court held that the seller was entitled to the amount claimed plus the cost of handling and resale.

BREACH OF CONTRACT

If ownership of the goods has passed to the buyer—whether he has taken delivery or not—and he refuses or is unable to pay for them, the seller may sue for the price; if ownership has not passed, the seller may sue only for damages for breach of contract.

NOTE In Alberta, Saskatchewan and Manitoba the sale of farm machinery and implements comes under a special statute. A statutory form of contract is provided which includes a vendor's warranty as to material, workmanship, and other such matters. The law applies only to sales from dealers, not from another farmer or individual; nor does it apply to second-hand machinery. Also in the same provinces, a licensed grain dealer acquires good title to grain delivered to him if he buys in good faith and without notice of any defect in the seller's title. In Manitoba, where sugar beets are sold and delivered to a person operating a beet sugar factory, the buyer acquires good title if he buys in good faith and without notice of any defect or want of title on the part of the seller.

APPLYING THE LAW

1. X received advertising literature offering seat covers for cars. The covers for particular makes and models of cars were identified by number. X ordered a set for his car according to the number given, and since the parcel arrived c.o.d., paid for the covers before examining them. When he did examine them, he found they did not fit his car at all. What are his legal rights?

2.

(a) At this point in the transaction, who owns the coat?
(b) Assume that when the purchaser calls for the coat it cannot be found but that the seller nevertheless bills the customer for the balance of the price. How would the law apply?

3. D, whose residence is heated by an oil furnace, orders 100 gallons of fuel oil. The delivery truck, while on its way to deliver oil to several residences including D's, was involved in an accident

which caused the loss of all the oil in the truck. Later, D received a bill for the 100 gallons of oil, the seller claiming that since it was D's oil that was on the truck, he should pay for it. Apply the law explaining D's legal position.

4.

How does the law apply to this situation?

DISCUSSION AND PROJECTS

1. Often in the field of retail merchandising the policy that "the customer is always right" takes the place of the old idea of caveat emptor (let the buyer beware). For example, in the matter of accepting returned purchases or cancellation of orders, the merchant often does not exercise his legal rights. Discuss any incidents of this nature of which you know or have heard.
2. Warranties and guaranties usually accompany sales of cars and household appliances such as stoves, washers, and refrigerators. Obtain some of these and examine them for "disclaimer" clauses. Does the disclaimer clause relieve the seller from fundamental liabilities which are implied by law?

Part 21
CONDITIONAL SALES AND CONSUMER PROTECTION

NATURE OF A CONDITIONAL SALE

A *conditional sale* is the kind of transaction which the ordinary consumer knows as the "time payment plan" or "buy on the instalment plan" and is the method commonly used today when purchasing automobiles, furniture, household appliances, and similar goods.

The contract itself is often found on either the front or back of the invoice used to record the sale and which the purchaser is required to sign. An example is illustrated.

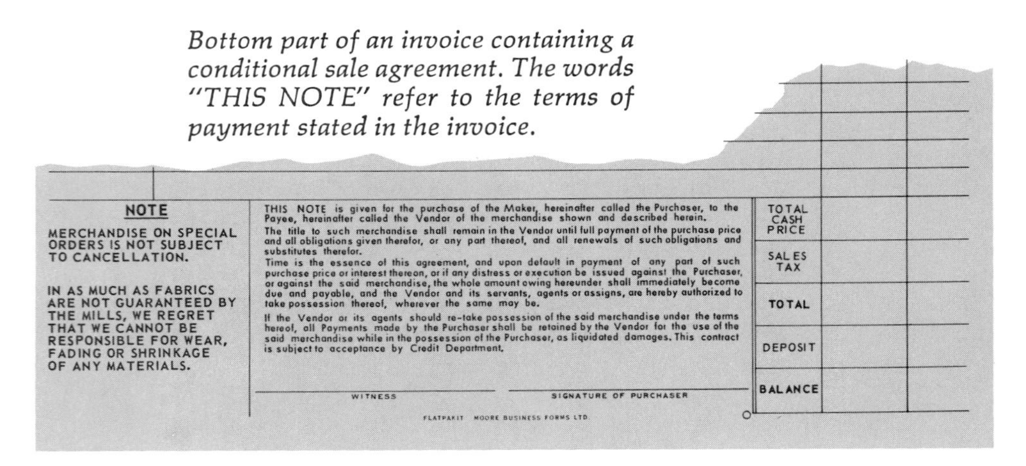

NOTE

MERCHANDISE ON SPECIAL ORDERS IS NOT SUBJECT TO CANCELLATION.

IN AS MUCH AS FABRICS ARE NOT GUARANTEED BY THE MILLS, WE REGRET THAT WE CANNOT BE RESPONSIBLE FOR WEAR, FADING OR SHRINKAGE OF ANY MATERIALS.

THIS NOTE is given for the purchase of the Maker, hereinafter called the Purchaser, to the Payee, hereinafter called the Vendor of the merchandise shown and described herein.

The title to such merchandise shall remain in the Vendor until full payment of the purchase price and all obligations given therefor, or any part thereof, and all renewals of such obligations and substitutes therefor.

Time is the essence of this agreement, and upon default in payment of any part of such purchase price or interest thereon, or if any distress or execution be issued against the Purchaser, or against the said merchandise, the whole amount owing hereunder shall immediately become due and payable, and the Vendor and its servants, agents or assigns, are hereby authorized to take possession thereof, wherever the same may be.

If the Vendor or its agents should re-take possession of the said merchandise under the terms hereof, all Payments made by the Purchaser shall be retained by the Vendor for the use of the said merchandise while in the possession of the Purchaser, as liquidated damages. This contract is subject to acceptance by Credit Department.

WITNESS

SIGNATURE OF PURCHASER

FLATPAKIT MOORE BUSINESS FORMS LTD.

TOTAL CASH PRICE	
SALES TAX	
TOTAL	
DEPOSIT	
BALANCE	

Bottom part of an invoice containing a conditional sale agreement. The words "THIS NOTE" refer to the terms of payment stated in the invoice.

The above agreement is very brief and to the point, but many business firms use longer and more detailed forms. In each case, however, the essential condition of the agreement which qualifies it as a conditional sale is that *the purchaser gets possession of the goods but the legal title (or ownership) remains with the seller until the buyer has completed the payments.*

Other subsidiary terms may be included in the contract at the option of the seller; for instance, almost invariably the contract contains the condition that the seller may repossess the goods on default by the purchaser, and that at the same time all payments which have been made by the purchaser are forfeited to the seller as liquidated damages for breach of contract.

As we shall see later in this section, the terms which the seller may enforce are subject to the provisions of the Conditional Sales Act of the province.

LEGISLATION CONCERNING CONDITIONAL SALES

A Conditional Sales Act is in force in all the provinces except Manitoba and Quebec. In Manitoba statutory provisions concerning conditional sales are included in its Consumer Protection Act; in Quebec, this type of sale is covered by the Quebec Civil Code. Most of the provinces have other statutes which directly or indirectly affect the rights and obligations of the parties to a conditional sale. Reference will be made to some of these in the course of this part.

Since all the Conditional Sales Acts have a common purpose, certain features of the law of conditional sales are fairly uniform throughout the provinces. For example, in all the provinces the contract must (a) be in writing and (b) identify the parties to the transaction; (c) be signed by the buyer; (d) contain a description of the goods sufficient to identify them; and (e) set forth the terms and conditions of the contract. In all the common law provinces (except Manitoba), provision is made for registration of the conditional sale contract. All the provinces provide for the right of repossession and resale in the event of the buyer's default on his contract.

At the same time, there are many variations in the law of conditional sales from province to province—so many, in fact, that within the scope of this text it is possible only to indicate the areas where differences exist. We must emphasize that when legal questions arise in connection with conditional sales in any particular province, reference should be had to the law of that province.

Registration of the Conditional Sale Contract

C—25

A sells his car to B under a conditional sale. Before B has completed his payments, and without A's knowledge or consent, B sells the car to C, who does not at the time know about the conditional sale agreement between A and B.

(a) Since cars are very often bought under conditional sale agreements, should C not be aware of the possibility that B may not have title to it? Could he say he had bought the car in good faith if he did not look into the matter of ownership?
(b) How could C find out who had title to the car?
(c) When A discovers that B has sold the car to C, what are his legal rights?

Notwithstanding that the conditional sale contract provides that the right of ownership to the goods remains in the conditional seller until the goods are fully paid for, the fact that the conditional buyer has possession and use of the goods (with the conditional seller's consent) makes him *appear* to be the owner.

The possibility then arises that the conditional buyer may sell the goods or otherwise dispose of them to a third party before payments under the first transaction have been completed. The question arises whether the conditional seller's right of ownership as provided in the conditional sale contract now holds goods as against the third party, the subsequent buyer?

The Conditional Sales Acts of all the provinces (except Manitoba) answer the question by providing that the condition in the contract which reserves the right of ownership to the seller is *void* as against the claim of a subsequent buyer who has purchased the goods in good faith; and that such subsequent buyer is deemed to be the owner of the goods *unless the conditional sale contract was properly registered* according to the requirements of the Act. Thus, by registering a copy of the conditional sale agreement, the conditional seller can protect his right of ownership.

Registration of the conditional sale agreement is deemed to be public notice, so that any person who intends to buy goods from someone who is *not* in the business of selling such goods, may check at the appropriate registry office to find out if a conditional sale agreement for the sale of these particular goods is on file. If there is such a document on file, he buys the goods at his peril, for he may be compelled to surrender the goods to their rightful owner (the conditional seller) or pay him the balance owing on the goods.

Time of Registration. Registration must take place within a specified period following the date of the contract. The period varies from province to province. In Ontario (at the time of this writing) it is five days for county areas and ten days for districts; in British Columbia it is 21 days; in Nova Scotia and Prince Edward Island, 20 days; and in the other provinces, 30 days. Most provinces make provision for late filing in certain circumstances. In order to keep the registration effective, it must be renewed at the end of a specified period, generally every three years (Nova Scotia, five years).

Removal of Goods to Another Province. Goods bought under a conditional sale in one province are sometimes removed to another province before title to the goods has passed to the conditional buyer. All the provinces (except Manitoba) provide for the registering of a copy of a conditional sale agreement originating in another province. The requirements vary from province to province.

Exemptions from Registration. As already noted, conditional sale agreements are not registered at all in Manitoba. In that province the conditional seller's title is protected if the goods have the manufacturer's name or some other distinguishing name painted, printed or stamped thereon or otherwise plainly attached thereto. It is the responsibility of the buyer of goods to use this information to obtain for himself the facts concerning the ownership of the goods.

In Alberta, a conditional sale of manufactured goods, including pianos and other musical instruments, need not be registered if the goods have the name of the seller affixed to them. Registration is not required at all if the amount of the sale is less than $15.

In Saskatchewan, New Brunswick and Newfoundland, registration is waived if the goods are sold directly by the manufacturer of the goods.

In Ontario, a conditional sale contract executed on or after January 1, 1971, is *exempt* from registration if the contract is for the sale of consumer goods, and the amount secured by the contract does not exceed $300. If the contract is for the sale of goods that are inventory or equipment, it is exempt from registration if the goods are manufactured goods (including musical instruments) that at the time of delivery have the name and address of the seller on the goods, or the goods are household furniture. (A refrigerator, for example, is "inventory" in the hands of an appliance dealer; "consumer goods" when used in your kitchen; and "equipment" when installed in a restaurant).

In some provinces special requirements apply to the registration of conditional sale contracts for the sale of automobiles, farm machinery, and for fixtures attached to the land; for instance, British Columbia, Alberta, Saskatchewan and Newfoundland require the serial number (strictly accurate) of a motor vehicle to be given in the contract.

From the few examples of exemptions from registration noted above it is quite clear that under the present law in any province a buyer of goods cannot assume from the absence of registration alone that he could get good title to the goods. Neither can he absolutely depend upon the fact that the seller's name does not appear on the article, for it has been held that the subsequent obliteration of the seller's name from the article does not affect the protection acquired by the seller when his name was affixed to the article at the time of its delivery to the conditional buyer.

Thus, in the case of these exemptions from registration, an intending purchaser is left to find out as best he can whether or not the goods he is interested in buying are legally owned by the seller. If this information is not available, he buys at his peril, particularly if the goods are of a kind which is often sold under a conditional sale agreement.

GOODS SOLD TO A TRADER FOR RESALE

C—26

An automobile manufacturer sells a number of vehicles to a dealer under a conditional sale contract. The contract is registered. In due course the dealer sells one of the cars to X.

Even though the dealer fails to pay the manufacturer and defaults on his agreement, does X get good title to the car?

In all the provinces, when goods are sold under a conditional sale agreement to a trader who deals in such goods and whose purpose is to resell them, the condition reserving ownership to the seller is void even though the conditional sales contract is registered. Hence, if such goods are resold by the trader to a third party in good faith and for valuable consideration, such third party gets good title and ownership to the goods notwithstanding that the terms of the conditional sale contract under which the trader obtained the goods reserves the title of the goods to that conditional seller until the trader has fully paid for them.

It is stressed, however, that the protection applies *only* where the conditional sale is to a trader *for the purpose of resale.* A reservation of title may have occurred prior to the sale to the trader, and, in that case, the purchase from a dealer affords no greater protection than from any other party.

C—27

A buys a new Thunderbird from City One Motors under a conditional sale contract whereby title will not pass to A until the vehicle is paid for. The contract is registered in the proper office. Six months later, and before the car is paid for, A trades the vehicle in on a new Comet at City Two Sales. Later, City Two Sales sells the Thunderbird to B.

B does not obtain a good title; the car is still subject to the claim of City One Motors. B is not protected because the original conditional vendor (City One Motors) did not sell to a trader for the purpose of resale. If the car is repossessed by City One Motors, B's only recourse will be to claim against City Two Sales for breach of warranty regarding its right to sell the goods.

(a) Draw a line diagram which shows the buyer-seller relationship between all the parties involved in this case.

(b) What should City Two Sales have checked on before taking the car as a trade-in?

Disclosing the Cost of Credit. All the provinces have enacted laws requiring the seller to disclose fully the cost of credit; that is, the carrying charges on credit sales. Since conditional sales are generally on the instalment plan, carrying charges are usually involved. The law, fairly uniform throughout the provinces, requires carrying charges, interest, etc., to be clearly shown in the contract both as a total amount and also as an annual percentage rate.

Conditions and Warranties Under a Conditional Sale. Generally, the implied conditions and warranties which apply to a sale under the Sale of Goods Act also apply to conditional sales. Saskatchewan law provides an exception in the case of second-hand goods where the contract of sale contains a statement to that effect. In such a case it is not implied that the goods shall be of merchantable quality or be fit for any particular purpose.

ASSIGNMENT OF CONDITIONAL SALES CONTRACTS

C—28

K buys a food freezer under a conditional sale contract, making a down payment and signing a promissory note for the balance. The seller assigns the contract to a finance company. Within the warranty period the freezer fails to function, but K cannot get any service or satisfaction from the seller. If K were still making his payments to the seller, he could withhold further payment until the seller honoured his warranty.

Does K have to continue making payments to the finance company regardless of the seller's breach of warranty?

It is a well established practice for merchants to assign their customers' conditional sales contracts to finance companies. It is then up to the finance company to register the contracts.

Since the merchant is assigning his right to receive money, he does not need the customer's consent to the assignment, although the customer must be notified. The customer then makes his payments to the finance company. At the same time, the merchant remains liable on conditions and warranties pertaining to the sale.

In taking the assignment of the contract the finance company cannot acquire a better right than the merchant had. The assignee takes the contract subject to the rights of the original parties. For this reason finance companies made it a practice to ask for not only an assignment of the conditional sales contract but also the endorsement to it of a promissory note made by the customer to the merchant. In the past, as a holder in due course of a promissory note, the finance company was not affected by the rights between the merchant and the customer. Now, however, a new law (an amendment to the federal Bills of Exchange Act) has recently been passed concerning promissory notes given by buyers under credit sales. The note must now be marked with the words "Consumer Purchase" to identify the purpose for which it was given. Further, a finance company to which the note has been assigned cannot enforce payment of the note if the seller of the goods for which the note was given cannot enforce it. Thus, if for some reason—for instance a defect in the goods—the conditional buyer would have a right to refuse to continue payment to the conditional seller, he now has that same right to refuse payment to the finance company to whom his contract was assigned. (See Consumer Bills and Notes, page 286).

Previous to the passing of this law, a finance company which had taken such a note in good faith could enforce its payment regardless of any right the conditional buyer had to refuse payment to the conditional seller.

STATUTORY RIGHTS AND REMEDIES IN THE EVENT OF DEFAULT BY THE BUYER

The rights and obligations of the parties to a conditional sale in the event of default by the buyer are strictly prescribed by each province's Conditional Sales Act. Again, as with the requirements for registration, there are provincial differences.

Repossession by the Conditional Seller (or His Assignee)

C—29

Is such a procedure legal?

The seller's right to repossess the goods if the buyer defaults follows logically from the terms of the contract; namely, that he is the owner of the goods until they are fully paid for. However, he is not entitled to use force in recovering the goods. In some provinces he must notify the defaulting buyer that he is going to repossess, and he must obtain a court order authorizing him to do so.

Some provinces restrict the right of the seller to repossess certain kinds of goods; for example, in Alberta there are certain restrictions imposed by that province's Seizures Act on the repossession of mobile homes. In Saskatchewan the Limitations of Civil Rights Act provides restrictions on the repossession of agricultural implements, farm trucks, cream separators, washing machines, stoves, heaters and sewing machines. The Consumers' Protection Acts of Ontario, New Brunswick and Nova Scotia provide that where a buyer has paid two-thirds or more of the purchase price, the seller may not repossess except by leave of a judge of a county or district court. Manitoba's Consumer Protection Act provides that where the balance owing by the buyer is less than 25% of the cash price of the goods at the time of the sale, the seller may not repossess the goods except by leave of the court or written consent of the buyer given at the time of repossession.

The examples given above are sufficient to indicate that many provincial variations of the law exist, so that to determine fully the right of repossession of any particular goods in any particular province one should have reference to the law of that province.

THE CONDITIONAL BUYER'S RIGHT TO REDEEM

C—30

The conditional sale agreement used by a certain retailer provides that in the event of default by the buyer, the seller shall have the right to repossess the goods and to resell them *immediately*.

(a) Is an *immediate* resale fair to the purchaser?
(b) Is the condition legal?

The Conditional Sales Act of each province provides that if the seller exercises his right to repossess the goods because of the buyer's default, he must keep the goods for a certain period before reselling them. In Newfoundland the period is one month; in Alberta (by the Seizures Act) the sheriff must keep the goods for fourteen days; in the other provinces the period is twenty days. During this time the conditional buyer may redeem the goods. This provision may not be waived even if the terms of the contract provide otherwise.

An important question is what payment will be sufficient to redeem the goods? Many conditional sale contracts contain an *acceleration* clause which provides that in the event of default the whole of the unpaid balance becomes due and payable.

In British Columbia, Nova Scotia, and Prince Edward Island, the Act provides that the buyer may redeem by paying the *balance of the contract price*, plus the expense of repossessing and keeping the goods. In Ontario and Manitoba, the buyer may redeem by paying the *arrears* plus the costs of repossession. In Manitoba, the buyer in default may, in certain circumstances, apply to the court for relief, and the court may, if it sees fit, relieve the buyer against the consequences of the repossession by ordering the seller to return the goods to the buyer under such conditions as the court sees fit to impose.

In Saskatchewan, Newfoundland and New Brunswick, the buyer may redeem by paying *the amount due on the contract price*. In Alberta (by the Seizures Act) a procedure is available by which the conditional buyer may apply to a judge who may suspend resale proceedings pending the payment of the debt by such means as he may prescribe.

In any case, an acceleration clause of this kind is of a penal nature and should be strictly construed; it may be enforced only if the parties proceed in strict compliance with the law.

Resale by the Seller (or His Assignee). Again, the fact that the ownership to the repossessed goods rests with the conditional seller suggests that he has the right to resell them. Nevertheless, he must allow the defaulting buyer the full statutory period of redemption and, as we have noted above, his right to resell may be restricted by a court order obtained by the buyer.

We shall now consider what remedies of the seller, if any, accompany the right of resale. In all the provinces except Saskatchewan the conditional seller may sue on the contract before repossessing the goods. In Saskatchewan, according to the Limitation of Civil Rights Act (which on this point supersedes that province's Conditional Sales Act), repossession and resale is the only remedy.

In Alberta, Manitoba and Newfoundland, if the conditional seller resells after repossession, he cannot hold the defaulting conditional buyer liable for any deficiency. In British Columbia, Ontario, New Brunswick, Nova Scotia and Prince Edward Island, the conditional seller may hold the defaulting buyer liable for a deficiency if the contract so provides. A clause in the contract stating that the proceeds of the resale will be *applied* on the unpaid balance of the price implies that the seller intends to hold the buyer liable for any deficiency.

In order to enforce liability for a deficiency on resale, the seller must give the buyer notice in strict compliance with the procedure outlined in the Conditional Sales Act. Briefly, the notice must indicate the seller's intention to sell; contain a detailed description of the goods; give an itemized statement of the payments made, the balance due, and the cost of taking and keeping possession; and warn the buyer that if payment is not made within a specified time the goods will be sold and that the seller intends to look to the defaulting buyer for any deficiency. This notice must be served on the defaulting buyer within a certain time before the sale strictly in the manner prescribed in the Act.

C—31

The buyer under a conditional sale defaulted on his agreement to purchase a gas washer and dryer from Consumers' Gas Co. The agreement was for a "Thor" machine, but the machine delivered and accepted was an "Inglis." Before the conditional buyer had completed his payments on the goods, he resold the appliance to another party. Eventually, the goods were repossessed by the gas company who then notified the defaulting buyer regarding the resale and the intention to hold him liable for any deficiency. When the amount realized on resale was less than the amount owing, there being a deficiency on the resale, the gas company sued. The Ontario Court of Appeal found that in the notice of resale the goods were described as "Thor," which was a mistake. The evidence also revealed that the notice of resale was sent by registered mail addressed in care of the buyer's solicitor at his office. This was not in compliance with the Ontario Conditional Sales Act which provides that "the notice shall be served personally upon or left at the residence or last known place of abode in Ontario of the purchaser or his successor in interest." The court held that the right to recover a deficiency arising out of a resale is purely statutory and accrues only if there has been strict compliance with the provisions of the Act which, in this case, had not been done. The gas company was therefore not entitled to recover the deficiency on the resale.

(a) Has the defaulting buyer lost all his payments on the machine?
(b) Does the decision in this case suggest that, as far as the law permits, the court leans toward protecting the consumer?

The Conditional Sales Act of Newfoundland and the Consumers Protection Act of Manitoba both state specifically that any surplus realized on resale after repossession must go to the defaulting buyer. The Acts of the other provinces are silent on this point, but it has been held that any surplus on resale belongs to the defaulting party.

HOUSE TO HOUSE SALES

CONSUMER PROTECTION LEGISLATION

C — 32

Once the contract is signed, is it possible to back out without being liable for breach of contract?

We have already referred to the "consumer protection" legislation which was enacted during the late '60's by all the provinces except Quebec. The titles of the statutes concerned vary from province to province: in some provinces it is The Consumer Protection Act, in others the Direct Sellers' Act, while some provinces have both Acts in force. Saskatchewan has a Cost of Credit Disclosure Act, and Alberta, a Credit and Loan Agreement Act. The details of these laws vary but two features are generally common to all: (1) the requirement that contracts of borrowing and of sales on credit must disclose fully the credit cost involved—interest, fees, carrying charges, etc.—expressed both as a total amount and also as an annual percentage; and (2) the provision (except in Prince Edward Island) that purchasers of goods or services from "house to house" salesmen may rescind their contracts within a specified time without making themselves liable for breach of contract.

The first feature offers some protection to the consumer in that it compels lenders and sellers on credit to reveal in full detail the cost of borrowing and buying on credit, facts heretofore often hidden in general terms. The second feature provides a means of escape for the victims of high-pressure selling by door-to-door salesmen.

Types of Sale to Which the Legislation Applies. Most of the provinces distinguish the type of sale which comes under this legislation as one that is made wholly or partly at a place other than the seller's place of business. In most cases this type of sale is made by the door-to-door salesman. In Alberta and Prince Edward Island, the sales to which the law applies are not exclusively of this type.

The salesman is required to be licensed under the Act which applies. In most provinces it is specifically provided that the contract is not binding unless the salesman is licensed.

Generally, the type of contract which is intended to be regulated is the *executory* type of agreement; that is, a contract where delivery or performance or payment in full is not made at the time the contract is entered into. Ontario and British Columbia specifically describe the contract as such. This type of contract includes conditional sales, which are governed in other respects by the Conditional Sales Act.

The statute concerned usually requires the contract to be in writing (in Newfoundland it may also be oral), and that it must describe the goods or services, state the price, terms of payment, and warranties and guarantees, if any, and fully disclose the cost of credit. Most provinces specifically require that a copy of the agreement be given to the buyer; if not specifically required, this rule would appear to be implied.

Statutory Right of Rescission. All the provinces (except Prince Edward Island) provide for a *cooling-off* period during which the buyer may cancel his agreement without making himself liable for damages for breach of contract. In Ontario and Manitoba the period is two days; in British Columbia, three days; in Alberta and Saskatchewan, four days; in New Brunswick and Nova Scotia, five days; and in Newfoundland, ten days. In Ontario and most of the other provinces, the time runs from the date the buyer received his copy of the contract; in other cases it runs from the date the contract was made. Notice of rescission must be given to the seller in writing.

A further provision (except in Ontario and Prince Edward Island) is that where there is no specified date of delivery, if the goods are not delivered within 120 days of the making of the contract the buyer may at any time within one year rescind the agreement. In British Columbia, Alberta, and Manitoba, if a delivery date is specified, and goods are not delivered within 30 days of that date, the same right of rescission is allowed.

Statutory Obligation to Inform the Buyer of His Right to Rescind. The provinces of British Columbia, Alberta, Manitoba and New Brunswick have made it a part of their law that the contracts which come under this legislation *must contain a notice* to the buyer of his right to cancel the contract, the time in which he may do it, and the manner in which it should be done. Manitoba and New Brunswick require the notice to be *on the face* of the contract; British Columbia and Alberta require the notice to be *as prominent as any other part of the contract.*

The importance of this requirement is obvious. If a person is not aware that the law gives him the right to cancel his contract he may allow the rescission period to lapse, in which case the protection intended by the law is lost.

Exempt Transactions. In this area we find many variations among the provinces, particularly in the number and kind of product to which the consumer protection statutes do not apply.

In some provinces the Acts do not apply to contracts of sale less than a specified minimum amount; in Ontario and some other provinces, the minimum is $50; in New Brunswick, $25; in Manitoba, $10.

The statutes of Manitoba, New Brunswick, Newfoundland and Saskatchewan contain a long list of goods and services (including motor vehicles, farm implements, and other products and services connected with agriculture) which are excluded from the provisions of the statutes as they apply to other sales.

However, one exemption is common to all the provinces: consumer protection laws do not apply to sales of goods made to a trader or person who is in the business of selling such goods.

APPLYING THE LAW

1.

Note that the seller has had the piano for only six months, and that the buyer is paying the full price, apparently without investigation.
(a) What risk is the buyer taking?
(b) How can the buyer avoid that risk?

2. Roberts purchases a console stereo set under a conditional sale contract. The seller immediately assigns the contract to a finance company. If some defect shows up in the stereo set and the seller fails or refuses to remedy it, is Roberts still obliged to make payments to the finance company? How does the law apply?
3. A house-to-house salesman obtains the signatures of a woman and her daughter to a contract for the purchase of a set of cookware on the instalment plan. (The cookware is for the daughter, but since the daughter is a minor, the mother signs also). The next day the mother and her daughter learn that the price they agreed to pay, including interest and service charges, is much higher than the usual retail price for such a set.
   (a) Do you think the two women can repudiate the contract on the grounds of fraud?
   (b) Is there any other legal recourse open to the purchasers?

DISCUSSION AND PROJECTS

1. Obtain copies of conditional sale contracts as used by different businesses in your area. Examine their terms. What terms are the same for all? Are there any unusual terms in any of them?
2. Discuss the justice of holding the buyer liable for a deficiency incurred by the seller as a result of repossession and resale.
3. Obtain a copy or copies of monthly bills submitted by merchants to customers who have charge accounts. Are service charges shown both as an amount and also as an annual percentage rate?

Part 22
CHATTEL MORTGAGES AND BILLS OF SALE

CHATTEL MORTGAGES

C—33

Desperately needing cash, Kapp goes to a finance company for a loan. The finance company gives the loan but requires as security for the loan a chattel mortgage on Kapp's new car which he has fully paid for and owns outright.

(a) How does the mortgage affect Kapp's title to the car?
(b) How could the finance company protect itself against loss of or damage to the car?
(c) Since the car is still in Kapp's possession and will be used by him as if it were fully his own, how may the finance company protect its interest if Kapp were to sell the car privately to another party?
(d) If Kapp does not pay off his loan as agreed upon, what will be the finance company's rights with regard to the car?

As a general rule, things that may be sold may be mortgaged, a transaction often arising from the need of the owner to borrow money. As security for the loan the borrower may execute a mortgage contract which transfers to the lender the title and ownership of certain goods that belong to and are in the possession of the borrower. Another instance in which a chattel mortgage may be used is the sale and delivery of goods to a purchaser who, not having paid the price of the goods, gives as security for the balance owing a chattel mortgage on the goods purchased.

In Alberta, Saskatchewan, Manitoba and Prince Edward Island there are certain statutory restrictions and priorities with respect to mortgages on growing crops.

FORM OF THE MORTGAGE CONTRACT

There is no statutory form of chattel mortgage, but legal practice has standardized it so that blank forms may be obtained from stationers and bookstores.

The principal conditions of the standard chattel mortgage are as follows:

- The mortgagor (the borrower) assigns the title to the goods to the mortgagee (the lender) in consideration of the debt.

- The goods are properly described and their location identified.
- The mortgage provides that on payment of the debt and interest in the manner and at the times stipulated, the mortgage becomes void.
- The mortgagor gives his solemn promise (called his personal covenant) that he will pay the debt according to the terms of the mortgage.
- The rights of the mortgagee on default by the mortgagor are defined.
- The mortgagor agrees to insure the goods for an adequate sum, payable to the mortgagee.

REGISTRATION OF THE MORTGAGE

Between the parties to the mortgage, the contract is effective as soon as it has been made. However, as in the case of conditional sales agreements, in order for the mortgagee to retain his prior claim against subsequent purchasers or mortgagees, it is necessary to register the mortgage in the proper office within the statutory period. As long as the mortgage remains unpaid, the registration should be renewed periodically.

The registering of the mortgage must be accompanied by (1) an affidavit that the chattel mortgage was given in good faith and not for the purpose of defeating the rights of creditors of the mortgagor, and (2) an affidavit of a witness to the execution of the mortgage.

In Ontario the time allowed for registration is ten days, in British Columbia twenty-one days, and in the other provinces thirty days.

It should be noted than an innocent purchaser for value of goods bought from a recognized trader (including a trader in second-hand goods) gets good title to the goods regardless of any existing mortgage on the goods.

ASSIGNMENT OF CHATTEL MORTGAGE

It is not uncommon for business men (mortgagees) who have taken chattel mortgages from their customers (mortgagors) to assign the mortgages to a finance company. It is not necessary to get the mortgagor's consent but he must be notified, and he will then be required to make payments on the mortgage to the finance company (the assignee). It is also legal for the mortgagor (but only with the mortgagee's consent) to sell the mortgaged goods and assign the mortgage and the obligation of making the payments to the new buyer (the assignee). However, if the assignee under the mortgage defaults on the mortgage payments, the mortgagee can hold the original mortgagor liable on his "personal covenant," and the obligation to pay the balance of the mortgage falls back upon him. When this happens, the original mortgagor is entitled to repossess the goods or, alternatively, to be indemnified by the defaulting assignee.

THE MORTGAGEE'S REMEDIES ON DEFAULT

According to the usual terms of a chattel mortgage, if payment is not made at maturity, the mortgagee may take any one of the following courses:

- Renew the mortgage.
- Take possession of the goods and sell to recover principal, interest and costs.
- Enter upon the premises, take possession of the chattels and hold them pending redemption by the mortgagor.
- Arrange an extension of time for payment with the mortgagor.

- Obtain an order of foreclosure. When the mortgagee forecloses he is, in effect, taking the goods for his own absolutely as full satisfaction for the debt. In the case of chattel mortgages this procedure is seldom used.

Sale by the Mortgagee. The remedy which the mortgagee usually employs on default of payment is to sell the chattels. The following are the rules governing a sale:

- The goods may be sold by public auction or by private sale. Usually the mortgage provides that the mortgagor shall be given formal notice of the intention to sell and the place and date of the sale.
- A mortgagee under a power of sale may not purchase the chattels for himself.
- In selling, the mortgagee must secure the best price obtainable.

C—34

A mortgagee held a chattel mortgage for $125 on certain household effects on which he had advanced only $45 to the mortgagor. On default in payment by the mortgagor, the mortgagee seized the goods and sold them for $148. The mortgagor sued for damages for loss, claiming that the goods were worth $2,000. The court held that the mortgagee had acted in a reckless and improvident manner in selling the goods and was therefore liable to the mortgagor for the loss sustained.

- Any surplus over and above the amount due the mortgagee must be paid to the mortgagor. On the other hand, if the sale is properly conducted, and the proceeds of the sale are not sufficient to pay the mortgage debt, the mortgagor is liable for the balance owing.

Mortgagor's Right to Redeem. The mortgagor is allowed a reasonable time in which to redeem the goods he has lost through default on the mortgage. He may exercise this right while the goods are still in the possession of the mortgagee. Generally a final order of foreclosure extinguishes the right of redemption.

DISCHARGE OF A CHATTEL MORTGAGE

When the mortgage has been paid the mortgagor may secure a certificate of discharge from the mortgagee. The certificate should be attested by affidavit of a subscribing witness and filed in the office where the mortgage is filed.

BILLS OF SALE

A *bill of sale* is merely the written document representing a sale of any kind. However, we shall examine here the law governing a bill of sale given in a transaction of a particular kind, namely a sale where the ownership of the goods has been transferred to the buyer but the seller retains actual possession of them.

For example, A buys 1,000 bushels of oats from B, a farmer, under an arrangement whereby B keeps the oats stored on his premises for the next three months, after which A will take delivery.

In a sale of this kind, the seller, having possession of the goods, is in a position to dispose of them fraudulently to an innocent third party without the knowledge of the true owner. Some special protection is therefore needed by the buyer to whom the ownership had been originally transferred in order to protect his rights against such third parties.

To provide this protection each province (except Quebec) has adopted a Bills of Sale Act which requires that where a buyer acquires ownership but not immediate possession of the goods sold to him, a bill of sale covering the transaction shall be registered in a public office. The registration is considered public notice of the transaction. Any party interested in the buyer's title to the goods may inquire at the Registry Office to see if a bill of sale to the buyer is on file.

If a bill of sale is not registered, a third party obtaining the goods from the seller (the apparent owner) gets good title to them and the original buyer (the true owner) cannot assert his right of ownership against such third party.

FORMALITIES OF REGISTRATION

A bill of sale need not be under seal, but in practice it is usual to execute it in this manner. Two formal documents must accompany the bill of sale and be registered with it:

- An affidavit of a witness that he saw the seller sign the bill of sale. (In Ontario, if a corporation executes a document under its corporate seal, no affidavit of attesting witness is required).
- An affidavit by the buyer that the sale has been made in good faith and for good consideration, and not for the purpose of holding the goods against creditors of the seller.

In Ontario, the time for registration is within five days (in counties) or ten days (in provisional districts) from the date of execution; in British Columbia, twenty-one days; and in the other provinces, thirty days. Registration should be renewed every three years (Prince Edward Island, every five years) until the contract has been discharged. In some provinces special provisions apply to the registering of bills of sale for the sale of motor vehicles.

THE PERSONAL PROPERTY SECURITY ACT OF ONTARIO

PURPOSE OF THE LEGISLATION

This Act, passed in 1967, covers the field now covered by The Conditional Sales Act, The Bills of Sale and Chattel Mortgages Act, and The Assignment of Book Debts Act. Because the Act introduced a change in the registration system, a three-year transitional period following its enactment was provided for, at the end of which it is intended that the three Acts mentioned above will be repealed and The Personal Property Security Act proclaimed. At that time, also, a new Bills of Sale Act will be proclaimed, the part of the former Act dealing with chattel mortgages being incorporated into The Personal Property Security Act.

Although proclamation of the Act is still pending as at the time of this writing, a brief explanation of its purpose and general operation is included here in anticipation of its being proclaimed in the near future.

The purpose of the Act is to make uniform the legal procedures by which a secured party (a mortgagee under a chattel mortgage, or a seller under a

conditional sale) acquires and exercises his security interest in personal property which is in the possession of another person. At present, the rights of these parties are governed by separate statutes. We should mention here that the Act is patterned after Article 9 of the American Uniform Commercial Code which has been adopted by all the states except Louisiana.

Transactions to Which the Act Applies. The Act applies "to every transaction that in substance creates a security interest." In this context we are concerned with the application of the Act to conditional sale contracts and chattel mortgages, uniformly referred to as "security agreements."

Definitions. A *security interest* is the indebtedness or other right secured to a party by the terms of a security agreement; for example, the rights of a conditional seller under a conditional sale agreement, or the rights of a mortgagee under a chattel mortgage.

The personal property to which the security attaches is called the *collateral.*

A security interest is said to be *perfected* when the security agreement is properly registered. Possession of the collateral by the secured party also *perfects* the security interest; for instance, repossession of personal property by the conditional seller.

As an illustration, suppose a car dealer sells a car to K under a conditional sale and registers a copy of the conditional sale agreement in the local registry office. Under the new Act, the car dealer is the secured party. The conditional sale contract is the security agreement. The car dealer's rights with regards to K's indebtedness on the car is the car dealer's security interest. The car itself is the collateral. When the car dealer registers a copy of the conditional sale contract, he perfects his security interest, or putting it the other way round, his security interest is said to be perfected. If K defaults on his contract and the car dealer repossesses the car, the repossession also perfects the car dealer's security interest.

REGISTRATION

In order to perfect a security interest (for example, the conditional seller's rights under a conditional sale), the security agreement must be registered within *ten days* of the date the collateral (the personal property) comes under the control of the debtor. Registration is to be made in existing county registry offices and from these points data will be transmitted to a central registry office in Toronto. Registration at a central office for the whole province provides a central source of information to interested parties in any part of the province, no matter where the documents were originally registered.

If the security agreement is not registered as required by the Act, any subsequent purchaser of the goods sold or mortgaged under the agreement, or any person who assumes control of the goods by legal process, gets good title to the goods.

We may note here that two practices related to registration under the older statutes are to be dropped: (1) Affidavits will no longer be required to accompany the execution of a chattel mortgage for registration purposes. There are no prescribed forms for security agreements; (2) The marking of certain goods with the seller's or manufacturer's name will no longer be a substitute for registration. A security interest can be perfected only by registration or by actual possession of the goods by the secured party.

If the debtor assigns his interest (sells or otherwise disposes of the goods), he should have the secured party's consent first, and the secured party must register a notice of the assignment within 15 days of the time he consented to it. If the debtor assigns without the knowledge and consent of the secured party, that party must register a notice within 15 days of the time he learns about it; otherwise the secured party's interest is no longer protected.

The Registration Certificate and The Assurance Fund. Upon the request of any person and the payment of a fee, the registrar will issue a certificate containing information from the registered document. Those who thus *search* the title to personal property will have to rely upon this certificate.

In the event that an incorrect certificate is issued by the registrar and loss is suffered as a result, the injured party will be indemnified out of an *Assurance Fund* which is to be set up for that purpose.

Removal of Goods into Ontario. If personal property was already subject to a security interest when brought into Ontario, the validity of the security interest is to be determined by the law of the jurisdiction where the property was when the security interest attached. However, unless the secured party registers a *caution* (notice) in prescribed form within 20 days after the goods entered Ontario, the secured party's right of repossession and resale is unenforceable. In order to protect his rights the secured party should within 60 days register a copy of the security agreement.

Goods Purchased From a Trader. A purchaser of goods from a seller who sells them in the ordinary course of business takes the goods free from any security interest given by the seller, whether it has been registered or not. So if the trader is a conditional purchaser who has not paid for the goods, or if he has mortgaged the goods to a creditor and the mortgage is registered, a purchaser from him will still get good title. This is similar to the rule already in effect under the Conditional Sales Act.

RIGHTS AND REMEDIES ON DEFAULT

The following rights and remedies are provided by the Act:

1. The secured party has the right of repossession and resale.

2. The party repossessing may dispose of the goods by public sale, private sale, lease or otherwise. Pending disposition, he may also retain the goods in his possession for a reasonable time. Only at a public sale may the secured party purchase the goods for himself.

3. Unless the goods are perishable or there is danger of a speedy decline in value, the secured party shall give the debtor not less than 15 days notice of resale. The notice must be given as prescribed by the Act, the conditions being practically the same as those required for the same kind of notice under the Conditional Sales Act.

4. If the secured party chooses to retain the goods irrevocably, the debtor is discharged from any further obligation on the indebtedness.

5. The secured party must account to the debtor for any surplus realized on the sale.

6. Where the debtor has paid at least 60% of the indebtedness secured, he may demand that the secured party, within 90 days of taking possession, dispose of the goods instead of retaining them.

7. At any time before the secured party has disposed of the collateral, or irrevocably elected to retain them in satisfaction of the debt, the debtor may redeem the goods, unless he has agreed otherwise in writing after default.

APPLYING THE LAW

1. At a gathering featuring snowmobile races, Joe admires Ken's snowmobile and offers to buy it on the spot. Ken agrees, the price is paid and Joe takes the snowmobile to his home.
   A week later a representative from the Ekta Finance Co. calls on Joe and informs him that the Ekta Company holds a chattel mortgage on the snowmobile he bought from Ken, and that Ken is in default on his payments. The representative also explains that the chattel mortgage has been on file in the local registry office from the date on which it was given.
   (a) Does the finance company have the right to repossess the snowmobile from Joe?
   (b) What can Joe do in order to keep the snowmobile?
   (c) Is Ken under any liability if the snowmobile is repossessed from Joe?
   (d) If the chattel mortgage had not been registered, could the snowmobile have been repossessed from Joe?
   (e) How could Joe have avoided this awkward situation?

DISCUSSION AND PROJECTS

1. Obtain a copy of a chattel mortgage such as is used by a finance company, and examine its terms.
2. Under the new Ontario Personal Security Act there will no longer be exemptions from registration as there are under the Conditional Sales Act. What advantages or disadvantages do you see in this change?

UNIT TEN
BORROWING, HIRING OR STORING PROPERTY

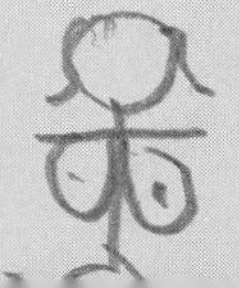

Part 23
THE LAW OF BAILMENTS

THE NATURE OF A BAILMENT

CASE 1

Leclair rents an electric lawnmower from the Ace Equipment Rental Co., and fails to notice that the wires are somewhat frayed. While he is cutting his lawn, sparks begin to shoot from the area of the handle. Leclair jumps back, twisting his ankle. The mower continues forward and is badly damaged through striking a baseball bat which had been left on the lawn.

Leclair takes out his rental receipt to find the telephone number of the Ace Rental Co. and for the first time notices that the receipt has stamped on it the words "Customer accepts full responsibility for loss or damage."

(a) This case involves a type of rental which in law is classified as a bailment. Who receives benefit from this bailment?
(b) Do you think Leclair should be responsible for the damage to the lawnmower?
(c) Would you make Ace Equipment Rental Co. liable for damages for Leclair's injury?
(d) Would the situation be different if the lawnmower had been borrowed from a friend?

A common type of transaction is the leaving of personal property with another person for some purpose. For instance, a person may loan or hire his property to another, or he may leave it in some person's possession to have something done to it or merely to have it stored for him. Also, goods may be delivered to someone for transportation.

Transactions of this nature are known in law as *bailments*, a word derived from the French "bailler" meaning "to give or to deliver."

A bailment consists of the delivery of personal property to another on the understanding that at the end of a specified or determined time, or when the purpose of the delivery has been fulfilled, the property is to be returned to the owner or to some other person according to the owner's direction. The person who owns and delivers the property is the *bailor*, and the person to whom the goods are delivered and who has the custody of them is the *bailee*.

Bailments are different from sales. In the case of a sale there is a transfer of ownership from seller to buyer, whereas in the case of a bailment the bailor continues to own the goods; he transfers only possession to the bailee. This distinction becomes important when it is necessary to determine on whom the loss should fall for damage to or destruction of the goods.

By law, all bailees have a duty to take care of the property entrusted to them. Essentially, it is a matter of contract between the parties concerned; and the terms that they agree on will govern the degree of care that must be taken of the goods and the responsibility for their loss or destruction. However, if the parties have not agreed on these specific conditions, the law of bailment establishes the standard of care which applies and the liability arising therefrom. On the other hand, it is quite possible that, where the parties choose to make their own agreement, they may agree on conditions that impose either a greater or a lesser degree of responsibility than would the law of bailment in the absence of an agreement.

CLASSES OF BAILMENT

Bailments may be divided into two main classes:

- Gratuitous bailments
- Bailments for reward

GRATUITOUS BAILMENTS

A bailment is said to be *gratuitous* when one of the parties to it receives some favour or service free of charge. Depending on who receives the benefit, this type of bailment may be further classified as either (a) bailment for the benefit of the bailor only, or (b) bailment for the sole benefit of the bailee. The distinction is important because, in the absence of a specific agreement otherwise, the standard of care imposed by the law of bailment on the bailee varies accordingly.

BAILMENT FOR THE BENEFIT OF THE BAILOR ONLY

C—2

(a) Who benefits from the above transaction, the bailor or the bailee?
(b) What degree of care do you think the bailee should take in this case:
    (i) The same care as he would take of his own property?
    (ii) A greater degree of care?
    (iii) A lesser degree of care?

This type of bailment is common, as when one person (the bailor) delivers goods or other property to another person (the bailee) to be kept in the bailee's custody and care without reward; or when a bailor delivers property to a bailee to have something done to it—again, free of charge; or when someone asks a friend to deliver a parcel for him, simply as a favour, and without reward.

Apart from a contract which provides specific conditions of care and responsibility, in bailments where only the bailor benefits while the bailee goes without reward, the standard of care imposed by the law of bailments on the bailee is, generally speaking, much less onerous than in other classes of bailments. In such cases the bailee is obliged only to take such care of the property as an ordinarily prudent person would take of his own property. If the property is lost, damaged or destroyed while in the bailee's care, he is not liable to the bailor unless the loss has occurred because of the bailee's gross negligence or because he has disobeyed or disregarded the instructions of the bailor.

C—3

Wills handed Brown a sum of money to buy certain tickets. Brown, instead of buying them himself as he was instructed to do, gave the money to one of his clerks, who instead of buying the tickets used a portion of the money for himself. Wills sued Brown for the return of the entire sum of money. Brown pleaded that the loss of the money was not his fault, and that he had not been grossly negligent.

An Ontario court held that once Brown had agreed to buy the tickets, he was required to use reasonable care and diligence with regard to the custody of the money, and was required to carry out that duty without negligence. The giving of the money to the clerk was a violation of this duty, and Brown was liable for the loss.

(a) Who was the bailor?
(b) Is this a gratuitous bailment?
(c) Who is benefiting from the bailment, the bailor or the bailee, or both?
(d) What degree of care is imposed on Brown in this case?
(e) Brown was held liable. Why?
(f) Suppose Brown had taken the money to a ticket agent who accepted the money and promised delivery of the tickets next day, but that next day it is discovered that the ticket agent is bankrupt, with no tickets and no money. Would the result be different?

BAILMENT FOR THE SOLE BENEFIT OF THE BAILEE

C—4

(a) Who receives the benefit in this transaction, the bailor or the bailee?
(b) What degree of care should the borrower exercise in this case?
  (i) The same care as he would take of his own property?
  (ii) Greater care?
  (iii) Less care?

This sort of bailment occurs when one borrows another's property without payment for its use. Since this type of bailment is entirely for the benefit of the bailee, the standard of care (in the absence of an agreement setting out specific responsibilities) required by the law of bailments is much higher than that required of a bailee for reward. The obligations of the borrower when the bailment is gratuitous are as follows.

• He must take the utmost degree of care of the article and is liable for his negligence, however slight.

• He must not use the article for any purpose other than that for which it was lent. If he does, he becomes liable for damage to the goods, no matter what the cause. Thus, if the borrower in turn lends the borrowed article to another person, the original borrower becomes liable for any and all damage to the article while it is so lent.

• Provided that the foregoing two rules are strictly observed, a bailee under a gratuitous bailment—even when the bailment is for the sole benefit of the bailee—is not liable for loss or damage to the goods caused by ordinary "wear and tear"; neither is he liable for loss or damage by fire or theft unless such events occur as a result of his negligence.

C—5

Anderson loaned Royer a tractor for use in threshing his crop. After the threshing was finished, the tractor was left upon Royer's premises at his request and with Anderson's consent, Royer having indicated that he might want to use the tractor again later. However, he did not drain the water from the tractor's radiator, and the water froze, damaging the engine.

From the evidence, it appeared that Anderson had telephoned Royer and had asked him to drain the radiator, and that Royer, thinking that one of his employees had done so, assured Anderson that it had been looked after. The Saskatchewan Court of Appeal held that Royer was liable for the damage to the tractor since he was negligent in not using due care to prevent damage.

(a) Who was getting the benefit from this bailment, the bailor or the bailee?
(b) Should the degree of care imposed by law on Royer be the same, or more, or less than that imposed on Brown in C—3, *Wills v. Brown*, above? Why?
(c) Would Royer's responsibility have been different if the tractor had been left on Royer's premises at Anderson's request?
(d) If Anderson had not phoned asking that the radiator be drained, would Royer's responsibility have been the same?

BAILMENT FOR REWARD

This type of bailment is sometimes described as bailment for the benefit of both parties, or bailment for hire.

As mentioned before, if the parties to a bailment agree on their own terms, these terms will govern. In the case of bailments for the benefit of both parties it is more common to find the parties entering into their own specific contract; in the absence of such an agreement, however, certain rules apply.

Renting personal property. When personal property is rented or hired, the owner of the goods is the bailor and the party hiring the goods is the bailee.

The bailor's responsibilities are:

- The article hired out must be reasonably fit and safe for the work for which it was rented. There is an implied warranty on the part of the owner that he will be liable for damage that results from defects of which he ought to have been aware.

- The bailor can be held liable for damage caused by hidden defects only where it is proved that he was negligent in not discovering the defects.

C—6

The owners of a crane rented it out to someone who employed Hadley (both young and inexperienced) to operate it. At the time the crane was rented out, there was a need for some adjustment, known to the owners, but the defect was not considered dangerous at the time. Later, the condition of the defect became worse,

and eventually caused an accident in which Hadley (the operator) was injured.
The court found the owners negligent and liable as bailors in that they had handed over a machine which needed adjustment without warning the bailee of that condition. The bailees were also liable to their employee, Hadley, in that they failed to service the crane properly before having it operated by an inexperienced employee. Damages were assessed equally against the owners and the bailees.

(a) What legal obligation as bailors did the court find the owners of the crane had failed to perform?
(b) In what respect did the court find the bailees had failed in their duty?
(c) Would the result have been different if the bailors had not been aware of the defect?

The bailee's obligations are:

- He must pay the full rental price even though he returns the property before the date agreed upon—unless, of course, the owner voluntarily agrees to a reduction of the rent.

- The bailee must exercise reasonable care over the property. He is liable for damage or loss caused by his negligence or that of his employees. Further, the onus of disproving such negligence rests upon the bailee. (This is an exception to the general rule that the plaintiff must prove his case rather than that the defendant disprove it. However, in this situation the onus appears to be reasonable in that the bailee, being in possession of the goods, is in a better position than the bailor to know just how the damage or loss occurred).

- Unless otherwise agreed, the bailee is not liable for damage or loss to the property due to ordinary wear and tear.

- He is not obliged to make repairs to the property except those incidental to taking reasonable care of it. If, however, he makes other repairs without the knowledge and consent of the owner, he cannot recover the cost of those repairs from the owner.

C—7

Smith agreed with Queens Sales to purchase a new car. The new car was not available immediately and, as part of the transaction, Queen Sales furnished Smith with another car to drive while he awaited delivery of the new one. Since the furnishing of the alternate car was part of the price, the court treated it as a bailment for reward just as if the car had been rented. Unknown to Smith, the brakes on the alternate car were faulty, and it was subsequently involved in an accident while being operated by Smith's girl friend. Queens Sales knew that the car would be driven by her as well as by Smith when they arranged for him to have it.

Since there was no negligence on the part of either Smith or his girl friend, and since the car was not used contrary to the instructions of the bailor (Queens Sales and Services Ltd.), the Nova Scotia Court of Appeal attached no liability to either Smith or the lady, and found Queen's Sales responsible.

(a) Why was Queens Sales held liable for the accident?
(b) What difference would it have made if, after taking the car but before the accident, Smith had discovered that the brakes were faulty?
(c) If Queens Sales claimed that the accident was Smith's fault, would the onus be on them to prove it or would Smith be obliged to disprove the charge?

Doing work on personal property. The owner of property who delivers it to someone for the purpose of having work done on it is the bailor, while the person who receives possession of the goods and does the work is the bailee.

The bailor's obligations are.

- He must pay the price agreed upon or, if not agreed upon, then a reasonable price.
- If the workman does more than the contract calls for, the owner (the bailor) does not have to pay any extra cost unless he consented to having the extra work done.

The bailee's (the workman's) duties are:

- The workman must do the work as agreed. If he implies that he has special skill or ability, he is liable for any loss caused by his failure to perform the work consistent with the skill and ability implied.
- The workman must take ordinary care of the property, and in the event of loss or damage, the onus of proving that he was not negligent is on himself as bailee.

C—8

A county school board delivered a motor vehicle to Stewart's garage for repairs. While in Stewart's possession the vehicle was destroyed by fire.
A New Brunswick court held that Stewart was liable. The burden was on him as a bailee for reward to show that the loss was not caused by his lack of reasonable care and skill. When he could not disprove negligence, he was held liable for the loss sustained.

(a) Would anybody be liable if Stewart had not been negligent?
(b) What facts would have helped Stewart show he was not negligent?

Unless there is an agreement to the contrary, an unpaid workman has a lien on the goods while the goods are still in his possession; that is, he may refuse to return the goods until the price agreed upon has been paid. Ultimately, he has the right to have the goods sold to satisfy the claim.

Storage.

C—9

(a) As bailee, what is the legal responsibility of the man who operates the pet boarding house?
(b) If the bird dies while in the care of the pet boarding house, and if the owner claims this was due to the negligence of the proprietor, upon whom will the burden of proof lie?

A person who is in the business of storing goods for a fee is called a *warehouseman*. Warehousemen as well as others who store goods for reward are subject to the following rules as bailees:

- The warehouseman must use reasonable diligence in caring for the goods deposited with him. The onus is on him as bailee to prove that loss or destruction of goods in his custody was not due to his negligence.
- If a warehouseman accepts for storage commodities that require special facilities (for example, meat and fruit), he is obligated to provide those facilities; otherwise he will be liable for loss or damage because of the lack of proper storage.

C—10

British Motor Corporation stored a large number of cars on the Judge Auto Transport lot, and paid three dollars per car per month. Judge employed a watchman to patrol the area, but, nevertheless, damage was done to the cars.
BMC sued for the damage, and a Nova Scotia court held that Judge did not exercise reasonable care. The patrol could not have been adequate if such extensive damage was done, and Judge could not disprove this assumption of lack of reasonable care.

(a) Why was the defendant, Judge Auto Transport, liable?
(b) What extra steps could have been taken to constitute reasonable care?
(c) Would the situation be any different if a friend stored a car in your garage and paid you $10 a month?

The same principles that apply to simple storage cases also apply to cases in which storage of goods is merely a part of a larger transaction, such as when a restaurant supplies racks for hats and coats and when a store provides

Notice on door reads: "CHARGES ARE FOR USE OF PARKING SPACE ONLY. This Company assumes no responsibility whatever for loss or damage due to fire, theft, collision or otherwise to the vehicle or its contents—however caused"

parking facilities. Generally, these cases are viewed as cases of storage for hire, since the business to be done indirectly involves some payment for the storage of one's goods.

C—11

Murphy, a customer in Hart's restaurant, hung up his coat and hat in one of the recesses provided for that purpose. When he was about to leave, he found that his hat and coat were gone. The Nova Scotia Court of Appeal held that this was a bailment for hire, and the onus was on the restaurant to show that the loss was not due to negligence on its part. The restaurant owner could not prove that he was not negligent in the matter, and he was held responsible.

(a) Would the restaurant owner be liable if the coat rack had been attached to the end of the booth in which the customer was sitting?
(b) Would a sign, "Not Responsible For Customers' Hats And Coats," have changed the situation?

Pledge or Pawn.

C—12

Connelly borrows $10 from McManus and gives him his watch as security for payment. McManus wears the watch while he awaits payment. On an unusually icy pavement, McManus slips and falls, damaging the watch.

(a) Is McManus obligated to repair the watch?
(b) If Connelly does not repay the $10, what may McManus do with the watch?

A *pledge* consists of depositing or pledging personal property as security for the payment of a debt. The usual condition is that the person to whom the property was pledged (for example, a bank) may sell the property if the debt is not paid according to the agreement between the pledgor and the pledgee. In the event that the property is sold, the pledgee may reimburse himself only for the amount of the unpaid debt and any expense involved in the sale; any surplus from the proceeds of the sale belongs to the pledgor. A common example of a pledge is the giving of bonds or other valuables as collateral security for a loan. As a bailee, the pledgee is responsible for reasonable care of the property while it is in his possession, and must return it when the debt is paid.

A *pawn* is similar to a pledge. The term is confined to transactions with pawnbrokers who are licensed to conduct such businesses. A pawnbroker is responsible for taking reasonable care of the property pawned with him, and is liable for loss due to his negligence.

Carriers. Carriers fall into two classes: private carriers and common carriers.

A *private carrier* is one who *occasionally* transports goods for other people and gets paid for the service, but who does not make it a business in a public way. Thus, he reserves the right to accept or reject either the customer or the type of goods to be carried, whether he has the facilities to carry them or not. For example, a company which operates a delivery truck in the course of its own business may, on occasion, make deliveries for others. On those occasions he would be a private carrier. However, a private carrier is a bailee for reward and, as such, has a duty to take reasonable care of the goods he carries. He is liable for loss caused by negligence whether it be his own or that of his employees.

Common carriers are those who hold themselves out to the public as being in the business of transporting goods; for example, railways and trucking companies. The law imposes two responsibilities on common carriers which do not apply to private carriers:

- A common carrier does not have the right to pick and choose his customers, and he must accept any and all goods offered for shipment—provided he has the necessary facilities for carrying them.

- A common carrier is an *insurer* of the goods during their transportation to the extent that he is liable for loss or damage occurring in the course of shipment, even though he has not been guilty of any negligence in the carrying of them.

There are three exceptions to the common carrier's liability as an insurer. A common carrier is not liable for loss or damage to goods caused by an "act of God," the King's enemies, or inherent defects in the goods.

An *"act of God"* is some unforeseen accident caused by the forces of nature—for example, a storm or flood or other forces over which man has no control—and which no reasonable care could have prevented.

C—13

(i) While crossing Northumberland Strait (which separates Prince Edward Island from New Brunswick and Nova Scotia) a ferry boat was struck by a huge wave, the like of which had not been known in that area for sixty years. Turgel Fur Company's truck, which was on the ferry boat, was damaged, as were also its contents. Turgel sued for damages.
A Nova Scotia court dismissed the case, holding that the damage was caused by an "act of God" which could not have been foreseen or prevented by the ferry boat owners.

(ii) The Canadian Wheat Board, an agent of the Crown, arranged to have a quantity of wheat transported by the Canadian Pacific Railway. The train carrying the wheat ran into a landslide covering the tracks, and was derailed. As a result, the wheat was lost. The landslide had been caused by a combination of weather conditions.
The Exchequer Court found the railway responsible on the grounds that, although the slide resulted from natural causes, information regarding the likelihood of slides and the potential danger to this area was available, and measures could have been taken to warn the crews or make the situation harmless.

(a) Why did the courts come to different conclusions in these two cases?
(b) Would damage caused by lightning be an "act of God"?

The second exception, *the King's enemies*, is self-explanatory. Carriers are not liable if goods are lost or destroyed by enemy action during war.

The third exception, *inherent defects in the goods*, means those defects which bring about deterioration of the goods. Examples might be defective packing, perishable products or unruly animals. In such cases the carrier is liable only if the loss or injury is due to negligence on the part of the carrier or his employees.

The common law liability of common carriers has been somewhat modified by statute. For example, the Railway Act contains rules and regulations for the operation of railways. One of the most important provisions is that a railway may modify its liabilities by contract, provided that the approval of the Railway Commission is obtained. A reading of the terms and conditions on the back of a railway bill of lading or a baggage check will reveal a number of clauses limiting the carrier's liability; for instance, one of the limitations is the amount which the railway will pay for lost or damaged goods. Other common carriers are also permitted to impose by contract certain limitations on their liability.

Any person shipping goods by common carrier is expected to make himself familiar with the terms of the carrier's contract. At the same time, common carriers cannot, by contract, escape liability for loss or damage caused by their own negligence; and any terms in the contract to that effect would be void.

A passenger's hand baggage must be distinguished from the baggage he checks with the carrier. A suitcase or handbag that a passenger elects to carry is

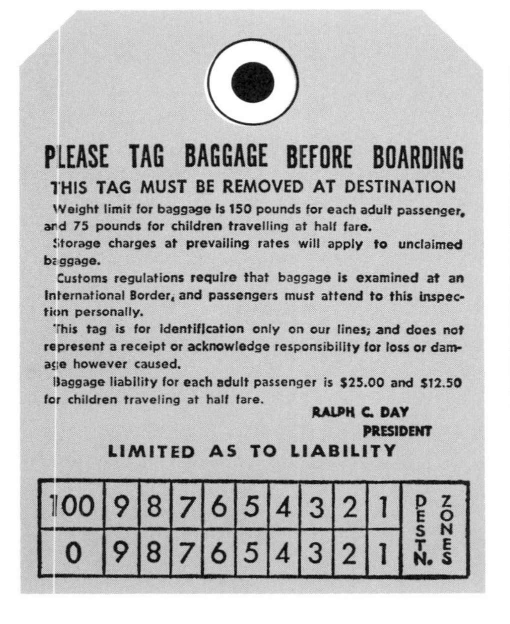

PLEASE TAG BAGGAGE BEFORE BOARDING

THIS TAG MUST BE REMOVED AT DESTINATION

Weight limit for baggage is 150 pounds for each adult passenger, and 75 pounds for children travelling at half fare.

Storage charges at prevailing rates will apply to unclaimed baggage.

Customs regulations require that baggage is examined at an International Border, and passengers must attend to this inspection personally.

This tag is for identification only on our lines; and does not represent a receipt or acknowledge responsibility for loss or damage however caused.

Baggage liability for each adult passenger is $25.00 and $12.50 for children traveling at half fare.

RALPH C. DAY
PRESIDENT

LIMITED AS TO LIABILITY

100	9	8	7	6	5	4	3	2	1	DEST N. / ZONES
0	9	8	7	6	5	4	3	2	1	

GRAY COACH LINES

Form 11-V

BAGGAGE IDENTIFICATION TAG

THIS IS NOT A BAGGAGE CHECK

To CALGARY
PRINT CLEARLY

Name BASIL STOWSKI
PRINT CLEARLY

Address 9 NEW MAIN ST.
PRINT CLEARLY

LIABILITY LIMITED TO $25.00

"FOR INSTRUCTIONS SEE REVERSE SIDE"

DEST N. / ZONES	1	2	3	4	5	6	7	8	9	100
	1	2	3	4	5	6	7	8	9	0

Gray Coach Lines

in the passenger's own custody; if it is lost, the passenger may not hold the carrier liable unless the loss was due to the carrier's negligence. On the other hand, if the baggage had been checked with the carrier, he would be responsible.

Once the goods have arrived at the point of destination, and the consignee (the person to whom the goods are shipped) is afforded a reasonable opportunity to take delivery of the goods, the liability of the transportation agency as a common carrier ceases. While the goods are being held in freight sheds or baggage rooms, the liability of a common carrier is that of a warehouseman. A warehouseman is not an insurer of the goods in his care, and is liable only if loss or damage is caused by his negligence.

C—14

George purchased a cargo of liquor in Scotland and arranged to have it shipped from Scotland to an Atlantic port by sea. A railway company then transported the liquor from that Atlantic port to Fort Frances, where George was to take delivery. When

the liquor arrived at Fort Frances, the shipment was placed in the railway company's warehouse under the supervision of customs officials, and George was sent a notice of arrival. Before the shipment was released by the customs officials part of it was stolen from the warehouse. George sued for damages for loss of the goods.
The Ontario Court of Appeal held that the railway company was still liable as a carrier, since the consignee, George, had not yet had a reasonable time to take the goods away after the carrier was ready to deliver. The railway company was not in a position to deliver the goods until after they had been cleared by customs.

(a) Would the result have been different if the theft had taken place despite the fact that the railway kept the liquor in a modern, supposedly theft-proof vault?
(b) Suppose the theft had taken place one week after clearance from customs. Would the railway still be liable?

C—15

Beausejour turned over a quantity of money to the Dominion Express Company for carriage. When the money arrived at the station to which it was destined it was placed in a safe in the railway station which was not protected against theft. The money was stolen and Beausejour sued the Express Company for the loss of the money.
A Quebec court held that the company's absolute liability as a common carrier had ended when the transportation had ended and there had been sufficient opportunity to take delivery of the money. However, the Express Company was still liable as a warehouseman and, since it was negligent in leaving the money in an unprotected place, it was obliged to compensate Beausejour for his loss.

Compare the facts and judgment in this case to those in C—14.

Hotelkeepers. A hotelkeeper, or innkeeper, as he is sometimes described in the law, is one who holds himself out to the public as ready to provide lodging and accommodations to all travellers. A guest is any transient who makes a contract, express or implied, with the hotelkeeper for accommodation.

By common law, an innkeeper may not refuse to receive any "fit and orderly" person as a guest, provided he has available accommodation. He must receive the guest's baggage as well.

As a bailee, the innkeeper's liability at common law is similar to that of a common carrier; that is, he is an insurer of the goods of a guest brought into the hotel. The questions of who may be a traveller, and what constitutes "within the hotel" have received broad interpretations from the courts.

C—16

(i) Williams, who was driving home in his automobile, stopped at Linnitt's hotel. He parked his car in the hotel parking lot, and had several drinks with friends in the hotel. About an hour later, when he left the hotel, he found that his car had been stolen. On

the parking lot, which immediately adjoined the hotel, was a notice which read "Cars parked. Patrons only."
The English Court of Appeal held that Williams—even though he resided in the immediate neighbourhood of the hotel, and visited it merely to have a drink—was none the less a "traveller" for the purpose of establishing Linnitt's liability as an innkeeper. The court further held that since it was part of Linnitt's normal business to provide accommodation for the cars of guests, the parking lot, being next to the hotel, and one in which a guest was customarily invited to leave his car, was "within the hotel." The owner of the hotel was therefore responsible as an insurer, and Williams was awarded damages to compensate for the loss of the car.

(ii) In this case, another Williams also travelling by automobile, became a guest at George's hotel in Cobourg, Ontario. When he arrived at the hotel, he saw an open area at the side of the hotel which was obviously used as a parking lot. On the lot was a prominent sign reading "Parking for Chateau Hotel Guests Free." Williams parked his car on the lot and left inside the car a travelling bag containing personal belongings and some clothing on hangers resting on the seat. He then went into the hotel premises where he stayed the night. The next morning he discovered that someone had broken into the car and stolen the travelling bag and clothing.
The Ontario Court of Appeal agreed that the innkeeper's liability would have extended to the loss of the car, but did not cover the contents of the car. And so Williams' case was dismissed. The Court indicated that the innkeeper had a right to expect that a guest would bring his goods into the hotel proper where the proprietor would have the opportunity of protecting himself against his common law liability.

(a) Explain the difference between the decisions in these two cases.
(b) In the case of a hotel which provides underground parking beneath the hotel, what is the responsibility of the hotel for the guest's car and its contents?

The liability of the innkeeper has been modified by statute. The Innkeepers' Act of Ontario provides that no innkeeper shall be liable to make good to his guests any loss or injury to goods or property (excepting a horse or other live animal) to a greater sum than $40, except where (i) goods or property have been stolen, lost or injured through the wilful act, default or neglect of the innkeeper or his servant; or (ii) such goods have been deposited with the innkeeper expressly for safe custody. The statute also provides that the innkeeper shall keep a copy of the Section of the Act limiting his liability posted in offices, public rooms and bedrooms. The innkeeper is entitled to the benefit of the Act *only* if these notices are posted.

Similar provisions to those of the Ontario Act are found in the Innkeeper's Acts of Nova Scotia and Prince Edward Island. In New Brunswick the

innkeeper's liability as an insurer is $100, and in Newfoundland, $150. In the other provinces, the innkeeper is not liable as an insurer for any amount; he is liable for loss or damage to his guests' belongings *only* if it is a result of his own negligence or that of his employees. In Alberta, Saskatchewan and Manitoba, the hotelkeeper's liability is further reduced in that he is not responsible for personal effects of any kind left by a guest in his room unless the room is locked during the absence of the guest and the key is left in the office.

A boarding house keeper is not classed as an innkeeper, and does not incur the same liability. A boarding house keeper reserves the right to accept or reject any person seeking board or lodging. As a bailee he is like any other bailee for reward; that is, he is liable for loss to his guest's property only if he fails to exercise reasonable care.

The question of whether or not a motel is an inn has received the attention of the courts. Note the decision in the following case:

C—17

King was refused accommodation at a motel in Alberta and sued for damages for refusal to provide accommodation. King's case relied on the assumption that the hotel was an inn, and on the common law duty of inns to provide accommodation.
An Alberta court held that the motel was not an inn since it did not provide food. Inns, as contemplated by the common law, provide full accommodation for travellers, and the simple provision of rooms without food did not constitute the keeping of an inn.

Some motels provide breakfast only. Are they "inns" at common law?

LIMITING LIABILITY BY CONTRACT

As previously mentioned, the law of bailment provides certain rules that govern the relationship between bailor and bailee in the absence of a specific agreement concerning the bailment. The parties are free to agree on a different standard of care or to provide that there shall be no responsibility whatever on the bailee. In cases where the parties freely agree on this alteration of their rights under the common law, there is seldom any problem. If the parties sign an agreement, they will in most cases be bound by the terms of the agreement despite the fact that they may not have understood its legal implications, and even if they were not fully aware of its contents.

The cases that cause considerable difficulty are those in which the bailee seeks to introduce a term into the contract of bailment by the display of a sign or by the printing of conditions on the back of a ticket. In many of these cases the bailor takes the position that he did not know of the special terms that applied to the bailment. Courts have held that bailees seeking to rely on this type of limitation of liability must demonstrate that reasonable steps were taken to bring the special term or condition to the attention of the bailor.

C—18

(i) Spooner parked his automobile in a parking lot operated by Starkman. He paid fifteen cents and received a ticket on which appeared in small type "Not responsible for car or contents." There were two signs on the premises, one bearing the same words as the ticket, the other saying "Car left at owner's risk."

The car was stolen from Starkman's lot, and was later recovered in a damaged condition. Spooner sued the parking lot operator on the grounds that he was negligent in allowing the car to be stolen. The parking lot operator defended on the grounds that the terms on the signs and on the ticket excluded liability.
The Ontario Court of Appeal awarded judgment to Spooner on the grounds that the parking lot operator was negligent, and that the terms on the signs and ticket were not adequate. The court suggested that the ticket was designed not to bring the terms to the attention of the customer but to conceal them.

(ii) Smith parked his car on Silverman's parking lot. While it was parked there it was damaged. At the time the car was parked, a ticket was issued that stated in bold black type "We are not responsible for theft or damage of car or contents however caused." In addition, there were four large signs bearing the same statement displayed in the parking lot.
The Ontario Court of Appeal held in this case that the words on the ticket and signs were a clear declaration, and that Silverman had done what was reasonably necessary to bring the terms limiting his liability to the attention of customers. Smith's claim for damages was dismissed.

Why did the decisions differ in these two cases?

THE RIGHT OF LIEN

The *right of lien* is the right to retain possession of another's goods until certain debts or charges against the goods have been paid. However, the right to retain the goods does not necessarily extend to the right to sell them unless the contract of bailment so provides, or unless the right is granted by statute. The Mechanics' Lien Act gives such a right to a workman who has repaired goods; the Innkeepers' Act provides that an innkeeper may, if necessary, hold and sell his guest's personal property to satisfy unpaid accommodation charges; and the Warehousemen's Lien Act gives a similar right to a warehouseman. When the right to sell goods under a lien is to be exercised, certain specific procedures dealing with such matters as advertising and notices must be observed.

APPLYING THE LAW

1. A rented a typewriter from B for three months. When A returned the typewriter, B noticed that it did not work properly and needed repairs. B claims that the typewriter must have received rough usage and that A should pay for the repairs. A argues that the repairs were needed as a result of ordinary wear and tear. Incidentally, the typewriter had been in use for five years. Apply the law to this case.
2. You park your car in a parking lot, leaving the keys in the car at the attendant's request. When you return to the lot, you find the car has been stolen. Explain the liability resting on the proprietor of the parking lot.

3. Ben borrowed his neighbour's lawnmower, an expensive tractor-mowing machine. When Ben had finished mowing his lawn he lent the mower to his friend, Jack, to try out the mower. When Ben returned the mower to its owner he did not know that Jack had damaged the machine. When the owner discovered the damage, he told Ben he expected him to pay the bill (an estimated $30). Ben refused, saying that since Jack had damaged the machine, the owner should look to Jack for redress. Explain the rights and liabilities of each of the parties to this case.
4. 

What is the liability of the railway company for this piece of personal luggage?

DISCUSSION AND PROJECTS

1. Survey the parking lots and restaurants in your area and check the existence and location of signs dealing with responsibility for cars, hats, coats, etc. Note whether the owners have done what is reasonably necessary to bring the signs to the attention of customers?
2. Obtain from a railway or airline, or from some traveller who may have them, a baggage check and passenger's ticket. Examine these documents to learn what limitations they contain regarding the carrier's liability for checked baggage.
3. Is it the practice of car dealers in your municipality to give the customer a "loaner" car when he leaves his car for service? If so, is the customer required to sign anything when taking the loaner? What are the conditions on the work order which he signs when leaving his car for service? Visit a local car dealer for answers to these questions.

UNIT ELEVEN SUBSTITUTES FOR MONEY

Negotiable instruments is a legal term for cheques, promissory notes and drafts. The term "negotiable" means that these instruments may be transferred from one person to another as payments. As a result they become practically a substitute for money. The same instruments are also referred to as *bills of exchange*; in fact, the statute which embodies the law pertaining to them is called the Bills of Exchange Act.

The use of bills of exchange developed in Europe during the Middle Ages, probably as a result of the risk of transporting gold or currencies from place to place at a time when routes were not safe and tavellers ran the risk of being waylaid by robbers and highwaymen. For example, if A in London owed a debt to B in Paris, and C in Paris owed A in London, A, by written document (a bill of exchange) could request C to pay B. By this means two debts were paid without running the risks involved in transporting currency. As trade and commerce increased, so did the use of bills of exchange. Today we have a highly developed, world-wide system.

During the Middle Ages in England and Europe, trade and commerce were largely controlled by organizations known as *guilds*. The merchant-members of the guilds developed their own rules and trading practices, and also their own system of enforcing them. This body of rules and practices had the force of law and was known as the *law merchant* (laws of the merchants). At the English fairs, which were important commercial events, disputes were settled in courts formed by officials of the fair. At these courts a great variety of cases came up, ranging from personal squabbles to important commercial suits. The traders who came to the fair from any one town or city were treated as a community. If disputes arose, the whole group was held responsible for each individual member. For example, the following entry was made in the roll of the fair of St. Ives in the year 1275.

William of Fleetbridge and Anne, his wife, complain of Thomas Coventry of Leicester for unjustly withholding from them . . . 55

> *shillings and 2 1/2 pence for a sack of wool. . . . Elias is ordered to attach the* community *of Leicester to answer . . . and of the said community, Allan Parker, Adam Nose and Robert Howell are attached by three bundles of ox hides, three hundred bundles of sheep skins, and six sacks of wool.**

In other words, Elias, an official of the fair, was ordered by the court to seize from Parker, Nose and Howell, who were also traders from Leicester, the rather large quantity of goods mentioned as security for the debt of their fellow-tradesman from Leicester, Thomas Coventry.

At first the law merchant was not recognized by the royal courts in which the common law was administered. But as trade and commerce spread beyond the confines of the fairs, and the power and influence of the guilds waned, the rules of the law merchant came to be administered by the common law courts. Eventually, for the benefit of merchants and bankers, the existing law on negotiable instruments was codified, and in 1882 the British parliament embodied the codification into the Bills of Exchange Act.

The Canadian Bills of Exchange Act, passed in 1890, is an adaptation of the British act. Since bills of exchange come under federal jurisdiction, the Act is a federal one, and applies to all of Canada.

It is interesting to note that the Uniform Negotiable Instruments Law of the United States is also based upon the British act. Here, again, there are only a few minor points of difference between the two acts.

* Cheyney, *Industrial and Social History of England*, page 66.

Part 24
CHEQUES

A cheque is a bill of exchange drawn on a bank, payable on demand.

A *bill of exchange* is defined by the Act as "an unconditional order in writing addressed by one person to another, signed by the person giving it, requiring the person to whom it is addressed to pay, on demand at a fixed or determinable time, a sum certain in money to or to the order of a specified person or to bearer."

The normal sequence of events in the life of a cheque is as follows:

- Issue
- Negotiation, or transfer
- Payment.

ISSUE OF THE CHEQUE

By issue is meant the writing of the cheque and the delivering of it.

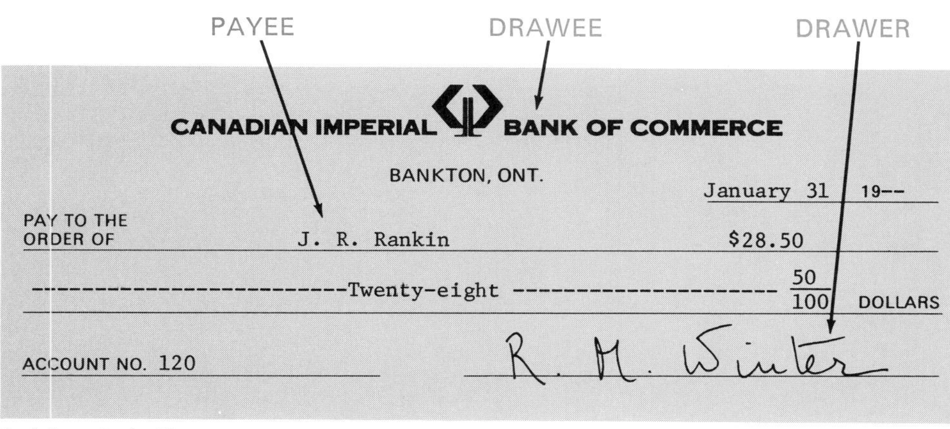

Bank forms in this Unit
courtesy Canadian Imperial Bank of Commerce

WRITING

The legal interpretation of writing includes words "printed, painted, engraved, lithographed or otherwise traced or copied." This interpretation also applies to the signature. According to the Act, the signature need not be in the handwriting of the drawer; it is sufficient if his signature is written thereon by some other person by or under his authority.

In practice, however, the bank keeps on file a specimen of the customer's signature or that of the person who has authority to sign for him, and if the signature on the cheque does not correspond with the authorized specimen, the bank may refuse to honour the cheque.

For the sake of convenience and also of uniformity, blank cheque forms are provided by all banking institutions free of charge (see illustration). At the same time, the law does not require that bank forms be used, and occasionally it is necessary to write a cheque when a bank form is not available. For instance, a farmer found it necessary to write a cheque in circumstances where neither bank forms nor other paper was available, so he wrote it on a shingle. Subsequently it was presented to the bank and honoured.

Sometimes unusual cheques have been drawn as part of a promotion scheme. For instance, to help put across the message of National Forest Products Week in 1961, the Federal Forestry Minister was presented with a cheque from a lumber company for the amount of one dollar in payment for a scroll copy of the Canadian Bill of Rights. The cheque was drawn on a sheet of plywood twelve feet long and four feet wide!

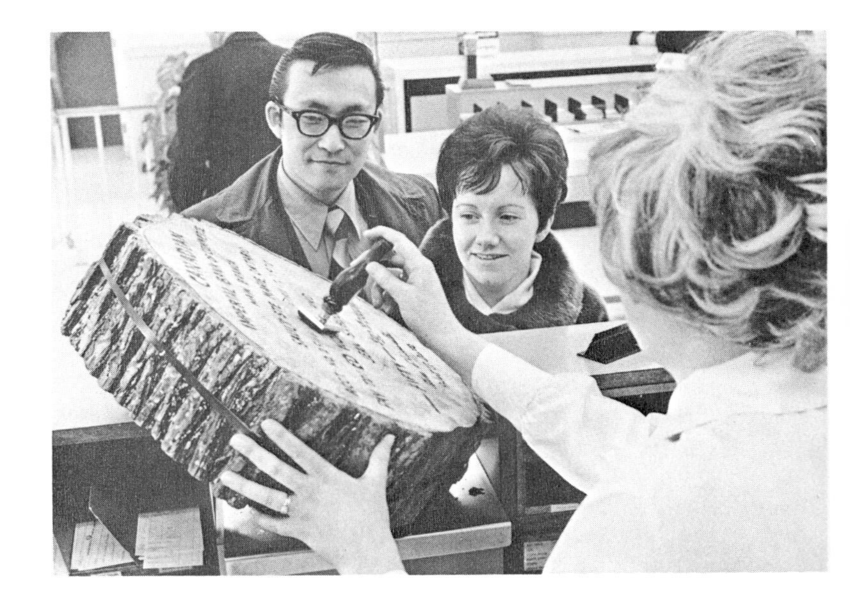

Bank teller cancels a 2 ft. wide dead elm slab. This cheque for $50 was a wedding gift from his colleagues to a Canadian Forestry Service employee working on a treatment for Dutch Elm Disease

Sault Daily Star and Canadian Imperial Bank of Commerce

It is not suggested, of course, that such irregular practices are to be encouraged, since it would create inconvenience for the bank. By law, a bank is entitled to require that its customers draw cheques in a form which is clear and free from ambiguity and which does not facilitate forgery.

NEGOTIATION OR TRANSFER OF THE CHEQUE

The legal procedure in negotiating a cheque (transferring it to another person) depends upon whether the cheque is (1) an order cheque, or (2) a bearer cheque.

An order cheque is written "Pay to the order of" (the payee), while a bearer cheque reads "Pay to (the payee) or bearer." By law an order cheque *must be endorsed* by the payee before it can be legally transferred. A bearer cheque may be transferred merely by delivery by the payee to another person.

In practice, banks and other well-advised persons require bearer cheques to be endorsed as well as order cheques, for the endorsement serves as an identification of the person negotiating it.

ENDORSEMENT

An endorsement is a signature, either alone or with other words, written on the back of the instrument. The forms of endorsements most commonly used on cheques are:

- Blank
- Special
- Restrictive.

In order to illustrate, we shall show endorsements as they might appear on the specimen cheque shown on page 265. (Note that the cheque is an order cheque).

ENDORSEMENT IN BLANK

Let us assume that the payee, J. R. Rankin, is transferring the cheque to a Mr. George Allen. A blank endorsement would appear as follows:

J. R. Rankin

The effect of a blank endorsement is to make the cheque a bearer instrument. It is now negotiable by the holder (George Allen) merely by delivery, and the cheque may pass legally from person to person without further endorsement. However, a bank would require the negotiator's endorsement for identification purposes.

Occasionally the name of the payee is misspelled or the wrong initials are used. In such cases the endorser will first endorse according to the name as it appears on the face of the instrument and then beneath it endorse his name properly spelt.

SPECIAL ENDORSEMENT

A special endorsement by Mr. Rankin would appear thus:

Pay to the order of
George Allen
J. R. Rankin

The effect of a special endorsement is that the holder (George Allen) must endorse the cheque before he negotiates it to another party. Allen may endorse it specially or in blank, and the instrument remains an order cheque or bearer cheque accordingly.

A point which may be noted here is that an instrument made payable to bearer on its face remains payable to bearer even though it bears a special endorsement.

RESTRICTIVE ENDORSEMENT

A restrictive endorsement restricts in some manner further negotiation of the cheque; for example:

For deposit only to
the account of
J. R. Rankin.

The above form is used most extensively by business concerns on cheques received from customers. This endorsement prevents anybody from cashing the cheque, which can only be deposited to J. R. Rankin's bank account.

Another form of restrictive endorsement is as follows:

Pay George Allen only
J. R. Rankin

This form of endorsement also restricts George Allen from negotiating the cheque to any other party. The cheque may now be presented to the bank for payment only by George Allen.

OTHER FORMS OF ENDORSEMENT

The following kinds of endorsement may be used as occasion demands:

1. *Identification Endorsement.* As the name implies, this endorsement is used to identify the person negotiating the instrument. The following are examples:

J. R. Rankin is hereby
identified by me.
W. A. Harris

J. R. Rankin
The above signature is
hereby guaranteed.
W. A. Harris

Note that W. A. Harris incurs no liability on the above endorsements as a party to the cheque, but he may be liable for fraudulent or negligent identification.

2. *Qualified Endorsement.* The following endorsement qualifies the endorser's liability on the instrument, but may not be generally acceptable since it evades liability for payment of the cheque:

> Pay to the order of
> George Allen
> without recourse to me
> J. R. Rankin

3. *Waiver of Protest.*

> Protest Waived
> J. R. Rankin

By the above endorsement Rankin is merely avoiding the costs incurred in formally *protesting* the cheque if it is not paid. *Protest* is explained on page 271.

THE ENDORSER'S LIABILITY

The Bills of Exchange Act specifically provides that the endorser's signature on the back of a cheque (or a bill of exchange) makes him liable to any subsequent holder or endorser for the amount of the cheque if default is made in its payment. Identification endorsements and qualified endorsements are exceptions to this rule.

For example, suppose a cheque is endorsed as follows:

> Pay to the order of
> George Allen
> J. R. Rankin
>
> For deposit only to the
> account of
> George Allen

If, after depositing the cheque, George Allen is notified by the bank that payment is refused, Allen may recover from the prior endorser, Rankin, who, as the original payee on the cheque, is left to recover as best he can from the drawer of the cheque.

PAYMENT OF THE CHEQUE

A cheque is payable *on demand.* According to the Act, a bill of exchange payable on demand should be presented for payment "within a reasonable time after its issue, in order to render the drawer liable, and within a reasonable time after its endorsement in order to render the endorser liable." In determining what is a reasonable time, ". . . regard shall be had to the nature of the bill, the usage of trade, . . . and the facts of the particular case."

THE BANK'S DUTY AND AUTHORITY TO PAY CHEQUES

A bank has a duty to honour its own customer's cheques on a current or a chequing account if there are sufficient funds in the account and the bank's authority to do so has not been terminated by any of the following:

- The drawer notifying the bank not to pay the cheque. This is known as *countermand of payment* or *stop-payment.*
- The bank having been notified or otherwise becoming aware of the death of the drawer.
- The bank learning that the drawer is bankrupt.
- The drawer's account being seized by order of the court.

A bank may refuse to honour a cheque if it is not regular on its face; for example, if the amount in words and figures do not agree or where there seems to have been an alteration on the cheque. Also, it may refuse to cash a cheque for a person who fails to produce satisfactory proof of identification when requested to do so.

Post-dated cheques will not be honoured until the date written on the cheque has arrived. In the meantime, the cheque may be retained by the holder or turned over to the bank to hold for deposit on the proper date.

The bank's regulations for savings accounts (usually printed on the inside of the pass book cover) generally permit the bank to require a specified number of days' notice before funds may be withdrawn. In practice, however, this rule is seldom enforced.

PROCEDURE FOLLOWING DEFAULT IN PAYMENT

If a bank refuses to pay a cheque (drawn on that bank) when presented for payment, the cheque is said to be *dishonoured.* The holder should then give notice of dishonour to the drawer and endorsers, if any, in order to hold them personally liable on the instrument. The following rules governing notice of dishonour should be observed.

- Notice must be made not later than the next following business day. All parties to the cheque are discharged from liability on it if they are not duly notified.

- Notice may be given orally or by letter posted within the proper time limit. Delay by the post office in delivering the notice does not affect the validity of the notice.
- If, after reasonable diligence, notice of dishonour cannot be given, it may be dispensed with.

A more formal method of notification of dishonour is a notice of *protest*. The protest is drawn up in legal form by a notary public or a justice of the peace and forwarded by him to the party or parties concerned, a fee being charged for this service.

The advantage of giving notice by formal protest is that it is the best evidence to a court that notice of dishonour was duly made. However, because the protest fees are added to the amount of the cheque under protest, the drawer or the endorser may waive protest by appropriate endorsement and avoid this expense.

RIGHTS OF THE HOLDER AND DEFENCES AGAINST HIM

The holder of a cheque, in the ordinary course of events, expects the cheque to be honoured. If this does not happen, the holder is obliged to give notice, as previously explained, and looks to the drawer and previous endorsers for payment. In most cases the holder will have a right to enforce payment, but in some cases the person from whom payment is sought may wish to resist payment—that is, set up a defence. The grounds of defence could, for example, be that the cheque was obtained by fraud, or that the signature was forged, or that the goods for which the cheque was given were never delivered. In fact any defence available to a person who is sued for breach of contract.

Many of the principles that we shall now consider are the same as those previously dealt with in the law of contract, but with one significant exception: the principal quality of a cheque (or note or draft) is its negotiability, and the policy of the common law, and later the Bills of Exchange Act, is to promote the free negotiability of these instruments. The result is that drawers of bills of exchange are often surprised to find that they are obliged to honour them despite the fact that the transaction leading to the instrument was unsatisfactory or even fraudulent.

CASE 1

A purchases an automobile from B and gives him a cheque in payment. Later, A learns that the vehicle is a stolen vehicle, and directs his bank to stop payment on the cheque. In the meantime, B has cashed the cheque at the Holiday Hotel where he was staying, and fled. Holiday Hotel presents the cheque to A's bank where payment is refused. Holiday Hotel, though, will be able to enforce payment from A. In this case, A, having been obliged to surrender the car to its rightful owner, may feel he is being treated unjustly when he is obliged to honour the cheque he gave B now that it is in the hands of the hotel.

At this point the reader is reminded of the title of this Unit, "Substitutes for Money." If A had paid B cash for the vehicle, and B in turn had paid the

very same currency over to the Holiday Hotel in settlement of his bill, A would not likely suggest that he was entitled to recover his money from the hotel; like most of us, he would recognize the free negotiability of money.

While the analogy between money and negotiable instruments is not exact, it illustrates the point that the drawer of a cheque begins the circulation of his private currency which he will likely have to honour.

DEFENCES AGAINST PAYMENT

The law dealing with the bases upon which payment may be refused on a negotiable instrument is complex. It depends to a large extent on the seriousness of the defence and the position of the holder relative to that defence. The available defences fall into three classes, and will be dealt with in more detail in the course of this Unit. They may be classified as follows:

(1) *Mere personal defences.*
- Set-off or contra account—A owes B, but B also owes A, and the two amounts cancel each other.

(2) *Defects in title.*
- Fraud, misrepresentation, undue influence, duress or illegality.
- Some kinds of incapacity—most commonly lunacy and drunkenness.
- Absence of consideration.
- Absence of delivery or conditional delivery.

(3) *Real defences.*
- Forged or unauthorized signature.
- Material alteration of a document.
- Absence of delivery of a blank or incomplete instrument.
- Absolute incapacity of the drawer—usually infancy.
- Discharge by payment in due course, or cancellation.
- Fraud or illegality of a nature to make the cheque void, and not merely voidable.

It now becomes necessary to consider the relationship of the holder to the drawer of the cheque.

IMMEDIATE PARTIES AND REMOTE PARTIES

The illustrations show a cheque drawn by Winter in favour of Rankin, and Rankin's endorsement of the cheque to Allen.

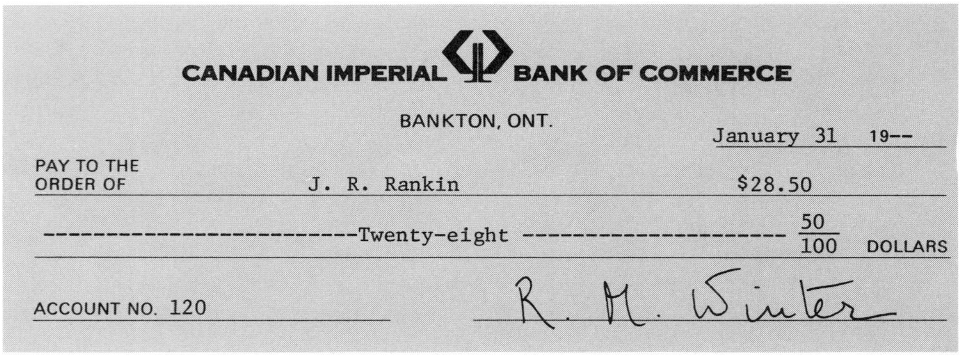

CANADIAN IMPERIAL BANK OF COMMERCE

BANKTON, ONT.

January 31 19--

PAY TO THE ORDER OF J. R. Rankin $28.50

------------------------Twenty-eight -------------------- 50/100 DOLLARS

ACCOUNT NO. 120

R. M. Winter

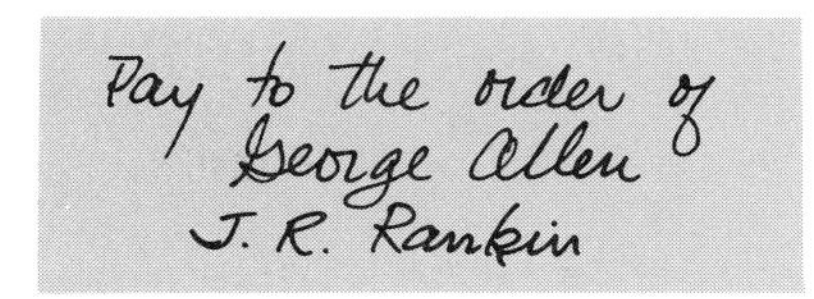

Since Winter and Rankin have direct dealings with each other (each is a party to the transaction for which the cheque was given), they are known as *immediate parties.*

For the same reason Rankin and Allen (to whom Rankin personally endorsed the cheque) are immediate parties.

The legal relationship between immediate parties is similar to that between the parties to a contract. As a result, Winter may stop payment on his cheque to Rankin for any of the defences listed in Classes 1, 2, and 3, above.

On the other hand, Winter (the drawer) and Allen (the endorsee) have had no direct dealings with each other about the transaction for which the cheque was given to Rankin; thus, they are known as *remote* parties. As a result, the reasons for which Winter may refuse to pay the cheque to Allen are more limited than those he could use against Rankin; for instance, he cannot use the defence of set-off (Class 1).

Here we must distinguish between a remote party who is a *holder in due course* and one who is not, because the defences in both Class 2 and Class 3 may be raised against a remote party who is not a holder in due course.

HOLDER IN DUE COURSE

A holder in due course is a remote party who has taken a cheque under the following conditions:

- the cheque was complete and regular on its face—that is, with respect to its form and content—and was not overdue;
- the holder took the cheque in good faith and for value (consideration);
- the holder had no notice that the cheque had been previously dishonoured;
- the holder took the cheque without notice of any defect in the title of the person who negotiated it to him.

Under these conditions, a holder in due course is in a preferred position; the only defences that can be successfully raised against him are those listed in Class 3, the "real defences."

C—2

> A buys a car from B, but stops payment on his cheque when he learns that the car has been stolen. However, A finds that the holder of the cheque is the Holiday Hotel which cashed the cheque for B. If the Holiday Hotel can show that it is a holder in due course, it is entitled to recover payment from A regardless of the defence A could have raised against B.

ENDORSERS

So far we have dealt with the liability of the drawer of a cheque to a holder; however, the same principles apply to the liability of an endorser to a subsequent holder. Of course, the position of a holder relative to an endorser, immediate or remote, may be different from the relationship between holder and drawer. The liability of the endorser should therefore be considered separately from the liability of the drawer.

The endorser of a cheque (or any bill of exchange) by endorsing it—unless by the form of the endorsement he negatives or limits his liability (see the preceding section of endorsements)—engages that on presentment the cheque will be paid according to its tenor, and that if it is dishonoured, he will compensate the holder or a subsequent endorser who is compelled to pay it (provided that the required proceedings on dishonour are duly taken). Thus if a cheque drawn by A payable to B is negotiated and endorsed in turn by B to C, C to D, and D to E, the liability of the endorsers is usually a simple reversal of the steps by which the cheque was negotiated; that is, D becomes liable to E, C to D, and B to C.

REAL DEFENCES

The real defences (those already listed under Class 3, above) are distinguished from other defences in that they are made with respect to the genuineness of the cheque itself as a bill of exchange rather than on the contract for which it was given. We shall now deal briefly with each of these defences.

Forged or Unauthorized Signature. When the signature to a cheque or any other bill of exchange has been forged or made without the drawer's authority, he cannot be held liable by any holder.

C—3

A haberdasher sells a suit to a man who offers in payment a cheque which he says is his pay cheque. The cheque appears to have been issued by the Steel Co. Ltd., and seems to be a genuine payroll cheque. The haberdasher accepts the cheque and deposits it along with the other store receipts. Later, he is notified that the Steel Co. has declared the cheque is a forgery and has refused to pay it. The bank charges the forged cheque back against the haberdasher's account, while the haberdasher is left to recover from the forger—if he can find him. Although the haberdasher may claim to be a holder in due course, he cannot enforce payment by the Steel Company on a forged cheque.

At the same time, it is the duty of the person whose signature has been forged to notify the bank and/or any other parties involved as soon as possible after he is aware of the forgery; otherwise, he may be precluded from denying liability.

C—4

Keech discovered from his passbook on April 28 that six cheques which he had not drawn had been charged against his bank account for a total of $510. Instead of informing the bank immediately and asking to see the cheques, he merely told the bank not to charge any more cheques against his account. Moreover, he would not put these instructions in writing even though the bank requested it. On June 12, Keech learned that his son-in-law had forged the six cheques and also ten additional cheques since April 28. He then notified the bank of the forgeries, and sought to recover from the bank the amounts paid out on all sixteen cheques. The court allowed his claim for the six cheques forged prior to April 28, but denied his claim for the other ten on the grounds that he had failed to notify the bank of the forgeries when he had first known about them. If he had not kept silent on the matter, the bank would not have cashed the additional ten cheques.

How could Keech have avoided liability for the cheques which were forged after April 28?

Forged or Unauthorized Endorsement. A forged endorsement has no effect against the party whose endorsement is forged; he remains the true owner. The drawer and prior endorsers remain liable to him even if the instrument has been paid. Those who endorse the cheque *after* the forgery, however, are liable to the holder.

C—5

Harris draws a cheque for $20 payable to Wilson, and gives him the cheque. Wilson places the cheque temporarily in the glove compartment of his car. Yates steals the cheque from Wilson's car and forges Wilson's endorsement. Yates then endorses the cheque and gives it to his sister (who has no idea that it was stolen) to cash at the corner grocery store. The sister endorses the cheque to Whipple's Grocery. By this time the theft of the cheque has been discovered and the bank has been notified to stop payment. If Whipple has deposited the cheque, the bank will charge it back to his account. Whipple may then recover from Yates' sister on her endorsement, while she, being the first person who took the cheque from the forger, must bear the loss if she cannot recover from her scoundrelly brother. Wilson, whose endorsement was forged, remains the true owner of the cheque and may recover payment on it from Harris.

A person who loses a cheque made payable to him, or has it stolen from him should anticipate the possibility of his endorsement being forged. He, therefore, has a duty to notify the paying bank immediately so that the bank can take the necessary steps to stop payment on the cheque. Unreasonable delay in giving such notice may be interpreted as negligence, and may prevent the party whose endorsement has been forged from asserting his claim for payment as the true owner of the cheque.

C—6

At about 5:00 p.m. Thomson discovered he had lost a cheque that was payable to him. He did not notify the paying bank until about 11:20 the next morning, although he had ample time and opportunity to do so. When he did notify the bank, he learned that his endorsement had been forged and the cheque had already been paid. Thomson sued the bank to recover on the forged endorsement, but the court denied his claim on the grounds that he had been negligent in not notifying the bank as soon as he discovered the cheque had been lost. If he had done so, the cheque would not have been paid.

Material Alteration of a Document. A material alteration, such as increasing the amount of a cheque, is forgery, and the same principles apply as explained above. There is one important difference, however: the cheque is still valid according to its original, genuine form against those who were parties to the instrument before the alteration was made. Also, any holder who takes it after the alteration may recover its altered value only from those who endorsed it subsequent to the alteration. However, any holder in due course may avail himself of the cheque as if it had not been altered, and enforce payment of it according to its original form. Suppose a cheque for $10 was drawn on Bank A, then raised by forgery to $100 and cashed at Bank B. Bank B presents the cheque to Bank A and is paid $100. Later, when the forgery is discovered, Bank B must repay $90 to Bank A, and is left to recover from the forger—if it can.

Absence of Delivery of a Blank or Incomplete Instrument. When a cheque, which is complete in form, gets into circulation without being delivered by the drawer (as for example, when such a cheque is stolen), the mere lack of delivery is not a good defence against a holder in due course, although it is an effective defence against the payee, an immediate party. However, when an *incomplete* cheque is not delivered by the drawer (as for example, a stolen cheque that does not have the amount filled in), completion by the person taking it would amount to forgery. If proved, these facts would constitute a real defence by the drawer, good against even a holder in due course. The holder's only recourse then is against a person who endorsed it subsequent to the forgery.

Absolute Incapacity of the Drawer—Infancy. An infant cannot incur personal liability upon a negotiable instrument even though it is given for necessaries. The creditor cannot sue upon the negotiable instrument; he may sue only on the contract for which it was given. However, the instrument as a whole is not invalid because it is drawn by an infant. For example, if a minor draws a cheque upon a bank that has sufficient funds in the infant's account, the bank is justified in making payment to the holder. Also, any adult endorser of a cheque drawn by an infant is liable to a subsequent holder. An infant endorser, however, cannot be held liable by any holder. Infancy is a real defence, good against even a holder in due course.

Incapacity by reason of mental illness or drunkenness may be a good defence against any holder except a holder in due course.

Discharge by Payment in Due Course (or Cancellation). Payment of a cheque in due course means payment to the holder *in good faith.* Such payment is a real defence against anyone who may present the cheque again for payment. Intentional cancellation of a cheque will discharge it only if the cancellation is apparent on it. If it is not apparent on the cheque, it is not a good defence against a holder in due course.

Fraud or Illegality Making the Cheque Void. If it can be shown that the person who places his signature on a bill of exchange *intended* to sign something of an entirely different character, and *did so in circumstances that do not imply negligence on his part,* the bill of exchange, as far as the signer is concerned, is void. He cannot be held liable on it, even by a holder in due course. The classic example happened in England just over a century ago:

C—7

The defendant, an elderly gentleman, had been induced to put his name upon the back of a bill of exchange. Because he had been led to believe that he was signing a guarantee similar to one he had signed previously at the request of the same party, he did not read the document. Later, he was sued as an endorser by a holder in due course. The court held that his signature had been obtained by fraudulent misrepresentation, and that he had had no intention of putting a bill of exchange into circulation. The court also found that, in the circumstances, the defendant was not guilty of any negligence in signing the paper. On these grounds the court held that the holder of the bill of exchange, although a holder in due course, was not entitled to recover from the old gentleman.

CERTIFIED CHEQUES

It is a common practice for business concerns, when advertising for tenders for construction projects, to require that the tender be accompanied by a *certified* cheque for some specified amount or a percentage of the tender price. Again, in many public offices where payments are made, one may see a conspicuous sign to the effect that "All Cheques Must Be Certified."

A certified cheque is one that has been marked "certified" by the drawee bank. At the time the cheque is certified, it is charged to the drawer's account in order to ensure that funds of the drawer will be available to pay it. By certification, that bank undertakes to pay the cheque when presented for payment.

Either drawer or holder may obtain certification. Payment of a cheque certified by a drawer may be countermanded by him before it is paid if he hands the cheque to the bank. If he has not the cheque to hand over, the bank is entitled to ask the drawer for security to indemnify it against the holder, in case the cheque has already been cashed or deposited at another bank.

Any holder of a cheque may have it certified by presenting the cheque at the drawee bank. (Of course, he might at that time have chosen to have it paid instead). As a result, the drawer and any endorsers are discharged from further liability on the cheque, and the bank becomes solely liable to pay.

A holder may choose to have the cheque certified instead of having it paid, particularly if it is for a large amount, because he may not wish to carry a large amount of currency on his person, or may intend to negotiate it to someone else, or to deposit it at another bank. When the holder has the cheque certified, the drawer can no longer stop its payment.

C—8

The plaintiff had received a cheque drawn on the defendant bank, and went to that bank to have it certified. By coincidence, at the very same time the certification was being made, the drawer of the cheque was at another wicket of the bank stopping payment on it. However, moments before the countermanding formalities had been completed, the cheque was certified and handed back to the plaintiff. Immediately after having handed it back, the clerk who had done the certifying was told of the countermand of payment and, since the plaintiff had not yet left the bank, called him back, requested the cheque, and stamped "cancelled" across the certification. The clerk then handed the cheque back again to the plaintiff. On being refused payment on the cheque, the plaintiff sued the bank on the grounds of certification. A Quebec court held that once the cheque had been certified, the bank no longer had the power to comply with the drawer's order to stop payment—not even if it was only a moment late. Therefore, the cancellation of the certification was null and void, and the bank was liable to pay the holder.

APPLYING THE LAW

1.

If this cheque has other endorsements on it besides that of the man cashing it, what should he do in order to protect his rights?

2. (a) A bought a second-hand radio from B (a private party, not a dealer in radios) and gave him a cheque in payment. A did not test the radio before taking delivery, depending on B's assurance that it would be in good order, but when he received it he found it would not work and that it was, in fact, useless. A then called his bank to stop payment on the cheque. The next day when B went to the bank to cash the cheque, he was told of the countermand of payment. What is B's legal position with regard to enforcing payment of the cheque?

   (b) Assume in (a), above, that B, immediately after receiving the cheque, had it cashed by C, the person from whom he had obtained the radio and who knew that it was useless—and who also knew that B had sold it to A. When C attempts to cash the cheque at the bank, he learns of the countermand of payment. What is C's legal position with regard to enforcing payment of the cheque?

(c) Assume in (a), above, that B, on the same day on which he received the cheque, cashed it at a store as payment for a purchase of goods. The store knew nothing about the transaction for which the cheque was given, but learned later that payment of the cheque had been stopped. What is the store's legal position with regard to the cheque?

DISCUSSION

1.

What particular difficulties could be encountered by accepting a minor's cheque?

2. The fact that a holder in due course may enforce payment on a cheque which the payer could legally refuse to pay to the payee could impose hardship on the drawer of the cheque. Discuss this feature of the law of bills of exchange.
3. Your neighbour is worried because her children's allowance cheque is long overdue. She is afraid someone has stolen it from the mail box. Can you advise her what to do? Can you reassure her that even if the cheque has been stolen and cashed, she will eventually receive the money?

Part 25
PROMISSORY NOTES

Our study of the law concerning promissory notes follows the same sequence as for cheques; namely, issue or the bringing of the note into existence, negotiation or the transferring of it to another party and payment.

ISSUE

As is the case with cheques, our banks provide blank notes in approved legal form which merely have to be filled in and signed. The bank form usually provides that the note will be paid at the bank out of the maker's account.

It is by no means necessary to use the bank form or to pay the note at a bank. The nature of a note is primarily that of a direct contract between the maker and the payee whereby the maker promises to pay the payee at some future time in connection with some transaction that has taken place between them.

While the instrument representing the promise may be a good contract between the maker and the payee, it may be phrased in such a way that it cannot be used as a negotiable instrument to be passed freely from person to

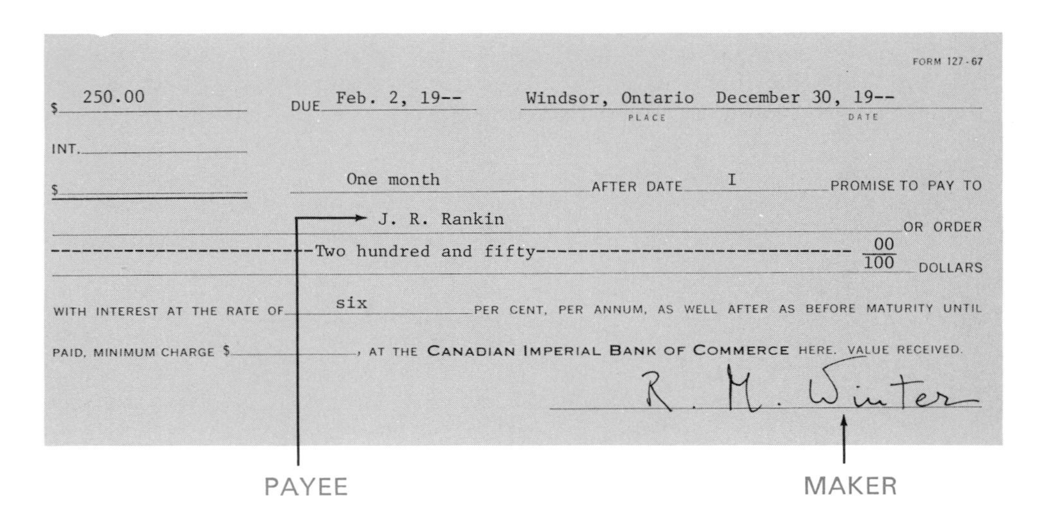
FORM 127-67

$ 250.00 DUE Feb. 2, 19-- Windsor, Ontario December 30, 19--
PLACE DATE

INT.

$ One month AFTER DATE I PROMISE TO PAY TO

J. R. Rankin OR ORDER

Two hundred and fifty 00/100 DOLLARS

WITH INTEREST AT THE RATE OF six PER CENT, PER ANNUM, AS WELL AFTER AS BEFORE MATURITY UNTIL PAID, MINIMUM CHARGE $, AT THE CANADIAN IMPERIAL BANK OF COMMERCE HERE. VALUE RECEIVED.

R. M. Winter

person by endorsement or delivery. To be negotiable, its form must comply with the essentials of negotiability as laid down by the Bills of Exchange Act.

The Act defines a promissory note as "an unconditional promise in writing made by one person to another, signed by the maker, engaging to pay, on demand or at a fixed or determinable future time, a sum certain in money to or to the order of a specified person or to bearer."

ESSENTIALS OF NEGOTIABILITY OF A PROMISSORY NOTE

A typical form of promissory note provided by banks is here illustrated. The statutory requirements are as follows:

1. *It must be in writing and signed.* The legal interpretation of "writing" has already been explained, on page 266. It applies to notes in the same way in which it does to cheques.

Actually, the signature need not appear at the end of the instrument. It is sufficient if it is written in the body of the note, as for example: "I, John Smith, promise to pay . . ."

2. *The promise to pay must be unconditional.* A note which promises to pay subject to some condition is not negotiable. The following is an example:

> Windsor, Ontario, December 30, 19--
>
> One Month after date I promise to pay to the order of A. WILLIAMS Five Hundred Dollars ($500.00) for repairs to the roof of my residence, provided it does not leak after it is repaired.
>
> E.S. Casman

This note is not negotiable because of the condition embodied in it. No endorser could compel Casman to pay if he refused. The instrument is therefore merely a contract between Williams and Casman.

The familiar *I.O.U.* is not a negotiable instrument unless it contains words which can be interpreted as a promise to pay. For example, "I.O.U. $20, payable on January 30, 1970," when signed, would be sufficient; but a mere "I.O.U. $20" would not be negotiable.

3. *The time of payment must be certain or determinable.* It is possible to express the time of payment in various ways and still satisfy the legal requirements. For example, "thirty days after my grandfather dies" is determinable because the event is sure to happen. However, a note payable "thirty days after I sell my house" would not be negotiable because the event is not sure to happen. The Act provides that a note may be payable "on demand," which means that the payee may request payment at any time. However, if the payee negotiates a demand note to another person, that person should present it for payment within a reasonable time after receiving it.

C—9

> The defendant, C, had given a promissory note to Parkway Holdings which read, "On demand I promise to pay . . . $17,000 . . . payable at $1,000 per month commencing on December 1, 1964." Shortly afterwards Parkway Holdings endorsed the note over to the plaintiff as collateral security for a loan. Subsequently, the bank (the plaintiff) sued to recover on the note, claiming the status of a holder in due course. A British Columbia court held

that the note was not a negotiable instrument within the meaning of the Bills of Exchange Act. The wording on the note provided for payments on demand *and also* on specified and fixed instalment dates, whereas the Act defines a promissory note as payable "on demand *or* at a fixed or determinable future time." The Act does not permit both times on the same note. Therefore, the court dismissed the case.

4. *It must be for a sum certain and payable in money only.* The value of a note cannot be determined for purposes of negotiation unless it is for "a sum certain in money." For example, a note that read in part, "This note is payable in merchantable timber, but if not so paid at maturity, becomes payable in cash," was held not to be a negotiable instrument since it was not payable in money only.

The effect of declaring a note not negotiable is that a party to whom the note has been endorsed (or delivered, if it is a bearer note) has no recourse against the maker. The note is useful only as evidence of a contract that existed between the immediate parties concerned.

NEGOTIATION OF A PROMISSORY NOTE

Notes are usually made payable to the order of the payee, although they may be made payable to bearer. As with cheques, order notes must be endorsed to be legally transferable, while bearer notes may be negotiated merely by delivery.

ENDORSEMENTS

Notes may be endorsed in blank or specially, and the endorser incurs the same liability on the note as has already been explained in the part dealing with cheques, page 267. Notes may be endorsed restrictively; for example:

Pay to George Allen only
J. R. Rankin

The restrictive endorsement, "For deposit only," does not apply to notes. However, notes are sometimes left at the bank for collection, in which case the holder may use the following restrictive endorsement:

Pay to the (name of bank)
for collection only
J. R. Rankin

The holder of a note may also *discount* the note at the bank. ("Discounting" means that the bank will buy the note at its maturity value minus interest on that value from the date of discount to the date of maturity). The proceeds may then be deposited to the holder's account. The bank then becomes the new holder and will collect from the maker.

If the person taking the note desires additional security, the maker may be able to find some other person willing to guarantee payment who will also be acceptable to the other party. The guarantee is usually given in the form of an endorsement, and since the guarantor is receiving no consideration, the endorsement is known as an *accommodation* endorsement.

In order to identify himself as such, a guarantor should make the endorsement in the following or in a similar way:

I hereby guarantee
payment of this note
George Allen

The guarantor becomes liable only if the maker does not pay. At the same time there is an implied contract on the part of the maker to indemnify the guarantor if he has to pay the note.

C—10

At the request of the maker of a promissory note, G agreed to sign his name on the back of the note in order that the maker could borrow money on it at the bank. When the maker failed to pay the note at maturity, the bank sued G as an endorser. The Court held that when the bank took the note it was entitled to G's liability as endorser, and he had to pay the bank.

How can G recover his money?

PAYMENT OF THE NOTE

PARTIAL PAYMENTS

In the case of a demand note the maker may make partial payments from time to time. An endorsement should be made on the note for each payment; for example, "October 21, 1959, received on this note, fifty dollars. J. R. Rankin."

TIME OF PAYMENT

A note should be presented for payment on its due date. All notes except those payable on demand have three *days of grace* added to the time specified on the note, and the due date is the last day of grace.

If the last day of grace falls on a legal holiday or *non-juridical* day, such as Sunday, the last day of grace is the day next following which is not a legal holiday or non-juridical day.

If the time on the note is expressed in days, the actual number of days plus the three days of grace must be counted. When the time is expressed in months, calendar months are meant. For example, a note dated January 30, 1972, and payable one month after date, becomes nominally due February 29th, and legally due on March 3rd, the last day of grace; a note dated February 29th, and payable one month after date, would become nominally due March 29th and legally due on April 1st.

PLACE OF PAYMENT

Where the place of payment is specified in the note, it must be presented for payment at that particular place in order to hold the endorser liable. Where no place of payment is specified, the note should be presented at the maker's known place of business or at his residence; and if neither is known, then at the post office of the place at which it is drawn.

Unavoidable delay in presentment for payment is excused, and in some special cases presentment is dispensed with.

PROCEDURE FOLLOWING NON-PAYMENT

If, on presentment for payment, the note is dishonoured, the holder should immediately give notice of dishonour to any endorsers in order to hold them liable. The method of giving notice is the same as that already explained for cheques. See page 270.

RIGHTS OF THE HOLDER AND DEFENCES AGAINST HIM

The same personal defences and real defences described in the previous part on cheques also apply to notes. Thus where the maker's defence against payment is a personal one, or a defect in the payee's title, a holder in due course may be able to enforce payment even though the payee (an immediate party) cannot do so.

C—11

A gives B a promissory note complete except for filling in the amount. A authorizes B to fill in the amount later according to the agreement for which the note was given. B fills in the amount for a greater sum than the authorized sum and in due course he presents it for payment. A may refuse payment to B because B has not completed the note strictly according to his authority. However, if in the meantime B has negotiated the note to C, who can successfully claim to be a holder in due course, A is not entitled to refuse payment to C.

The defences which the maker of a note may successfully use to avoid payment to a holder in due course are the real defences: forgery, material alteration, absence of delivery of an incomplete note, absolute incapacity of the maker, discharge by payment or cancellation and fraud or illegality which makes the note void from the beginning.

C—12

A makes out a note to B but leaves the amount blank. A does not give the note to B, but B gets possession of it without A's knowledge, fills in an amount and endorses it to C, a holder in due course. When C presents the note for payment, A has a real defence—ABSENCE OF DELIVERY *of an incomplete note*—and may successfully refuse payment to C even though C is a holder in due course.

KINDS OF NOTE

JOINT NOTE

A joint note is one signed by two or more makers. The specimen shown below is a common form.

FORM 127-67

$ 250.00 DUE Feb. 2, 19-- Windsor, Ontario December 30, 19--
PLACE DATE

INT.

$ One month AFTER DATE We PROMISE TO PAY TO

J. R. Rankin OR ORDER

-------------------------Two hundred and fifty--------------------------- 00/100 DOLLARS

WITH INTEREST AT THE RATE OF six PER CENT. PER ANNUM, AS WELL AFTER AS BEFORE MATURITY UNTIL PAID. MINIMUM CHARGE $, AT THE CANADIAN IMPERIAL BANK OF COMMERCE HERE. VALUE RECEIVED.

George Allen
R. M. Winter

Each joint maker is liable individually for the full amount of the note. At the same time, if default is made on a joint note, all joint makers should be sued together, for the law permits only one judgment to be obtained on a joint note. Consequently, if a judgment were given against one maker only, and he could not satisfy the claim, the right to sue the other maker would be barred. If one of the makers has to pay the full amount of the note, he is entitled to recover from the other maker or makers that part which he has paid on their behalf.

If the above note read, "*I* promise to pay" instead of "we", it would be a "joint and several" note. The chief legal difference is that a judgment against one maker, unless it is paid, is not a bar against suing another maker.

INSTALMENT NOTE

An instalment note is payable in instalments. The usual form is illustrated below.

Windsor, Ontario, December 30, 19--

On the first day of each month hereafter for Six months consecutively, I promise to pay to the order of E.A.DAY the sum of Fifty Dollars ($50.00) the whole amounting to Three Hundred Dollars ($300.00) with interest at the rate of Six per cent both before and after maturity until paid. Roger L. Crossley

Each instalment is treated as a separate note for the purposes of presentment, and three days of grace are allowed on each. Each payment should be properly endorsed on the back of the note.

If default is made on any instalment, the holder is entitled to take action to recover the overdue payment only. For that reason a clause known as an *acceleration clause* may be added to an instalment note. The usual wording is as follows:

In the event of default in making any of the above payments when due, the whole of this note shall thereupon become due and payable forthwith.

The acceleration clause makes it legally possible to sue for the full remaining balance if default is made on any instalment.

LIEN NOTE

A lien note is a promissory note, given in connection with a sale of goods, which contains a clause to the effect that the title (ownership) to the goods does not pass from the seller to the buyer until the note is fully paid. Under such a sale the buyer usually takes possession of the goods even though the seller retains the right of ownership. Lien notes are sometimes incorporated into the body of a contract; in other cases it may be a separate document. The following illustration is a simple form of lien note:

Windsor, Ontario, January 4, 19--

$150.00

Three months after date I promise to pay to the order of J.R.RANKIN One Hundred and Fifty Dollars ($150.00).

Value received.

The title of the Johnson Outboard Motor, No.11630, for which this note is given, shall not pass but shall remain in the said J.R.Rankin until this note is fully paid.

R. H. Winter

CONSUMER BILLS AND NOTES

The above heading is the title of a new part (Part V), added to the Bills of Exchange Act in 1970 as an amendment to that Act.

A *consumer bill* is a bill of exchange issued in connection with a consumer purchase, on which the purchaser or anyone signing to accommodate him is liable. This does not include a cheque that is dated the date of issue or is post-dated not more than 30 days.

A *consumer note* is a promissory note issued in respect of a consumer purchase on which the purchaser or anyone signing to accommodate him is liable.

A *consumer purchase* is a purchase of goods or services, other than a cash purchase, from a person who is in the business of selling or providing such goods or services. It does not include a purchase by an individual for resale or for use in his own business or profession.

The amendment was passed to remedy the use (particularly by finance companies) of bills of exchange in consumer credit transactions "in a way," as one court expressed it, "which was not contemplated when the Act was created."

The rapid growth of retail credit buying in modern times had to be accompanied by a method of financing such transactions: hence the development of a well-known pattern: The consumer (the buyer) buys goods under a conditional sale agreement (see Unit 6) which requires the giving of a promissory note, usually in instalments. The merchant-seller then discounts this note with a finance company, and the buyer is notified to make his payments to that company.

The unsatisfactory feature of this practice, before the passing of the new amendment, was that the finance company, being a "remote party," could in many cases claim to be a holder in due course. As a result, the buyer—although he may have had a good reason for refusing to continue making his payments on the note if the note were still held by the seller (for example, the failure to honour warranties, or the seller being guilty of misrepresentation or fraud)—could not rely on these defences against a holder in due course, and the finance company was entitled to enforce payment of the note regardless of the plight of the unfortunate buyer.

To remedy this situation the new amendment to the Act (Section 190) provides that

> *(1) Every consumer bill or consumer note shall be prominently and legibly marked on its face with the words "Consumer Purchase" before or at the time when the instrument is signed by the purchaser or by anyone signing to accommodate the purchaser.*
>
> *(2) A consumer bill or consumer note that is not marked as required by this section is void except in the hands of a holder in due course without notice that the bill or note is a consumer bill or a consumer note.*

The new law also provides that in any consumer purchase transaction, any defence which the purchaser had against the seller may also be used against any holder of a consumer purchase bill or note. This means that a finance company, or any other holder, could not enforce payment on a consumer purchase note if the seller of the goods for which the note was given could not enforce it. And further, this right of the purchaser cannot be waived, regardless of an agreement to the contrary.

The Amendment also contains a clause covering the possibility of the seller directing the buyer to a finance company (or other lender) to borrow money in order to make a purchase. In such a situation, if the seller and the lender are dealing with each other at less than "arms length" (that is, if they are in collusion with each other), the purchase will be considered a consumer purchase, and the promissory note given for the loan will have to be marked accordingly. The purpose of this clause is to plug a possible loophole whereby an unscrupulous merchant in collusion with a similarly unscrupulous lender could sidestep the safeguard written into the law. It does not apply where no such collusion exists and where the purchaser obtains on his own a loan to be used in making a purchase.

Anyone who obtains a signature on an unmarked instrument given in respect of a consumer purchase is liable to a heavy fine.

APPLYING THE LAW

1.

What risks does the friend take if he "backs" the note?

2. A approaches B offering him a new color TV set for $100. A had stolen the set and B knows it. Nevertheless, B agrees to buy it, but he persuades A to take his promissory note for one month for the amount, saying he is temporarily out of funds. A takes the note and later endorses it over to C who gives him $100 for it.
   (a) If A had kept the note and B refused to pay it, could A enforce payment at law? Why or why not?
   (b) If B refuses to pay C, what are C's legal rights
      (i) if C knows about the transaction for which the note was given by B?
      (ii) if C knows nothing about the transaction and has taken the note in good faith?

DISCUSSION AND PROJECTS

1. Obtain specimens of promissory notes used when people borrow from banks and finance companies. What might these lenders require in order to avoid loss if the borrower is unable to pay the note when it comes due?
2. Discuss the way in which consumer purchase notes will be of advantage to the consumer.

Part 26
COMMERCIAL DRAFTS

Up to comparatively recent years the use of commercial drafts was quite common. In fact it was from the use of the draft that the early law of bills of exchange developed. Today the use of drafts is declining markedly, although they are still being used, and the law concerning them still applies.

The legal definition of a draft is the same as that for a cheque; both are bills of exchange under the Act. However, a cheque is always drawn on a bank; a draft is drawn on another person.

In order to explain the law as it applies to drafts, we shall follow the normal progress of a draft step by step from issue to payment.

ISSUE

Like cheques and notes, drafts must be drawn in a form that complies with the essentials of negotiability.

Let us look at an example to illustrate the use of a draft:

C—13

> Industrial Supplies, Limited, wholesalers, sold Rogers' Hardware, Ltd., retailers, goods invoiced at $1,000. The invoice was dated January 4, 19—; terms, 30 days. Industrial Supplies immediately drew a draft on Rogers' Hardware, payable to the Canadian Imperial Bank of Commerce, discounted the draft at the same bank and deposited the proceeds to their account.

Although not required by law, it is convenient to use the blank forms provided by the bank for the use of its customers. The draft for the above transaction is a commercial draft and would appear as shown on the following page.

In this particular case, Industrial Supplies, Limited, have made the time on their draft correspond with the terms of the invoice for which it was drawn. However, the time specification may vary with the drawer's wishes, subject, of course, to the terms of the transaction. Drafts may be made payable *on demand*, *at sight*, or any stated number of months or days *after sight* or *after date*.

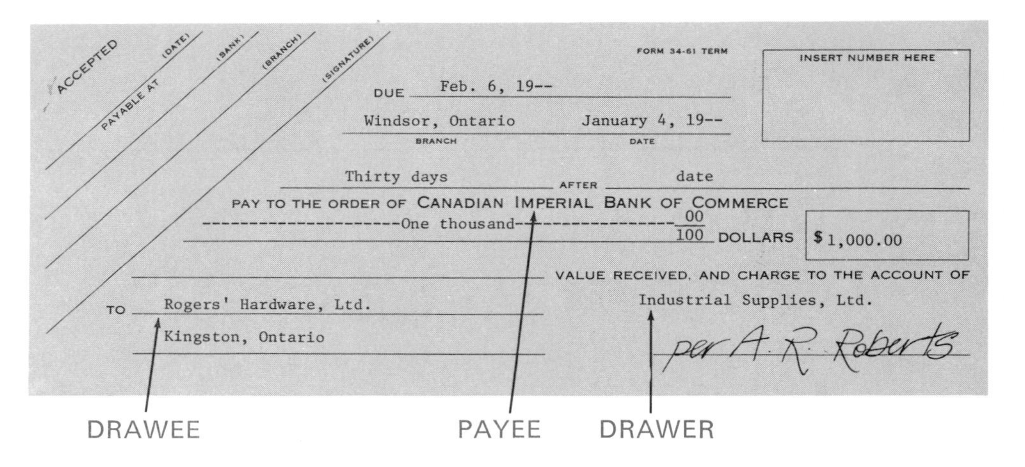
ACCEPTED (DATE) PAYABLE AT (BANK) (BRANCH) (SIGNATURE)

FORM 34-61 TERM

INSERT NUMBER HERE

DUE Feb. 6, 19--

Windsor, Ontario January 4, 19--
BRANCH DATE

Thirty days AFTER date

PAY TO THE ORDER OF CANADIAN IMPERIAL BANK OF COMMERCE

---------------------One thousand--------------- 00/100 DOLLARS $1,000.00

VALUE RECEIVED, AND CHARGE TO THE ACCOUNT OF

TO Rogers' Hardware, Ltd.
Kingston, Ontario

Industrial Supplies, Ltd.
per A. R. Roberts

ACCEPTANCE OF THE DRAFT

Normally, the next step in our example is to obtain an acceptance from Rogers' Hardware, Ltd. The acceptance signifies the drawee's intention to pay and is equivalent to the promise of the maker of a promissory note.

In order to secure the acceptance, the Canadian Imperial Bank of Commerce at Windsor will endorse the draft and forward it to a branch of the same bank in Kingston, or to some other bank there which will act as their agent, with the request to obtain an acceptance from the drawee and later to collect the amount of the draft.

The form of the acceptance may vary. The mere signature of the drawee without additional words is legally sufficient. The customary form, however, is made as provided for in the top left-hand corner of the specimen draft already shown.

RULES OF PRESENTMENT FOR ACCEPTANCE

The following rules respecting acceptance should be observed:

- Except for drafts payable at sight or after sight, presentment for acceptance is not legally necessary to hold any party liable on the draft. Drafts payable at sight or after sight *must* be presented for acceptance in order to fix the maturity date of the instrument. Notwithstanding the rule, it is customary to present a draft for acceptance as soon as convenient so that the drawee's intention concerning it may be determined. Once a draft is accepted, the payee acquires the same rights as on a promissory note.
- The drawee has two days in which to decide whether or not to accept the draft. If acceptance is refused, the draft is then treated as dishonoured, and the holder acquires an immediate right of recourse against the drawer and endorsers. In order to hold these parties liable, the holder must comply with the rules governing notice of dishonour and protest.

Again referring to our example C—13, if Rogers' Hardware, Ltd. refuses to accept the draft, the bank at Kingston will return the draft to the Canadian Imperial Bank of Commerce at Windsor, who may then recover from Industrial Supplies, Limited.

PAYMENT OF THE DRAFT

There are certain rules to be observed in presenting a draft for payment.

- The draft should be presented for payment on its due date, not before. As in the case of promissory notes, days of grace apply to all except demand drafts.
- The draft must be presented for payment at a reasonable hour on a business day.
- The draft must be presented for payment at the place specified in the acceptance. If no place is specified, it should be presented at the drawee's place of business; or if he has no place of business, at his residence.

The draft is considered dishonoured if payment is refused or cannot be obtained. The holder then should give proper legal notice of dishonour in order to hold the drawer and endorsers liable. By law, notice of dishonour of foreign bills of exchange must be made by formal protest.

Although it is customary to use the bank as an agent for the collection of drafts, the draft may be drawn payable to the drawer himself and presented for acceptance and payment by the drawer or his agent. The drawer may also make the draft payable to some creditor and require the drawee to pay that creditor. At any time before maturity, the acceptance may also be negotiated by endorsement to another party who, not being an immediate party to the instrument, may acquire the rights of a holder in due course and thus recover from the drawee even though the drawee has a good defence against the drawer.

Let us assume in respect to case C—13 that Industrial Supplies, Limited, owes Standard Machine Company of Kingston. The draft drawn on Rogers' Hardware, Ltd. could be made payable to Standard Machine Company and forwarded to Rogers' Hardware to obtain acceptance and payment.

APPLYING THE LAW

1.

What procedure will now be followed with respect to the draft?

UNIT TWELVE
THE LAW OF REAL PROPERTY

OWNERSHIP OF LAND

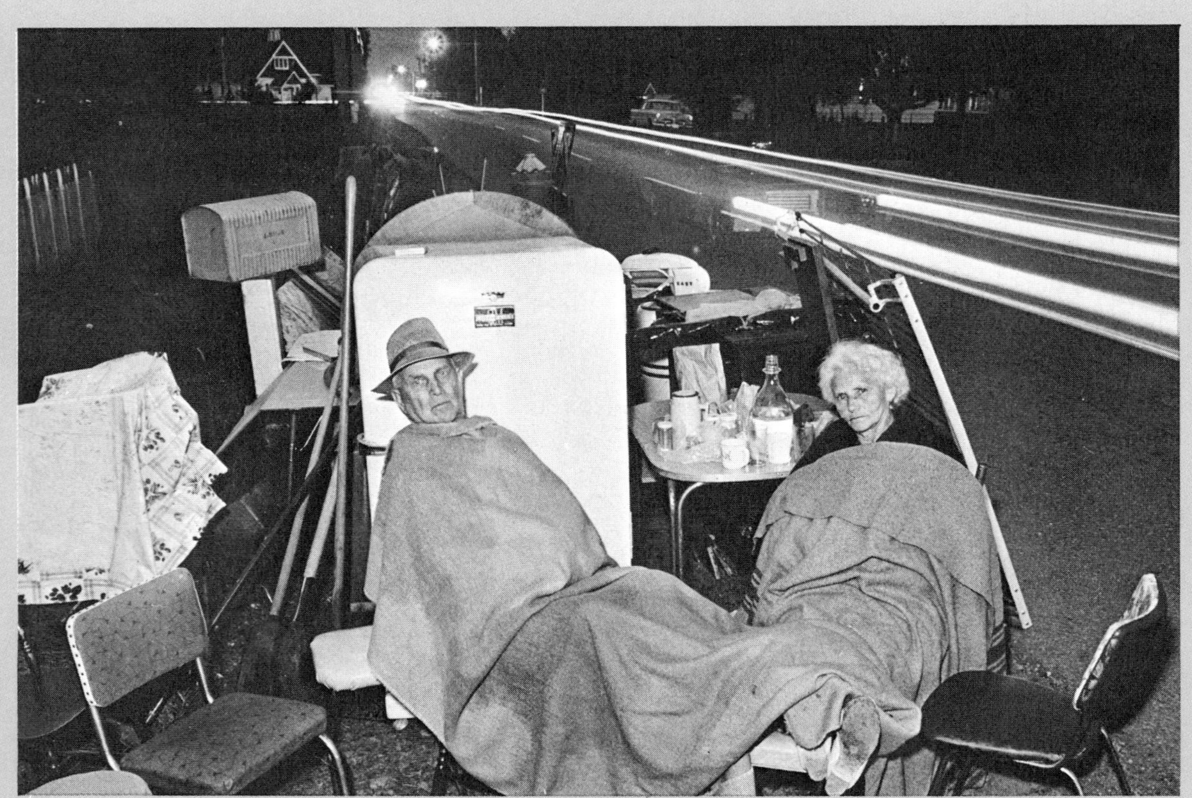

Photo Vancouver Sun

Still resisting an exproriation order even after their eviction by sheriff's men, this couple camped among their belongings on a British Columbia roadside. They were demanding twice as much for their property as had been paid to them by the municipality.

Since earliest times men have greatly prized the ownership of land. Land was a place on which to live, grow food and graze animals. In simple terms, land represented shelter, food and clothing. As the control of land increased beyond those immediate needs it came to represent wealth and power.

In a modern society that is more industrial and commercial and less agrarian the economic importance of land has declined, but its cultural importance has remained high. Home ownership is considered desirable and the mark of stability. One may defend his land and his home against intruders even if in doing so it is necessary to use a reasonable degree of force. Ordinarily, even public authorities may enter a home only by permission or under the authority of a warrant. It has been said that "an Englishman's home is his castle," and to a large extent the theory of the common law that underlies this statement continues to be true.

THE FEUDAL ERA

Because of the early importance of land, laws respecting it became necessary and were developed at an early stage in our history. In the feudal era, when laws with respect to other matters were few and primitive, a complex system of laws regulating land was developing. The law which evolved so early continues to be the basis on which our present land law is founded. Many changes and amendments have been made, but concepts formed in feudal times continue to affect our land law and supply much of the terminology.

In feudal England, at least after the Norman Conquest, no one "owned" land except the King. The King, to consolidate his strength, retained ultimate ownership but gave grants of land to his lords, called "estates" (derived from *status*, meaning "position") which was subject to certain duties. As long as the lord performed his duties to the Crown (e.g., military service) he would continue to hold his estate in the land. Lords, in turn, granted the estates to vassals who similarly held them subject to various duties.

The lords and vassals were tenants (from the Latin *teneo*, "I hold") of land according to the nature of their various estates. This theory continues to underlie our modern land law. A modern deed will contain the following language: ". . . to have and to hold unto the said grantee his heirs and assigns to and for their sole and only use forever."

It is in accord with the same principle that when a person dies leaving no heirs and not having disposed of his land by will, the land *escheats* to the Crown; that is, the property interest reverts to its ultimate owner.

TYPES OF ESTATE

One of the distinguishing features of an estate in land that might be granted by the Crown to a lord was the type of duty that went with it (e.g., military, agricultural, monetary, etc.). The duties attending estates and land have long ago dropped away and are no longer important. The other distinguishing characteristic was the length and duration of the estate. The estate might be permanent (forever) or indefinite (for life) or for a fixed period of time (a number of years).

The first two of these estates were termed "freehold estates"; that is, they were subject only to duties which free men would perform as opposed to duties performed by serfs. The permanent freehold estate is of such an ample character that, for all practical purposes, it amounts to absolute ownership. Nevertheless, the Crown has the right to take away or expropriate the land if it is required for public purposes. The holder will be paid a fair price on the expropriation. Both the Federal and the Provincial Governments possess this power, and they have delegated the same power to municipalities and a number of other public bodies such as school boards, hospital boards, and others. Freehold estates will be discussed further under the heading, "Buying." Estates in land for a fixed time are called "leasehold estates." The leasehold interest will be dealt with under the heading of "Renting a Home."

In the course of time, the feudal system gradually disappeared from England, giving place to the practice of selling and renting land, and culminating in our present system. This evolution was accompanied by the growth of a voluminous body of law. Literally dozens of statutes are to be found in the various provinces dealing with real property. To deal with the law of real property fully is far beyond the scope of this book. We will attempt only to deal with certain general principles of concern to anyone contemplating buying or building or renting a home.

REAL PROPERTY

The term "property" has two meanings: the common meaning is everything which is the subject of ownership and would include the land itself; the other meaning is the *right of ownership* in a thing such as land.

The word "real" (from the Latin *res*, meaning "thing") as used in the term "real property" is derived from the manner in which the early courts dealt with rights. Thus, a lawsuit in which the courts dealt with the rights to a thing itself was called a *real action*, while a law suit involving rights that were resolved by the award of a sum of money was called a *personal action*. Land ownership was usually the subject of a real action.

The term "real property," therefore, can mean either land or the ownership in land. The more modern terms "real estate" and "realty" are derivative terms. Leasehold interests, on the other hand, were not considered real property since violations of leasehold rights were compensated simply by the award of money.

Technically speaking, there is no real property in Newfoundland. A statute in that province entitled "Of Chattels Real" provides that "all land, tenements and other hereditaments in the Province of Newfoundland which by common law are regarded as real estate, shall . . . be held as chattels real and shall go to an executor or administrator as other personal estate." The significance of this law will be better understood after a study of this Part and that on wills and inheritance, Unit 13.

LAND

CASE 1

As an antenna for his short-wave radio, A strings a single wire from his upstairs bedroom to a telephone pole about 100 feet away. The wire crosses above a corner of B's back yard.

(a) Can B prohibit A from using the air space above his land?
(b) How far up or down do B's rights extend?

Thus far we have been using the term "land" without reference to its full legal meaning. Ordinarily, the term suggests the surface of the earth. As a legal term, however, it includes everything below the land; that is, minerals, gas, oil, etc. The land also includes anything permanently affixed to it, such as buildings, fences, trees. shrubs, etc., and even fixtures (things affixed to buildings). Land also includes the air space above the land. Common law courts stated that the land included the air space above the land extending to the heavens. This concept was sufficient to prevent others from extending buildings into the air space above another's land. In modern times, however, the doctrine could not be continued. Various statutes have cut down the ownership of the air space above the land by allowing aircraft to pass freely, and by limiting the height of buildings that may be erected.

LAND USE

C—2

Bruce, who has become very wealthy, sets out to fulfil a childhood ambition. He buys a large piece of land in a residential area in Winnipeg, intending to build a medieval castle complete with moat, drawbridge, etc.

(a) Will he be allowed to do this?
(b) What may interfere with his plans?
(c) Should Bruce be allowed to use his land as he pleases?

In a less complicated era a holder of land might use it as he pleased. It is true that it could not be put to a use which would unreasonably interfere with his neighbours by the belching of smoke or odours, but beyond that an owner could erect any type of building and put it to any use he chose. Growing urbanization has, however, spawned a large number of community regulations. Zoning bylaws control the use to which land can be put; building by-laws prescribe the size, location and quality of buildings; other regulations deal with complex restraints as to the use of land, in order to accomplish such purposes as the prevention of pollution and the enhancement of the general area by proper planning.

Part 27
BUYING

GENERAL PROCEDURE IN THE TRANSACTION

For the majority of us the purchasing of a home is something we may do only once or twice in a lifetime. It usually involves a considerable sum of money, and is not the kind of transaction one can afford to learn about by making mistakes.

The volume, intricacy and complexity of the body of law on this subject is understandable when one considers the great variety of conditions which may accrue to the ownership of a piece of property which, down through the years, may have had a succession of owners either by purchase or inheritance.

It is important, therefore, to emphasize at this point that any person intending to buy a house should engage a lawyer to pilot him through the transaction.

A home—or for that matter, any other real property—may be purchased under one of the following plans:

- *Obtaining a deed upon payment in full.* (A *deed* is a document recording the transfer of ownership or title of real property from one person, called the *grantor*, to another person, called the *grantee*. Each province has prescribed a legal form of deed to be used within its boundaries).
- *Obtaining a deed with a mortgage* back to the vendor for the balance.
- *Under Articles of Agreement*, popularly described as "paying like rent."

According to the Statute of Frauds, a contract for the sale of real property must be in writing to be enforceable at law. The usual practice, therefore, is for the purchaser to submit to the seller a signed *Offer to Purchase* which has added to it a form of acceptance to be signed by the seller.

THE OFFER TO PURCHASE

The form of an Offer to Purchase has been standardized to the extent that printed forms may be obtained at any stationers. The standard form contains the following:

1. An offer to buy certain specified property of the seller.
2. The price offered and the manner of payment.
3. A stipulation as to how long the offer is to be open—usually to the exact hour.
4. A provision that all taxes, and where applicable, water rates, insurance and any rent due from existing tenants shall be adjusted as of a certain date.
5. The date on which possession shall be given.
6. A condition that the seller shall not be bound to produce any abstract of title or any deeds or any other evidence of title except such as are in his possession.
7. A condition that the purchaser shall search the title at his own expense and within a specified time; and that if the purchaser makes any objection to the title within that time, the seller shall have a reasonable time to remove it; and if unwilling or unable to remove it, the contract shall be cancelled and the deposit returned without any further liability to the purchaser.
8. That if the offer is accepted as aforesaid, the contract shall be binding; and that time shall be of the essence thereof.

The form of acceptance added to the document may be in some such words as, "I hereby accept the above offer according to the terms thereof," followed by the signature of the seller.

It can be seen by the terms of the Offer to Purchase that if the seller signs the acceptance, only one thing remains conditional to concluding the deal, and that is the satisfaction of the purchaser with the seller's title as revealed by the search.

SEARCHING THE TITLE

C—3

A is interested in buying B's house. Before completing the deal, should A check whether B is really the owner of the house?

(a) Should he also check to see if the house is fully paid for?
(b) How can these things be verified?
(c) Are there any other matters that should be investigated?

The object of searching the title is to discover what kind of ownership the seller has to the property in question. The procedure includes the following:

1. A search of the records at the local Registry Office for documents registered against the property—deeds, mortgages, leases, etc. The purposes of this search are:

- To ascertain whether there is a good chain of title. One must ensure that each succeeding owner has properly transferred the land to the next person in the chain of ownership, and that there are no breaks in the chain or interests unaccounted for. This process is much simplified under the land titles system. (The land titles system is explained later in this Part, page 299).
- To ascertain if there are any encumbrances or claims against the property; for example, outstanding mortgages or mechanics' lien claims which will have to be paid or adjusted before the transaction is closed. (See page 314).

- To ascertain if there are any claims to possession of the property; for example, registered leases or easements (rights of way over part of the property).

2. Inquiring at the sheriff's office to ascertain if any writs of execution for unsatisfied judgments have been filed against the vendor or previous owners.

3. Getting information from the local municipal offices regarding taxes prepaid or in arrears, water rates, building restrictions, zoning by-laws, and similar matters.

C—4

R was the owner of certain lands in the City of Windsor. On the land was a dwelling and a small building to the rear. R made substantial improvements to the rear building and rented it to tenants. R then agreed to sell the property to B, and this transaction was completed. A short time later B discovered that the premises were in breach of a by-law which allowed only one dwelling per lot.

The Ontario Supreme Court held that if the breach of the by-law had been raised as an objection to the title before the transaction had been completed, the purchaser could have refused to go through with it. Since the transaction was completed without complaint, no relief could be granted the buyer.

(a) What should B have done before completing the transaction?
(b) What other restrictions might there have been?

4. Finding out if a tenant is renting the property. Not all leases are registered or have to be registered by law, and apart from the document search referred to above, it should be ascertained whether in fact a tenant is in possession of the property and, if so, the tenor of his lease.

5. A survey of the property to show that the building is on the land conveyed, and whether there are encroachments or apparent easements, as perhaps a laneway or driveway, or a telephone company's right to run cables over part of it.

C—5

(i) Fowler agreed to sell a house to Caulfield, but it appeared that part of the house projected six inches beyond the southerly limit of the property. The purchaser objected to the title unless the seller could arrange to obtain the extra six inches of property and include it in the sale. In a court action which ensued the Ontario Supreme Court held that the objection was valid and that the purchaser was not obliged to complete the transaction.

(ii) H agreed to sell a house to G. The offer to purchase provided that the time for making objections to the title would expire on the date for closing the transaction. Before the transaction was closed, G discovered that the front of the house was flush with the street line, and that in order to gain entrance to the house two cement steps had been placed on the street right of way extending into the street. G refused to go through with the transaction. H argued that this was a minor matter and that the steps could be changed and the cost deducted from the sale price. However, the change would have reduced the size of one room of the house. An Ontario Court held that the purchaser was not obliged to accept the house and was entitled to the return of his deposit.

The search requires a careful examination of all the documents concerning the property which are on file or which may be otherwise discovered. The result of the search may be summarized in a document known as an *abstract of title*. Again we emphasize that this is a task for those trained in legal matters; ordinary laymen are not qualified to understand the meaning and legal import of the terms and phraseology usually contained in such documents.

CONCLUDING THE TRANSACTION

If the purchaser is satisfied with the title which the seller can convey, the deal will be closed by the seller giving the purchaser a deed to the property, and, assuming it is a cash deal, by the purchaser paying the balance of the price. Following the conclusion of the transaction, a copy of the deed should be filed immediately with the local Registrar.

Failure to Register. The purpose of registration is to create a public record of the ownership of and claims to land. If a person fails to register the document evidencing his interest in the land, he may lose that interest. Documents (other than some leases) which are not registered are deemed to be void as against subsequent purchasers or mortgagees *who have no notice* of the unregistered transaction.

Let us suppose, for example, that A sells his house to B and gives him a deed which B doesn't bother to register, and that before B takes possession he leaves for Europe. While B is absent A sells the house to C who, in searching the title, finds that A appears to be the owner of the property. So C, not knowing of the sale to B, closes the transaction and pays A in full. B will not be able to assert his ownership rights against the land which is now owned by C.

TITLE TO REAL PROPERTY

A person who purchases a home is variously described as "being the owner" or as "having title to the property." As outlined in the earlier part of this Unit, these are simply ways of referring to the fact that one holds an estate in land.

An *owner* is the holder of a *freehold estate*. The number of types of freehold estates has declined; for all practical purposes there are now only two:

- Estate in fee simple, and
- Life estate.

Estate in Fee Simple. An estate in fee simple is the highest estate that can be held in land and, in our legal system, is the closest thing we have to absolute ownership. A holder of an estate in fee simple may dispose of the property as he wishes by deed or will. The overwhelming majority of those who purchase real property in Canada obtain an estate in fee simple.

Life Estate. A life estate is the right of possession and use of the property by the grantee for the rest of his or her life. It often arises where a man having wife and children wills his property to his wife for her use as long as she lives and at her death to the children in "fee simple." The wife, therefore, has only a "life estate" in the property and cannot by selling or leasing the land convey a title extending beyond her lifetime unless the children named in the will join with her in conveying the property. Unless the children are of competent legal age, the conveyance would not be binding.

In Ontario, New Brunswick, Nova Scotia and Prince Edward Island, a life estate may also arise through (a) a wife's estate by "dower" and (b) a husband's estate by "the curtesy."

The *wife's right of dower* is a life estate in one-third of the real property which her husband owned in fee simple during the marriage. A wife has no right of dower in (a) real estate not yet improved by clearing, fencing or cultivation, (b) real estate owned by a partnership of which her husband was a member, or which he held with another as joint tenants.

The life estate accruing to a wife by dower does not come into actual effect until her husband's death. At that time she has the right.

- To have one-third of the real estate marked out for her use as long as she lives; or
- To receive one-third of the rents or profits from the property; or
- To accept a lump sum calculated as the equivalent of her dower rights according to her life expectancy.

The wife's right of dower cannot be taken from her without her consent. Therefore, when a married man sells real estate, the purchaser should make sure that the wife signs the deed waiving her dower rights. This is known as *barring her dower.* If the wife does not bar her dower in property in which she has dower rights, a purchaser would not get good title to it, since at the death of the husband, the wife could claim her life estate in the dowable property.

The *husband's estate by the curtesy* is the right of the husband on his wife's death to a life estate in all her real property. The right exists only where there is a child of the marriage capable of inheriting the property. In contrast to the husband's inability to take away his wife's dower rights, the wife may dispose of her property by sale or will during her lifetime without her husband's consent.

The provinces of British Columbia, Alberta, Saskatchewan and Manitoba have abolished the common law rights of dower and curtesy as described above and have substituted therefor certain rights in the *homestead.* The rights are not entirely uniform in these provinces, but the common features are:

- The extent of property which constitutes the homestead is established.
- The husband may not dispose of the homestead or certain rights in it during his lifetime without his wife's consent.
- On the death of the husband the homestead passes to the wife exempt from certain charges against the deceased's estate which might otherwise apply.

In Alberta and Manitoba the widow is entitled to a life estate in the homestead. There is no right of dower in Newfoundland, all lands being held as *chattels real.*

CO-OWNERSHIP OF FREEHOLD ESTATES

C—-6

These people have just finished paying for their home. Why would they be called tenants?

When two or more persons are co-owners of an estate, they are either (1) joint tenants or (2) tenants in common. Here, again, we can discern the historical basis of our law of real property in the use of the word "tenant" (holder) to refer to an owner.

Joint Tenants. A joint tenancy may be created by a deed or a will which specifically states that the owners hold as joint tenants. The property is not divided among the owners so that each has a separate part; instead, each owner is said to have an *undivided* interest in the estate.

The most important characteristic of a joint tenancy is that on the death of one of the owners the property passes to the surviving owners. For this reason husband and wife usually prefer to be named in a deed as joint tenants, since on the death of one of them, the entire property goes to the other without any legal formalities except the satisfying of death duties (where they apply). If occasion arises whereby any legal action is commenced concerning the ownership of the land, all joint tenants must sue or be sued together. Similarly, if the land is sold, all joint tenants must join in the sale.

Tenants in Common. Co-owners are tenants in common if they are not joint tenants. Again the owners hold an *undivided* interest in the estate.

The chief difference between joint tenants and tenants in common is that on the death of one of the tenants in common, the other or others do not automatically become the owner or owners of the deceased tenant's interest. Any tenant in common may dispose of his undivided interest by will, and the beneficiary then assumes his right as a tenant in common of the property. A tenant in common may also sell his interest to another.

As in the case of a joint tenancy, when legal actions are taken relating to the property, all tenants in common must sue or be sued together. If the whole property is sold, all tenants in common must join in the sale.

SPECIAL RIGHTS AFFECTING OWNERSHIP OF LAND

Certain common law rights affecting ownership arise in connection with the following:

- Water flowing through the land.
- Fixtures on the property.
- Easements.

Water Rights. An owner of land which has a stream flowing through it has a right to the continued flow of the stream in its natural state. He is entitled to take the water for domestic use, for his animals and for irrigation of crops on land which borders the stream. He may not use the water otherwise so as to interfere with the rights of other adjacent owners through whose property the stream flows. Therefore, he may not pollute the water to the degree that it is unfit for its natural use by other owners. He may divert the water from its natural course, but the diversion and the return to its natural course must take place within the boundaries of his own land.

Fixtures. Fixtures are chattels or personal property which have been attached to the land so that they become part of the "real" property. The general rule is that when real estate is sold, fixtures go with the property.

The question whether some particular chattel is or is not a fixture is often difficult to determine. The general distinction is that things which merely rest on the land or the floor of a building are chattels not fixtures, and may be removed by the owner on giving up possession of the property. Where chattels are attached to the property in a temporary manner, the question as to whether they have become fixtures may depend upon the intention of the owner at the time they were affixed to the property or upon the contract of the parties to the sale.

Easements. When purchasing property it is a wise precaution to ascertain whether or not any *easements* exist. An easement is a right which some person or persons other than the owner may have acquired to the property. The most common easements are a *right of way* over the land and a right to encroach on the land.

A right of way is the right to cross the land. It may be acquired by the express consent of the owner or even by a grant. It may also be acquired by *prescription*. In Ontario and most of the other provinces, if a person has openly enjoyed the use of a right of way across another's land for twenty years, he acquires the right by prescription, and thereafter his right cannot be denied. To be effective the use must have been *openly* assumed as if it were a right; be uninterrupted and undisputed, and *not* by any implied or express permission of the owner.

Common forms of *encroachments* are eaves overhanging another's property, a building which rests wholly or partly on another's land, etc. As with a right of way, the right to encroach may be established by grant, by permission or by prescription. (Easements may not be acquired by prescription in those areas where the land titles system of regisration is in effect).

C—7

L and H were joint owners of a farm and agreed to divide the property. There was a road on the property which was used as a means of access to the public road. After the division of the property, both parties continued to use the road for about 30 years. A dispute then arose as to whose property the road was on. The Nova Scotia Court of Appeal held that it didn't matter much whose land the road was on. Since there had been continuous *user* (the exercise of a right of use) by both parties for more than 20 years, both parties and those claiming under them had a right of way over the road.

(a) Why should twenty years *user* give L or H any rights?
(b) Some owners of land over which others use a right of way close the right of way for one day a year. Why?

REAL ESTATE MORTGAGES

When the purchaser of property is unable to furnish the complete purchase price, the seller may be willing to accept a down payment and take a *mortgage* on the property for the balance. As an alternative, the purchaser may borrow the necessary funds from a third party who will accept a mortgage on the property as security for the loan. The borrower who mortgages his property is known as the *mortgagor*; the lender is the *mortgagee*.

A distinction must be drawn between mortgages on land registered under the *old* system and those registered under the *new* (Land Titles) system. The land titles system prevails in British Columbia, Alberta, Saskatchewan, parts of Manitoba and parts of Ontario. All crown lands in these provinces come under this system.

In the provinces where the old system prevails, a mortgage is a document which provides that in consideration of a certain sum of money given by the mortgagee to the mortgagor the said mortgagor *conveys legal title to the property to the mortgagee*. Before accepting the mortgage, the mortgagee should have the title to the property searched in order to satisfy himself that the title conveyed to him is good.

In the provinces where land is registered under the Land Titles system, a mortgage does *not* convey legal title to the mortgagee. The mortgage is known as a *charge* upon the land in consideration of the debt. Except for this difference, a mortgage and a charge are practically the same.

Terms of the Mortgage Contract. Each province prescribes a statutory form of mortgage conforming to the law and system in effect in that province. The principal terms of the statutory form of mortgage for Ontario and those provinces where the "old" system is in effect follows:

1. The names of the parties to the mortgage are shown. If the mortgagor is married, his wife should also be a party to the mortgage in order to bar her dower.

2. In consideration of the loan the mortgagor "grants and mortgages" the property. The property must be properly identified and described. By this clause the mortgagor actually transfers the legal title to the property to the mortgagee.

3. The wife of the mortgagor bars her dower.

4. The mortgage will be void on payment of the loan and interest thereon according to the contract.

5. The mortgagor *covenants* with the mortgagee to pay the mortgage money and interest as provided in the mortgage. This is the mortgagor's *personal covenant*, of which more will be said later.

6. The mortgagor has good title to the property and has the right to convey it.

7. The mortgagor will insure the buildings on the land. In practice the minimum policy will be at least equal to the amount of the mortgage debt, and the loss under the policy must be made payable to the mortgagee as his interest appears.

8. On default of payment as provided in the contract, the mortgagee may take possession of the property and lease it or sell it to satisfy the debt.

9. The mortgagee may *distrain* for arrears of interest. (The procedure of distraining is the same as for landlord and tenant. See page 325).

Obviously, some of the above terms would not be found in a mortgage under the Land Titles System; for instance, the transferring of title. Also, the barring of dower would not apply in those provinces where dower has been abolished.

Registration of the Mortgage. In order to protect the mortgagee's priority of interest against subsequent purchasers or mortgagees, the mortgage should be registered immediately after it is executed. Along with the mortgage there should be registered also an affidavit of the marriage status of the mortgagor and an affidavit of a witness as to the execution of the instrument. These affidavits have been added to the statutory form of mortgage already referred to.

Discharge of Mortgage. Provided that the mortgagor makes his payments according to his contract, no legal difficulties should appear. On the completion of the payments, the mortgagee is required to give the mortgagor a certificate of *discharge of the mortgage*. This certificate should then be registered. If, however, the mortgagor defaults on his payments, certain legal procedures are open to the mortgagee.

The Mortgagee's Remedies on Default. If the mortgagor defaults on his payments, the mortgagee has the following rights:

- He may sue for the payment due.
- He may sue the mortgagor on the personal covenant which is the mortgagor's solemn promise to pay.
- He may take possession of the land, secure a tenant and apply all rent and profits on the debt. If he takes this action, he must pay all expenses such as taxes, insurance, etc., which are incurred in the holding of the property. He may retain possession in this manner only until the net rents received liquidate the amount of the debt. The property must then be given back to the mortgagor.
- He may ask for a sale of the property under the power of sale given in the mortgage. Any amount realized over the debt must be paid to the mortgagor.

In Ontario if an express power of sale is omitted from the mortgage contract, there is an *implied* power of sale when payments of interest are six months in arrears or payments on principal are four months in arrears, or if the mortgagor fails to keep the property insured.

If the sale does not realize a sufficient sum to cover the debt, the mortgagor may be held liable for any deficiency. At the same time, the mortgagee must use reasonable diligence to secure as high a price as possible for the property. He may be held liable for damages if he sells in such a manner as to sacrifice the property unnecessarily.

It is important to note that the mortgagee may not buy the property himself, nor his agent nor his solicitor for him.

- The mortgagee may apply to the court for an order of foreclosure. If the property is foreclosed, the mortgagor loses all his equity in it and it passes into possession of the mortgagee; however, if a mortgagee sues for foreclosure, the mortgagor may demand that the property be sold instead, but must make a deposit to cover the cost of the sale.

In all of the provinces the mortgagor has the right to redeem the land by paying off the entire debt before the foreclosure or sale. If a mortgage provides that the whole amount falls due in case of default in the payment of a single instalment, statutes in many of the provinces provide that the mortgagor may cure the default by paying up the arrears and then continuing to pay the regular instalments. This right becomes somewhat more restricted if the mortgagee has already started sale or foreclosure proceedings.

We should point out that the above remedies apply under the "old" system and also that there are some provincial variations. Under the Land Titles System, the remedies open to the mortgagee are fundamentally the same as above; that is, he may sue on the debt or take possession or take action for sale or foreclosure according to the procedure prevailing in his province.

Prepaying a Mortgage. A mortgage is a contract and as such may be enforced according to its terms. Therefore, a mortgagor is not entitled to prepay his mortgage and so avoid the burden of paying interest unless the mortgage contract provides that right. However, by the Federal Interest Act if the term of the mortgage is more than five years, it may be prepaid at the end of five years or any time thereafter by paying three months' bonus interest.

Sale of Mortgaged Property. A person who has mortgaged his property is not prevented thereby from selling it. At the time of the sale the mortgagee must be notified, and the new purchaser assumes the mortgage and liability for the unpaid portion of the debt.

The original mortgagor is not entirely relieved, however, from all liability under the mortgage. If the new purchaser—who is now the mortgagor—defaults on his payments on the mortgage, the original mortgagor remains liable on his *personal covenant*. This liability remains until the entire mortgage debt is paid.

In the event that the original mortgagor has been compelled to pay on his personal covenant, he may assert his right to recover from the defaulting party either the amount paid or the property itself.

Assignment by the Mortgagee. A mortgagee may sell or assign his mortgage rights, and the assignee takes his place with reference to the mortgagor and the title to the property. The mortgagor should be notified so that subsequent payments will be made to the assignee instead of to the original mortgagee. The assignment must be in writing and under seal and should be registered in the proper office.

Second Mortgages. It is not unusual for a person who has already given a mortgage on the property to borrow further on the security of a *second* mortgage. The previous mortgage is then known as a first mortgage. Although it is unusual to go beyond a second mortgage, there is no law limiting the number of mortgages that may be given.

If a second mortgage is registered before a first mortgage, the second mortgage takes priority in the event that action has to be taken against the mortgagor for default in payment. Otherwise, claims under second and subsequent mortgages have to be postponed until the first mortgage is satisfied, following which each remaining mortgage is met according to the order of its registration.

PURCHASE UNDER AN AGREEMENT FOR SALE

Homes may be offered for sale under a plan which requires a small down payment and the balance in monthly instalments which usually approximate what would be a reasonable monthly rental for the property. Under the agreement the seller retains the title to the property and does not convey the deed to the buyer until the purchase price is fully paid or until a specified sum has been paid. The buyer, therefore, cannot mortgage the property since he cannot convey title to the mortgagee.

The document representing the contract is known as an *Agreement of Sale* or *Articles of Agreement.* The usual terms of an Agreement of Sale are as follows:

1. The names of the parties to the agreement.
2. A specific description of the property to be sold.
3. The price agreed upon and the manner and times of payment.
4. A personal covenant by the buyer that he will pay the price as agreed upon with interest at a specified rate.
5. A promise by the buyer to pay taxes and to keep the property adequately insured. (The seller may decide to take care of these matters personally in order to ensure that no default may arise to jeopardize his equity in the property. The cost of the taxes and insurance is then included in the regular instalments made by the buyer.)
6. A covenant by the seller to convey good title to the buyer on completion of his payments of principal and interest.
7. A clause providing that if payments are not made punctually, the agreement will become void and the seller shall be at liberty to re-sell; and that any payments made to that date shall be the property of the seller as liquidated damages.
8. A provision that the buyer may search the title at his own expense within a specified period, and if his lawful objections to defects in the title cannot be met and the defects cured, the agreement to be void.

Assignment of an Agreement of Sale. A person buying property under this plan is entitled to sell the property to a third party by assignment of the contract of sale. The amount paid to the seller will be that amount by which the selling price of the property exceeds the amount owing on the Agreement of Sale.

Agreements of Sale should be registered for the same reasons as have already been explained in the case of deeds and mortgages.

APPLYING THE LAW

1.

Is it wise to buy a lot "on sight"? What risks are involved?

2. A and B are owners of adjoining farms. For 22 years A has used a lane through B's farm. Now, as a result of a rift in their friendship, B forbids A to use the lane. Apply the law to this situation.

3.

Explain the legal rights of the parties concerned in the above situation.

4. A buys his house by giving a down payment and a mortgage for the balance. B buys his house under an Agreement of Sale, giving a down payment but no mortgage. A needs money and borrows it by giving a second mortgage on his house. B needs money but cannot give any mortgage on his house. Explain.

DISCUSSION AND PROJECTS

1. The following report appeared in a newspaper: ". . . Council on Tuesday reaffirmed its new policy of restricting residential development when it turned down two more requests, one for a building permit and one for a watermain extension. . . . Council's policy is to curtail residential development while at the same time attempting to attract new industry to give the township a healthier assessment base."
   Suppose that the applicant for the building permit has had the lot for 10 years and has paid taxes on it during that period. He has just arrived at the point where his financial position allows him to build, and argues that the township rule denies him the right to build on his own property. Discuss this problem.
2. The following advertisement appears in a newspaper:

   > HOUSE FOR SALE. Three-bedroom split level. Attached garage. Large lot. Will take mortgage. Phone 600-7000.

   Obtain specimen copies of the legal documents that ordinarily would be used in this sale.

Part 28

BUILDING

The two matters on which a person may need legal advice when proceeding to build a home are (1) the acquiring of the land, and (2) the building contract.

ACQUIRING THE LAND

Before concluding the purchase of the land on which the house is to be built, the title to the property should be searched to learn if it is free and clear and if any easements exist. (See the preceding Part on Buying).

It is also necessary to determine what building restrictions, if any, are in effect. Building restrictions may have been imposed by an owner of the property—either the immediate seller or one of his predecessors—in connection with a building scheme of which this particular parcel of land is a part. Such restrictions frequently affect the type of building to be erected, its price range and its proximity to the lot lines. In Ontario, building restrictions of this type may be modified upon application to a Judge under the terms of the Conveyancing and Law of Property Act, provided that the modifications desired are reasonable and that there is no serious opposition from neighbouring owners. Similar procedures apply in the other provinces.

C—8

> An early deed from E to W contained a promise by W not to build on the land nearer than 15 feet from the street line. A subsequent purchaser applied to a Judge for a modification of this restriction. It appeared that the character of the neighbourhood had changed since the condition was first imposed and, as a result, the building restriction was removed.

(a) Why should a judge be able to modify this type of building restriction?

(b) What kind of character change in an area might lead a judge to remove building restrictions? Does the age of a neighbourhood make any difference?

Building restrictions may also be established by municipal by-laws. This type of restriction may not be changed by a judge's order, but can be varied or repealed only by the municipal authority which imposed the building restrictions in the first instance.

THE BUILDING CONTRACT

Building contracts, although they are almost invariably in writing, do not have to be in writing unless they come within the provisions of the Statute of Frauds.

C—9

Leatherdale agreed to build a house for Mitchell at a certain price. Part of the contract was an oral agreement that Mitchell was to transfer the title to the land to Leatherdale with the understanding that Mitchell would pay for the house in instalments, and that when it was paid for, the land would be reconveyed to him. Mitchell did not convey the land as promised, and action was commenced by Leatherdale. Mitchell pleaded the Statute of Frauds, and argued that the agreement was unenforceable since it was not in writing.

The Ontario Supreme Court agreed and held the contract unenforceable, indicating that although a contract to erect a building was not within the Statute of Frauds, the part of it dealing with the transfer of land was included in the agreement, and therefore the whole agreement was unenforceable.

(a) How could the problem in this case have been avoided?
(b) Suppose in the above case that the house had been built. Would the builder have any remedy?

Implied Terms. A contract to perform any work, in the absence of any stipulation as to the manner in which it is to be carried out, implies a condition

that the work shall be done in a good and workmanlike manner. A person who contracts to do work and supply materials generally warrants that the material which he uses will be of good quality and reasonably fit for the purpose for which he is using them.

So where a builder contracts to sell a house to be erected, or a house in the course of erection, there is an *implied* warranty that the house will be completed in a workmanlike manner with proper materials. In the case of a completed house, however, there is no implied warranty.

C—10

S, a building contractor, orally agreed with M that he would build a basement for M, who intended to erect a house on it himself. When the basement was finished, M began to erect the superstructure of the house. It was not until the work was well under way that serious defects were discovered in the concrete work performed by S, to the extent that building experts advised M that the basement would not properly support the house. M then sued S for damages.

The Court of Queen's Bench in Saskatchewan held that even in the absence of an express term in the oral agreement that good materials and good workmanship were to be used, there was an *implied* term that the work and materials would be of good quality. M, the plaintiff, was awarded damages to cover the expense of moving the structure from the basement walls, demolishing the old basement, erecting a new one and moving the house back on to the new foundation.

(a) What is an implied term?
(b) If the house had been completed on the defective foundation, and then sold to X, would X have any claim for damages?

A Written Contract. Despite the fact that building contracts do not have to be in writing, prudence and common sense indicate that they should be. Since the framing of the contract requires some technical knowledge of building operations, it is usually prepared by an architect who has been retained to draw up the plans and specifications for the job. A standard form of contract has been approved by the Royal Architectural Institute of Canada and the Canadian Construction Association. The contract forms are readily available and are in common use, being adaptable to practically all classes of construction. This form of contract, however, is not a statutory requirement and the owner may, if he wishes, draw up his own contract.

It is important that the building contract include the following:

1. Clearly defined plans and specifications covering the style of building, details of construction and finish, kind and quality of materials to be used and the quality of the workmanship.

C—11

Gearing agreed to build a house for Nordheimer according to certain plans and specifications prepared by an architect. A contract was signed, but the specifications were not signed. Gearing completed the house according to the specifications, but sought more money than the contract called for, claiming that since he had not signed the specifications the contract price was not binding, and that he was entitled to be paid according to the value of the work done and the material provided rather than by the terms of the contract. Nordheimer insisted on holding to the contract price and Gearing sued.

The Ontario Court of Appeal held that the specifications were a part of the contract since they were clearly identified, even though they were not signed or initialled, and that Gearing was bound by the terms of the contract.

(a) How could this problem have been avoided?
(b) Does the question whether the contractor made or lost money on the job affect this case?

C—12

What would have prevented this misunderstanding?

2. A specified time for the job to be completed.

3. An agreement as to sub-contracting any specialist work such as heating and electrical installations, and the contractor's liability therefor.

4. An agreement concerning "extras." It is wise to have written into the contract a term providing that the owner will only be responsible for extras if they are ordered by him in writing.

5. A clear statement with respect to warranty. A person who has a house built for himself may assume that the builder is obliged to return and repair defects, while this may not be the case. The written contract should therefore expressly cover this matter and further set out the period of time for which the builder will continue to be responsible for defects.

6. Insurance. The agreement should deal with the responsibility for insuring the building as it progresses. If the owner assumes the responsibility of insuring the building, the building contract should further provide for the disposition of the insurance monies. Otherwise the owner may be able to retain the proceeds of the insurance money while the building contractor is obliged to complete the building according to his contract and for the contract price.

C—13

Smith agreed to build a house for Dawson for $6,464, but when the house was nearly finished a fire took place causing extensive damage. Dawson had insured the building and, after the fire, was paid $2,150. Smith had neglected to take out insurance coverage on the work although he was entitled to do so. Dawson pressed for completion of the house (including repairs of damage from the fire) and the builder, after some conversation with Dawson on the matter, complied. On completion of the work, Smith requested additional money to cover the extra cost caused by the fire. Dawson refused and the builder sued, claiming that from the conversations he had with Dawson after the fire he understood that it was agreed that if he completed the house he would receive the insurance money.

The Ontario Court of Appeal held that even if there had been a promise by Dawson to pay the insurance money, Smith was not entitled to enforce it, because he was simply fulfilling his obligations under the original building contract, and had given no consideration for Dawson's promise.

(a) How could the problem in this case have been avoided?
(b) If a promise by the owner to pay the insurance money had been in writing, would it have been enforceable?

7. A clear agreement as to the complete price and the times at which certain payments will be made to the contractor. A stipulated amount should be withheld for a specified period after the house is completed in order to have security against mechanics' liens which may possibly ensue. (See Mechanics' Liens later in this Part).

Some Legal Rules Which Apply to Building Contracts. The following points should be considered with respect to the rights and obligations of the parties to a building contract:

• Unless otherwise provided in the building contract, a sub-contractor employed by the general contractor to do certain specialist work cannot sue the owner for the price of his work. There is no contract between the owner and the sub-contractor; the sub-contractor must look to the person with whom he made his agreement. However, the unpaid sub-contractor may recover all or part of his claim by filing a lien.

• Even though a contract may not provide for a completion date, the contractor is nevertheless under an obligation to do the work within a reasonable time. If he fails to do so, the owner may treat the contract as not performed, or elect to sue for damages if he can prove that the delay has caused him to suffer loss.

• A promise to pay a contractor for work which by contract he is already bound to do is not binding unless consideration can be shown for the promise. For example, a building contractor, as a result of strikes or bad weather, falls behind schedule. The owner promises him a bonus if he can finish the job on time. The contractor hires extra men and does finish on time; nevertheless, the promise to pay the bonus is unenforceable since there was no consideration. The building contractor in completing his contract on time is only performing his obligation under the original contract.

• Oral evidence is not admissible to alter or qualify the effect of a written contract, but oral evidence is admissible to qualify the meaning of words apparently a part of the contract. The purpose is not to alter the contract, but to show what it is. The meaning of words by usage or local custom may therefore be shown.

MECHANICS' AND WAGE EARNERS' LIENS

In the ordinary course of building a house an owner makes an agreement with a contractor who undertakes the general responsibility of erecting the house. The general contractor in turn makes agreements with other tradesmen, called sub-contractors, to do certain parts of the work, such, for instance, as plumbing, brick-laying, and electric wiring.

On the basis of contract alone, the general contractor has a claim for payment from the owner, and the sub-contractors can claim only from the general contractor pursuant to their agreements with him. If upon completion of the house the owner sells the house to another, the contractual claim against the owner may not be worth much if he flees or dissipates his money.

If the general contractor becomes bankrupt, the sub-contractors have no claim against the owner since they have no contract with him. In these cases the unfortunate result is that contractors, sub-contractors and the suppliers of material could easily go unpaid despite the fact that their effort and material had gone into the construction of the house.

In order to remedy the situation, the various provinces have passed Mechanics' and Wage Earners' Lien Acts. These Acts give to mechanics, labourers, contractors and suppliers of material a *lien* (derived from Latin *ligare*, "to bind") for work done upon or material furnished to be used in the erection of any building or the performance of any other work of construction.

C—14

K, a lumber dealer, delivered lumber to a site where a contractor was erecting a house for H. The contractor failed to pay for the lumber, and K claimed a lien against the house. H opposed the lien on the grounds that there was no evidence that the lumber was actually used in the construction of the house.

The Ontario Court of Appeal held that it was not necessary to show that the material actually went into the building in order to have a right to attach a lien. It was enough if the lumber was furnished to the property "to be used" in the construction of the building. The supplier was therefore entitled to a lien.

(a) Why should the lumber dealer have a claim against the house?
(b) Is his claim against the contractor for the price of the lumber not sufficient?
(c) What would be the position of a lumber dealer who delivered materials to the site of a housing project of 100 homes?

A right of lien arises as soon as work is begun or material has been furnished. However, the right ceases unless the lien is filed in the Land Registry Office within a certain period after the completion of the work or the furnishing of the material. The period is fixed by provincial statute; in Ontario, it is 37 days.

C—15

Rossiter made a contract with Rich Construction Company for them to build an addition to his premises. Rich sub-contracted the plumbing work to Robinson. Subsequently, the Rich Construction Company went into bankruptcy and Robinson registered a lien claim for the plumbing work against the property and claimed payment from Rossiter. Rossiter defended on the basis that the lien was registered too late—later than the allowed 37 days after the completion of the work. Robinson established that certain tests and repairs were performed within the 37-day period. The Ontario Court held that the right to file a lien continued to exist, since the work was not finished until these repairs and tests were performed.

Would the result be different if a contractor deliberately left some small part of his job unfinished for the purpose of protecting his lien rights?

It is important that any person wishing to take advantage of his right of lien should place the matter in the hands of a lawyer for action before the statutory period has elapsed. Once the period has ended, the claimant ranks only as an ordinary creditor, and loses all the advantage that a properly registered lien would give. A properly registered lien has priority over all mortgages, assignments, etc., which are unregistered at the time the lien is filed.

PRIORITY OF LIENS

Liens for wages are given priority over all other liens. In Ontario and some of the other provinces the priority of wage earners is for 30 days wages; in Alberta and British Columbia, six weeks; in Newfoundland, 12 days. Liens for wages beyond these periods rank with other lien claimants.

Following liens for wages, liens for material or other services and sub-contractors' claims, generally speaking, rank equally.

LIABILITY OF THE OWNER FOR LIENS

In all the provinces except Quebec, there is a statutory requirement that the owner retain a certain percentage of the value of the work done for a specified period after the work has been completed. There are provincial variations with respect to percentage and time. In most of the provinces 20% must be retained if the contract does not exceed $15,000, and 15% if over that amount. In Ontario the "hold-back" is now a straight 15%.

The period of retention also varies: for Ontario it is 37 days; British Columbia, 40 days; Alberta, 35 days; New Brunswick, 60 days; and the other provinces (except Quebec), 30 days.

The purpose of retaining part of the price is to cover claims which may arise out of mechanics' liens. If the owner does not hold back a portion of the contract price (or of the value of the work done if the contract is not completed), he will still be responsible to the lien claimants for the amount that he should have held back. It will be seen, therefore, that the owner can protect himself by complying with the statutory hold-back provisions; and if he does so, his total obligations should never exceed the contract price. For example, the owner who has paid the general contractor the allowable percentage through the progress of the building and then finds that the general contractor has not paid his sub-contractors is responsible only to the extent of the hold-back—the 15% or the 20%, as the case may be. If this amount is not sufficient to pay in full all of the lien claims, the proceeds are shared proportionately among them and the owner is discharged from any further responsibility. If there are no lien claims by the time the statutory period governing the hold-back has expired, the owner may safely pay the balance to the general contractor since the liens will have expired if they are not filed within that time.

The law concerning the incidence of liens on real property and their priority over other claims suggests that any purchaser of a newly completed building should, in searching the title, give consideration to the period in which liens may be registered against the property, and investigate the possible existence of such claim. Otherwise, the purchaser may find himself liable to satisfy such claims in place of the original owner. For example, the purchaser of a house that has been completed only a few days before he buys it may find that in the first 37 days after completion (or the relevant statutory period) that liens will be filed against this house which he will be obliged to pay, despite the fact that he may have already paid the entire purchase price.

LIENS FOR REPAIRS

In concluding this topic it should be mentioned that every mechanic or other person who has repaired any article for the owner thereof has a lien on the article for labour, material and other costs applied to the repair of the article. It is important to note that in most cases a lien for repairs may be enforced *only* if the article repaired is retained in the possession of the repairer.

Generally, if the amount owing for repairs is left unpaid for three months (there are provincial variations of the time), the article may be sold by the repairer at public auction. The sale must be advertised according to the statutory requirements of the province concerned. Any surplus resulting from the sale must be paid to the debtor, after deducting costs incident to the sale. At the same time, if a deficiency results from the sale, the debtor remains liable for the unrealized portion of the debt.

APPLYING THE LAW

1. A few days after Mr. Long had moved into his newly completed house, he paid the general contractor in full. The following week Mr. Long was advised that a lien had been placed on the house by the sub-contractor who had done the electrical work but had not been able to collect from the general contractor. Under the law, what is Mr. Long's position?
2. When the owner of a house being built for him saw the type of windows being installed, he objected strenuously. The contractor explained that the specifications did not specify any particular type of window and that his contract figure had been based on the type being installed. Legally, where does the owner stand in this case?

DISCUSSION AND PROJECTS

1. Your new house has been built for you on general contract. Soon after moving in, you notice that after every heavy rain small leaks appear in the basement walls. The contractor assures you these will clear up eventually. You suspect they will not. Discuss your legal position regarding the situation. Consider such matters as the building contract, implied warranties, statutory hold-back, etc.
2.

Discuss the possible consequences suggested in this illustration. Have one of your class or group obtain a copy of the building code for residences in your municipality. Read and circulate this among your colleagues.

Part 29
RENTING

THE LAW OF LANDLORD AND TENANT

As we have seen, the word "tenant" applies generally to anyone who is a holder of an estate in land and, strictly speaking, includes owner as well as one who rents property. In modern times the word generally indicates a person who holds a leasehold interest in the lands of another. Even the legislatures have come to accept this meaning of "tenant", so that in the various provinces legislation dealing with the renting of property is usually entitled "The Landlord and Tenant Act."

With the exception of Quebec, all the provinces derived their landlord and tenant law from England. The law has been modified by provincial statutes, but remains reasonably uniform throughout the common law provinces. The most important provincial variations will be noted as they occur.

CLASSES OF TENANCY

C—16

Jim owns a summer cottage on the shore of Lake Simcoe. He agrees to rent it to Tom for the summer season (June 1st to October 1st) at a rent of $200 a month. In the course of the summer, Jim and his friends continue to come to the property to swim and picnic.

(a) Can Tom prohibit Jim from using the property during his period of tenancy?

(b) If Tom decides he does not want the cottage, may he end the agreement by giving one month's notice?

The estate held by the tenant who rents land from the owner is termed a *leasehold interest.* A leasehold interest entitles the tenant to exclusive possession of the property during the term of the lease. The leasehold interest must begin at a fixed date and end at a fixed or ascertainable date. This type of interest in land may be divided into the following classes:

1. *Lease for a definite term.* A tenancy for a definite term is one which expires on a specific day without any further act or agreement by the landlord or tenant. A lease of a house from January 1st, 1971, to January 1st, 1976, or

the lease of a summer cottage from August 1st to September 1st of a specific year are examples of tenancy for a definite term. The duration of the term is not significant and can range from a very short time (for example, one day) to a very long term (for example, a hundred years). The important feature is the certainty of the term.

If the tenant remains in possession after the expiration of the term and the landlord accepts rent, a new periodic lease is implied. If the original lease was for a period of months, the new lease is from month to month.

2. *Periodic tenancy.* A periodic tenancy is a leasehold interest which renews itself on the last day of the term for a further period of time of the same length. Periodic tenancies continue from year to year, month to month, week to week, etc. Periodic tenancies may be expressly agreed upon, but in most cases are implied from the manner of paying the rent; for example, if a tenant moves into a house or apartment and begins paying rent at regular monthly intervals, a monthly tenancy is implied even though no specific periodic term had been agreed upon.

As indicated above, a periodic tenancy may be created after the expiration of a tenancy for a definite term if the landlord continues to accept rent. Periodic tenancies continue indefinitely until proper notice is given to terminate them.

3. *Tenancy at will.* A tenancy at will is not a true leasehold interest since it does not involve a definite period of time. It arises when a person is in possession of property with the landlord's consent but without any express or implied lease. This frequently happens when an intending purchaser of property gains possession of the property and is allowed to remain pending completion of the sale. A tenant at will may be required to vacate the premises on demand.

4. *Tenancy at sufferance.* A tenancy at sufferance is really not a tenancy at all, since the "tenant" occupies the property without the owner's consent. An example of a tenant at sufferance is a tenant who, after the end of his term, continues to stay in possession wrongfully. Since there is no true tenancy, no "rent" is payable, but the owner is entitled to be paid for the use and occupation of the premises.

THE RENTAL CONTRACT

The relationship of landlord and tenant is established by contract, known in law as a *lease.* The landlord is referred to as the *lessor* and the tenant as the *lessee.* The consideration in the lease is called *rent.* An agreement relating to the renting of premises at a future time is an *agreement for a lease.* Leases and agreements for leases of real property are covered by the Statute of Frauds, which means that in many cases they must be in writing to be enforceable. Nevertheless, many people rent their homes or other properties under oral agreements which become valid leases. It is therefore necessary to consider each of the following:

- The agreement for lease,
- The oral lease,
- The written lease.

THE AGREEMENT FOR LEASE

An agreement for lease is one which relates to the renting of a property to commence at a future time. In most of the provinces an agreement for lease of any duration must be in writing to be enforceable; in Ontario, an agreement for lease need be in writing only if the duration exceeds three years.

However, even if the agreement for lease offends the Statute of Frauds, it may still be enforceable if the tenant has taken possession or has partly performed the agreement.

C—17

Anderson was the owner of certain lands in Saskatchewan and had rented the land to Carlson, under an oral agreement, for three years ending November, 1939. According to evidence given by Carlson, in May of 1938 Anderson inspected the land and suggested that it should be summer fallowed (plowed, but not planted) in 1939. Carlson pointed out that since his lease expired in 1939, he would receive no benefit from the plan even though it would improve the land. Anderson then promised that if the summer fallowing were done as suggested, he would give Carlson another three-year lease, starting in November of 1939. Carlson accepted and the summer fallow operation was accomplished. Subsequently, Anderson refused to give the additional three-year lease and demanded possession. Although Anderson contradicted Carlson's evidence, the court accepted it and held that the agreement for lease, while not reduced to writing, was nevertheless enforceable because the summer fallow operation was part performance of the agreement.

(a) What should Carlson have done to protect himself?
(b) Would the result have been the same if Anderson had not mentioned summer fallowing, but Carlson had done it of his own accord, relying on an oral agreement from Anderson to give another three-year lease?

The Oral Lease. In Ontario and most of the common law provinces, a lease for a term *exceeding* three years is required to be in writing to be enforceable. If the term is three years or less, an oral lease is valid. Even in the case of oral

leases where the term exceeds three years, when the tenant has taken possession or partially performed the agreement the courts, as a general rule, hold the lease is enforceable despite the fact that it was not in writing.

C—18

B orally agreed to become a tenant of certain premises in Toronto for a period of five years at a rent of $90 a month. A lease was prepared but was never signed. B went into possession, paid one month's rent and spent $12 on fixtures. Subsequently, because of certain circumstances which arose, the landlord desired to take possession and claimed he was entitled to do so because there was no effective written agreement. An Ontario Court held that there was part performance of the agreement, and that it was enforceable despite the fact it was not in writing.

(a) What is part performance? Why does it make any difference in this case?
(b) If B had spent the $12 on fixtures but had not taken possession, would he have been able to enforce his oral lease?

Oral leases are not always satisfactory; for example, the tenant may take it for granted that the landlord has certain obligations with respect to such items as taxes and repairs, and then finds that he is mistaken. Even if the oral agreement includes such matters, it may be difficult to establish the terms of the agreement.

The Written Lease. A lease for a period *exceeding* three years is not valid unless it is in writing. With certain statutory exceptions, in the Western provinces the lease must also be under seal. If such a lease is in writing but not under seal, it does not operate immediately to make the tenant a holder of an estate in land, but it will be regarded as an *agreement for a lease* and may be enforced as such.

Requisites of a Valid Lease. A valid lease should contain the following:

1. The names of the parties (the lessor and lessee).
2. A description of the premises (the street address or lot and concession number).
3. The commencement date and the term.
4. The duration of the term.
5. The rent and how it is to be paid.
6. The material terms of the contract dealing with other matters (heat, light, responsibility for damage, etc.).

THE SHORT FORMS ACTS

Ontario and some of the other provinces have passed Acts referred to as the Short Form of Leases Act. These statutes authorize the use of certain forms of covenants (solemn promises) which may be used by persons preparing leases. The parties, if they wish, may refer to the Short Forms Act and thus incorporate the provisions of the Act into their lease. These Acts are for the convenience of those who draw up leases, and can be used or not as the parties choose. In practice, however, the Acts set the pattern of leases that are most often followed.

The various Short Forms Acts provide leases whereby the lessee promises as follows:

1. To pay rent.
2. To pay taxes, except for local improvements.
3. To pay water rates.
4. To repair the premises, reasonable wear and tear and damage by fire and tempest excepted. (In Ontario, by virtue of a recent amendment to the Landlord and Tenant Act, the landlord is now obliged to repair in the case of residential tenancies) See Page 327.
5. To keep up fences.
6. Not to cut down timber.
7. That the lessor may enter and view the state of repair.
8. That the lessee will repair the premises according to notice in writing, reasonable wear and tear and damage by fire and tempest excepted. (See No. 4, above, re Ontario).
9. Not to assign or sublet the premises without permission (it is implied by law that the landlord will not withhold unreasonably his consent to assign or sublet the premises).
10. To leave the premises in good repair, reasonable wear and tear and damage by fire, lightning and tempest only excepted (see No. 4, above, re Ontario).
11. That the lessee may remove his fixtures.
12. That in the event of damage by fire, lightning or tempest making the premises unfit for the tenant's purposes, rent shall cease until the premises are rebuilt.
13. To allow re-entry by the lessor on non-payment of rent or non-performance of covenants.

The lessor covenants with lessee for quiet enjoyment of the property leased.

RIGHTS AND OBLIGATIONS OF LANDLORD AND TENANT APART FROM CONTRACT

Apart from the lease certain rights and obligations of both landlord and tenant are either implied under common law or provided by statute. In many cases these provisions apply where the parties to the lease have not agreed on something to the contrary. In other cases, however, the law will override the agreement of the parties and lay down a rule which governs the landlord and tenant despite their agreement to the contrary. We shall consider some of the principal rights and obligations.

RENT

The amount of rent to be paid is a matter of contract between the parties to the lease. Rent may be paid *in kind*, as when the janitor of an apartment house agrees to pay his rent in the form of services; or when a farm is rented for a consideration of part of the crop.

Rent is not payable in advance unless the lease so provides; however, it must be paid strictly when due according to the lease or the landlord may be entitled to take action for possession of the premises for non-payment.

PURSUANT TO THE LANDLORD & TENANT ACT:
THE LANDLORD HAS TAKEN POSSESSION OF THESE PREMISES FOR NON-PAYMENT OF THE RENT.
ANYONE TRESPASSING ON THIS PROPERTY OR TAMPERING WITH THE LOCKS OR DOORS IS LIABLE TO ARREST AND PROSECUTION.
Dated at Toronto this day....
30th March
....

Above is the wording of a notice posted on the shop door.

C—19

Robertson, the owner of a building, agreed to rent a part of it to Milan to be used as a butcher shop, with Milan also to have the use of a room behind the shop. In return, Milan agreed to act as caretaker of the whole building. Later, the landlord attempted to dismiss Milan as caretaker and to recover the premises, claiming that Milan was not carrying out the caretaking duties properly, and that the agreement between them was one of employment and not a lease.

A Manitoba court held that the agreement was a lease and the services were rent. From the evidence the court found that the services were being adequately performed and the rent was not in arrears; consequently, the landlord was not entitled to recover possession.

(a) Does rent have to be in money?
(b) Give other examples of rent payable in kind.

C—20

(i) For two years Hill paid his rent by sending a cheque through the mail to his landlord. In August of 1949 a cheque was mailed but went astray. The landlord brought an application to recover possession of the property, claiming that the rent was overdue and unpaid.

The Ontario Court of Appeal held that "unless there is an express or implied agreement between the parties, or an express or implied authorization by the landlord that the rent may be paid by remitting the same by post, the tenant assumes all the risks if he adopts that method, and the rent is not paid by him when he places the letter in the post office. Here there was no such agreement or authorization expressed or implied. Neither does the course of conduct between the parties amount to a recognition by the landlord of the tenant's right to remit by post." The landlord's application for possession for non-payment of rent was therefore granted.

(ii) A landlord always called at the rented premises to collect the rent, but in May and June of 1946 he did not do so. When the landlord did not call, the tenant sent a boy with the rent, but the landlord refused to take it because (as he said) he had a pending application with the rental control board for an increase in rental. This increase was granted in June, but still the landlord did not call for the rent, neither did the tenant send it although he was always ready to pay. Subsequently, the landlord gave the tenant notice to vacate, but the tenant refused to give up possession. The landlord then took proceedings for possession of the premises, alleging that the rent was in default.
The British Columbia Court of Appeal stated that while as a general rule the creditor must seek out the debtor, in this case the circumstances implied that the payment of the rent was to be made at the rental premises. The court therefore refused the landlords claim for possession.

(a) Is the landlord under any obligation to collect the rent?
(b) These two cases appear to have been decided differently. What fact was the key to each decision?

Raising the rent is usually a matter of negotiation between landlord and tenant. In the absence of an agreement, rent may not be changed during the currency of the lease. Any notice to change the rent at the end of the current lease is subject to the right of either party to give notice of termination of the lease if he does not agree to the proposal. In the case of a lease for a lengthy fixed term, the ability to change the amount of the rent at the end of the term may be of little practical consequence. In the case of the short term lease, the question is more immediate, and new rent may be negotiated as a part of the new lease. Where the tenancy is periodic, for example, month to month, and the parties fail to agree on a change for succeeding periods, either party may terminate the lease by giving the appropriate notice (see Termination of the Tenancy).

RENT CONTROLS

During World War II the federal government enacted regulations which restricted the ability of landlords to increase rent. This was necessary during the war and for some time thereafter because of the housing shortage.

After the war the federal government repealed those regulations, but they were then adopted by the various provinces. Eventually, most of the provinces also repealed these controls. However, in British Columbia, Newfoundland and Quebec, forms of rent control continue to exist. In Ontario, the Landlord and Tenant Act now provides that any municipality may set up a landlord and tenant advisory bureau whose primary function is to conciliate disputes. Since rent increase could be a matter of dispute, the bureau will no doubt attempt to restrain rent increases, although it has no actual authority to prevent them.

DISTRESS

When a tenant allows rent to fall into arrears, the landlord may either sue for the rent or exercise his right of distress or right *to distrain.* These terms mean the right to seize the tenant's goods which are on the rented premises and sell them to satisfy the arrears of rent. This is an old common law right which became the law in all the provinces. In 1969, however, Ontario abolished the right of distress in so far as it applied to residential tenancies, allowing it to continue only for non-residential tenancies. In the other provinces (at the time of writing) this right of the landlord continues to exist for all types of leases. There are some statutory variations between the provinces, and these variations, however slight, may be important in a particular case. Where the right of distress is to be exercised in any province, a lawyer should be consulted.

In general, the following rules apply to non-residential leases in Ontario and to all leases in the other provinces.

1. *The seizure.* The seizure is usually made through a bailiff; however, by law the landlord may exercise the right personally. Neither the landlord nor the bailiff may force his way on the property to seize the goods. They may enter through an unlocked door or an open window, but they may not legally put their hands through a broken door or window in order to unfasten it from the inside. If they cannot enter other than stated above, a court order will be necessary to gain legal entry.

The landlord does not have the right to distrain goods until after the rent is due, and then only between the hours of sunrise and sunset. However, if he finds the tenant removing his goods on the day the rent is due, he may forbid their removal; but he has no right to prevent removal of goods prior to this date.

C—21

The plaintiff was a tenant of a building in Humboldt, Saskatchewan. In December, the landlord had seized some of the tenant's goods for non-payment of rent, but the tenant paid up the arrears. On the same day that this matter was settled, the tenant moved his goods from the building to his own home. On January 30 (the following month), a bailiff, on the instructions of the landlord, seized the goods that had been removed to the tenant's home to satisfy rent again owing. The tenant then took action for wrongful distress.

The Saskatchewan Court of Appeal held that since at the time of removal of the goods from the rented premises there was no rent owing (the previous arrears having been paid), the landlord was not entitled to follow the goods and to distrain them at the tenant's home.

(a) Apart from seizure of the goods, does the landlord have any other way of collecting his rent?
(b) What change in the facts of this case would have made the seizure legal?

2. *Goods which may be seized.* Generally, only goods found on the premises may be seized. However, if the goods have been fraudulently removed on

the day the rent is due, or clandestinely removed after sunset of that day, the landlord may follow the goods and seize them wherever they are at any time within a certain period.

The landlord may seize any of the goods and chattels of the tenant except those which are exempt; namely, certain household furniture and utensils which are necessary to his living, a limited supply of food, tools of his trade, etc. Any goods belonging to the tenant's wife, children or near relatives who live on the premises as members of his family are also subject to seizure for distress. The goods of a lodger or subtenant may also be seized, but only to the amount these parties owe the tenant for lodging or rent, as the case may be. Goods which the tenant is buying under a conditional sale agreement may be distrained (seized for distress) subject, however, to payment of the balance owing to the seller under the contract.

3. *Wrongful distress.* If the landlord distrains the tenant's goods wrongfully, in an irregular manner, or more goods than are reasonably necessary to cover the rent overdue and the cost of the seizure, the landlord and/or the bailiff is liable for damages.

4. *Exemptions.* Certain property is exempt from seizure in order that the tenant may continue to survive and earn a living. These exemptions include:

- necessary household furniture, utensils and equipment;
- necessary wearing apparel of the tenant and his family;
- a limited supply of fuel and food;
- a limited number of tools and implements of the tenant's trade or occupation; and
- in the case of a farmer, a limited supply of seed, livestock and implements.

QUIET ENJOYMENT

A tenant has the right to quiet enjoyment of the property rented. A written lease usually contains a clause to this effect; but if it does not, or if the lease is oral, then the law implies such a right to the tenant. The right to quiet enjoyment does not mean undisturbed by noise, but rather free from interference with the use or possession of the property.

C — 22

MacLennan leased to an insurance company a suite of offices immediately over his place of business in the City of Toronto. The door from the street, which also gave access to stairs leading to the company's office, was locked by the caretaker of the building at 6 p.m. MacLennan would not consent to the tenant having a key to the outer door unless the tenant arranged for the caretaker to be present while the offices were in use after 6 p.m. Thereupon, the company took action, claiming that they were wrongfully prevented from obtaining access to the offices they had leased. MacLennan contended that any difficulty experienced by the tenant was a breach of duty on the part of the caretaker, and not his fault.

The Ontario Court of Appeal held that MacLennan could not avoid liability for the actions of the caretaker, and that since there was no stipulation in the lease regarding the closing of the street entrance at 6 p.m., to enforce this rule was a breach of the tenant's right to quiet enjoyment of the premises.

(a) Generally speaking, why is a tenant entitled to access to his premises at all times?
(b) Most office buildings lock their doors at night and on Sundays. How do lessors and lessees of such premises avoid problems arising similar to the above case?

C—23

(i) Jenkins rented from Jackson two rooms in a building. Jenkins used the rooms as an office for his business as accountant. After granting the lease, Jackson rented the premises immediately above for the purpose of a dance hall. Jenkins complained that his premises could not be enjoyed or used in comfort. An English court held that the landlord by renting the premises above as a dance hall was in breach of his covenant of quiet enjoyment.

(ii) Walton was the owner of a building in Winnipeg, and Biggs was the tenant. Biggs had moved out and was being sued for rent due under the lease. Biggs said he owed nothing because he had not had quiet enjoyment of the premises, due to the fact that the occupier of the suite overhead carried on the business of dress-making which necessitated a constant use of sewing machines and pressing irons, causing vibration and thumping. A Manitoba court agreed that there was a breach of the tenant's right to quiet enjoyment; consequently, the tenant was not liable for rent.

(a) Does quiet enjoyment mean only free from noise?
(b) What other circumstances could amount to a breach of the tenant's right to quiet enjoyment?

THE OBLIGATION TO REPAIR

The question of putting and keeping rented premises in repair has in the past proved to be one of the more common points of friction between landlord and tenant. In many cases the obligation rested on no one.

In 1969, as a part of a general overhaul of landlord and tenant law, the Ontario Landlord and Tenant Act was substantially amended with respect to residential property. The landlord is now obliged to provide and maintain the rented premises in a state of good repair, fit for habitation, and in accord with health, safety and housing standards. The tenant is responsible for ordinary cleanliness of the premises and for the repair of any damage caused either wilfully or negligently by the tenant or by anyone permitted on the premises by him. Further, the new amendment provides these rights and obligations cannot be varied or altered by agreement between the landlord and the tenant. In the other provinces, and in the case of a non-residential lease in Ontario, the following principles apply:

1. *Agreement to Repair.* The landlord and the tenant are free to agree on any terms they choose with respect to repair. If a written lease is prepared, the question of who is responsible for repair should be clearly defined.

Example of tenant neglect of premises

Toronto Telegram

Many forms of lease contain a clause which imposes the duty of repair on the tenant. The same form usually excludes the tenant's responsibility due to reasonable wear and tear and to damage by fire or tempest. A tenant not wishing to assume responsibility for repair should look at the form of lease carefully before signing it.

C — 24

Rempel was a tenant of certain premises owned by Bartram, and had covenanted to repair, reasonable wear and tear excepted. Bartram complained that the fence in front of the premises was falling down, and sued Rempel for breach of covenant to keep the premises in repair. Rempel's defence was that the condition of the fence was due to "wear and tear." Evidence was given that the fence was 28 years old and that the posts had rotted.

The British Columbia Court of Appeal held that "reasonable wear and tear" included the normal progressive action of the forces of nature, and that the tenant was not obliged to repair the fence.

(a) If there is no agreement dealing with repair, who has the obligation to repair—landlord, tenant, or nobody?

(b) If the fence were still standing despite its age and condition and Rempel had knocked it over with his car? Would Rempel be obliged to repair the fence?

If the landlord agrees to make repairs (as is sometimes done), the general rule is that the tenant must notify the landlord when repairs are needed, and that then the landlord will repair. If the landlord does not make repairs when so notified, the tenant may make the repairs himself and deduct the amount from the rent, provided that the tenant gives the landlord reasonable notice of his intention to do so and the landlord still fails to make repairs. The tenant has the alternative right of suing for damages for non-repair, but he is not entitled to consider his lease terminated by this breach of warranty, since he is entitled to make repairs himself and deduct the cost from rent.

2. *In the Absence of an Agreement to Repair.*

C — 25

G Company leased part of its building to the S Company. A water pipe which served the whole building passed through the leased premises. During severe winter weather the pipe froze and burst, damaging goods of S Company. The lease contained no provision with respect to heat or duty to repair, but the S Company sued for damages, alleging negligence on the part of G Company in failing to take measures to prevent such damage.
The Supreme Court of Canada said there was no duty on the part of G Company, the landlord, to prevent the pipe from freezing or to keep it in repair. The claim of the S Company for damages was dismissed.

(a) What should the S company have done to protect itself?
(b) Suppose the break had taken place in a part of the building retained and occupied by the landlord, and the water had run from that part into the leased premises. Would the tenant have had a claim?

C — 26

McDonald rented a house to Hamilton as a tenant from month to month. There was no written lease. The house had a hot water heating system and in January one of the pipes burst. The landlord sued the tenant for the cost of repairs, alleging that the tenant was negligent and had not kept the fire burning properly.
A Nova Scotia court agreed that the tenant had a duty to use the premises in a tenant-like manner, but said that in this case there was no negligence in the care of the furnace, and held that the damage was the result of a poor heating system. MacDonald's case was dismissed.

(a) What do you think "tenant-like manner" means?
(b) For what sort of thing would the tenant be responsible on the grounds of failure to use the premises in a tenant-like manner?

In the case of a furnished dwelling it is implied by law that the house must be in a habitable condition at the commencement of the tenancy, but the landlord is not obliged to make any further repairs unless there is an agreement to do so.

In the case of an unfurnished dwelling or other premises, the landlord is under no obligation to put the premises into a habitable condition at the beginning of the tenancy or to make repairs during the tenancy. The tenant is expected to examine the property before he agrees to rent it and, if it is not to his liking, to bargain with the landlord regarding the repairs. If he enters into a lease without an agreement as to repairs, he must take the property as he finds it, and is liable to pay the rent for the duration of the lease, regardless of discomfort caused by non-repair. (As already noted, in Ontario this rule has been changed for residential property).

The tenant of either furnished or unfurnished premises, while under no duty to repair, is obliged to treat the premises in a tenant-like manner and is responsible for damages which he causes either wilfully or negligently.

Example of landlord neglect

Toronto Telegram

LIABILITY FOR INJURY

The responsibility for the safety of premises is generally the burden of the occupier and not of the owner. A person suffering damage or injury, therefore, will usually have a claim against the occupier who may be a tenant (See Unit 2, Torts).

In many cases the owner of the premises is not liable. If he has covenanted to repair, however, he will be responsible, but then only to the tenant and not to the tenant's family, friends, or employees. In Ontario, the 1969 amendment to the Landlord and Tenant Act has imposed the duty to repair residential property on the landlord, and this will likely lead to the landlord's responsibility for damage or injury caused by failure to repair.

The foregoing applies to the leased premises themselves, but where the landlord retains control of a part of the building (the entrance, hallways, etc.), he continues to be responsible for those areas and he is governed by the ordinary law of torts.

C—27

An Express Company driver called at a building to collect parcels from a tenant. He was injured because of a defective elevator which serviced the whole building. When the injured driver sued for damages, the landlord's defence was that he was not responsible for the accident. He argued that the driver's business was with a tenant, and his accident was due to his own failure to take care. The Supreme Court of Canada held that the driver was an invitee of the landlord while in the elevator. As owner of the building, he was held to be negligent in the maintenance of the elevator, and damages were awarded to the express driver.

(a) Ordinarily, who is responsible for injury to third parties caused by defective premises, the landlord or the tenant?
(b) Would the result be different in the above case if
  (i) the tenant rented the whole building?
  (ii) there was a sign on the elevator reading "Out of Order"?

SECURITY DEPOSITS

C—28

A, a young high school teacher in the city of Toronto is in desperate need of an apartment for himself, wife and child. He finally finds one, but has to sign a three-year lease and pay a $500 deposit to the landlord as a "security deposit." In addition to the deposit A pays the rent regularly. At the expiration of the three years, A buys a house and moves out of the apartment. A demands the return of his deposit, but the landlord says the apartment has to be redecorated and that this will cost $500.

(a) Is A entitled to the return of the $500, or part of it?
(b) Is the landlord entitled to the interest on the $500 for the three years?
(c) Is there any limit on the time the landlord has to repay the deposit or account for it?

In recent years a practice has arisen whereby a landlord as a condition of leasing property obtains a deposit of money from the tenant to be held by the landlord and used to pay the costs of repairs to the premises on the expiration of the lease. In many cases, the deposits were large, and in some cases tenants experienced difficulty in obtaining the return of the deposit either in whole or in part at the conclusion of the tenancy.

In Ontario, the Landlord and Tenant Act as amended in 1969 prohibits security deposits for residential property, excepting only a deposit of one month's rent to insure the payment of the last month's rent. Further, the landlord must pay 6% interest on the deposit of the one month's rent while he holds it. In the case of non-residential property in Ontario and all types of property in other provinces, the security deposit remains a matter of agreement between the parties. However, the Alberta Landlord and Tenant Act provides that within ten days after the termination of the tenancy the landlord must deliver to the tenant the deposit in full or a statement of the expenditures for repairs, either actual or estimated, and the balance of the deposit, if any.

TAXES AND SERVICES

Generally speaking, the questions of who shall pay the taxes and who is responsible to pay for services such as heat and electricity, etc., are matters of agreement between the landlord and the tenant. Most of the Short Forms of Leases Acts contain clauses whereby the tenant assumes the responsibility of paying taxes (except for taxes for local improvements). Generally, in the absence of an agreement, the obligation to pay the real property taxes rests with the landlord; however, custom and practice in the community may be looked to and can furnish implied terms of the agreement. In the case of services also, common practice and custom can be referred to from which an agreement can be implied. If an agreement cannot be implied, liability will rest upon the person who contracts for the service; for instance, the landlord would pay for the fuel he orders to heat a building, the tenant would pay for the telephone he orders installed, and so on.

FIXTURES

C—29

A, built a house and stable upon the land he rented. Later, a dispute arose between the creditors of A and the owner of the land as to the ownership of the buildings. Both buildings were of wood and rested on loose stones, and could be removed without injury to the land.
A Saskatchewan court held that these buildings were not attached to the land and were still the property of A, the tenant, and therefore available to his creditors.

(a) Why was the question of "attached to the land" important?
(b) How does the ruling in this case apply to the mobile home?

As we have seen earlier, some goods when attached or affixed to the land or a building become a part of the real property, and the ownership to the goods vests in the owner of the land. Therefore, when tenants instal things in a building, erect fences or plant trees, etc., problems occasionally arise as to the right of the tenant to take them away when the lease expires. Generally speaking, anything that is attached in a permanent way to the building is considered to be a fixture and part of the real property. On the other hand, articles simply resting of their own weight are presumed not to be fixtures and remain the property of the tenant.

Even if the object is attached to the land or building, a tenant may still be able to remove it if it was

- attached only for the purpose of convenience of the tenant or better enjoyment of the object; or
- a trade fixture—an object brought on to the land or building for the purpose of carrying on some business or trade.

Both the above are classed as tenants' fixtures and may be removed if a tenant can do so without leaving the premises in a damaged condition.

ASSIGNMENT AND SUBLETTING

C—30

A tenant applied to a landlord for permission to assign his lease, but the landlord withheld consent saying that the rent was too low, and she could get a higher rent per month. She said simply "it is my apartment building and I wish to choose my own tenants." However, she had no specific objections to the proposed assignee.
The Ontario Court of Appeal said the consent was unreasonably withheld. The landlord simply wanted to regain possession in order to obtain a higher rent from a new tenant.

(a) Does a tenant have the right to assign a lease?
(b) What legitimate objections might a landlord have with respect to a proposed assignee of a lease?

Situations may arise in the currency of the lease causing a tenant to wish to assign his lease to another. As the holder of an estate in land, he has the right to sell or

Greenwin Construction Co. Ltd.

assign his interest to someone else. A person employed in Vancouver may be transferred to Halifax and no longer have any need for his rented premises in Vancouver. His covenant, however, binds him to continue paying the rent. He may, therefore, *assign* his lease to another who will occupy the premises and pay rent and, in effect, become the new tenant, subject to the same rights and obligations. By doing this, the old tenant does not escape the primary liability of paying the rent. If the assignee does not pay, the obligation continues to bind the first tenant.

Occasions may also arise when a tenant may wish to *sublet* the premises. This is somewhat different from an assignment. In the case of the assignment, the tenant transfers his whole estate; in the case of the sublease, the tenant transfers only a part. The part transferred may be a part from the standpoint of either time or space. For example, a tenant of a house for a longer term may sublet it for the summer and re-occupy it in the fall; or a tenant of a ten-room house may sublet five of the rooms to someone else.

A landlord, of course, has a very real interest in the question of who becomes an assignee of a lease or a subtenant. These may be people to whom he would not have rented the premises in the first instance. Landlords therefore almost invariably extract a promise from the tenant that he will not assign the lease or sublet without the consent of the landlord. In many of the provinces (Ontario, Manitoba, Saskatchewan, New Brunswick, Prince Edward Island) the consent may not be unreasonably withheld.

SALE OF THE LEASED PREMISES AND REGISTRATION OF LEASES

A holder of a fee simple estate in land (or owner) who leases property grants away the right to possession for the term of the lease, but he remains the holder of the ownership estate in the land; that is, he is the owner. He is, of course, free to sell or mortgage this ownership interest without regard to the tenant's consent.

Generally, if the premises are sold, the new owner takes ownership subject to the tenancy. In the case of long-term leases, the tenant's right to retain possession may depend upon whether the lease has been registered. In Ontario, a lease for seven years or more must be registered, otherwise it is void as against a subsequent purchaser or mortgagee who did not know of the lease. In the other provinces, except Quebec, the same rule applies to leases exceeding three years.

TERMINATION OF LEASES

A leasehold interest by its very nature is temporary and in due course will come to an end. It may terminate simply through the passing of a definite time, or the giving of notice, or by some default.

1. *Lease for a definite term.* A tenancy for a definite term terminates automatically without notice at the end of the term. If, however, the tenant remains in possession and the landlord accepts rent on the former plan, a new periodic lease is implied. If the original lease was for a year or more, the new implied lease may be from year to year. If the original lease was for a period of months, the new lease is from month to month.

When the tenant remains in possession without the landlord's consent, he is known as an overholding tenant. The landlord may allow an overholding tenant to remain in possession until the tenant finds new premises, and to pay rent meanwhile, but the overholding does not imply a new tenancy either by the landlord or by the tenant.

If the landlord does not wish to permit the overholding, he may demand possession by written notice. If this fails, he may then take the necessary action to evict the tenant.

During the period of a lease for a definite term, both landlord and tenant may agree to earlier termination of the tenancy. This voluntary termination may be accomplished by a payment of money. For example, a landlord who requires the premises for his own use and who wishes to be rid of the tenant, may pay the tenant to surrender his lease; or a tenant who finds he no longer needs the premises may pay his landlord to release him from the lease. In some cases, of course, the cancellation of the lease may be mutually advantageous.

2. *Periodic tenancy.* As we have seen, a periodic tenancy is one that goes on from month to month or year to year, or other periods. A tenancy of this type continues indefinitely until either the landlord or the tenant gives the appropriate notice, called a *notice to quit.*

The length of notice that must be given is largely dependent on the type of periodic tenancy. Generally, sufficient notice is as follows:

- In the case of a weekly or monthly tenancy, notice must be given on or before the last day of a tenancy period in order that the tenancy be terminated on the last day of the next tenancy period. Hence, in the case of a weekly tenancy the notice must be at least one clear week, and in the case of a monthly tenancy, one clear month.
- In the case of a yearly tenancy, notice must be given to terminate the tenancy at the end of a tenancy year. The minimum amount of notice varies with the provinces as follows: six months in Newfoundland, Manitoba, Saskatchewan and British Columbia; three months in Quebec, New Brunswick, Nova Scotia and Prince Edward Island; and sixty days in Ontario and Alberta.

Where the notice to quit has been given by the landlord and the tenant does not vacate the premises, he becomes an overholding tenant and the landlord may take the appropriate eviction proceedings.

3. *Forfeiture.*

C—31

A tenant under a written lease for a definite term was in the habit of paying the rent several months at a time instead of every month as required by the lease. In the course of this irregular procedure he fell in arrears from time to time. On one of the occasions when the tenant was in arrears, the landlord took steps to re-enter the premises. The tenant applied to a British Columbia court for relief against forfeiture of the lease and, as a part of the application, tendered all of the arrears of rent. The court granted the application on the grounds that it was equitable to do so, and held that the lease remained in force.

(a) Does breach of a duty under the lease automatically result in the tenant forfeiting his lease?
(b) What were the equitable grounds in this case upon which the tenant retained his lease?

If a tenant is in breach of one of his duties under the lease (for example, the payment of rent), he may forfeit his tenancy and give the landlord the right to re-enter the premises. In some cases the landlord may first give the tenant a notice of the breach of covenant.

In the case of failure to pay the rent, the rent must remain unpaid for a prescribed period of time before the right to re-enter arises. The period runs from 15 days in most provinces to six months in Newfoundland.

In most cases the right of re-entry is not carried out by the landlord personally; instead, he takes legal proceedings. In Ontario, the re-entry must be pursuant to a court order. The courts of the various provinces have jurisdiction to grant relief against forfeiture of the lease when it would be equitable to do so.

APPLYING THE LAW

1.

I PLANTED THESE EVERGREENS
I'M NOT LEAVING THEM
FOR THE
NEW
TENANT!

May the tenant legally remove the evergreens? What about other things which the tenant may have installed in the house; for example, an air conditioner, or a kitchen fan? Explain how the law applies.

2. The owner of a four-apartment dwelling, who occupies one of the apartments, rents the others usually without a written agreement. He tries to select his tenants carefully and always gives them to understand that he will not allow subletting of rooms. How does the law apply in these circumstances?
3. A landlord wishing to be rid of a tenant tried to make the tenant leave by creating a series of incidents designed to inconvenience

the tenant; for instance, at various times he broke a padlock, removed a door to part of the premises occupied by the tenant, interrupted the electrical supply and cut off the heat. Is any legal recourse open to the tenant? Explain.

DISCUSSION AND PROJECTS

1.

Discuss the landlord's liability according to the law in your province.

2. At considerable expense and with much hard work Jones converted his house into a duplex with a view to deriving some income from rental. Jones, now retired, depends on this rental to supplement his pension, but his present tenant is two months in arrears with the rent, claiming he has been laid off and cannot get work. Jones, however, feels that the tenant is not much concerned about being in arrears. Discuss the legal aspects of this problem.
3. Obtain, if you can, a copy of an actual lease. Examine its terms. What does it say about making repairs?

UNIT THIRTEEN INHERITANCE OF PROPERTY

Part 30
WILLS AND INHERITANCE BY LAW

Although there is some variation, the same general principles and design of the law concerning wills and inheritance apply in all the provinces. The scope of this text necessarily limits our treatment of what is a broad and in many respects intricate body of law to a brief outline of some of its chief aspects. The outline given in this Unit follows the law of Ontario except where specific references are made otherwise.

Wills are governed by the Wills Act, a title used in all the provinces. The inheritance of property not disposed of by will, known as *intestate succession* is covered in Ontario by the Devolution of Estates Act; in Prince Edward Island it comes under the Probate Act; in the other provinces the title is either The Devolution of Estates Act or The Intestate Succession Act.

MAKING A WILL

A *will* is a document by which a person directs how his property is to be disposed of after his death. The person who makes a will is called the *testator* (feminine, *testatrix*).

Those named in the will to receive gifts are known generally as *beneficiaries*. In more technical terms, a gift of personal property made by will is known as a *bequest* or a *legacy*; the person to whom it is given is called the *legatee*. A gift of land or real property is called a *devise*, and the person who receives it, a *devisee*.

The *executor* is the person appointed by the testator to administer the estate and distribute the property. A woman who acts in this capacity is called an *executrix*.

FORM AND WORDING

CASE 1

A home-made will made by the testator provided as follows:

> *This is my last will.*
> *I give my soul to God.*
> *I give all I belong to my wife.*
> *I want her to pay my debts—raise the family.*
> *All will belong to my wife until the last one comes to the age of 21 years old.*
> *If my wife marries again she should have her share like the other children; if not, she will keep the whole thing and see that every child gets his share when she dies.*

Following the death of her husband, the widow carried on the family business, a retail store, and raised the family until they were all past the age of 21. At that time the question arose as to what was the widow's interest in the estate after "the last one comes to the age of 21 years old," and application was made to the court for advice and direction as to the proper construction of the will.

The court, after considering all the circumstances existing at the time the will was made, held that the widow had been given a life interest in the estate with the right to carry on the business and to encroach on the capital, if necessary, for the maintenance and support of herself and the children—not only until the youngest child became 21 years of age, but afterwards as well, until her remarriage or her death. On her death the estate should vest in the children in equal shares.

(a) What did the court consider besides the actual will itself?
(b) What is a life interest in the estate?
(c) What is meant by the right to encroach on capital?
(d) What does this case indicate about home-made wills?

No particular form or wording is prescribed by law for the construction of a will; it is necessary only to show clearly the intentions of the party making it.

The above statement, however, implies an over-simplification of the matter. The testator may *think* the words he uses express his intentions, but those who read these words after his death may be uncertain as to what he really meant; or, since their individual interests are involved, they may not agree among themselves on the interpretation; and the testator is not around to explain things.

It cannot be stressed too strongly, therefore, that wills should be drawn by lawyers or those with sufficient knowledge of the law for the intentions of the testator to be clearly expressed in appropriate language. Then, again, proper legal advice will enable the testator to frame his will so that it will take care of circumstances and effects of which he may not be aware, such as inheritance taxes. Generally the cost of having a lawyer draw up a will is very modest.

The following examples illustrate the importance of these points:

- A motor car used principally for pleasure was held to be included in a bequest of "household goods and effects."
- A bequest of "wearing apparel and personal effects" was held *not* to include money or securities for money.
- A bequest of "my old clothing" was held not to mean all clothing.
- A bequest of "contents of a house" was held to include a ring on the finger of the testatrix at her death, and a motor car in a garage adjoining the house.
- A bequest of "personal belongings" was held to include a motor car but not a government bond.

The courts, when called upon for direction in the interpretation of the terms of a will, try to determine the true intentions of the testator and, as far as possible, give effect to those intentions.

LEGAL CAPACITY TO MAKE A WILL

In order to make a valid will the testator must qualify as follows:

- He must have reached his majority, unless he is a member of the armed services on active service or a sailor at sea, in which case he may make a will disposing of personal property.
- He must be of sound and disposing mind; that is, he must understand what he is doing.
- He must be free from "undue influence" by another person.

C—2

Mrs. Lamphier, a woman 80 years of age, who during the period of 1903 to 1911 had drawn four wills which differed only slightly, made another will in 1912 which was radically different from all the others.

For instance, whereas former wills included her husband as a beneficiary, the 1912 will did not mention him at all in spite of the fact that she was on good terms with him. However, at the time this will was made her memory was so impaired that at times she forgot his existence. Again, while former wills provided for specific bequests (unequal in amount) to some of the children, the 1912 will provided for an equal distribution of the property among all the children, and also included the widow of a deceased son who had not been given anything in former wills.

These radical changes, coupled with the fact that the old lady's health had progressively deteriorated, were questioned by some of the heirs. For their part, the executors—one of whom was Murphy, a brother of the aforementioned widow of the deceased son,—took action to have the will established by the court as the true will.

The court found that the will had been made

(a) during the temporary absence of the testatrix from her husband;

(b) without reference to or communication with her natural protectors;

(c) whilst she was in the hands and under the care of two married daughters who were dissatisfied with a former will and had recently sought to have it changed;

(d) by an old lady verging on eighty years of age, suffering from a double process of deterioration from impairments of senility and the inroads of a progressive disease affecting her brain;

(e) with the aid of a solicitor who could not be regarded as an independent advisor and who had not been chosen by the testatrix;

(f) on the spur of the moment where the method of testamentary disposition (disposition according to the will) originating nine years before and carried through a series of wills down to the one made in 1911, was displaced and superseded by a method of distribution desired by the two married daughters in whose care the testratrix was when the disputed will was made.

Considering these findings, the court held that the evidence given by the plaintiffs (the executors) fell far short of satisfying the onus resting on them to show that Mrs. Lamphier understood the effect of the will or intended it to have such effect. The court therefore dismissed the action and ruled that the 1912 will was invalid.

(a) Why did some of the heirs question the 1912 will?

(b) What facts suggest very strongly that the will was made under undue influence?

EXECUTION OF A WILL

C—3

MISS JONES, WILL YOU PLEASE SIGN HERE, AS WITNESS TO MY WILL?
(SHE DOESN'T KNOW I HAVE LEFT HER $1000 BY THE WILL.)

What is your opinion of the validity of this will?

The execution of a will is the signing of it by the testator and the witnesses. If the formalities of execution as provided by statute are not strictly observed, the will may be declared null and void. The rules of execution are as follows:

1. The will must be signed by the testator personally or by someone whom he directs to sign for him and in his presence. A testator who cannot write makes *his mark* ("X") to his name, which is written by the other person.

2. The testator's signature must be made or acknowledged in the presence of two witnesses who must both be present at the same time; and both witnesses must attest and subscribe their names to the will after the testator's signature has been so made or acknowledged in their joint presence.

An exception to the above rules is that no witnesses are required to a will made by a soldier on active service or by a sailor at sea.

C—4

Mrs. B wrote out her will in longhand and signed it in the presence of her nurse, Mrs. V. Mrs. V then signed her name as a witness in the presence of Mrs. B. This took place in an upstairs room and immediately afterwards the two went downstairs to another room where they were joined by a Mrs. M. The testatrix, Mrs. B, told Mrs. M she had made her will and asked her to witness her signature, which she then acknowledged. Mrs. V similarly identified her own signature as a witness. Mrs. M then signed her name as a second witness.
When these facts were revealed in the course of proving the will in Surrogate Court, that court held that not only was it necessary for the testatrix to acknowledge her signature in the presence of the witnesses both present at the same time, but it was also necessary for both witnesses to sign their names as witnesses to the will *after* the testatrix had acknowledged her signature in their joint presence. This had not been done. Mrs. V had failed to subscribe her name as a witness to the will *after* the testatrix had acknowledged her signature in the joint presence of Mrs. M and Mrs. V, and this failure rendered the will invalid.

(a) What error of procedure made the execution of the will invalid?
(b) Why does the law require that the rules of procedure in executing a will be strictly observed?

An important point to remember is that by law a competent witness to a will, or the wife (or husband) of such witness, is not entitled to take any benefit under the will. The will is not thereby made invalid, but the gift is void and becomes a portion of the estate not covered in the will. In Alberta, Saskatchewan, New Brunswick, Nova Scotia and Newfoundland, if there are three witnesses, a gift to one only is not void.

An executor, however, may be a witness to a will and it does not affect his status as such. An executor may also benefit under a will if he is not also a witness thereto.

HOLOGRAPH WILLS

A holograph will is one written and signed by the testator in his own handwriting. In Newfoundland, Quebec, Manitoba, New Brunswick, Saskatchewan and Alberta, holograph wills are not required to be witnessed.

C—5

Mr. Webber, a resident of Saskatchewan, made a holograph will. After his death the administrator, when examining the will, noticed that the fraction "$\frac{1}{12}$" in a bequest of "$\frac{1}{12}$ of my net estate" had been changed to "$\frac{1}{6}$". The administrator and beneficiaries thereupon applied to the court for an interpretation of the will.

The question was not whether the alteration had been made by any means other than the testator's own handwriting, but whether the change had been made before or after the document was signed. A Saskatchewan court expressed the opinion that the legislature in providing for holograph wills did not intend the rules of execution prescribed in the Wills Act for the English type of will to apply to holograph wills; rather it was intended in the case of holograph wills that "the courts would try in every way to give effect to the expressed intentions of the testator. The court's sacred duty is to protect a man's last will and to give effect, if possible, to his intentions."

In this case the court ruled that the intention of the testator was clear: he wanted the beneficiary to get $\frac{1}{6}$ of the net estate. It was immaterial whether the alteration was made before or after the testator had affixed his signature as long as it was clear that the alteration had been made by the testator.

(a) What particular fact influenced the court in declaring that the change in the will would stand?
(b) What risk does the testator take if he makes a holograph will?

CHANGING A WILL

C—6

Eliza, a spinster, has had her will drawn by a lawyer and properly executed some years ago. She now wishes to make some changes in the bequests but does not want anyone else to know about it. She believes she may do this simply by privately crossing out certain portions and inserting others, and putting her initials in the margin near the changes.

Do you think she is correct in this assumption?

According to the Wills Act, an alteration made in the body of a will by inserting new words or crossing out words has no valid effect unless the change is signed or initialled by the testator and attested by witnesses in the margin near the alteration. Otherwise, the will is valid according to its terms as first executed. If certain words have been obliterated and are not ascertainable, it will be interpreted according to its terms without such words.

C—7

The executors of Alvina East applied to the court for a ruling as to whether certain alterations in her will were valid. The will was drawn on a printed form supplied by a stationery store. In drawing up the will the testatrix did not consult a lawyer, but was assisted by two clergymen who were also named executors. Some time later the testatrix privately changed certain specific bequests and signed her name in the margin opposite the alterations, but did not have this signature witnessed.

The court held that "the provisions of the Wills Act not having been observed (the signature in the margin had not been witnessed), the obliterations and alterations were of no effect, and the will must be read as if the pen had not been drawn through the words."

How does the court's decision here answer the question following C—6?

The proper way to change a will is by making a new will, at the same time destroying the previous will, or by executing a *codicil* to the current will.

A codicil is a supplement to a will, and by its terms adds something to or changes some part of the will to which it is attached. A codicil must be executed (signed and witnessed) in the same manner as prescribed for a will.

REVOCATION OF A WILL

A will may be revoked by:

1. A new will which revokes any previous will.

2. Tearing, burning, or otherwise destroying a will with the intention of revoking it. (Note that the intention to destroy must be evident. Mutilation of a will by accident, or by a person whose mind has become deranged, does not make the will invalid if the content of the will can still be sufficiently determined).

C—8

Eighty-year-old Mr. McGinn suffered a stroke which seriously impaired his ability to speak and his thinking processes. About a month later, at a time when he was emotionally disturbed, he tore his will into several pieces but immediately put the pieces back into an envelope. Upon his death, an application was made to the court to determine whether or not the will had been revoked by his act.

The court held, on the evidence submitted, that there was no intention on the part of the testator to revoke the will—and "the intention to revoke is all important." The application to prove the will was granted.

Why did the court ignore the tearing up of the will?

3. The subsequent marriage of the testator, unless the will declares that it was made in contemplation of such marriage.

DUTIES OF THE EXECUTOR

At the death of the testator, the property included in the will comes under the authority and control of the executor. It is then his duty to take the necessary steps to carry out the provisions of the will.

More than one executor may be named in a will. If an executor is unable to act, he may be released from his duties by formal declaration in writing. If an executor is deceased, or none of them is able to act, the court will appoint an administrator to carry out the necessary duties.

The executor's duties involve certain legal formalities, and it is usual for the executor to engage a lawyer to act for him.

The first matters to be attended to are (1) probating the will, and (2) paying *death duties* (where they apply).

Probating the will means the proving of the execution and authenticity of the will. If this can be done, the grant of *letters probate* will be made to the executor, and the whole estate vests in him for distribution according to the will.

No distribution of the estate may take place until the death duties have been assessed and paid. When the governmental departments concerned have been satisfied in this respect, they will forward *releases* which permit bank accounts, etc., to be released into the custody of the executor for distribution to the beneficiaries.

DISTRIBUTION OF ASSETS

The order of distribution of assets is as follows:

1. Funeral expenses. The undertaker's claim comes first.

2. Costs of administration. The executor is entitled to a fee as determined by the Surrogate Judge.

3. Debts of the testator. In order to inform creditors, it is customary to give public notice of the distribution of the estate by advertising three times in successive weeks in the local newspaper. The usual notice includes a clause to the effect that after a specified date the assets of the estate will be distributed having regard only to those claims which have been received.

4. Distribution of remaining assets to beneficiaries under the will. In case of estates where cash and personal belongings comprise the only assets, few, if any, legal difficulties may be encountered. In the case of an estate including such assets as real property, securities, and partnership equities, the legal work involved may be considerable.

SOME OTHER POINTS OF LAW CONCERNING WILLS

LOST WILL

If on the death of a person his will cannot be found, it is presumed to have been revoked unless evidence can be produced to the contrary. If a copy of the will can be produced, or other proof of the testator's intention can be furnished to the satisfaction of the court, the court may act upon such evidence as if it were a will.

C—9

Following the death of the deceased, no will could be found. However, a friend of the deceased claimed to be his beneficiary and produced a letter which stated that the deceased had made a will leaving everything to him (the friend). The lawyer who made the will was traced, but he had not kept a copy and could not remember its contents.

A Manitoba court ruled that the letter did not qualify as a "testamentary document" and, even though in the deceased's own handwriting, did not possess the essential requirements of a holograph will. The court ruled that "if a will was last traced to the possession of the testator and is not forthcoming at his death, it is presumed to have been destroyed by the testator." The deceased, therefore, was declared to have died intestate.

(a) Was the letter intended to be a will?
(b) Was there any proof that the letter contained all the terms of the lost will?
(c) What possibilities could arise if, in such circumstances, letters were allowed to serve as wills?

CONDITIONAL GIFTS

If a gift is made subject to some condition that must be fulfilled either before or after taking the gift, such condition must be observed unless it is an *invalid* condition. Generally, a condition to a bequest is valid if it could be a valid part of a contract.

A gift by the testator to his widow on condition of her not marrying again, and a gift to a daughter on condition that she not marry under a certain age have been held to be valid conditions.

DOMICILE

The place where a person is born is his *domicile of origin.* This remains his domicile regardless of the fact that he resides in another place or country, unless his intention is to remain permanently in such place or country; in which case it becomes his *domicile of choice.* A married woman acquires the domicile of her husband whether of origin or of choice.

A change of domicile of the testator does not affect a will in so far as his real property is concerned. In order to dispose of real property, the will must be executed according to the law of the place where the land is situated, and the land must be disposed of according to that same law. Thus a devise of land situated in a foreign country (for this purpose any other province in Canada is also a foreign country) may be invalid according to the law of that country although valid according to the law of the testator's domicile.

In the case of personal property, however, a will is valid if made and executed according to the law of the testator's place of domicile at the time the will was made, or of the place at which the will was made; and the personal estate of the testator is administered according to the law of the place where the testator was domiciled at the time of his death.

ADMINISTRATOR

If the testator does not name an executor in his will, an *administrator* must be appointed by the Surrogate Court to administer the affairs of the testator. The duties of an administrator are the same as those of an executor.

MORTGAGED PROPERTY LEFT BY WILL

A beneficiary receiving a devise of property on which a mortgage exists must assume the obligation of the mortgage if he takes the property. He has no legal right to require that the mortgage be paid out of the personal estate of the testator.

RELIEF FOR DEPENDENTS

In most of the provinces, legislation has been passed which intervenes when the testator has left his immediate dependents out of his will. Dependents include wife or husband or a child under sixteen years of age, or a child over sixteen unable through infirmity to earn a livelihood.

The law provides that, on application by the dependents declaring that the testator has by will so disposed of his property that adequate provision has not been made for the future maintenance of his dependents, a judge of the Surrogate or County Court may make an order charging the testator's estate with proper maintenance of dependents.

Before making the order, the judge will consider any matters which he deems should be fairly taken into account in deciding upon the application. The limit of allowance ordered shall not exceed the amount the applicants would have been entitled to if the testator had left no will.

INHERITANCE BY LAW

C—10

A, a comparatively wealthy man, dies without leaving a will. A is survived by his widowed mother, a brother and a sister, neither of whom is wealthy by any means; also by his wife, an adopted son 12 years of age, and a married daughter who has one child.

Who do you think would inherit A's estate?

A deceased person having left no will, or a will which is invalid, is said to have died *intestate*. His property then succeeds to those entitled to inherit according to law.

Real estate is inherited according to the law of the province or country in which the real property is located; personal property is inherited according to the law of the testator's place of domicile at the time of his death.

FORMALITIES

Before any disposition of the property of the intestate can be made, an administrator must be appointed. The usual procedure is for the next-of-kin to apply through a lawyer to the court for *letters of administration* to be given to one of themselves, thus keeping the administration fees "in the family." The alternative procedure is to ask the court to appoint some person to act as administrator. Certain trust companies specialize in this class of business.

The administrator's duties are the same as those of an executor. These have been outlined in the previous part to this unit.

DISTRIBUTION OF THE PROPERTY

Those entitled to inherit are wife or husband and relatives. Relatives are either *lineal descendants* or *collateral relatives*, each of the two classes being divided into different degrees of relationship.

Lineal descendants are recognized according to a descending scale: the intestate's children are in the *first* degree, grandchildren are in the *second* degree and so on. An adopted child shares equally with natural children of the intestate. Except in British Columbia and Ontario an adopted child is also entitled to inherit from his natural parents and kindred. Stepchildren, having no blood-relationship with the intestate, do not inherit by law, although they may inherit by will.

Collateral relatives are recognized according to an ascending scale: the intestate's parents are in the *first* degree; brothers, sisters and grandparents are in the *second* degree; nephews, nieces, uncles and aunts are in the *third* and so on.

The wife or husband of an intestate, although not in either of these classes, has a preferred position with regard to inheritance. You will note in the details of distribution which follow that practically every province provides that the widow (or widower) receive a certain sum "first." This is his or her *preferential* share of the estate. If the estate does not exceed the preferential share, the widow (or widower) receives the whole estate; when it does exceed the preferential share, the widow or widower receives a fractional share of the residue.

If there are no heirs or next-of-kin (relatives) living, the estate escheats to the Crown; that is, to the province in which the intestate is domiciled. In Alberta, the University of Alberta has been granted the right to such estates.

Each province has its own statute governing inheritance. In Quebec, the law of community of property between husband and wife prevails, and its rules of inheritance differ considerably from those of the other provinces. The law of Quebec is not quoted in this Part. In the other provinces the statutory rules of distribution are as follows:

- Where the intestate, being a man, leaves

no wife or child: In Ontario, father, mother, brothers and sisters share equally. If any brother or sister is deceased leaving child or children, such child or children take their parent's share, but representation does not go beyond this point unless the only other living heirs would be in the same degree of relationship.

In all the other provinces, except Quebec, the estate goes to the intestate's father and mother in equal shares. If one parent is deceased, the other takes all. If both parents are deceased, the estate goes to brothers and sisters equally. If a brother or sister is deceased, the child or children of such brother or sister, that is, nephews or nieces of the intestate, take their parent's share. However, children of a nephew or niece cannot represent their parent so as to take that parent's share if other nephews or nieces are living.

a widow, but no child: In British Columbia, Alberta, Saskatchewan and Manitoba, the whole estate goes to the widow.

In Ontario, the widow gets the first $20,000 and two-thirds of the remainder; the other one-third goes to the intestate's collateral relatives (see above). If there are no collateral relatives, that share escheats to the Crown.

In New Brunswick, if the estate is not more than $50,000, the widow gets all. When it exceeds $50,000, the widow gets $50,000 and the personal chattels first; one-half of the residue goes to the widow, while the remainder goes to the intestate's collateral relatives. If there are no collateral relatives, the widow takes all.

In Nova Scotia, the widow gets $25,000 first; the remainder is divided equally between the widow and the intestate's next-of-kin. If there are no next-of-kin, the widow takes all.

In Prince Edward Island, the widow gets $50,000 first and one-half of the remainder; the other half goes to the intestate's next-of-kin. If there are no next-of-kin, the widow takes all.

In Newfoundland, the widow get $30,000 first and one-half of the remainder, the other half going to the intestate's next-of-kin.

In all the provinces which retain the right of dower the widow must elect either to take her dower—in which case she has no further claim on the real property—or accept her statutory share in lieu of dower. (The Dower Act of Manitoba now provides that the rules concerning the widow's usual dower rights do not apply if her husband has left her an annual income of $9,000, or property and insurance of not less than $150,000, or has left her $75,000 plus an annual income of $4,000).

a widow and one child: In Ontario, British Columbia and Alberta, the widow gets $20,000 first; in Saskatchewan and Manitoba, $10,000 first; in Nova Scotia, $25,000 first. In each of these provinces the remainder is divided equally between the widow and the child.

In New Brunswick, the widow gets the personal chattels and one-half of the residue; the other half goes to the child.

In Prince Edward Island and Newfoundland, the estate is divided equally between the widow and the child.

a widow and children: In Ontario, British Columbia and Alberta, the widow is entitled to $20,000 first; in Saskatchewan and Manitoba, $10,000 first; in Nova Scotia, $25,000 first. The remainder in each case is divided by giving one-third to the widow, and two-thirds to the children in equal shares.

In New Brunswick, the widow gets the personal chattels and one-third of the residue; the remaining two-thirds go to the children in equal shares.

In Prince Edward Island and Newfoundland, the widow gets one-third of the estate, the other two-thirds going to the children in equal shares.

a child or children only: In all the provinces the children share equally in the estate, descendants of a deceased child taking their parent's share. An only child would inherit all the estate.

- Where the intestate, being a woman, leaves

no husband or child: In all the provinces the same rules apply as when a man dies leaving no wife or child.

a husband but no child: In Ontario, the husband is entitled to $20,000 first and half of the remainder; the balance goes to the deceased wife's collateral relatives.

In each of the other provinces, except Quebec, the husband inherits from his deceased wife leaving no child in the same manner and proportion as a widow would inherit from her deceased husband leaving no child.

a husband and child or children: In Ontario, the husband receives $20,000 first and one-third of the residue; the other two-thirds go to the child or children. In each of the other provinces, except Quebec, a husband and child (or children) inherit from a deceased wife in the same manner and proportion as a widow and child (or children) would inherit from her deceased husband.

In provinces where the husband's right "by the curtesy" prevails, the husband, in order to take his statutory share in that part of the estate which is real property, must abandon his right "by the curtesy." If he elects to take his right "by the curtesy," he must abandon his share of the real property as outlined above.

We should note here that if the heirs of the estate wish to divide the property differently from the statutory plan, the law will not interfere. It would be most important that any such change be made in the form of a written agreement signed by all parties concerned.

The foregoing outline of the law of intestate succession is fragmentary and extremely brief. More would be beyond the scope and purpose of this text. Enough has been written, it is hoped, to suggest the importance of consulting a lawyer and making a will whereby the testator may dispose of his property as he wishes—which, incidentally, may not be at all like the statutory plan of distribution.

THE SURVIVORSHIP ACTS

All the provinces have enacted legislation generally known as Survivorship Acts. The Acts, which are uniform, provide that "where two or more persons die at the same time or in circumstances rendering it uncertain which of them survived the other or others, such deaths shall, for all purposes affecting the title to property, be presumed to have occurred in the order of seniority, and, accordingly, the younger shall be deemed to have survived the older."

Also where the death of a testator and a beneficiary under his will, through accident or otherwise, occurs at the same time so that it does not appear which died first; and if the will makes disposition of the property in the event that the beneficiary predeceased the testator, then it shall be presumed that the beneficiary died first.

It should be noted also that the Insurance Act provides that unless a contract or a declaration declares otherwise, where the person whose life is insured and the beneficiary under the policy die at the same time or in circumstances rendering it uncertain which of them survived the other, the insurance money is payable as if the beneficiary had predeceased the person whose life is insured. This means that unless other beneficiaries are named in the insurance policy and survive the insured, the insurance money reverts to the insured's estate.

C—11

Mr. and Mrs. Cane, residents of Manitoba, died at the same time in a highway accident, the circumstances of which were such that it could not be determined who died first. The couple had no children and neither of them left a will. Mrs. Cane was younger than Mr. Cane.

Mr. Cane's next-of-kin was his mother; Mrs. Cane's next-of-kin was her mother. Mr. Cane had two life insurance policies, both of which named his wife as beneficiary. After their deaths, the administrators of the estates of Mr. and Mrs. Cane applied to the court for direction.

The court held that by virtue of the Insurance Act of Manitoba the insurance money was payable as if the beneficiary had predeceased the person whose life was insured; consequently, the insurance money reverted to Mr. Cane's estate. Since Mr. Cane died intestate, his estate would be divided according to the Manitoba Devolution of Estates Act. Moreover, by the terms of The Survivorship Act Mrs. Cane was deemed to have survived her husband since she was the younger. According to the Devolution of Estates Act of Manitoba a surviving wife (when there are no children) inherits the whole of her deceased husband's estate. Thus Mrs. Cane inherited the proceeds of the insurance policies plus any other property owned by her husband. Then, since Mrs. Cane also died intestate, her estate (according to the law of Manitoba) would go to her parents equally. However, since her father was deceased, her whole estate went to her mother.

(a) Can you think of a reason why, in the circumstances described in this case, insurance law provides that the insurance money reverts to the insured's estate?
(b) Is it likely Mr. Cane would have wanted all his estate to go to his mother-in-law while his own mother was living? How could he have avoided it?
(c) How would Mr. Cane's estate have been inherited if he had been a resident of your province?

APPLYING THE LAW

1. The deceased testator, K, was survived by a son and a married daughter, and had lived with this daughter for several years preceding his death. K's son was a wealthy business man but his daughter and her husband had only a modest income. K's will left all his estate to his daughter. When the will was probated it was seen that K's daughter and her husband had signed the will as witnesses. How does the law of your province apply to this case?

2. X died intestate leaving an estate appraised at $100,000. He was survived by his wife. The next closest relative was a nephew whom X had always considered a "no-good." Divide the estate according to the law of your province.

3.

What is the law in your province governing this situation?

DISCUSSION AND PROJECTS

1. Discuss the possible benefits arising from giving a preferential share of an *intestate* estate to the widow.
2. Make a chart to show the manner in which an intestate estate is divided according to the law of your province.
3. Check the legal notices in your newspaper. Is there one by the executors of a will?

UNIT FOURTEEN
INSURANCE

Part 31
LIFE, PROPERTY, AND CAR INSURANCE

THE INSURANCE POLICY

Insurance may be defined as a contract (known as the *policy*) whereby for a stipulated consideration (called the *premium*) one party (the insurer — usually an insurance company) agrees to pay another party (the insured) a certain sum or indemnity on the happening of some event (called the *risk*).

If the insurance is directed by the insured to be paid to some person other than himself, that person is known as a *beneficiary*.

LEGISLATION GOVERNING INSURANCE COMPANIES

Insurance legislation is largely under the control of the provinces, and any company incorporated in any one of the provinces may carry on business in the other provinces. With the exception of Quebec, the statute law of the provinces concerning insurance is almost uniform, with few variations.

In the interests of the public, the promotion and organization of insurance companies is strictly prescribed by law. All insurance companies except certain mutual companies are required to make a deposit with the provincial treasurer for the protection of policy holders.

Insurance companies must also build up adequate reserves to safeguard the payment of the amount of policies in case of loss, or in the case of life policies to pay the policy at maturity or on the death of the insured. The Act imposes strict regulations as to the kind of securities in which insurance companies may invest their funds, and requires that a bona fide audit of their books and records be made annually by qualified accountants.

KINDS OF INSURANCE

CASE 1

The career and also the financial security of a concert pianist might be jeopardized if some accident or disease were to cripple his hands.

Do you think he could obtain insurance against such a risk?

One can insure against almost any risk in which one has an *insurable interest*. For example, a person has an insurable interest in his own life or in the life of another person whose death might cause him some loss, in the risk of loss or damage to his own property, or in the risk of liability for injury or loss to other persons.

There are several classes of insurance, the three most widely known being life insurance, property insurance—commonly called fire insurance although risks other than fire are included—and automobile insurance. Among other kinds of insurance available are: marine insurance (insurance against loss of ships and cargo), crop insurance, plate glass insurance, robbery, burglary and theft insurance, personal accident and sickness insurance, and liability insurance covering a variety of risks. The famous "Lloyd's of London" will insure against almost any eventuality.

LIFE INSURANCE

Every insurance company may draw up its own contract of insurance; benefits and conditions differ accordingly. At the same time, the Insurance Act provides that certain conditions must apply to a life insurance policy, and usually these are incorporated into the policy and form part of the contract. Some of these conditions are given below as they concern misrepresentation in the application, insurable interest, lapsing of the policy, minors and beneficiaries.

MISREPRESENTATION IN THE APPLICATION

C—2

When applying for life insurance X does not disclose that he has had a serious operation for cancer. X feels quite well now and believes he is permanently cured.

Might this non-disclosure constitute material misrepresentation?

Sometimes the applicant for life insurance is required to have a medical examination, and sometimes not; but in either case he will be required to answer questions on the application form concerning his medical history. The Act provides that "an applicant for insurance and a person whose life is to be insured (one person may insure the life of another in whose life he has an insurable interest) shall each disclose to the insurer . . . every fact within his knowledge that is material to the insurance and is not so disclosed by the other." It is also provided that "a failure to disclose, or a misrepresentation of, such a fact renders the contract voidable by the insurer."

For example, in submitting a proof of loss in connection with a claim on a life insurance policy, it was admitted that the insured party was suffering from a heart ailment at the time he applied for the policy, but he had not disclosed this fact in his application. The non-disclosure was considered a material misrepresentation sufficient to disentitle the beneficiary from recovering on the policy.

In another case the applicant, in applying for a policy of life insurance, stated that she was in good health when, in fact, she was aware at the time that she was suffering from tuberculosis. This misrepresentation and concealment was revealed when the applicant died within six months of the issue of the policy. Consequently the insurance company refused to pay the policy.

The Act provides, however, that statements made in the application (except errors in regard to age) are, in the absence of fraud, incontestable after two years from the date of the policy. Misrepresentation of age would mean an adjustment to the premium cost, and possibly to the amount of insurance payable.

Usually, a life insurance policy contains a condition to the effect that the policy is void if the insured commits suicide within a certain period (generally two years) of the date of the policy.

INSURABLE INTEREST

C — 3

Do you think this type of policy would be legal?

Life insurance can be obtained only on persons in whose life the applicant has an *insurable interest*. The Act states that every person has an insurable interest in

(a) his own life;

(b) the life of his child or grandchild;

(c) the life of his wife (the wife also has an insurable interest in the life of her husband);

(d) the life of another upon whom he is wholly or in part dependent for support or for education;

(e) the life of any person in whom he has a pecuniary interest.

For example, the members of a partnership may insure the lives of each other in order to be able to pay off the share of a deceased partner. By this means the surviving partners may avoid being compelled to liquidate the assets of the partnership for that purpose. Also, a person who makes a loan may insure the life of the borrower for the amount of the loan. In these cases the insurable interest must exist at the time of the application for the insurance, but if the insured dies before the debt has been repaid, the full amount of the policy may be payable even though only part of the debt remains unpaid.

LAPSING OF THE POLICY

C—4

A's life insurance premium is due on March 1. A forgets to pay it until March 15.

Would the delay cause the policy to lapse?

The policy may lapse if premiums are not paid when due. Thirty days of grace are allowed for the paying of premiums on life insurance policies—but only on life policies. However, where a policy has lapsed, the insured, upon application within two years from the date of the lapse, may have the contract reinstated, provided that the cash value rights or other rights have not been exercised and that no change has taken place in the insurability status of the insured.

A MINOR'S CAPACITY TO DEAL WITH INSURANCE

C—5

John is 17 years of age and is steadily employed. He wants to take out a life insurance policy, but a friend has told him that, since he is a minor, only his father can obtain life insurance on him.

Is this friend correct?

A minor, after attaining the age of sixteen years, has the legal capacity of a person of full age to effect a contract of insurance on his own life or, if married, to effect a contract of insurance on the life of his wife and children.

BENEFICIARIES

C—6

Benny, an unmarried man, names his mother as the beneficiary of his life insurance policy.

If Benny marries, may he change this and make his wife the beneficiary?

A beneficiary is the party named in the policy to receive the insurance money. In naming a beneficiary the insured should consider the possibility that at some future time he may wish to change the beneficiary—for instance, he may wish to borrow money using his life insurance policy as collateral security. To do this it is necessary to assign the proceeds of the policy to the lender until the loan is repaid. In 1962, changes were made in the Insurance Acts of the provinces which have given the insured greater freedom in this respect. For policies issued since these changes came in effect, unless the insured designates a person as his beneficiary *irrevocably*, he is free at any time by declaration to alter or revoke the designation. Before the change, if the beneficiary was a wife, husband, child, grandchild, father or mother of the insured (classed as *preferred beneficiaries*), such designation could not be changed to any party outside this class without the beneficiary's consent. This older law still applies for policies issued prior to the change.

Before paying out the proceeds of a life insurance policy, the insurer will require *proof of loss* (proof of the death of the insured). However, the Act provides that if the party insured has not been heard of for seven years, he may be *presumed* dead, and the beneficiary is entitled to apply to a court for a declaration as to *presumption of death*, and for an order for the payment of the insurance.

If the insured had the policy payable to himself as beneficiary, it is made payable to his estate and becomes part of his estate at his death. Thus the proceeds of the policy would be disposed of by a will, or according to law if he dies intestate.

A further important point regarding beneficiaries is that when the insured and the beneficiary both die at the same time in such circumstances that it is not known which died first (for instance in an automobile accident or other disaster), it is presumed that the beneficiary died first. The insurance then reverts to the insured's estate.

FIRE (PROPERTY) INSURANCE

Although fire is possibly the greatest risk against which property is insured (hence the name generally used), such policies usually insure also against loss or damage to the property from several other causes—water, windstorm, explosion, lightning, burglary and some other specified risks.

Toronto Telegram

A contract of fire insurance is *indemnity* insurance; that is, the insured is entitled to be reimbursed for not more than the amount of the loss, no matter how large the amount of the policy. On the other hand, in no case will the insurer pay more than the amount of the policy, no matter how great the loss.

A fire insurance policy is primarily a contract between the insurer and the insured. At the same time, the Insurance Act provides that certain conditions are deemed to be part of every fire insurance contract, and must be printed on the policy under the heading "Statutory Conditions." In this text space does not permit more than a brief reference to a few of these conditions as prescribed by the Act.

MISREPRESENTATION IN THE APPLICATION

C—7

Mr. Speiling applying for fire insurance misrepresented the value of the property and said he owned it when, in fact, it was owned by his sister. In defence of a claim, the insurance company contended that the policy would not have been issued if the facts had been truly stated. The court held that the insurance contract was voidable because of the misrepresentation.

(a) Why would this misrepresentation be considered sufficient to avoid the policy?
(b) What other type of misrepresentation could be made on an application for fire insurance?

A statutory condition states:

If any person applying for insurance falsely describes the property . . . or misrepresents or fraudulently omits to communicate any circumstance which is material to be made known to the insurer in order to enable it to judge of the risk to be undertaken, the contract shall be void as to any property in relation to which the misrepresentation or omission is material.

From the insurer's point of view, it is very important to know any particulars about the property or its use which might affect the hazards and risks against which the property is insured. Certain uses of the property increase the hazard of fire or explosion, and the premium cost or even the insurability of the property may be materially affected thereby.

MATERIAL CHANGE

C—8

(a) Would a fire insurance policy on a dwelling permit keeping gasoline in a basement?
(b) In what circumstances might keeping gasoline in the basement constitute a material change in the risk?

Again quoting from the statutory conditions:

Any change material to the risk and within the control and knowledge of the insured shall avoid the contract as to the part affected thereby unless the change is promptly notified in writing to the insurer or its local agent; and the insurer when so notified may return the unearned portion, if any, of the premium paid and cancel the contract, or may notify the insured in writing that, if he desires the contract to continue in force, he must, within fifteen days of the receipt of notice, pay to the insurer an additional premium; and in default of such payment the contract shall no longer be in force and the insurer shall return the unearned portion, if any, of the premium paid.

C—9

By the terms of a fire insurance policy, the furniture insured was covered only while the premises were "occupied as a private dwelling." When a fire occurred causing loss to the furniture, the insured, Kozlik, presented a claim to the insurer. It was then discovered that at the time the insurance was taken out Kozlik was using the premises not only as a dwelling but also for the illegal sale of liquor, a fact which Kozlik had not disclosed to the insurer at the time he applied for insurance. Furthermore, at the time of the fire, the premises were being leased to another person who (with the knowledge of Kozlik) was also running an illegal liquor business on the premises—a change material to the risk which had not been reported to the insurer.

As a result, the insurance company successfully defended the claim on the grounds that there was fraudulent non-disclosure at the time the insurance was applied for, and also subsequent failure to report a change material to the risk.

(a) What was the change material to the risk?
(b) If when applying for the insurance Kozlik had disclosed the true facts, would he have been able to obtain insurance on the property?

PROPERTY OF OTHERS

According to the statutory conditions, "unless otherwise specifically stated in the contract, the insurer is not liable for loss or damage to property owned by any person other than the insured, unless the interest of the insured therein is stated in the contract." The ordinary insurance policy provides that household and personal effects of the insured's spouse, the relatives of either, and any other person under the age of 21 in the care of the insured—and then only while on the premises—are covered by the insured's policy. Property of persons other than those mentioned is not covered unless specifically provided in the policy.

LIMITATION OF ACTION

According to the Act, "every action or proceeding against the insurer for the recovery of any claim . . . shall be absolutely barred unless commenced within one year next after the loss or damage occurs."

EXTENT OF COVERAGE AND EXCLUSIONS

Apart from the statutory conditions applying to a policy, the insurance contract sets forth the extent of the coverage. At the same time, certain losses are excluded from that coverage. Note the following examples of exclusions which appear in a standard composite dwelling insurance policy:

Smoke: "There is no liability under this Section for loss or damage directly or indirectly caused by smoke from a fireplace." (Smoke damage due to sudden, unusual, and faulty operation of any apparatus vented to a chimney is covered.)

Rupture of a water system or public watermain: "There is no liability under this Section for loss or damage directly or indirectly caused by rupture of or escape of water from a sewer or drain, nor by rupture or escape of water from a sump, septic tank, eavestrough or downspout."

Vandalism: "There is no liability under this Section for loss or damage occurring while a building is vacant . . ."; or "to glass constituting part of a building"; or "to property insured directly or indirectly caused by theft or attempt thereat."

Windstorm or hail: "There is no liability under this Section for loss or damage to an outdoor radio or television antenna . . ."

We have mentioned only a few exclusions out of the many that appear in the insurance contract. Of course, if the insured wishes, he may by paying an additional premium be covered for many of the losses that are otherwise excluded.

SUBROGATION

The Insurance Act provides that "the insurer, upon making a payment or assuming liability therefor under a contract of fire insurance is *subrogated* to all rights of recovery of the insured against any person and may bring action in the name of the insured to enforce such rights." To illustrate, let us suppose that A, who carries ample fire insurance, suffers a fire loss because of B's negligence, and that A has a cause of action against B in tort for causing the fire. Since A is insured, his insurance company will indemnify him for the fire loss, but at the same time the company acquires A's right of action against B and may take such action to recover from B the amount paid to A because of B's tort.

AUTOMOBILE INSURANCE

This part is confined to automobile insurance as it applies to owners of automobiles of the private passenger or station wagon type.

C — 10

When operating his car, A runs many risks; for instance:

(i) He may be the cause of an accident in which people are injured or killed. He may be injured himself as well.
(ii) He may cause a collision with another car which, although no one is hurt, results in damage to that car and also his own.
(iii) His car may be damaged by fire, or it may be stolen.
(iv) The windshield of his car may be broken by a flying stone.
(v) A tire could blow out after hitting an obstruction in the road.

How many of these risks do you think are covered by the standard automobile insurance policy?

THE INSURANCE CONTRACT

Private passenger automobile insurance ordinarily covers three different types of risk:

- Loss or damage to the insured automobile;
- Accident benefits—medical expenses, death, dismemberment and total disability suffered by the insured; and
- Third party liability—legal liability for bodily injury or death, or damage to the property of others.

Third party liability insurance may be obtained without purchasing the other two types, these being optional. Because of the additional premium cost, some people carry only third party liability insurance.

Like fire insurance, automobile insurance is indemnity insurance, the insurer paying only the actual loss suffered, subject to the amount of coverage and certain statutory conditions. The insurance contract sets forth the risks covered (and those excluded) and the benefits available, much of which is specifically prescribed by the Insurance Act.

Again, as with fire insurance, certain statutory conditions prescribed by the Act are deemed to be part of every policy and must appear therein under the heading of "Statutory Conditions." A brief reference to some of these conditions follows, in particular to those which, if they are not observed by the insured, will cause forfeiture of his right to indemnity.

MATERIAL CHANGE IN RISK

C — 11

A carries insurance on his car. Before the insurance has expired, he sells the car to B.

Does A's insurance cover B as owner of the car?

The insured must promptly notify the insurer in writing of any change in the risk material to the contract and within his knowledge which takes place after the policy has been issued. "Change in the risk material to the contract" includes any change in the insurable interest of the insured; for example, the sale of the automobile to another person; the giving of a chattel mortgage on the car in consideration of a loan; the placing of a lien or other encumbrance on the car by a creditor; and the taking out of any other insurance on the automobile covering loss or damage which is already covered by an automobile insurance policy.

In the event of the death of an owner insured under an unexpired automobile insurance policy, the coverage of the policy is extended temporarily to the spouse of the deceased if residing in the same premises as at the time of his death, or to any other person having proper custody of the automobile until the estate has been probated.

Failure to notify the insurer of a material change in the risk may entitle the insurer to avoid the policy.

PROHIBITED USES

The insured shall not drive or operate the automobile, nor shall he permit another person to do so

- while under the influence of intoxicating liquor or drugs to such an extent as to be for the time being incapable of the proper control of the automobile; or
- while he is not qualified or authorized by law to drive; or
- for any illicit or prohibited trade or transportation; or
- in any race or speed test.

If the insured is involved in an accident while violating any of the above prohibited uses, he may forfeit his right to indemnity for loss or damage.

REQUIREMENTS WHERE LOSS OR DAMAGE OCCURS

The insured must give prompt written notice to the insurer of any accident in which he is involved, with all available particulars. This condition is important even in the case of accidents where damage or injury appears at the time to be negligible. Not infrequently injuries or damages which were not noticeable at the time of the accident appear later, and the insured may jeopardize his coverage under his policy if he fails to notify the insurer about the accident promptly.

LIMITATION OF ACTION

Any action against an insurer with respect to loss or damage to an automobile or loss or injury to persons must be commenced within one year after the cause of action arose.

MISREPRESENTATION IN THE APPLICATION FOR AUTOMOBILE INSURANCE

There are several factors which affect the possibility of obtaining insurance on an automobile and the premium rate to be charged. These include the age of the applicant and of any other person who is allowed to drive the car; the use to which the car is put (pleasure driving, driving to work, average annual mileage, etc.); and the insured's accident record.

In connection with the above, the applicant for automobile insurance should be aware that the Insurance Act provides that the following warning must appear on the face of every automobile insurance policy:

> *Where (a) an applicant for a contract gives false particulars of the described automobile to be insured to the prejudice of the insurer, or knowingly misrepresents or fails to disclose in the application any fact required to be stated therein; or (b) the insured contravenes a term of the contract or commits a fraud; or (c) the insured wilfully makes a false statement in respect of a claim under the contract, a claim by the insured is invalid and the right of the insured to receive indemnity is forfeited.*

EXCLUDED USES OF THE AUTOMOBILE

The Insurance Act provides that unless coverage is expressly given by an endorsement of the policy (for an additional premium), the insurer is not liable when the automobile is

- rented or leased to another;
- used to carry explosives or radioactive material; or
- used as a taxicab or for carrying passengers for compensation or hire.

The following uses, however, are not considered as carrying passengers for hire, and are thus not excluded from coverage under the policy:

- The ordinary car-pool arrangement where two or more persons take turns in driving each other to work.
- The occasional carrying or transportation of a person who shares the cost of a trip.
- The carriage of a temporary or permanent domestic servant; for example, taking the baby-sitter home.
- The carriage of customers or clients or prospective customers or clients.

LOSS OR DAMAGE TO THE INSURED AUTOMOBILE

Under this Section of the policy, the insurer agrees to indemnify the insured against loss or damage to his own automobile.

The standard classification for coverage coming under this heading is as follows:

1. All Perils—covering loss or damage to the automobile from all causes.
2. Collision or Upset—caused by collision with another object or by upset.
3. Comprehensive—covering loss from any peril other than by collision with another object or by upset.
4. Specified Perils—including fire, lightning, theft and a number of other separately specified risks from which an automobile could suffer damage.

The reason for the separation of these risks is that "All Perils" (total coverage) is rather expensive. Consequently, some owners carry only collision insurance, or only comprehensive, or only certain specified perils, or perhaps a combination of collision and specified perils. Such owners are thus assuming personally those risks for which the automobile is not insured.

The insured should be aware that certain losses are excluded from the above coverages: for example, the insurer is not liable under this Section for loss or damage to car radios, or contents of trailers, or to rugs or robes, or to tapes and equipment used with a tape recorder. If the car owner wishes to be covered for these exclusions he may take out special insurance for that purpose.

Incidentally, if the insured intends to use his automobile for towing a trailer, he should check with his insurance company to see if special coverage is required for liability incurred when the car is being used for that purpose.

Usually special insurance is required to cover liability incurred when towing a house-trailer.

Another point to be remembered is that the insured forfeits any right to recover from the insurer for loss or damage to his own automobile from any peril under this Section if the loss occurs while the insured is guilty of violating certain statutory conditions of the policy. For example, if A, although carrying "all perils" insurance, damages his car by collision or otherwise when engaged in a race or speed test or in any other "prohibited use," he forfeits his right to be indemnified for his loss.

ACCIDENT BENEFITS

This Section of the policy provides certain specified benefits for the insured and his passengers if he is injured in an automobile accident. Benefits include compensation for medical expenses, loss of wages, etc. There are exceptions to this coverage; for instance, the insurer is not liable for those portions of such expenses which are payable or recoverable under any medical, surgical, dental or hospitalization plan or law or under any other insurance contract. Again, it should be noted that the insured forfeits his right to accident benefits if the accident occurs while he is in violation of one or other of the statutory conditions of the policy.

Accident benefits now include indemnity (under certain circumstances) for injuries or loss suffered by the insured as a result of an accident caused by an uninsured motorist (see under the next heading).

UNINSURED MOTORIST COVERAGE

In each of the provinces of Canada, if a person suffers injury or loss resulting from an accident caused by the driver or owner of an uninsured or unidentified automobile, such a person has recourse to a victims' indemnity fund (or unsatisfied judgment fund) for compensation up to the minimum prescribed by the province for third party liability in an automobile insurance policy. See Victims' Indemnity Funds, page 52. Similar plans are in effect in some of the states of the United States of America.

Prior to a recent amendment to The Insurance Act, no such recourse was available to the victim of an accident caused by an uninsured motorist if the accident took place in a jurisdiction where no such indemnity fund was in effect. This gap has now been filled (at least for such victims as carry automobile insurance themselves) by the standard automobile policy which, by law, now provides that when the insured is entitled to recover damages from an uninsured motorist (except in Canada or any jurisdiction of the United States where recovery from an unsatisfied judgment fund is in effect), the insurer will compensate the insured or, if he is fatally injured, any other person legally entitled to recover damages thereby, up to the prescribed minimum of third party liability insurance applicable to the jurisdiction in which the accident occurred—provided that this limit is not greater than the limit for the jurisdiction in which the insurance policy was issued.

For example, let us suppose that A, a motorist from Ontario who carries automobile insurance, is motoring in a part of the United States where no unsatisfied judgment fund is in effect, and that he is injured in an accident caused by an uninsured motorist. A's own insurance policy will now cover the

loss he suffers up to $50,000 (the Ontario minimum). A's insurance company is then subrogated to A's rights against the party who caused the accident, and is entitled to recover from him the amount paid to A. This right may be of little value if the uninsured motorist is incapable of making payment.

THIRD PARTY COVERAGE

C — 12

Mack, while driving his automobile, causes an accident which results in serious injury to the driver and occupants of the other car, and damage to both cars. The occupants of Mack's car (his wife, his daughter, and a friend) are also injured, while Mack suffers only a few bruises. Mack's car insurance is for the minimum amount of third party liability under the standard policy. Under his policy Mack is also covered for collision.

(a) What is the minimum third party liability under car insurance in your province?
(b) If the combined claims of the occupants of the other car amount to more than the minimum third party liability under the insurance policy, who is responsible for the difference?
(c) Would claims by Mack's wife and daughter and the friend be covered by the standard car insurance policy?
(d) Would Mack's insurance cover the damage to his own car?

This is the primary risk under an automobile insurance policy. Under the terms of this Section of the policy the insurer agrees to indemnify the insured (and every other person who with his consent personally drives the insured automobile) against the liability imposed by law upon the insured (or upon any such other person) for loss or damage arising from the ownership, use or operation of the automobile, and resulting from bodily injury or death of any person, or damage to another's property. Incidentally, the insured's policy covers him (and his wife) for this risk when he (or she) is operating another person's automobile with that person's consent and in accordance with conditions set forth in the policy.

Again there are some exclusions from coverage: for example, the insurer is not liable for loss or damage resulting from bodily injury to or the death of the son, daughter or spouse of the insured while an occupant of the automobile; neither is the insurer liable for injury to or the death of gratuitous passengers carried on or in the insured automobile unless the accident from which the injuries or death resulted was caused by the gross negligence of the driver of the automobile. (In British Columbia, by a recent amendment to the law, proof of ordinary negligence will now be sufficient to render the insurer liable).

The minimum amount of third party liability insurance is prescribed by provincial law. In most of the provinces (at the time of this writing) the minimum is $35,000; in Ontario and British Columbia, it is $50,000. Since the liability incurred in an accident may exceed the provincial minimum—particularly if several people are injured in a single accident—many automobile owners carry third party liability insurance for substantially larger amounts, often $200,000 or more.

Earlier in this part it was pointed out that the insured forfeited his right to accident benefits or to be indemnified for damage to his automobile if the

loss was due to the insured's violation of a statutory condition of the contract. This rule is considerably modified in the case of third party liability. To illustrate, let us suppose that A carries third party liability insurance of $100,000, and that he causes an accident for which he is held liable for a total of $75,000 damages. If, in causing the accident, A has not contravened any conditions of his policy, his insurance will take care of his total liability. However, if A caused the accident while under the influence of intoxicating liquor or drugs to the extent that he was incapable of the proper control of the automobile (a violation of a statutory condition), the law requires that the insurance company must pay the insured's liability for the accident up to, but *only* up to, the minimum coverage prescribed by law (in Ontario, $50,000). At the same time, the insurer may set up A's violation of the conditions of the contract as a defence against paying any excess over that prescribed minimum. Furthermore, the insurance company is entitled to recover from A the amount paid out on his behalf when, in fact, A had forfeited his right to any indemnification. It should also be remembered that A is also liable for that part of the damages which the insurance company did not pay.

GENERAL PERSONAL LIABILITY INSURANCE

C—13

> The postman who delivers mail to A's house slips on icy steps leading to the mail box, and severely injures himself. The postman suffers a loss of earnings as well as medical costs. He sues A for $3,500 damages.

Could A insure himself against such claims?

It is not only by reason of automobile accidents that a person may incur liability for loss or injury suffered by another. For instance, a business man runs the risk of customers being accidentally injured on his premises, either as a result of his own negligence or that of his employee. Similarly, a home-owner could incur liability for injuries to a person entering on his property; or a hunter could be liable for a hunting accident.

Personal liability insurance covering a variety of risks is available and should be carried both for the protection of the insured who, in the event of a claim that he is unable to meet, could be faced wih a lifetime debt; and for the benefit of the injured party who otherwise might never collect damages if the party to blame is financially unable to meet the obligation.

APPLYING THE LAW

1. A has his house insured under the standard dwelling policy. In order to supplement his income, A decides to set up a repair shop for lawn mowers in his basement. However, A does not notify his insurance agent of this move. If fire loss occurs because of a gasoline explosion in the repair shop, what is A's legal position with regard to recovering the fire loss? See C—9, page 361.
2. Suppose that B, who carries automobile insurance himself, is the victim of an accident caused by an uninsured motorist. To what

source may B look for compensation (a) if the accident takes place in a jurisdiction where an automobile accident indemnity fund has been established? (b) if the accident takes place in a jurisdiction where no such fund is in operation?

3. While A was visiting at a friend's house, an expensive car tape recorder was stolen from A's car which was parked unlocked outside the house. A carries fire and theft car insurance. Will he recover the loss from his insurance company? Explain.
4. Driving his car while intoxicated, D lost control of it and collided with another car, causing damage to that car and bodily injury to its driver. D's car was damaged but he escaped personal injury. D carries ample insurance both for third party liability and for collision:
   (a) What is D's legal position with regard to recovering from his insurance the cost of the damage to his own car?
   (b) Can the victim of the accident expect to be compensated by D's insurance company? Explain.

DISCUSSION AND PROJECTS

1. Obtain a copy of a standard form of Composite Dwelling Insurance Policy and examine the coverage offered by the "Comprehensive Personal Liability" section of the policy.
2. Consult an automobile insurance agency to find out which of the States of the U.S.A. do not have a motor vehicle accident fund or unsatisfied judgment fund in operation, and what happens if a Canadian driver has an accident outside Canada.
3. Obtain a copy of an automobile insurance policy and find to what extent the insured party is covered by his policy with respect to liability to third parties when
   (a) he is towing a trailer with his car;
   (b) he has just turned in his insured automobile for a "newly acquired car";
   (c) he is using a substitute automobile (for example, a "loaner" while his car is being repaired);
   (d) he is driving a friend's automobile (for example, when he is accompanying a friend on a motor trip and is assisting with the driving);
   (e) his son or daughter is driving his car.

UNIT FIFTEEN
GOING INTO BUSINESS

Part 32
SINGLE PROPRIETORSHIP AND PARTNERSHIP

SINGLE PROPRIETORSHIP

This is the type of business owned and operated by one person, as distinct from a partnership which is owned and operated by two or more persons, or a corporation which is owned by a number of shareholders ranging from a few to many thousands.

NAMING A SINGLE PROPRIETORSHIP

CASE 1

> G. R. West opens up a repair shop business as the sole owner. He puts up a sign over the store, "G. R. WEST." By a coincidence, in the same town another proprietor named G. R. West has been using an identical sign.

Would there be any legal difficulties involved in the use of the same name?

A person carrying on business as sole owner may designate his business under his own name. However, if he desires to use some other name to distinguish his business, and/or to add the words "and Company" to it, he must register that name in the local registry office, giving the required particulars as to the ownership and the nature of the business. Registration serves as a source of information to the public; for instance, to a person who has an interest in knowing who owns the business, what its nature is, and how long it has been operating.

If the name chosen conflicts with one already registered, he may not be allowed to use it (unless it is his own name) if the person whose right to that particular name is infringed takes legal action to prevent the infringement.

Subject to the above requirements and the by-laws of his municipality as to business license, and related matters, a single proprietor may carry on any legitimate business, and his rights and liabilities are matters of contract with the people with whom he deals.

THE PROPRIETOR'S PERSONAL LIABILITY

Ordinarily, a person in business for himself will keep business liabilities and business assets separate from his personal affairs; that is, the business will "stand on its own feet"—pay its own bills, etc. However, if the business gets into

financial difficulties, the creditors may claim against the proprietor's personal financial resources and any property he owns. When faced with such a situation, the proprietor cannot avoid liability simply by "putting his property in his wife's name," or by transferring it to some other person. According to law, such a transfer would be null and void since its purpose would be to defraud his creditors.

C—2

Two years prior to going into bankruptcy, Mr. K. had transferred his house to his wife. In view of the circumstances surrounding the transfer, the trustee in charge of the bankruptcy proceedings declared the transfer void, and ruled that the property should be available to meet the claims of creditors. Mr. K. appealed this ruling.

The court found that (1) at the time the transfer was made, the debtor was not meeting his obligations as they became due, and was unable to pay all his debts without the aid of the property transferred to his wife; (2) the transfer was made for one dollar and "natural love and affection"; (3) the wife knew at the time that her husband was not meeting his obligations and that his creditors were pressing for payment. From this evidence it was concluded that in transferring the house to his wife, "the debtor had the guilty intent to place the property beyond the reach of his creditors for the benefit of his wife or for their joint benefit." Since it was apparent that the wife also knew of this purpose, the court held that a transfer of the property in these circumstances was void when the transferor became bankrupt, and that the property was to be available to the trustee for settling the accounts of the bankrupt debtor.

(a) If K had not become bankrupt, would the transfer of the house to his wife have been void?
(b) What facts suggest that the transfer was made to avoid having the house seized by the creditors?
(c) If the transfer had been made ten years before the bankruptcy, would it have been declared void?

PARTNERSHIPS

CODIFICATION OF PARTNERSHIP LAW

Prior to about the middle of the nineteenth century and the emergence of the limited company as the principal method of organizing the larger business ventures, the *partnership* was the usual form of organization. The single proprietorship, of course, predominated in the field of small businesses, but the amount of capital required by the larger enterprises, and the diversity of talent sometimes necessary, could be provided only by the pooling of the resources of two or more persons.

Up to the end of the nineteenth century, the source of the law of partnership was the voluminous body of case law which had accumulated over many years. By this time the principles of common law and equity relating to partnerships had become so well established that in 1890 the English Parliament enacted a codification of the law, The Partnership Act. This Act was subsequently adopted in substantially the same form by all the common law provinces of Canada. In Quebec, the law of partnership is part of the Civil Code.

CREATING A PARTNERSHIP

C—3

Arthur and Henry inherit the family farm as joint owners. Arthur lives on the farm and operates it, while Henry works in the city. The agreement between the brothers is that Arthur will bear the cost of maintaining and operating the farm, and that Henry will share only in that part of the net income which exceeds an agreed upon amount.

(a) Does this arrangement constitute a partnership?
(b) If Arthur and Henry work the farm together, sharing costs and income, would the legal relationship be different?

When two or more persons combine to carry on a business with a view to sharing resulting profits, the legal relationship of these persons is that of a partnership. It may be created by an express or an implied agreement between the parties concerned. The agreement may be oral or in writing or even by conduct.

A partnership may be *general* or *limited*.

GENERAL PARTNERSHIP

When two or more persons are engaged in an undertaking without any express partnership agreement, the following facts are considered evidence of a *general partnership*:

1. They are carrying on a business in common.
2. Each of them participates in the management of the business.
3. They share—not necessarily equally—in the profits of the business. (While the taking of a share of the profits of the business may not of itself make the person taking it a partner, if he disputes the partnership relationship, that act will impose on him the onus of proving that he was not a partner. Generally, the sharing of the gross receipts of a business does not create a partnership; for example, if a farm owned by one person is worked by another, the mere fact that the owner's "rental" consists of a share of the gross proceeds of the crop does not create a partnership).
4. Each party is prepared to bear part of any loss incurred by the business. Generally, the sharing of losses as well as of profits is sufficient evidence that a partnership relationship exists.

The Partnership Act of each province declares that certain circumstances do *not* in themselves create a partnership unless there is further proof that the parties intended to be partners. Included in these circumstances are the following:

1. Joint or common ownership of property, whether or not the tenants or owners share the profits or gross returns from its use.
2. An agreement to pay a debt by instalments or otherwise out of profits.
3. Sharing of profits by a servant or agent as remuneration for services rendered.

4. Receipt by a widow or child of a deceased partner of an annual payment out of the profits of the business.

5. Receipt of interest by the lender of money to the firm at a rate varying according to profits.

THE PARTNERSHIP AGREEMENT

C—4

Bill and Dick begin a trucking business as partners. Bill provides the truck while both participate in the driving and other work involved. When profits are to be divided a dispute arises. Bill insists the understanding was that he was to get a greater share than Dick because he provided the truck. Dick denies there was any such agreement.

How might this dispute have been avoided?

As far as outside parties (the parties with whom the partnership does business) are concerned, the partnership agreement is of little concern, at least insofar as it concerns the rights of the partners between themselves. But as between the partners themselves, the partnership agreement is very important. The agreement should be in writing and should contain specific provisions concerning:

- The name of the firm.
- The investment each partner is to make.
- How profits and losses are to be divided.
- The particular duties and authority of each partner.
- The beginning and ending of the term of the partnership.
- The settlement to be made on the retirement or death of a partner.
- The procedure to be followed in the event of disagreement or dissolution.
- Generally, any particular matter which might be anticipated from the nature of the partnership.

The importance of having the above terms specifically agreed upon is emphasized by the fact that where they have not been expressed certain statutory rules apply. In all the common law provinces, *unless the agreement provides otherwise*, the following rules govern:

1. The partners are entitled to share equally in the profits and capital of the business and must contribute equally towards losses, whether of capital or otherwise. This rule applies *even though the original investments of the partners were not equal.*

2. The firm must indemnify every partner in respect of payments made and personal liabilities incurred by him in (a) the ordinary and proper conduct of the business of the firm, or (b) about anything necessarily done in the preservation of the business or property.

3. Every general partner may take part in the management of the business.

4. A partner is not legally entitled to receive a salary (in the ordinary sense of the word) for acting as a partner. The remuneration which a partner receives from the partnership business is charged against his share of the profits.

5. No person may be introduced as a new partner without the consent of all the existing partners.

6. A majority of the partners may decide any differences arising out of the ordinary business of the partnership, but no change can be made in the nature or membership of the business without the consent of all existing partners.

7. Where no fixed term for the duration of the partnership has been agreed upon, any partner may terminate the partnership by giving notice of his intention to do so to the other partners.

8. If a partner, without the consent of the other partners, carries on any business of the same nature as, and competing with, that of the firm, he must account for and pay over to the firm all profits made by him in that business.

WHO MAY BE A PARTNER

C—5

Elaine's mother operates a small beauty shop. When Elaine reaches 17 years of age, her mother takes her into the business as a partner.

How does the fact that Elaine is a minor affect her legal rights and responsibilities?

Persons legally capable of making binding agreements may enter into a contract of partnership.

A minor may be a partner, but he cannot be held liable for the debts of a partnership unless he commits fraud in his capacity as a partner. If, however, he accepts benefits in the form of a share of the profits, he cannot avoid his liabilities. He may repudiate his partnership contract any time before he attains his majority or within a reasonable time thereafter. If he does not so repudiate, he will be bound as a partner and be liable for debts incurred by the firm.

A married woman may be a partner; she may also be a business partner with her husband. At the same time, the marriage relationship does not of itself create a partnership coming under the Partnership Act even though a wife may work with her husband in the operation of his business. There must be evidence that a business partnership was intended and, in fact, existed.

C—6

After a rift in her marriage and separation from her husband, Mrs. K. sued him demanding the dissolution of an alleged partnership with him and the sale and division of the proceeds of the family property. The husband and wife had conducted farming operations for more than thirty years, during which time the wife had contributed her work and time in the operation of the farm.
From the evidence given, the court found that Mrs. K. had not made any financial contribution to the purchase price of any of the property acquired; that the title to the property acquired was solely in her husband's name; that there was no express partnership agreement between the husband and wife; and no evidence whatever that it was ever intended that the wife was to have any interest in the property. The court held that "a wife does not acquire any interest in property unless she makes a financial contribution or there is an agreement with her husband that she should acquire such an interest; i.e., where there is a partnership between the husband and wife." The court therefore dismissed the action.

(a) Why did the court conclude Mr. and Mrs. K. did not operate the farming operation as a partnership?
(b) If there had been a partnership agreement between K and his wife, would the fact that she had made no financial contribution to the business affect the validity of the agreement?
(c) What would have been a definite proof of a partnership relationship?

REGISTRATION OF A GENERAL PARTNERSHIP

Registration consists of filing in the registry office a declaration signed by all the partners containing:

1. Names in full and addresses of all partners. If any partner is under twenty-one years of age, the date of his birth must be given.

2. The firm name. (The name under which a partnership may register may consist of the names of its members or of any other distinctive name as long as it does not conflict with a name already registered).

3. A declaration that the partners named are the only partners.

4. The date when the partnership was formed.

The purpose of registering a declaration of partnership is to provide a source of information to those persons such as creditors who have an interest in knowing the names and addresses of the partners and any other information pertinent to the rights of outside parties who have dealings with the partnership.

Most of the provinces require that partnerships formed for the purpose of carrying on trading, manufacturing and mining businesses must be properly registered within a prescribed time, otherwise a penalty (a fine) will be incurred. Nova Scotia exempts fishing and farming partnerships from registration requirements. Manitoba and Prince Edward Island do not restrict registration to the above three classifications of trading, manufacturing and mining; their Acts include "every trade, occupation or profession" (except where a profession is regulated by a governing body of that profession under statutory authority).

The Partnership Acts of Ontario and Nova Scotia further provide that if a partnership is not registered as required by the Act, neither the partnership firm nor any member thereof may maintain any court action in respect of a contract made in connection with the partnership business. However, this does not mean that outside parties cannot maintain an action against the partnership; it simply means that the partnership cannot bring legal action against outside parties with regard to contracts made with such outside parties if the partnership declaration has not been filed. As an example, in Ontario and Nova Scotia a partnership for the manufacture of furniture for sale is required to be registered. However, a partnership formed to carry on an auditing business (a professional enterprise) is not subject to this requirement. It should be remembered that the provincial Acts are not uniform in this respect. (See the note on Manitoba and Prince Edward Island, above).

Once the partnership agreement has been filed, no person who signed the declaration ceases to be a partner (even if he withdraws from the firm) until a new declaration, either of a change in the partnership or of its dissolution, has been filed.

POWERS, RIGHTS AND LIABILITIES OF A GENERAL PARTNER

LIABILITY TO THIRD PARTIES

C—7

THE DEAL IS IMPOSSIBLE.
IT WOULD RUIN THE FIRM.
BUT YOUR PARTNER HAS SIGNED THE CONTRACT!

Should the partner shown above be able to refuse to take any responsibility for the deal?

With respect to third parties, a partner is in the position of an agent and has power to bind his firm on any contract which comes within the apparent scope of his authority. Of course, if the third party were aware that the partner did not have the authority he assumed, the contract would not be binding.

This liability extends to wrongful acts done in the name of and for the benefit of the firm. For example, if one of the partners of a firm, acting within the scope of his authority, receives from a client money which should be held in trust for that client or another person, and then without the other partners' knowledge uses that money in the partnership business, the partnership firm is liable to the client for the misapplication of the funds.

The liability of the partners is *joint*—not joint and several. Thus if any partner is sued separately, and the creditor's claim is not fully satisfied, he loses his right to sue the other partner or partners; therefore, in any action against a partnership, it would appear wise to sue all partners together.

LIABILITY OF A RETIRING PARTNER

C—8

Baxter, a partner in the firm of Phee, Hirsett, Mure & Associates, is only 42 years old when he suffers a heart attack. After some weeks' rest he is able to go in to work on three days a week, but after a year even this proves too fatiguing, and Baxter's doctor recommends that he retire from work completely. Baxter resigns his partnership exactly 18½ years after first joining the firm.

(a) Could the retiring partner be held liable for future debts of the firm?
(b) What should he do to protect himself?

A partner who has retired does not thereby cease to be liable for partnership debts incurred *while he was a partner* unless there is an agreement to that effect between himself, the other members of his firm and also the creditors.

A partner who has withdrawn from the business may still be held liable by third parties on liabilities incurred by the firm *after his retirement* unless such third parties have been informed of his retirement. However, if the retired partner participates in the payment of such liabilities, he is entitled to be indemnified by the other partners who, after all, knew of his retirement.

To avoid subsequent liability, a retiring partner should have the change in membership advertised in the official publication of the province, known as the Gazette. This is sufficient notice to persons who had no dealings with the firm before his retirement. In the case of old customers, notice should be sent by letter. A notice in a newspaper is not effective when it cannot be proved that the persons concerned have seen it.

The Partnership Acts of all the provinces (except Newfoundland) require that a declaration shall be filed whenever any change is made in the membership of the firm (this includes the change when a member retires from the partnership) or in the name of the firm. Failure to file the declaration of change incurs the same penalties as provided for failure to register the original declaration of partnership. In Newfoundland it is sufficient to publish a notice in the Newfoundland Gazette and one other newspaper published in the province, as to persons who had no dealings with the firm prior to the change in membership.

C—9

Mr. Whynot and his son had carried on a business dealing in meat which they peddled to the public, the father by horse and cart, the son by motor truck. They were well known by the public as being in the business together, although there was no formal partnership agreement between them. About five years before this case, the father orally gave the business over to his son, at the same time offering to peddle meat if the son wanted him to do so. There was no notice to the public of this arrangement, and father and son continued in the business of buying and selling meat on the same premises. Eventually, Mr. Whynot's son became indebted to Mr. Fancy, who finally sued both father and son as partners to recover the debt.

The father denied liability on the grounds that he had given the business to his son and was not a partner. The court, however, held that the father, by not giving notice to Mr. Fancy (who had had dealings with the father prior to his retirement) had continued to hold himself out as a partner, and was, therefore, liable as a partner whether he actually intended to be or not; and according to the Partnership Act (of Nova Scotia) "Everyone who by words, spoken or written, or by conduct, represents himself, or who knowingly suffers himself to be represented, as a partner in a particular firm, is liable as a partner to any one who has on the faith of any such representation given credit to the firm. . . ."

(a) What evidence was there that father and son had operated as partners?
(b) On what facts did the court base its decision that the father was liable in this case?

C—10

P had entered into partnership with M under the firm name of Anahim Lake Store. P invested $4,500, but soon after decided to withdraw from the partnership. An agreement was drawn up between P and M whereby M would pay P $5,000 in instalments over a period of time. The promise was secured by a chattel mortgage on the stock-in-trade, furnishings and equipment of the store.

The first partnership agreement had been duly registered, but the agreement covering the withdrawal of P. was not. Subsequently, M went bankrupt, and P claimed as a creditor.

The trustee in bankruptcy disallowed P's claim on the grounds that in the absence of a registration of the agreement dissolving the partnership, P must be considered a partner and, as such, liable along with M to the other creditors. The trustee based his ruling on sections of the Partnership Act of British Columbia as follows: *Section 70.* "A similar declaration shall in like manner be filed when and so often as any change or alteration takes place in the membership of the firm . . ." and *Section 72.* "Until a new declaration is made and filed by him or his partners, . . . no such signer (of the declaration of partnership) shall be deemed to have ceased to be a partner; . . . ."

(a) What was the oversight which involved P in such an adverse situation?

(b) What hope is there of P enforcing payment of the unpaid instalments?

LIABILITY OF A PARTNER PERSONALLY

(c) Does the decision in the McGinnis case, above, mean that P was required to pay the partnership debts from his own private resources?

If the firm is sued by a third party and the partnership assets are not sufficient to satisfy the claim, the creditor has a claim against the *private estate* of any and all general partners. The rule is that a partner's personal assets are first applied to that partner's personal debts, and any surplus thereafter becomes available for the partnership debts along with that of the other partners according to the ratio in which their agreement states that losses must be borne.

If it so happens that one of the partners has no personal assets, the other partners must nevertheless bear his share of the loss in satisfying the claims of creditors. The paying partners may assert their claim against the defaulting partner for the amount they have paid on his behalf—if they think there is any possibility of recovering from him.

LIABILITY OF A DECEASED PARTNER'S ESTATE

(d) Again referring to the McGinnis case (C—10), if P had died just before M went bankrupt, would any liability rest on P's personal and private estate?

The estate of a deceased partner is liable for debts of the firm contracted up to the time of his death, subject to the prior claims of creditors against the deceased's personal estate. Any value remaining in the estate after the personal creditors have been satisfied, is then available to creditors of the firm of which the deceased was a partner. The estate is not liable for partnership debts contracted after the date of death.

A NEW INCOMING PARTNER

A new partner is not liable for debts incurred by the partnership before he became a partner unless he has assumed such liability by signing an agreement to that effect.

Since the admission of a new partner creates a change in the partnership, a new declaration of such change must be filed in the same office in which the original declaration of partnership was filed.

DISSOLUTION OF A GENERAL PARTNERSHIP

All the Partnership Acts provide a number of implied terms which concern the dissolution of a partnership. Generally, a partnership is terminated or *dissolved* in any of the following ways:

1. By expiration of the term of the partnership or the completion of the work for which it was formed.
2. Where there is no fixed term, by notice of a partner of his intention to retire from the partnership.
3. By the death of a partner.
4. By a partner being declared insolvent.
5. By a partner permitting his share of the partnership to be charged for his private debt.
6. By order of the court on application of one or more of the partners in the following cases:

    (a) Permanent incapacity of one of the partners due to insanity or other disability.
    (b) Misconduct of one of the partners which would prejudicially affect the carrying on of the business.
    (c) When the business can be carried on only at a loss. (This is for the protection of the creditors).
    (d) Whenever the court considers it just and equitable to decree a dissolution.

On the dissolution of a partnership or the retirement of a partner, a declaration of dissolution should be filed in the registry office, and public notice should be given in the official Gazette of the province. Old customers should be advised of the dissolution by private letter.

Settling Accounts after Dissolution. The Partnership Acts provide that, subject to any agreement otherwise, the following rules shall be observed in the settling of accounts and the distribution of assets of a dissolved partnership:

1. Losses must be paid first out of accumulated profits, next out of capital and lastly, if necessary, by the partners personally in the proportion in which they were entitled to share profits and losses.

2. The assets of the firm, including any sums contributed by the partners to make up losses or deficiencies of capital, are to be applied in the following manner and order:

(a) In paying the debts of the firm to those who are *not* partners therein.

(b) In paying to each partner what is due to him according to the amount of capital to his credit after his share of loss or deficiency has been charged to his capital account. For example, suppose A, B and C decide to dissolve their partnership, their capital investments being $9,000, $6,000 and $3,000 respectively. Suppose also that they share profits and losses equally. If in selling out the business the partners take a loss of $9,000, their capital accounts would appear as follows:

A—(*Capital Account*)	*Dr*	*Cr*
Investment in the business		$9,000
One-third of loss on dissolution	$3,000	
Cash received to balance	6,000	
	$9,000	$9,000

B—(*Capital Account*)	*Dr*	*Cr*
Investment in the business		$6,000
One-third of loss on dissolution	$3,000	
Cash received to balance	3,000	
	$6,000	$6,000

C—(*Capital Account*)	*Dr*	*Cr*
Investment in the business		$3,000
One-third of loss on dissolution	$3,000	
Cash received to balance	nil	
	$3,000	$3,000

(c) If the partnership is not bankrupt and the dissolution results in a profit, this profit shall be divided among the partners in the same way in which regular profits have been divided.

(d) The balance, if any, shall be divided among the partners in the proportion in which profits were divisible.

In the event that on dissolution a partner is financially unable to pay his share of the liabilities of the firm, the other partners must pay it for him. The amount which they pay on his behalf is considered as a personal debt rather than a business loss. This interpretation follows the decision in the English case of *Garner v. Murray* (1903) when the courts ruled that on the dissolution of a partnership, if one of the partners is insolvent and his financial interest in the partnership is not sufficient to pay his share of the firm's liabilities, the other partners must pay it for him—not in the proportion in which they share profits or losses, but in the ratio of their capital investment in the business as at the date of dissolution. Presumably, this rule is based on the assumption that the party having the greatest amount of capital to his credit is best able to bear the highest proportion of the defaulting partner's liability.

The paying partners, of course, are entitled to recover from the defaulting partner, if and when he is able to pay. For example, suppose that in the case of the partnership of A, B, and C (above) the loss and deficiency on dissolution was $12,000 instead of $9,000. After dissolution the accounts would appear as follows:

A—*(Capital Account)*	*Dr*	*Cr*
Investment in the business		$9,000
One-third of the loss on dissolution	$4,000	
*5/7 of $1,000 (C's default)	714	
Cash received to balance	4,286	
	$9,000	$9,000

B—*(Capital Account)*	*Dr*	*Cr*
Investment in the business		$6,000
One-third of the loss on dissolution	$4,000	
*2/7 of $1,000 (C's default)	286	
Cash received to balance	1,714	
	$6,000	$6,000

C—*(Capital Account)*	*Dr*	*Cr*
Investment in the business		$3,000
One-third of the loss on dissolution	$4,000	
Amount of default (borne by A and B)		1,000
	$4,000	$4,000

* After business losses have been charged to the capital accounts, A's capital is $5,000 and B's, $2,000, a total of $7,000. Therefore A bears 5/7 of C's default while B bears 2/7. (The amounts have been calculated to the nearest dollar).

Rights of a Retired Partner on Dissolution. Every partnership agreement should provide for the situation where one of the partners dies or retires and the surviving partners wish to continue the partnership business. Provision may be made for the buying out of the deceased or retiring partner's share on such terms as will still allow the business to continue to operate. The various Acts provide that where any partner dies or otherwise ceases to be a partner, and the surviving partners carry on the business pending a final settlement of accounts between the firm and the out-going partner or his estate, then, in the absence of any agreement to the contrary, the deceased partner's estate is entitled either to an equitable share of the profits made since dissolution, or to interest on the amount of his share of the partnership assets. Eventually, if the retired partner or the beneficiaries of a deceased partner insist on payment of that partner's share, the business may have to be sold in order to raise the necessary cash.

LIMITED PARTNERSHIPS

NATURE OF A LIMITED PARTNERSHIP

A partner who contributes only cash to the partnership but who takes no part in the management is known as a *limited* partner. It is obvious that a partnership cannot be wholly composed of limited partners; there must be one or more *general* partners who have the power of managing the business.

All the provinces except Prince Edward Island have enacted legislation for the creation of limited partnerships. In Quebec the civil code contains the necessary provisions for this form of organization.

LIABILITY OF A LIMITED PARTNER

The chief characteristic of a limited partnership is that the limited partner is exempt from any liability with respect to the debts of the firm beyond the amount he invests in the business.

In order to retain this exemption, it is essential that he comply with the following provisions of The Limited Partnership Act:

1. There must be one or more general partners whose liability is unlimited.

2. He may invest only cash in the business.

3. His name must not appear in the firm name. If it appears on the firm's stationery, he must be designated thereon as a limited partner.

4. He must take no part in the management of the business. However, he may be an employee and he is entitled to examine the firm's books.

5. He must not withdraw any part of the amount he contributed during the continuance of the partnership. He is, however, entitled to draw his share of the profits.

6. The partnership must be registered by filing a declaration signed by each and all partners before a notary public which states:

   (a) The name and general nature of the business.
   (b) The names and addresses of all the partners, indicating which are limited partners.
   (c) The investments of the limited partners.
   (d) The date and term of the partnership.
   (e) The principal place of business of the partnership.

It is important to note that if any of the above provisions is not strictly observed, a limited partner becomes liable as a general partner.

Any change in the membership, nature of the business, the investment of the limited partners, or in any other matter specified in the original registration certificate requires the filing of a new certificate. Failure to do this makes the limited partners liable as general partners.

APPLYING THE LAW

1. A, B and C were partners in a business operating two branches. C, the manager of one branch, borrowed money and gave the lender a promissory note signed in the firm's name. The money was used in the branch of the business managed by C. When the note came due C's branch could not pay it and A and B refused to be bound by C's act, claiming it was unauthorized. On the basis of the facts as given, how does the law apply?
2. D and E were partners in a business. D died and the partnership was dissolved and the business sold, unfortunately at a considerable loss. Explain how the law applies to the liability of D's estate: (a) to his personal creditors; (b) to the partnership creditors.

DISCUSSION AND PROJECTS

1. Discuss the implication of the statement "A partnership is a risky ship to sail in."
2. Smith carries on a small upholstery business in his home. His wife spends most of her time assisting him in the work; in fact, Smith depends on her to do certain operations because she can do them better than he can. Does this of itself create a partnership? Discuss.
3. (a) Survey your local area and determine the number of single proprietorships and partnerships that exist.
   (b) Based on your survey can you draw any conclusions as to the types of business in your area that use these forms of business organization?
   (c) Interview a sole proprietor and a partner. Have each one tell you why he chose the form of organization he did and what he sees as its advantages and disadvantages.

Part 33
LIMITED COMPANIES

NATURE OF A LIMITED COMPANY

A limited company (or corporation) is an *artificial person* created by law. A group of individuals may apply to the appropriate department of government asking for the creation of such a corporate being, but the limited company is and remains separate and distinct from those who petitioned its formation, direct its affairs, or own its stock.

The word "limited" signifies that the liability of the owners of the company, the shareholders, is limited to the amount they paid for their shares. Thus, if the company becomes insolvent, the shareholders may lose to the extent of the value of the stock which they hold, but the loss stops there.

Limited liability of shareholders is a comparatively modern development. The liability of the shareholders of the earlier companies was similar to that of partners; that is, they were personally liable for the debts of the company if it failed and could not pay its debts. One of the best known examples of this was the "South Sea Bubble," a speculative scheme by which a company known as the South Sea Company was chartered in 1719 to carry on whale fishing and the slave trade to the West Indies. A great number of investors and speculators were ruined by its failure. An example of a company which succeeded is the Hudson's Bay Company, whose history is bound up with that of Canada. This company was founded in 1670 and continues to this day, the last remaining of the great trading companies of an earlier era.

It was not until 1862 that the British Companies' Act granted the full privilege of limited liability to joint-stock companies; and not until 1879 that the same privilege was granted to banks—too late to save the shareholders of the City of Glasgow Bank which failed in 1878. Those shareholders "were called upon to pay (to the creditors) no less than 27½ times the par (face) value of their stock in the bank."*

*Cudmore, *History of the World's Commerce*; page 167; (Pitman).

Charles the Second by the grace

Hudson's Bay Company

The Royal Charter granted in 1670 by King Charles II to "the Governor and Company of Adventurers of England tradeing into Hudson's Bay."

Reproduced here is the first of the document's five sheets of parchment measuring about 31 by 25 inches.

The status of a corporation as an "artificial person" or legal entity means that its managing officials are agents through whom the corporation may make contracts in its own name and, if necessary, sue on these contracts in its own name. By the same token, a corporation may be held liable for contracts made by these agents, and also for torts committed by them within the scope of their apparent authority.

Practically all matters concerning the organization and operation of limited companies—except their actual trading or manufacturing activities—are closely prescribed by statute. Company law (also called corporation law) exists on both federal and provincial levels. Limited companies operating on a nationwide scale are usually incorporated under the Canada Corporations Act. Companies operating within the confines of any one province are usually incorporated under the law of that province. Notwithstanding the common purpose and general outline of the law, there are variations from province to province.

Involved as it is with the technicalities of business and finance, the field of corporation law is both broad and intricate. In this text we shall not attempt to do more than give a very brief outline of some of its features.

CLASSES OF COMPANIES

Public companies are those which offer their shares to the general public, placing neither limitation on the number of shareholders nor restriction upon the transfer of shares. This structure makes the public company particularly useful for the promotion of large enterprises.

Provision for the incorporation of *private* companies is made in the Canada Corporations Act and also in most of the provincial Companies' (or Corporations) Acts. (Ontario has abolished the distinction between public and private companies. However, the sale of stock to the public is controlled by provincial securities laws (The Ontario Securities Act), while stock distributed privately to the members of a company does not come under the same control).

Private companies do not offer their shares to the general public. The ownership of these shares must be kept within the membership (the shareholders) of the private company. The number of members is restricted to a specified number, generally fifty. (In British Columbia, when a private company has 15 members or more, it is deemed to be a public company).

The transfer of shares of a private company is also restricted. As a rule, such shares may not be transferred without the consent of the board of directors.

The private company form of organization is often used for the operation of "family" businesses (where the business is owned and operated by the members of a family). It is also a suitable alternative to the partnership form of organization, changing the unlimited personal liability of the individual partners of a partnership to the limited liability of the shareholders of a corporation.

One of the drawbacks to incorporation as a company by a small group of persons is the cost involved, which includes incorporation fees and legal expenses. Another is that management control of a corporation is more restricted and not as flexible as that of a partnership. For example, the powers of the board of directors of a corporation are closely prescribed by law, whereas each of the members of a partnership is entitled to share in the management of the partnership business, subject only to the terms of his own partnership agreement.

Non-trading companies (sometimes called *non-profit* companies) are those whose object and purpose is of a social, religious, sporting or other similar nature, and as distinct from trading companies, *not* for the purpose of pecuniary gain. Any profits realized by such an organization are used for the improvement and benefit of the organization itself.

The members of a non-profit company acquire *memberships* instead of shares of stock. At the same time, the members have limited liability; that is, they will not be held personally liable for debts of the company beyond the amounts they have invested therein. On the other hand, neither do they receive dividends.

PROCEDURE IN FORMING A LIMITED COMPANY

In Canada, two systems of incorporation are used. Manitoba, Quebec, New Brunswick and Prince Edward Island and the federal government incorporate a company by *Letters Patent,* a document which is issued under the authority of the government. This system is an inheritance from the original method of incorporation whereby the king personally granted a royal charter to bring a company into existence. British Columbia, Ontario, Alberta, Saskatchewan, Nova Scotia and Newfoundland have adopted the *registration* system, whereby the applicant registers a document called a *Memorandum of Association* (in Ontario, *Articles of Incorporation*). Although there are some differences between the two systems, these are not considered significant for the purpose of this text.

The procedure of incorporation is similar for both systems. In either case it will be necessary to employ a lawyer to prepare the necessary documents and to complete the required legal formalities involved in organizing a company. Briefly, the procedure of incorporation is as follows:

1. Filing the application with the proper government official. Public companies are also required to file a prospectus.
2. Issue of the Letters Patent or Certificate of Registration by the said official.
3. Internal organization of the company.

The Application. The prescribed documents and forms required for application must be obtained from the Provincial Secretary. These forms require certain information to be given, including the names of the present shareholders, the number of shares to be authorized, the purpose of the business and the name of the company.

The name selected must not be the same as that used by another company, neither may it resemble another name so closely that it may be confused with it. The use of words suggesting royal patronage, such as "King's," "Queen's," "Royal" or "Imperial" may not be used without the consent in writing of the appropriate authority. All limited companies (except non-trading companies) must use the word, "Limited," as the last word in the company name.

All the applicants named in the "petition" must have subscribed for shares in the company, and a prescribed number of them shall be named as *provisional directors* who are to act until the shareholders elect their regular board at their first meeting. Some of the provinces, require only three applicants for incorporation; other provinces require five. (In Ontario, an Ontario corporation need have only one shareholder).

The Prospectus. If the company is to offer its shares to the general public, it must file a *prospectus* along with its application. The prospectus is the company's advertisement to attract investment in the company.

The various acts concerning companies specify in detail what shall be set forth in the prospectus, and a penalty is provided for any material misrepresentation of facts.

The Letters Patent. If all legal requirements have been fulfilled to the satisfaction of the Provincial Secretary, *Letters Patent* will be issued to the company. The letters patent, also called the *charter,* is a formal document certifying that the company has been duly incorporated under the name and according to the facts set forth in the application.

As already noted, in some of the provinces the application and *Memorandum of Association* (or *Articles of Incorporation*) are registered with the proper authority and a certificate of registration is granted instead of letters patent. It may also be noted here that banks and railways may be incorporated only by special act of the Federal parliament.

Internal Organization. The letters patent having been received, the provisional directors meet to prepare by-laws for the regulating of company affairs. These are to be presented for confirmation by the shareholders at their first meeting which will be called as soon as conveniently may be after incorporation. At their first meeting the shareholders also elect a board of directors who now take over from the provisional directors.

THE BOARD OF DIRECTORS

The duties and liabilities of the members of the board of directors are prescribed by law.

Duties. The directors are charged with the management of the affairs of the company. Their first duty is to elect from among themselves those who will hold office for the current year as president, vice-president, secretary and treasurer, according to the by-laws of the company.

Authority is given to directors to transact all necessary business of the company in connection with the following:

- The allotment of stock and the making of calls thereon.
- The issue of stock and the transfer of shares.
- The declaration and payment of dividends.
- The general conduct of the affairs of the company.

If it is necessary for the directors to pass new by-laws, these shall have effect only until the next annual meeting of the shareholders, at which time the shareholders may confirm them or reject them. The Act requires that by-laws on certain matters must have the approval of at least two-thirds of the votes cast at the annual meeting.

A director's first duty is to the company, and he must not make use of his position for his own private advantage. If he has an interest in any contract made by the company, he will be obliged to account for or pay to the company whatever personal profit he makes on the contract. This is a common problem since some people are members of the boards of directors of several companies. A director, however, will not have to be accountable to the company for such profits if he first discloses his interest in the contract to his fellow directors and abstains from voting on the contract at the meeting of the board at which the contract is considered.

Liabilities. In order to protect the interests of creditors of the company, certain liabilities are imposed upon the directors, including the following:

1. It is within the powers of directors to declare dividends out of profits, but if they declare any dividend which impairs the capital fund, they

shall be jointly and severally liable to the company and to the creditors of the company for all debts of the company then existing or thereafter contracted. This requirement does not apply to mining companies, for which the Act makes special provisions.

2. Directors are jointly and severally liable to the creditors of the company if they consent to the transfer of shares not fully paid to a person who is insolvent.

3. The directors are liable if they make a loan to a shareholder except as provided in the Act.

4. If the company becomes insolvent, the directors are liable for unpaid wages due to employees for a specified period, generally six months.

5. If the directors allot bonus shares or sell shares at a discount contrary to statutory requirements, they become liable for any loss suffered thereby by the company.

6. Should the directors fail to make annual returns to government agencies as required by law, they are liable to a penalty.

C — 11

Although no profits were available, the directors of a company which was engaged in the theatre business declared a dividend of 2% on the paid-up capital. The dividend amounted to $1,500 and was paid on May 1. On February 27 of the following year the company was declared insolvent. It was found that the company had, in fact, been insolvent when the dividend was paid, and that the payment reduced the company's capital. The directors were held liable to make good to the creditors of the company the dividend illegally declared and paid, together with interest thereon.

Considering that usually the directors of a company are large shareholders, do you see a good reason for this rule?

SHAREHOLDERS

It has already been pointed out that the shareholders of a limited company, in contrast to the individual partners of a partnership, do not participate directly in the management of the company. However, at the *annual meeting* the shareholders may exert certain statutory rights.

Annual Meetings of the Shareholders. The law provides that every corporation shall hold an annual meeting within a specified time and at regular intervals.

Each shareholder entitled to vote must be notified according to statutory regulation as to the time and place of the annual meeting and must be sent a copy of the annual financial report of the company which is to be considered at the meeting. A shareholder has one vote for each *voting share* that he holds (some classes of shares do not carry voting rights). If his shares are not fully paid for, he is not entitled to vote.

If a shareholder does not attend the meeting personally, he may vote by *proxy*. A proxy is an authorization in writing given to another person to vote in the place of the absentee. Proxy forms are usually sent to shareholders along with the notice of the annual meeting.

The business ordinarily transacted at an annual meeting includes the following:

- The president's report.
- The report of the auditors.
- The confirmation (or rejection) of by-laws passed by the directors since the last meeting. (This right represents a substantial degree of control over the powers of the directors and their policies).
- The election of the directors for the ensuing year. (Again, the right to elect or reject a person seeking the office of director is to some degree a safeguard for the shareholders).
- The appointment of the auditors. (We should note that choice of auditor rests with the shareholders—not with the directors).

In the case of private companies with their limited number of shareholders (sometimes closely linked by family connections), it is obvious that the shareholders by exerting their rights at the annual meeting could wield a strong influence over the activities of the company. It is equally obvious, that in the case of large corporations whose shares are bought and sold on the open market, and whose shareholders, possibly in the thousands, are scattered far and wide, only those shareholders who own substantial blocks of shares will go to the trouble and expense of attending the annual meeting. Thus, in practice, it is the *majority* shareholders who exert the real influence at the annual meetings. However, if the *minority* shareholders can show that the controlling group have been guilty of fraud or discriminatory action against the minority, they may appeal to the court for redress.

Liability of a Shareholder for Unpaid Shares. When a person who has applied for newly issued shares receives notice that his application has been accepted and the shares have been allotted to him, he becomes liable on the contract and may be sued for any balance owing. If the company becomes insolvent while any balance remains unpaid, the subscriber is liable to creditors of the company for such unpaid balance. (Partly paid shares can no longer be issued by an Ontario corporation).

When payments on shares are not made when due, the subscriber may be compelled to forfeit his shares and any payments made thereon. The company may then dispose of the forfeited shares in any way they wish. The subscriber, however, remains liable for the deficiency if the shares are sold at a loss.

Transfer of Shares. A shareholder may sell or otherwise transfer shares to another person. This transaction may be carried out directly between the two parties or it may be done through a licensed stockbroker.

If the transferee wishes to be registered in the company's books as a shareholder and to receive dividends on the stock he holds, it will be necessary for him to return the stock certificates to the company and request that new certificates be issued in his name.

NUMBER 0013475

SHARES 20

CANADIAN PRODUCTS COMPANY LIMITED

Incorporated under the ——— Companies Act
Authorized capital $2,000,000
Divided into 50,000 Common Shares par value $25 and 15,000 Preference Shares par value $50

This Certifies that ----- Xavier Q. Zedorus ----- is the owner of ---------- Twenty Common ---------- Shares of the Capital Stock of CANADIAN PRODUCTS COMPANY LIMITED transferable only on the books of the Corporation by the holder hereof in person or by Attorney upon surrender of this Certificate properly endorsed.

IN WITNESS WHEREOF, the said Corporation has caused this Certificate to be signed by its duly authorized officers and its Corporate Seal to be hereunto affixed this fifth day of April A.D. 19--

Secretary

President

SHARES $25.00 EACH

CORPORATE SECURITIES

A *share* is simply one of the equal fractional parts into which the capital of a corporation is divided. The size of the fraction depends on the total number of shares issued. Thus, one share in a corporation which has issued a million shares represents a one-millionth interest in the capital of the company. The document representing ownership of a share is called a *share certificate.*

Shares may be issued having a certain value shown on them known as *par value*, or without any stated value, in which case they are known as shares *without par value.*

The Act provides that, except in the case of mining companies, shares having a stated par value may not be issued at a discount. Shares without par value may be sold at any price decided upon by the board of directors.

All corporations issue *common shares;* some also issue *preferred shares.* As a means of borrowing money, a corporation may also issue *bonds* or *debentures.*

Common Shares. The common stockholders share pro rata in the net profits of the business after the stipulated dividend, if any, on preferred shares has been paid.

Preferred Shares. Shares may be issued giving the holder certain preferred rights as compared with the rights of common shareholders. The preferences are such as the directors—subject to the provisions of the Act—may by by-law declare. Those usually given are:

- The right to a fixed rate of dividend out of earnings before such earnings are available for dividends on common shares.
- A priority over common shareholders on the assets of the company in the event of insolvency.

Bonds or debentures. These securities are written promises to pay issued by corporations (usually in denominations of $100, $500 or $1,000), bearing interest at a fixed rate, and payable in full at a future date. The terms "bonds" and "debentures" are used almost interchangeably but debentures are usually secured by a floating charge on the general assets of a corporation while bonds are secured by a mortgage on real property. Interest on the bonds or debentures, and eventually the principal, is payable whether or not the corporation makes a profit.

DIVIDENDS

The mere fact that the company has made a profit does not mean that the shareholders must receive it in the form of dividends. *Dividends* are declared at the discretion of the board of directors, who must also consider the advisability or the necessity of setting aside a portion or all of the profits for contingent liabilities or for future expansion of the business.

Dividends may be paid in the form of a *stock dividend* which the shareholders receive in fully paid up shares of stock instead of in cash.

Dividends may be paid only out of profits. If the directors should pay them out of the capital fund, they become personally liable for the amount so paid.

SUPPLEMENTARY LETTERS PATENT

If a company desires to change its name, the purpose for which it was incorporated, or any other matter not authorized in the original letters patent, or to increase or decrease its shares, it must obtain *supplementary letters patent.* These may be obtained from the Provincial Secretary after the directors have passed the necessary by-law and have had it confirmed by the required majority vote of the shareholders. Similarly, a company incorporated under a memorandum of association may file an *alteration of the memorandum* (in Ontario, Articles of Amendment).

GOING OUT OF BUSINESS

Winding-up the Company. The shareholders of a company—although it may be solvent and able to pay its creditors—may for some reason decide to *wind-up* operations and surrender its charter; that is, to discontinue the business. Procedure for the winding-up operation is laid down in the various provincial Companies (or Corporations) Acts.

BANKRUPTCY

If a company is insolvent, it may make a voluntary assignment of its assets or it may be compelled to submit to bankruptcy proceedings by a petition of its creditors. Bankruptcy proceedings are taken under the federal Bankruptcy Act.

Bankruptcy proceedings are open to individuals as well as to companies. To quote from the statement of a judge in a bankruptcy case,* ". . . if a debtor is so burdened by debts that he cannot properly support his family or otherwise perform the ordinary duties of citizenship, he is entitled to go into

*Re White (1964), *Canadian Bankruptcy Reports,* Vol. 7, page 111.

bankruptcy because of such debts, whatever the debts are, whether arising from a judgment with respect to a motor vehicle accident or however they may arise."

Individuals engaged solely in fishing, farming or the tillage of the soil, or any individual whose income from wages or commission does not exceed $2,500 a year, and who does not on his own account carry on business cannot be compelled to submit to bankruptcy proceedings under a court order, although they may do so voluntarily.

Voluntary Assignment. A debtor, knowing that he will not be able to meet his financial obligations as they become due, may of his own accord make an assignment of his property to the official Receiver in Bankruptcy for the district. This official then appoints a custodian who will take charge of the debtor's business until the creditors appoint a trustee who will complete the dissolution of the business.

Compulsory Receiving Order. Any creditor having claims against the debtor amounting to $1,000 or more may present to the court a bankruptcy petition. If the court is satisfied with the proof of the claims of the creditors and is convinced that the debtor has committed an *act of bankruptcy,* it will issue a *receiving order,* and the debtor's property is then placed in the hands of a custodian until a trustee is appointed by the creditors.

Acts of Bankruptcy. An act of bankruptcy is some act by the debtor which constitutes grounds for a creditor to demand bankruptcy proceedings. The following are considered acts of bankruptcy:

- A voluntary assignment.
- A fraudulent transfer by the debtor of part or all of his property.
- A fraudulent preference to one or more particular creditors.
- An attempt to abscond.
- An attempt to remove his goods with intent to defraud his creditors.
- A bulk sale of his goods contrary to the Bulk Sales Act.
- Ceasing to pay his liabilities as they become due.

Duties of the Trustee. The trustee is an officer of the court who takes charge of the debtor's business and administers it as trustee for the creditors.

The Bankruptcy Act prescribes the powers and duties of the trustee. In brief, the trustee either carries on the business for the benefit of the creditors or winds it up so as to realize as much as possible in satisfaction of their claims. Priorities as to claims are prescribed by the Bankruptcy Act.

Discharge from Bankruptcy. The effect of a discharge from bankruptcy is to free the debtor from any unpaid portion of his debts after the trustee has disposed of the debtor's assets. Subject to certain provisions of the Act, a discharged debtor may commence his business life anew.

After three months and within a period of twelve months following bankruptcy, the trustee will apply to the court for a hearing of an application for the bankrupt debtor's discharge, at which time he will present a report on the bankrupt's affairs. The debtor and his creditors will be notified of the hearing.

After hearing the report, the court may grant the discharge if it is shown that the debtor's bankruptcy has been due to misfortune and not to dishonesty. Generally, the court will refuse a discharge if the unsecured creditors have not received at least fifty cents on the dollar, or if the bankrupt has been guilty of some offence in connection with his insolvency as laid down in the Act.

In some cases the court will grant a *conditional* discharge; that is, the discharge will be suspended subject to certain conditions imposed by the court.

C—12

At a hearing of an application for discharge from bankruptcy, the court found that the debtor and his wife had been irresponsible with regard to their business affairs, and that their bankruptcy was the result of their mismanagement of household affairs and a judgment against them of $11,559 arising out of an automobile accident. It appeared to the court that the chief reason for going through bankruptcy proceedings was to avoid the judgment debt. In view of the reasons for the bankruptcy, and the fact that the debtor was still earning in the neighbourhood of $7,500 a year, the court granted a discharge only on the condition that the bankrupt debtor pay his unsecured creditors an amount equal to twenty-five cents on the dollar, the discharge to take effect only when this had been done.

In making this ruling the court commented: ". . . the Bankruptcy Act must not be considered to be a clearing house for the liquidation of debts . . . nor must it be considered a summary and expeditious means of avoiding payment of damages arising out of automobile collisions." And further "although the Bankruptcy Act is available to an insolvent not engaged in business, the Act was never intended to enable a judgment debtor to get rid of a judgment for damages and with no other purpose to serve than the convenience and comfort of the debtor."

(a) In view of the facts, do you think that having to pay 25 cents on the dollar was a harsh ruling?

(b) When your debts get too large, why not just declare yourself bankrupt?

We should note here that a corporation may not be given a discharge from bankruptcy unless it has paid its creditors in full. Although, as in the above case example, the court may require a natural person to continue to pay his debts from future earnings, such a condition is not possible against the shareholders of a company which has limited liability.

A discharge in bankruptcy does not release an individual from liability to pay (a) alimony, (b) maintenance and support of a wife or child living apart from him, or (c) claims arising from the debtor's fraud or dishonesty. And it has been held that although a debtor could be discharged from a debt owing to the Unsatisfied Judgment Fund, he was not entitled to get his driver's license back until he had repaid in full the amount paid out by the Fund in his behalf.*

*Re Caporale (1969), *Canadian Bankruptcy Reports*, Vol. 13, page 57.

SPECIAL CLASSES OF COMPANIES

Cooperative companies and credit unions merit mention in this part because of their rapidly increasing growth in our business life and because of some distinctive features which apply to them.

Cooperatives. A cooperative company is organized in very much the same way as any other company. However, in many respects cooperatives are different from other types of companies. In Ontario and Manitoba, a special division of their companies acts deals with cooperatives; the other provinces have a separate act, The Co-operative Associations Act, for the same purpose.

Some of the distinctive features of cooperatives are:

- A member has only *one* vote regardless of the amount of his investment.
- There is no voting by proxy.
- Surplus funds are distributed to its members in the form of (1) interest on investment, and (2) a division of the remainder among the members in proportion to the volume of business which they have done with or through the cooperative.
- Shares may not be transferred unless authorized by the directors.
- Capital for the company may be obtained by the sale of shares to the members or by securing from them promissory notes payable on demand. The notes may be used as collateral security for loans obtained by the company. The members are liable on their promissory notes whether the notes are used as collateral or not, but they are not directly liable for the debts of the cooperative; that is, they have limited liability.

Credit Unions. The forming and operation of a credit union is also prescribed by statute law. Like other cooperatives, no member has more than one vote and voting by proxy is in most cases not allowed.

APPLYING THE LAW

1.

Compare the personal liabilities of the owners of these bankrupt businesses.

2. Jones is a director of both A Company and B Company, holding a large number of shares in each. It develops that A Company is in need of a certain machine manufactured by B Company (as well as by other companies). Obviously, it is in Jones' interest that A Company enter into an agreement to purchase the machine from B Company. How does the law apply to Jones as a director of A Company?

DISCUSSION AND PROJECTS

1. The Athletic Sportsmen's Club has only twenty members at present. The members are considering incorporation of the club. Discuss the advantages of having the club incorporated. What are the disadvantages?
2. Obtain a specimen copy of (a) a stock certificate, (b) Letters Patent (or other equivalent document). Examine their form and content.
3. From time to time bankruptcy notices appear among the legal notices in newspapers. Check your newspaper for one of these notices and examine its content.

REFERENCES TO REPORTED CASES

REFERENCES TO REPORTED CASES

Unit 2	C—3	Conn v. David Spencer Ltd., 1931 Dominion Law Reports, page 805.
	C—4	Russell Transport Ltd. v. Ontario Malleable Iron Co. Ltd., 1952 Ontario Reports, page 621.
	C—5	Shuttleworth v. Vancouver General Hospital, 1927 British Columbia Reports, Vol.38, page 300.
	C—8	McQuire v. Western Morning News Co., 1903 King's Bench, Vol.2, page 100.
	C—10	Blyth v. Birmingham Waterworks Co., 1856 Exchequer, Vol.11, page 781.
	C—12	Hay (or Bourhill) v. Young, 1943 Appeal Cases, page 92.
	C—14	Donahue v. Stevenson, 1932 Appeal Cases, page 562.
	C—16(i)	Such v. Dominion Stores, 1963 Ontario Reports, Vol.1, page 105.
	C—16(ii)	Campbell v. Royal Bank, 1964 Supreme Court Reports, page 85.
	C—17	City of Glasgow v. Taylor; 1921 Appeal Cases, Vol.1, page 44.
	C—19(i)	Murray v. Harringay Arena Ltd., 1951 King's Bench, Vol.2, page 529.
	C—19(ii)	Payne v. Maple Leaf Gardens, 1949 Ontario Reports, page 26.
Page 54, Applying the Law, Q. 1		Hart v. Dominion Stores Ltd. and Coca Cola Ltd., 1968 Ontario Reports, Vol.1, page 775.
Unit 3	C—1	Magda v. Her Majesty the Queen, 1964 Supreme Court Reports, page 72.
	C—2(i)	Fouché v. Landry; 1960 Quebec Practice Reports, page 337.
	C—2(ii)	R. v. Churchman and Durham; 1955 Ontario Weekly Notes, page 90.
	C—3	Benning v. The Attorney General for Saskatchewan, 1963, Western Weekly Reports, Vol.41, 497.
	C—4	Regina v. Drybones; 1970 Western Weekly Reports, Vol.71, page 161.
	C—5(i)	Robertson and Rosetanni v. Her Majesty the Queen, 1963 Supreme Court Reports, page 651.
	C—5(ii)	Teretolkin v. Superintendent of Child Welfare, 1958, Dominion Law Reports, Vol.11 (2d), page 417.
	C—6(i)	The Alberta Press case, 1938 Supreme Court Reports, page 100.
	C—6(ii)	Aimé Boucher v. His Majesty the King, 1951 Supreme Court Reports, page 265.
Unit 4	C—4	Nane v. Sykiotis; 1966 Ontario Reports, Vol.2, page 428.
	C—5	Moss v. Moss; 1897 Probate Division, page 263.

Unit 4 C—6 Pascuzzi v. Pascuzzi; 1955 Ontario Weekly Notes, page 853.
C—8 Alspector v. Alspector; 1957 Ontario Reports, page 454.
C—12 Kaakee v. Kaakee; 1915 Ontario Weekly Notes, page 648.
C—16 R. v. R.; 1969 Ontario Reports, Vol.2, page 857.
C—17 Stark v. Stark; 1910 Probate Division, page 190.

Unit 5 C—3 Re Dervishian; 1968, Exchequer Court, Vol.2, page 384.
C—4 Regina v. Leach; Ex Parte Bergsma; 1966 Ontario Reports, Vol.1, page 106.
C—5 Re B. Almaas, E. Almaas, E. Nielson, and T. Nielson; 1968 Exchequer Court Reports, Vol.2, page 391.

Unit 6 C—3 MacLean v. Kennedy; 1965 Dominion Law Reports, Vol.53, page 254.
C—6 Wattie v. Lytton; 1945 Ontario Weekly Notes, page 57.
C—7 Parrish & Heimbecker Ltd. v. Gooding Lumber Ltd.; 1968 Dominion Law Reports, Vol.67 (2d), page 495.
C—8 Finelli v. Dee; 1968 Ontario Reports, Vol.1, page 676.
C—9 McManus v. Cooke; 1887 Chancery Division, Vol. 35, page 681.
C—10 McSweeny et al v. The Windsor Gas Co. Ltd.; 1941 Ontario Weekly Notes, page 367.
C—11 Loft v. Physicians' Services Inc.; 1966 Ontario Reports, Vol.2, page 253.
C—12 Hyde v. Wrench; Beavan Reports, Vol.3; page 334.
C—13 Byrne v. Van Tienhoven; 1880 Common Pleas Division, Vol.5, page 344.
C—15 Garden v. McGregor; 1945 Ontario Weekly Notes, page 691.
C—16 Governors of Dalhousie College v. Boutilier; 1934 Dominion Law Reports, Vol.3, page 593.
C—17 Sargent v. Nicholson; 1915 Dominion Law Reports, Vol.25, page 638.
C—19 Eastwood v. Kenyon; 1840 English Reports, Vol.113, page 482.
C—20 Doyle v. White City Stadium Ltd.; 1935 King's Bench, Vol.1, page 110.
C—21 Beam v. Beatty; 1902 Ontario Law Reports, Vol.4, page 554.
C—22 Butterfield v. Nipissing Electric Supply Co. Ltd.; 1950 Ontario Law Reports, page 504.
C—23 Hilliard v. Dillon; 1955 Ontario Weekly Notes, page 621.
C—24 International Accountants' Society Inc. v. Montgomery; 1935 Ontario Weekly Notes, page 364.
C—25 Steinberg v. Scala (Leeds) Ltd.; 1923 Chancery Reports, Vol.2, page 452.
C—27 Nash v. Inman; 1908 King's Bench, Vol.2, page 1.
C—28 Jewell v. Broad; 1909 Ontario Law Reports, Vol.20, page 176.
C—31(i) Hardman v. Falk; 1955 Western Weekly Reports, page 337.
C—31(ii) Chait & Leon v. Harding; 1920 Ontario Weekly Notes, Vol.19, page 20.
C—32 Bawlf Grain Companies Ltd. v. Ross; 1917 Western Weekly Reports, Vol.3, page 373.
C—33 Dorsch v. Freeholders Oil Co.; 1963 Dominion Law Reports, Vol.40 (2d), page 307.
C—34 Cobb v. McKinlay Motors Ltd.; 1964 Maritime Provinces Reports, Vol. 51, page 198.
C—35 F & B Transport Ltd. v. White Truck Sales; 1964 Dominion Law Reports, Vol.47 (2d), page 419.
C—36 Morley v. Loughnan (1893) 1 Ch. 736.
C—37 McMurchy v. Harper; 1937 Dominion Law Reports, Vol.2, page 774.
C—38 Bank of Montreal v. Stuart et al; 1911 Appeal Cases, page 120.
C—39 R. v. Ontario Flue-cured Tobacco Growers' Marketing Board, Ex Parte Grigg; 1965 Dominion Law Reports, Vol.51 (2d), page 7.
C—40 McRae v. Commonwealth Disposals Commission; 1951 Law Quarterly Review, Vol.68, page 30.
C—45(i) Moorehouse v. Income Investments; 1966 Dominion Law Reports, Vol.53 (2d), page 106.

Unit 6	C—45(ii)	Miller v. Lavoie; 1966 Dominion Law Reports, Vol.60 (2d), page 495.
	C—46	Cope v. Harasimo; 1964 Western Weekly Reports, Vol.46, page 376.
	C—47	Re Giannone and Stampeder Motor Hotel Ltd.; 1963 Dominion Law Reports, Vol.41 (2d), page 242.
	C—48	Taylor v. McQuilkin; 1968 Dominion Law Reports, Vol.2 (3d), page 463.
	C—49	R. v. Howard Smith Paper Mills; 1957 Dominion Law Reports, Vol.8 (2d), page 449.
Page 146, Applying the Law, Q. 1		Green v. Stanton; 1969 Dominion Law Reports, Vol.3, page 358.

Unit 7	C—2	Allux Ltd. v. McKenna; 1962 Ontario Weekly Notes, page 258.
	C—4	Paramuschuk v. Meadow Lake; 1964 Dominion Law Reports, Vol.47, page 427.
	C—7	Mason & Risch Ltd. v. Christner; 1920 Dominion Law Reports, Vol.54, page 653.
	C—8	Downie & Hatt v. Norman; 1965 Maritime Provinces Reports, Vol.50, page 150.
	C—9	Giswold & wife v. Hill & wife; 1963 Western Weekly Reports, Vol.41, page 549.
	C—11	Detroit Football Co. v. Dublinski; 1957 Dominion Law Reports, Vol.7, page 9.
	C—13	Taylor v. Caldwell; 1863 English Reports, Vol.122, page 309.

Unit 8	C—2	The Cockshutt Plow Co. Ltd. v. A. J. Macdonald; 1912 Western Weekly Reports, Vol.3, page 488.
	C—4	Compagnie Equitable d'Assurance Contre Le Feu v. Gagné; 1966 Dominion Law Reports, Vol.58, page 56.
	C—5	R. v. Royal Bank; 1920 Western Weekly Reports, Vol.1, page 198.
	C—7	Agnew v. Davis; 1911 Western Law Reporter, Vol.17, page 570.
	C—8	Winnipeg Piano Co. v. Wawryshyn; 1935 Western Weekly Reports, Vol.2, page 220.
	C—9	Hastings v. Village of Semans; 1946 Western Weekly Reports, Vol.3, page 449.
	C—11	Ella v. Pearlman; 1961 Ontario Weekly Notes, page 200.
	C—12	O.K. Ladies Garment Co. Ltd. v. Edgecombe; 1934 Maritime Provinces Reports, Vol.9, page 27.
	C—13	Hal H. Paradise Ltd. v. Apostolic Trustees of the Friars Manor; 1966 Dominion Law Reports, Vol.55 (2d), page 671.
	C—14	Maneer v. Sanford; 1905 Western Law Reporter, Vol.1, page 128.
	C—15	Lloyd v. Grace, Smith & Co.; 1912 Appeal Cases, page 716.
	C—17	Alliston Creamery v. Grosdanoff and Tracy; 1962 Ontario Reports, page 808.
	C—18	H. B. Etlin Co. v. Asselstyne; 1962 Ontario Reports, page 810.
	C—19	McDonald et al v. Associated Fuels et al; 1954 Dominion Law Reports, Vol.3, page 775.
	C—21	Cummings v. Reister and Anderson; 1948 Western Weekly Reports, Vol.2, page 260.
	C—22	Renner v. Joyce et al; 1945 Dominion Law Reports, Vol.1, page 67.
	C—23	Neilsen v. Redel; 1954 Western Weekly Reports, Vol.13, page 416.
	C—24	Marshment v. Borgstrom; 1942 Supreme Court Reports, page 374.
	C—25	Finnegan v. Riley; 1939 Dominion Law Reports, Vol.4, page 434.
	C—26	Hoar v. Wallace & Viking Sprinkler Co.; 1938 Ontario Weekly Notes, page 401.
	C—27	Clayton v. Raitar Transport; 1948 Dominion Law Reports, Vol.4, page 877.

Unit 8	C—28	Carson v. Dairy and Poultry Pool; 1966 Western Weekly Reports, Vol.56, page 629.
	C—29	Rex ex rel Doeing v. Wagner; 1951 Western Weekly Reports, Vol.4, page 666.
	C—30	Woods v. Miramichi Hospital; 1967 Dominion Law Reports, Vol.67, page 757.
	C—31	Protective Plastics Ltd. v. Hawkins; 1965 Dominion Law Reports, Vol.49 (2d), page 496.

Unit 9	C—1	Winfield v. Stewart; 1909 Nova Scotia Reports, Vol.44, page 10.
	C—3	Goodwin Tanners Ltd. v. Belick and Naiman; 1953 Ontario Weekly Notes, page 641.
	C—4	Alkins Bros. v. G. A. Grier & Sons; 1924 Ontario Weekly Notes, Vol.26, page 407.
	C—5	McCutcheon v. Northern Fuel Co.; 1906 Western Law Reporter, Vol.4, page 57.
	C—6	Stevenson v. Colonial Homes Ltd.; 1961 Dominion Law Reports, Vol.27 (2d), page 698.
	C—8	Craig et al v. Beardmore et al; 1904 Ontario Law Reports, Vol. 7, page 674.
	C—9	McDill v. Hillson; 1920 Dominion Law Reports, Vol.53, page 228.
	C—10	Laurin v. Ginn; 1908 Eastern Law Reports, Vol.5, page 335.
	C—11	Caradoc Nurseries Ltd. v. Marsh; 1959 Ontario Weekly Notes, page 123.
	C—12	Orr v. Danforth Wine Co., Ltd.; 1936 Ontario Weekly Notes, page 306.
	C—14	Diamond v. B.C. Thoroughbred Breeders' Society and Boyd; 1965 Western Weekly Reports, Vol.52, page 385.
	C—16	Smith v. Goral; 1952 Ontario Weekly Notes, page 421.
	C—17	Roberts v. Wales; 1948 Western Weekly Reports, Vol.1, page 1034.
	C—18	Scottish Rubber Co. Ltd. v. Berger Tailoring Co. Ltd.; 1921 Ontario Weekly Notes, Vol.20, page 463.
	C—19	Thompson v. Schooley; 1932 Ontario Weekly Notes, Vol.41, page 107.
	C—20(i)	Buckley v. Lever Bros. Ltd.; 1953 Dominion Law Reports, Vol.4, page 16.
	C—20(ii)	Hopkins v. Jannison; 1914 Dominion Law Reports, Vol.18, page 88.
	C—21	Grant v. Australian Knitting Mills & John Martin & Co. Ltd.; 1936 Western Weekly Reports, Vol.1, page 145.
	C—22	O'Fallon v. Inecto Rapid (Canada) Ltd. et al; 1940 Dominion Law Reports, Vol.4, page 276.
	C—23	Chomyn v. American Fur Co.; 1948 Western Weekly Reports, Vol.2, page 1110.
	C—24	Lightburn v. Belmont Sales Ltd. et al; 1969 Western Weekly Reports, Vol.69, page 734.
	C—31	Consumers Gas Co. v. Atkins et al; Dingman et al., third parties; 1968 Dominion Law Reports, Vol.69 (2d), page 629.
	C—34	Ward v. Dickenson; 1912 Ontario Weekly Notes, Vol.3, page 1153.

Unit 10	C—3	Wills v. Brown; 1912 Ontario Weekly Reporter, Vol.20, page 880.
	C—5	Anderson v. Royer; 1928 Dominion Law Reports, Vol.3, page 248.
	C—6	Hadley v. Droitwich Construction Co.; 1967 All England Reports, Vol.3, page 911.
	C—7	Queens Sales & Services Ltd. v. Smith, Maritime Provinces Reports, Vol.48, page 364.
	C—8	Northumberland County School Finance Board v. Stewart; 1965 Dominion Law Reports, Vol.54 (2d), page 657.
	C—10	British Motor Corp. v. Judge Auto Transport Ltd.; 1966 Dominion Law Reports, Vol.56 (2d), page 625.

Unit 10	C—11	Murphy v. Hart; 1919 Dominion Law Reports, Vol.46, page 36.
	C—13(i)	Turgel Fur Co. v. Northumberland Ferries Ltd.; 1966 Dominion Law Reports, Vol.59 (2d), page 1.
	C—13(ii)	The Queen v. C.P.R.; 1965 Exchequer Court Reports, Vol. 1, page 145.
	C—14	George v. Canadian Northern Railway; 1922 Ontario Law Reports, Vol.53, page 94.
	C—15	Beausejour v. Dominion Express Company; 1899 La Revue de Jurisprudence, Vol.5, page 503.
	C—16(i)	Williams v. Linnitt; 1951 All England Reports, Vol.1, page 278.
	C—16(ii)	George v. Williams; 1956 Ontario Reports, page 871.
	C—17	King v. Barclay and Barclay's Motel; 1960 Dominion Law Reports, Vol.24 (2d), page 418.
	C—18(i)	Spooner v. Starkman; 1937 Ontario Reports, page 542.
	C—18(ii)	Samuel Smith and Sons Ltd. v. Silverman; 1961 Ontario Reports, page 648.

Unit 11	C—4	Keech v. Canadian Bank of Commerce; 1938 Western Weekly Reports, Vol.2, page 291.
	C—6	Re Imperial Bank of Canada; 1913 Western Weekly Reports, Vol.5, page 913.
	C—7	Foster v. Mackinnon; 1869 Law Reports; Common Pleas, Vol.4, page 704.
	C—8	Commercial Automation Ltd. v. Banque Provinciale du Canada; 1962 Dominion Law Reports, Vol.39 (2d), page 316.
	C—9	Toronto-Dominion Bank v. Parkway Holdings Ltd. et al; 1969 Dominion Law Reports, Vol.1(3d), page 716.
	C—10	Robinson v. Mann; 1901 Ontario Law Reports, Vol.2, page 63.

Unit 12	C—4	Bard v. Rasauskas; 1955 Ontario Weekly Notes, page 246.
	C—5(i)	Re Fowler and Caulfield; 1925 Ontario Weekly Notes, Vol. 29, page 245.
	C—5(ii)	Heifitz v. Gural; 1950 Ontario Weekly Notes, page 855.
	C—7	Horne v. Horne; 1905 Nova Scotia Reports, Vol.38, page 404.
	C—8	Re: Button; 1925 Ontario Law Reports, Vol.57, page 161.
	C—9	Leatherdale v. Mitchell; 1925 Ontario Weekly Notes, Vol.28, page 426.
	C—10	Mack v. Stuike; 1963, Western Weekly Reports, Vol.45, page 605.
	C—11	Gearing v. Nordheimer; 1876 Upper Canada Queen's Bench, Vol.40, page 21.
	C—13	Smith v. Dawson; 1923 Ontario Law Reports, Vol.53, page 615.
	C—14	Kalbfleisch v. Hurley; 1915 Ontario Law Reports, Vol.34, page 268.
	C—15	Robinson Plumbing and Heating v. Rossiter; 1955 Ontario Weekly Notes, page 29.
	C—17	Anderson v. Carlson; 1942 Western Weekly Reports, Vol.1, page 652.
	C—18	Bell v. Chartered Trust; 1919 Ontario Law Reports, Vol.46, page 192.
	C—19	Robertson v. Milan; 1951 Western Weekly Reports, Vol.3, page 248.
	C—20(i)	Davidovich v. Hill; 1948 Ontario Weekly Notes, page 201.
	C—20(ii)	Browne v. White; 1947 Dominion Law Reports, Vol.2, page 309.
	C—21	Zerouvinski v. Duke; 1924 Western Weekly Reports, Vol.3, page 49.
	C—22	MacLennan v. The Royal Insurance Company; 1876 Upper Canada Queen's Bench, Vol.39, page 515.
	C—23(i)	Jenkins v. Jackson; 1888 Chancery, Vol.40, page 71.
	C—23(ii)	Walton v. Biggs; 1912 Western Law Reporter, Vol.19, page 895.
	C—24	Bartram v. Rempel; 1949 Western Weekly Reports, Vol.2, page 1183.
	C—25	Scythes and Company Limited v. Gibsons Limited; 1927 Supreme Court Reports, page 352.

Unit 12	C—26	McDonald v. Hamilton; 1911 Eastern Law Reports, Vol.9, page 395.
	C—27	Hillman v. MacIntosh; 1959 Supreme Court Reports, page 384.
	C—29	Hamilton v. Chisholm; 1909 Western Law Reporter, Vol.11, page 134.
	C—30	Cowitz v. Siegel; 1954 Ontario Weekly Notes, page 833.
	C—31	Balagno v. Leroy; 1913 Western Weekly Reports, Vol.3, page 1124.
Unit 13	C—1	Re S; 1967 Ontario Reports, Vol.2, page 275.
	C—2	Murphy v. Lamphier estate; 1914 Ontario Law Reports, Vol.31, page 287.
	C—4	Re B; 1954 Ontario Weekly Notes, page 301.
	C—5	Re Webber Estate; 1969 Western Weekly Reports, Vol.70, page 670.
	C—7	Re East; 1923 Ontario Weekly Notes, Vol.24, page 394.
	C—8	Re McGinn Estate; 1969 Western Weekly Reports, Vol.70, page 159.
	C—9	Kennedy v. Piekoff; 1966 Western Weekly Reports, Vol.56, page 381.
	C—11	Re Cane estates; 1968 Western Weekly Reports, Vol. 63, page 242.
Unit 14	C—7	Speiling v. Germanic Insurance Co. of New York; 1932 Dominion Law Reports, Vol.2, page 634.
	C—9	Kozlik v. Northern Assurance Co.; 1940 Ontario Weekly Notes, page 21.
Unit 15	C—2	Vasey v. Kreutzweiser; 1966 Canadian Bankruptcy Reports, Vol.8, page 225.
	C—6	Klutz v. Klutz; 1969 Dominion Law Reports, Vol.2(3d), page 332.
	C—9	Fancy v. Whynot et al; 1938 Dominion Law Reports, Vol.3, page 655.
	C—10	Re McGinnis; 1950 Dominion Law Reports, Vol.1, page 853.
	C—11	Re Metropolitan Theatres Limited; 1920 Ontario Weekly Notes, Vol.18, page 72.
	C—12	Rice et Ux v. Copeland; 1965 Western Weekly Reports, Vol.51, page 227.

GLOSSARY

GLOSSARY

ABSTRACT OF TITLE A summary of all the successive conveyances (deeds, mortgages, etc.), affecting a person's title to a parcel of property.

ACQUITTAL Discharge of an accused person upon a verdict of "not guilty."

ACT OF GOD An event caused by the forces of nature beyond human foresight and control.

ACTION A civil proceeding commenced by writ or notice, as permitted by rules of court.

ADMINISTRATOR A person appointed by a court to manage the property or affairs of another.

AFFIDAVIT A written statement sworn to by the maker.

AFFINITY Relationship by marriage.

AGENT A person who is authorized to act on behalf of another.

ALIEN A person who has not attained the citizenship of the country in which he lives.

APPEAL A proceeding taken to correct an erroneous decision by taking it to a higher court.

ARM'S LENGTH, AT In law, a relationship of parties as if they were strangers.

ARRAIGN To call a person accused of a crime before a court, read to him the charge, and ask for a plea of guilty or not guilty.

ARREST To seize or take into custody by authority of the law.

ASSAULT Intentional application of force to another person, or an attempt or threat thereof by act or gesture with the apparent ability to do so.

ASSIGN To transfer or make over to another.

ATTACH To take by legal authority.

ATTEST To certify an act; e.g., to witness the signing of a document.

BAIL Money or credit deposited with a court to ensure the appearance of an accused person who is temporarily released from custody.

BAILMENT A delivery of goods on condition that they be returned.

BANNS Proclamation of a proposed marriage.

BARTER An exchange of goods for other goods—not a sale of goods.

BENEFICIARY A person named to receive benefit from a will, insurance policy, trust agreement, etc.

BIGAMY Entering into another marriage while already legally married.

BONA FIDE In good faith.

BOND A contract under seal to pay a sum of money.

BY-LAWS Rules or "laws" made by a corporation for its own management; e.g., municipal by-laws.

CAVEAT EMPTOR Let the buyer beware.

CHATTEL Moveable property—any property except real estate.

CIVIL ACTION An action between private citizens as opposed to criminal actions initiated by the state.

CIVIL LAW Law governing relations between individuals as opposed to criminal law, which governs the relations of the individual to the state.

CODICIL A document made by a testator adding to or altering a will.

COHABITATION The state of living together; e.g., husband and wife.

CONSANGUINITY Relationship by blood.

CONSORTIUM The normal association of husband and wife.

CONVERSION Wrongful assumption and exercise of the right of ownership of another's property.

CONVEYANCE An instrument (document) used to transfer the title of land from one person to another.

COVENANT A promise made in writing under seal.

CREDITOR A person to whom a debt is owing.

CROWN ATTORNEY The public prosecutor.

DAMAGES Compensation or indemnity in money for loss suffered owing to tort or breach of contract.

DEBENTURE A document issued by a corporation or public body as security for a loan.

DEBT A sum of money due from one person to another.

DEED A written document which is signed, sealed and delivered; e.g., a deed to a parcel of land.

DEFAMATION The publication of a false statement with respect to another person without lawful justification.

DEFENDANT A person who is sued or against whom a legal proceeding is commenced.

DEVISE A gift of real property by will.

DIRECTORS The persons who direct the affairs of a corporation.

DOMICILE The place where a person has his permanent place of residence.

EASEMENT A right enjoyed by the owner of land over the land of another.

ENCUMBRANCE A charge or liability attached to property.

ESCHEAT The reversion of property to the Crown if there are no heirs.

ESCROW, TO HOLD IN The holding of a document by a third party until certain conditions have been fulfilled.

ESTOPPEL In law, a rule which prevents a person from affirming or denying some fact because of previous conduct.

EXECUTOR A person named in a will to carry out its provisions.

EXPRESS Direct communication as contrasted with communication by implication.

EXPROPRIATE To take property, with compensation, for public purposes.

FEE SIMPLE A freehold estate denoting full ownership—subject to the rights of the Crown. (From old Anglo-French: *fee*, meaning land granted to a man and his heirs for services rendered; and *simple*, meaning absolute or unconditional).

FIXTURE Something annexed or attached to the land.

FORECLOSURE To take action to eliminate the right to redeem a mortgage.

GARNISHEE To attach debts (money) owing to a debtor (for example, wages) pursuant to a court order, so that this money can be used to pay the creditor.

GIFT A gratuitous transfer of property.

GUARANTEE A promise to answer for the debt of another.

HABEAS CORPUS A prerogative writ directed to a person who holds another in custody commanding him to produce that person (have the body) before the court.

HEIR One who succeeds by right of relationship to the property of another who is deceased.

HOLOGRAPH WILL A will entirely handwritten by the testator.

HOMICIDE The killing of a human being.

I.O.U. A written acknowledgment of a debt.

IMPLIED Suggested or understood without being openly expressed.

IN CAMERA The hearing of a case in private.

INDEMNIFY To reimburse; to make good a loss.

INDICTMENT A written accusation of the committing of a crime presented to a Grand Jury.

INDORSEMENT The signature and writing on the back of an instrument.

INFANT A minor. (See Unit 6, Part 11).

INJUNCTION A court order whereby a person is required to do or to refrain from doing a particular act.
INSOLVENT Unable to pay debts which are due.
INSTRUMENT A written legal document.
INTESTATE Without a will.

JOINT TENANCY Ownership of land in common with a right of survivorship.
JUDGMENT The decision of a court in a legal proceeding.

LEASE The grant of possession to land for a fixed or determinate period.
LEGACY A gift of personal property under a will.
LESSEE A person to whom a lease is granted; a tenant.
LESSOR One who grants a lease; the landlord.
LIBEL Defamation by printing, writing or other permanent form.
LIEN The right to hold or charge the property of another as security for an obligation.
LIQUIDATED DAMAGES Damages agreed upon in a contract in the event of a breach of that contract.
LITIGATION A law suit.

MAJORITY With reference to age, means full legal age. (See Unit 6, Part 11).
MINOR See Unit 6, Part 11.
MORTGAGE The transfer of the title to property for the purpose of securing payment of a debt.

NEXT FRIEND A person who acts for a minor in a legal action.
NISI (Meaning "unless"). With reference to divorce (e.g., a decree nisi), means a divorce not to take effect *unless* within a certain period of time the person affected by it fails to show cause why it should not take effect.
NOVATION The substitution of a new contract in consideration of the cancellation of an old contract.

ONUS Responsibility; burden.

PAROL By word of mouth; not written.
PARTY A person who takes part in a legal proceeding or transaction.
PERJURY The giving of false testimony under oath.
PERSONAL PROPERTY Moveable property; goods and chattels.
PLAINTIFF One who sues or commences a legal proceeding.
PRIMA FACIE Evidence sufficient "on its face" to establish a fact.
PRINCIPAL A person for whom another is an agent.
PROBATE The procedure of proving a will.
PROXY A document authorizing one person to exercise another person's right to vote at a meeting; one who represents another at a meeting.

QUANTUM MERUIT As much as it merited—what he has earned.
QUITCLAIM DEED A deed in which one person releases and transfers his claim to a piece of real property without warranting the validity of his interest.

RATIFICATION The act of adopting a contract or other transaction by a person who was not otherwise bound by it.
REAL PROPERTY Immoveable property; an interest in land other than leasehold.
REALTY Real property; real estate.
RECOGNIZANCE A bond given by a person before a court binding that person to do or not to do something, such as to appear in court at a certain time, or to keep the peace.
REDEMPTION The paying off of a mortgage debt or charge.
RENT The payment due from a tenant of land to the landlord.
REPLEVIN, AN ORDER OF A court order directing one person to give up possession of goods to another who claims it is wrongfully withheld.
RIPARIAN RIGHTS Rights to property abutting a stream, river, or other body of water, including legal rights regarding the use of the waterway itself.

SHARE A specific portion of the capital of a corporation.
SLANDER Defamation by means of a spoken word or gesture.
SQUATTER'S TITLE The title acquired

by a person who, without original right, occupies another's land in such circumstances and for such length of time that he acquires ownership of it.

STATUTE An Act of Parliament or of a Provincial Legislature.

SUBPOENA Writ (under penalty if not obeyed) directing a person to appear in court for a specified purpose.

SUBROGATION Substitution of one person for another so that certain rights which attach to one person now attach to the other.

SUE To bring civil proceedings against another.

TENANT One who holds land.

TENDER An offer.

TESTATE Having made a will.

TESTATOR The maker of a will.

ULTRA VIRES In excess of legal authority and therefore invalid.

USURY An excessive rate of interest.

UTTER An attempt to pass a forged document or counterfeit money.

VENDOR A seller.

VENUE The place where a case is to be tried.

VERDICT The answer of the jury in a civil or criminal case.

VOID Of no legal effect; a nullity.

VOIDABLE Capable of being rescinded.

WARRANTY A term of a contract.

WILL A written declaration whereby the person making it provides for the distribution of his property after his death.

WRIT OF SUMMONS A process issued by a court at the request of a plaintiff to give the person sued notice of the claim made against him.

INDEX

INDEX